234.2

REASON, SCIENCE AND FAITH

In this fascinating and thorough book, the authors demonstrate how reason, science and faith are not opposed to each other but rather complimentary. *Rev Nicky Gumbel (National Alpha Courses Leader).*

This is a most useful work, written in a student-friendly style. Though readers may not agree with all the authors' conclusions, and some may find some parts hard-going, it should interest and stimulate students and others wanting to explore and understand these science-faith topics. *Prof Gordon Wenham (Professor of Old Testament and author of the 'Word' reference commentary on Genesis).*

This book covers a great deal of ground, and the treatment is not superficial. The arguments are well set out, and the style of writing is clear. It is going to be a demanding read for people, but one out of which they will get a great deal. Its great strength is the clarity of thought it brings to the issues dealt with. It ought to help people sort out some of the muddled ideas that are around regarding science, Christianity and the Bible. I hope it gets well advertised and widely read. *Rev Dr Ernest Lucas (PhD in Biochemistry, PhD in Hebrew Bible Studies, Lecturer at Bristol Baptist College).*

In an age of relativism Marston and Foster remind us of the need to rediscover the Gospel as public truth. At a time when Evangelicals and Charismatics together need to rediscover a thoughtful faith, this book will make you think. It is not a text for the intellectually lazy. Read it and grow. *Dr Mark Bonnington (New Testament Tutor in St John's College Durham and a Leader in the New Churches movement).*

In this excellent book, Marston and Forster robustly expose the intellectual and moral poverty of the scientistic atheism of a number of science popularisers inhabiting the strange world of 'Denkinsland'. They are equally devastating in their critique of so-called 'scientific creationism', which they show to be neither scientific, nor Biblical, nor to represent mainstream Christian thinking over 2 millennia. At the same time, they provide an incisively reasoned defence of their own evangelical Christian theistic position, which is non-physicalist, allows for libertarian free-will and divine action, and is true both to the Bible and Christian tradition. I ca~ ~h~r~~~hl~ r~c~mmend the book to all who are interested in the rel_____hy and faith. *Rev Dr Rodney Ho_____s, and Church of England Minister*

WEBSITE

This book has its own dedicated website.

- Articles in extra depth on some issues
- Updates and latest info'
- Invitation for counter-articles and papers
- Invitation for supporting-articles and papers
- Opportunity to put email questions to the authors
- Comments section

---

www.reason-science-and-faith.com

---

in the 3rd millennium
a book can be an ongoing
experience and interchange...

Reason, Science and Faith

PAUL MARSTON AND
ROGER FORSTER

MONARCH
BOOKS

First published by Monarch Books 1999

ISBN 1 85424 441 8

Editorial office: Monarch Books,
Broadway House, The Broadway, Crowborough.
East Sussex TN6 1HQ

British Library Cataloguing Data
A catalogue record for this book is available
From the British Library.

Designed and produced for the publisher by
Gazelle Creative Productions,
Concorde House, Grenville Place, Mill Hill, London NW7 3SA.
Printed in Great Britain.

CONTENTS

AUTHORS

Paul Marston

Paul studied economics, philosophy, and statistical and scientific methodology at London University's L.S.E. where his tutors included Karl Popper, Imre Lakatos and Paul Feyerabend. He completed a London Masters degrees in statistical theory and one in the history and philosophy of science. His PhD concerned interactions between science (geology), scientific methodology, and Christianity. As a Senior Lecturer in the Faculty of Science at the University of Central Lancashire, his current teaching includes courses on statistical theory, philosophy of science, and the Copernican and Darwinian Revolutions. His course 'Christianity Science and History' won a prestigious Templeton prize in 1998. Paul and his wife Janice have a daughter Christel, and a son Justin who is founder/chair of CSIS (Christian Students in Science). His solo books include one on statistics and *God and the Family*.

Roger Forster

Roger completed studies in theology and mathematics at Cambridge University, and then did national service as an RAF officer before entering teaching. In 1957 he became a full time evangelist and teacher, ministering in numerous conferences and meetings of church and student groups at home and abroad. He has served on councils of various inter-denominational bodies such as the Evangelical Alliance, as a vice-president of the UCCF, and currently a vice-president of Tear Fund. He was a founder member of March for Jesus. With his wife, Faith, he currently leads the London based Ichthus Fellowship in its programme of spiritual development, youth training and social action. There are currently about 200 Ichthus linked churches, UK and overseas. Roger and Faith have a son and two daughters: Christen, Juliet and Deborah. His solo books include *Saving Faith, Fasting,* and *Saturday Night, Sunday Morning...*

Previous Joint Books: *Yes But..., That's A Good Question, God's Strategy in Human History, Reason and Faith, and Christianity, Evidence and Truth.*

*We demolish arguments and every pretension
that sets itself up against knowledge of God,
and we take captive every thought
to make it obedient to Christ.*

(2 Corinthians 10:5)

Usually even a non-Christian knows something about the earth, the heavens, and the other elements of this world... and this knowledge he holds to as being certain from reason and experience. Now, it is a disgraceful and dangerous thing for an unbeliever to hear a Christian, presumably giving the meaning of Holy Scripture, talking nonsense on these topics, and we should take all means to prevent such an embarrassing situation, in which people show up vast ignorance in a Christian and laugh it to scorn.

Augustine of Hippo

Two rules are to be observed, as Augustine teaches. The first is, to hold the truth of Scripture without wavering. The second is that since Holy Scripture can be explained in a multiplicity of senses, one should not adhere to a particular explanation, only in such measure as to be ready to abandon it if it be proved with certainty to be false; lest Holy Scripture be exposed to the ridicule of unbelievers, and obstacles be placed to their believing.

Thomas Aquinas.

In this vanity some of the moderns have with extreme levity indulged so far as to attempt to found a system of natural philosophy (science) on the first chapter of Genesis, on the book of Job, and other parts of sacred writings; and repression of it the more important, because from this unwholesome mixture of things human and divine there arises not only a fantastic philosophy but also an heretical religion.

Sir Francis Bacon

After the revival of learning, as all other branches of philosophy, so this in particular received new light. And none was more serviceable therein than Lord Bacon: who... incited all lovers of natural philosophy to a diligent search into natural history... Proofs of a wise, a good and powerful Being are indeed deducible from everything around us.

John Wesley

FOREWORD

Ever since Darwin, or so the popular myth has it, science has disproved Christianity. In a celebrated argument between the followers of Darwin, represented by Professor T. H. Huxley, and the church, represented by Bishop Samuel Wilberforce of Oxford, the Bishop was (it is popularly believed) left looking foolish. Since Darwin's day science has advanced enormously in its understanding and explanation of the world, but many still hold that science has disproved the Bible, especially in what it has to say about the creation of the world; so they believe that Christianity is not credible. It makes little difference that many scientists are believing Christians, or that they don't speak with a united voice about their explanations of the natural world. The damage is done.

Christians have reacted to this in a variety of ways. Some have sought to uphold what they see as the 'literal' truth of the Bible and so have argued for a young earth, six twenty-four hour days of creation and a universal flood. Others have sought to engage with contemporary science and tried to interpret the Bible's teaching more in harmony with contemporary science. Others have bowed down at the altar of science and, quite wrongly for Christians, sacrificed the Bible.

Forster and Marston are among those who seek an intelligent engagement with science. They demonstrate masterly comprehensiveness, genuine expertise, realistic humility and appealing persuasiveness. They explain how one's scientific perspective is shaped by a number of broader questions concerning our understanding of truth and rationality. They show how one's scientific views have wide implications for Christian faith and experience including what we believe it means to be human, what we believe about miracles and what we believe about God speaking to us through Jesus Christ.

They do not write as detached guides, but I can think of no better guides. They write as those committed to believing the Bible is God's word to us and that science can reveal God's ways to us. They also write as 'critical realists', believing, rightly, that such a common sense approach to the world makes much better sense of our experience than other philosophical stances. So they are critical of other philosophical viewpoints, not least some of those recently thrown up by postmodernity. But they are not 'fundamentalists' in the modern sense. They argue against those who would want to interpret the early chapters of the Bible strictly literally. In a couple of very illuminating chapters they show that those who have attempted to handle Genesis 1-3 literally do not represent the mainstream history of the (even evangelical) church and that they are forced, in the end, to be inconsistent in their arguments. They present us with some very revealing evidence which undermines the anti-evolutionary young-earth creationist thinking of Christians like H. M. Morris.

The book contains a wealth of detail. For those who do not know their way around the field it will open their eyes. For those who do, it will make them interact with careful argument and specific evidence, enabling them to reflect again on their own position. For the experts who differ it will mount a case which has to be answered. For the Christian believer it will give confidence and hope that, even if Marston and Forster are not right in every respect, there are ways of harmonising science and the Bible which show respect for modern science and remain faithful to what the Bible teaches. For those who do not believe, on the grounds that modern views of truth or science are stumbling blocks, it will clear a path to faith.

I was brought up to believe that you can never argue anyone into the Kingdom of God. From one viewpoint that is exactly right. To become a citizen of the Kingdom of God requires a work of the Holy Spirit. Argument alone will not do it. But those who taught me this were quite wrong to allow anti-intellectualism to reign supreme and to conclude that argument has no place in commending the faith. God gave us minds to enquire, to study, to understand, and he calls us to love him with our minds as well our hearts, souls and strength. Commending the Christian faith today requires more than a simple ABC presentation of the gospel. In truth, it always has. The Apostle Paul did not only state positively the case that Jesus was the Messiah, the Saviour, but en route he demolished arguments which would have led people to think otherwise and he sought to persuade people in their minds, as well as their hearts, about the truth he was preaching. It led him to expose erroneous thinking and to seek to enlighten darkened minds. He entered into some of the current religious debates and put forward a case that Christianity, whilst ultimately a matter of faith, was credible.

Marston and Forster stand in that tradition. They challenge undue scepticism on the one hand and discredit naive literalism on the other. They construct a convincing case that reason, science and faith can happily fit together. We owe them a debt because they have constructed the case with such care. This book should help to make sure that the myth that science is opposed to the Bible is debunked once and for all. I warmly commend it, believing that anyone would profit from reading it.

Derek J. Tidball
Principal of London Bible College
March 1999

INTRODUCTION

The authors of this book are Conservative Evangelicals who believe that biblical Christianity (ie Christianity which takes the Bible as authoritative) 'makes sense' and is consistent with modern science and historical study. This question is, of course, of interest not only to committed Christians but also to anyone else who wants to consider Christianity seriously. We will not, therefore, assume that our readers share our acceptance of the authority of the Bible. Where we cite it (in translation or in reference to the Biblical Hebrew or Greek original languages) this will be to show what 'biblical Christianity' *is*, not to prove its truth.

Our general approach is that where more detail on a topic would be useful but is prevented for reasons of space, then supplementary articles will be put on our specialised website www.reason-science-and-faith.com. Opportunity for counter argument, questions, and interaction will also be on the site.

Though written unashamedly from an evangelical viewpoint, we have tried honestly neither to misrepresent nor to treat with any disrespect those with whom we do not agree. We have also attempted throughout our work to maintain proper standards of citation and the careful objective checking of any 'facts' given. Our claim is that we represent a 'traditional' approach, in the sense that it is in harmony with the Bible itself and with the approach to understanding what it says on creation and nature taken by the earliest Jewish and Christian commentators. To sympathise with their *approach*, does not, of course, mean that we agree with all their particular conclusions. We, like they, have to come to terms with what is known about natural phenomena and origins through the study of nature. With present scientific knowledge the particular conclusions may differ, but we contend that our approach is in the mainstream tradition of Bible believing Christianity, and that this is the view which in the end 'makes the most sense' of our world.

1

Reason & Faith

Reason and Faith

Reason is the process by which we see that one set of truths
logically implies another set. *Faith* (to paraphrase Hebrews
11:1) means to accept and act on the assumption that something
is real although we cannot strictly prove it. There are various
different approaches to the relationships between these aspects
of human thinking and experience, and our purpose here is to
assert and defend a balanced Christian view. As we shall
explore, both faith and reason are necessary to human life, but
neither is sufficient on its own.

We will first make a rather stark statement of our own views
(as critical realists) of the relevant issues:

1. There is a unique 'correct' form of **reason** applicable to any
    given subject area.
2. There is a unique **reality**.
3. As anyone experiences that reality (s)he interprets it using
    concepts built up throughout his/her life. Thus human
    observation involves interpretation and **perspective**.
4. '**Truth**' is a statement about reality made in human
    language and concepts. As such it too must involve
    interpretation and perception.
5. Individuals use reason to analyse and harmonise their
    experiences of reality, forming (consciously or
    unconsciously) a more or less consistent '**worldview**'.
6. If two people 'see things differently', reason can be used to
    determine whether these are indeed two valid perspectives
    on reality, or whether they are in such **contradiction** that at
    least one must be mistaken.

There is a lot in this and we need to unpack it.

The existence and reliability of a unique 'reason' as in (1)
cannot be 'proved'. In order to do so (or even to think in a way
that recognises 'truth' and reality) requires the use of that very
reason it tries to prove. Ultimately, then, any reliance on human

reason requires an act of faith. Keith Ward, for example, points out that in saying "there is nothing that cannot be understood" militant atheist Peter Atkins exhibits extraordinary faith![1]

The existence of a unique reality seems to be 'reasonable', and any other assumption seems incoherent - though again there is no way to 'prove' it in absolute terms.

The point (3) above about observation always involving interpretation may be less obvious to some readers. But, as a simple example, think about observing a falling stone. The ancient Greek philosopher Aristotle 'saw' a stone as a piece of one of the four basic elements (earth) returning to its natural place. Aristotle thought no forces were needed to make it move, as it was doing what came naturally. Newton 'saw' motion caused by a 'force of gravity' operating between the earth and the stone (or an apple!). Albert Einstein in his theory of General Relativity 'saw' in a falling stone a warp in space-time introduced by the presence of a large mass - the earth. To each one, 'seeing' and 'describing' also involved interpreting, though they all genuinely 'saw' the same reality. Whilst, though, there can be different 'perspectives' on one reality, this does not mean that any description is as good as any other. If, say, someone told us that what she 'saw' was a pink elephant floating upside down in custard, we would say that she was not experiencing 'reality' at all. Though this might indeed be 'her experience', she would be hallucinating, not 'seeing' reality. So how do we tell the difference between perspective, mistake and hallucination? Reason and coherence are the only means we know - a description has to 'make sense' in an overall context of a coherent worldview which maps onto general experience. We maintain this whilst recognising that there is no philosophically 'watertight' formulation of it, as we discuss below in section 10.

'Truth' is expressed in language, and different languages contain different concepts that mould how we 'see' things. There is therefore a dynamic interaction between our experience of reality and the language in which we express this. Human beings *invent* concepts to interpret their experiences and their language reflects the concepts they have invented. Ancient

---

[1] Ward (1996) p. 26.

Greeks, for example, had no *word* for 'inertia' as it appears in Newton's system of physics, because the *concept* had not been invented. Ancient Greeks simply did not 'see' moving objects in Newtonian terms. Some systems of concepts (and so some language) 'map better' onto experience of reality than others. Again, reason can help us to decide which maps best - though we must remember that, as human inventions, words and concepts are seldom perfect. Much of language is used in an analogical or metaphorical sense, experiences in one area colouring how we see those in others. Thus eg we speak of a 'hard' person, being 'broken hearted' or of light 'waves'. Today, linguists and philosophers recognise that languages and words are human inventions although all human languages have similar basic structures. Interestingly, the author of the book of Genesis may see *language* as part of being in the Divine image, but actually sees *particular* words/concepts as human inventions! (Gen 2:19,22).

We accept the validity of reason. Pure reason, however, cannot, on its own, tell us what *is* real. It deals only with relationships between truths - not with what *is* true. To know (or at least have some assurance of) what *is* true we need experience as well. Sensory perception, as everyone agrees, is a source of such experience, and Christians also believe that experience may come to us through a direct intuition or inner voice of God. Reason is part of the way in which we 'make sense of' or relate those experiences to our other experiences and our world-view. Inevitably a part of what goes to make up that world-view is assumption. Assumptions pass beyond pure experience and reason, requiring some kind of faith to accept something that is not strictly provable. But reason applied to wrong assumptions can come up with wrong answers or solutions. Reason, therefore, is vital but limited, and as a *human* activity it is also fallible. Human beings can make mistakes in their reasoning just as they can in mathematics.

How does all this relate to religion? Firstly, we believe that a personal creator God is a part of the one unique reality. God exists as a person and experiences personhood whether anyone else believes it or not. Secondly, language involves humanly created concepts through which religious experience is filtered and interpreted. Again, much of it is analogical. God is not 'really' a father, but the 'father' picture expresses something real about God's nature. Some of the most astute books from Christian critical realists in the late 1990's have compared the use of models and analogical language in science with that in Christianity.[2] Language based on analogy is not somehow inferior, it is a vital part of human understanding. Language, cultural perspective, and individual experience can all cause valid differences in an individual's perspective of God. Again, however, some alternative religious beliefs may simply be in contradiction - which implies that in such instances at least one must be mistaken. Which are truly contradictory, and which are simply perspectives, has to be determined by evidence and reasoning processes.

Finally, we may need to make clear (to avoid adverse religious conditioned reflexes!) that we are *not* saying that 'mankind can by unaided reason find out God'. It is God who reveals himself through nature, through the prophets, through the Holy Spirit, and supremely through Jesus Christ. It is through his eternal word and true light that God *chooses* to 'enlighten *every* man who comes into the world' (John 1:9). Nevertheless, the rational God has made us in his image, and reason is an *inevitable* part of the process by which each of us constructs a personal worldview.

Our kind of 'critical realism', and view of reason as essential but limited (which we believe to be in line with mainstream Christianity), is today subject to attack both from secular and religious sources. We will later be looking briefly at some of the main ones of these.

Some Philosophical Background

First, we need some philosophical background. René Descartes (1596-1650) is often regarded as the founder of modern philosophy. Central to his system were the ideas of:

- **Truth:** The belief that there was a truth to be known.
- **Rationality:** That human thinking and rationality were reliable.

---

[2] Barbour (1998) pp. 115ff; Jeeves & Berry (1998) pp. 82ff.

- **The Self:** The only thing of which he felt he could be sure was his own existence - he put forward the famous line: 'I think, therefore I am'.
- **God:** God is actually central to Descartes' system. It is because God would not deceive us that we know what we perceive clearly must be true (though there is a certain circularity here because the existence of God is one of the things we perceive clearly!)[3]

Descartes has been subject of an unusual number of misinformed attacks from both secular and Christian sources. He wrote partly in response to a movement which said that *nothing* could be known anyway, so the best thing to do was to live a moderate life according to our own cultures. Funnily enough, this sounds pretty familiar to us today! Beginning then, from a 'systematic doubt', Descartes claimed to be able to construct the system outlined above. Like the present Oxford philosopher Richard Swinburne[4], who might be seen as a modern parallel, Descartes was a committed Christian, and he wanted to see the church adopt his system.[5]

Similar ideas were developed in that great 'Age of Reason' the 18th century 'Enlightenment'. One modern (non-Christian) philosopher describes the 'Big Ideas' of the Enlightenment as truth, rationality and the self.[6] There was assumed to be a 'God's eye view of the world', a complete and objective account of all reality which was known in the mind of God and to which human knowledge tried to get ever closer. There was, they assumed, a single 'truth' about reality, so that in eg as one writer described the discoveries of Newton:

> We were unpicking the world's secrets, a world that was, to most Enlightenment thinkers, an object of divine creation. By learning to read the workings of the world, we were learning to read the mind of God.

In the foundations of this thinking, the world was rational, and human reason could be used to understand it, precisely because

---

[3] See Cottingham (Ed) (1992) ch. 7.
[4] The most 'accessible' of Swinburne's works is *Is There a God?* (1996). See also eg his (1979*)*, (1981), (1993), (1994*)* in the bibliography.
[5] See Cottingham (1992) p. 37 etc.
[6] Michael Luntley (1995) p. 9.

(to Newton himself, to sincere Christians like Kepler, Boyle, and to many others) it was created by a rational God in whose image humans were made. Unfortunately, some Enlightenment thinkers began to exaggerate the powers of reason and human capacities and some found God unnecessary, or gave him a minimal role. By the late eighteenth century the movement so exaggerated the power of reason, that finally it 'expired as the victim of its own excesses.' *(Brittannica)*. The atrocities of the French Revolution gave the lie to excessive belief in the power of Reason and the goodness of human nature.

Yet, some of the more moderate foundations remained intact, and it was generally assumed that there was one reality and truth, discoverable by human experience and reason. Descartes had shown how reason interpreted brute experience. For example, he said that through our reason we know that even though wax when heated may entirely change its physical properties (texture, colour, and smell), it is the 'same wax'. Our reason attributes an identity beyond pure experience. In contrast, the English empiricist philosopher David Hume (1711-1776) identified all *ideas* (or concepts) as corresponding one-to-one with experiences, and saw the mind as 'nothing but' a bundle of perceptions.[7] Hume abandoned the role of reason as actively interpreting experiences, the self, and God. His naiveté was breathtaking even in the eighteenth century. Today, when so many concepts in modern physics are far removed from a one-to-one correspondence with experiences, the claim of the atheist Professor Lewis Wolpert (chair of a Committee for Public Understanding of Science!) to be a follower of Hume is little short of amazing.

One response to Hume came from the philosopher Immanuel Kant (1724-1804), who pointed out that as humans we inevitably see all objects in human terms, and never experience what things are like 'in themselves'.[8] The Christian philosopher and scientist William Whewell (who invented the word 'scientist') extended this into discussion of the nature of science.[9] Philosophers of science came to recognise that human

---

[7] David Hume (1739) Bk 1, Pt 4.
[8] Francis Bacon's 'idols of the tribe' earlier hinted at this.
[9] William Whewell (1840).

perception inevitably involved interpreting, and that there was no pure 'seeing' without interpretation.

In the mid decades of the twentieth century there was an extraordinary resurgence of naiveté in the Logical Positivists, who looked back to Hume, but this was transient (it has to be said that the most naive of philosophical views do seem to be associated with atheism!) By the 1960-70s, however, philosophers such as N R Hanson, Michael Polanyi, and T S Kuhn reasserted a dynamic view of thinking and observation. It was recognised that different 'paradigms' could involve radically different ways of 'seeing;' reality (for example the perception of space-time within Einstein's theories differs from that in Newton's). Nevertheless, there was assumed to be some kind of 'reality', and whilst different 'paradigms' might perceive it differently there were limits to what made sense.[10] Our own critical realist view of knowledge in line with some of the current movements in the philosophy of science (Cf Section 10 below). But what other views are there?

Modernism and Postmodernism

In spite of a spate of books about them, the meanings of these terms remain far from clear. One writer cites claims that postmodernism started anywhere between the 1870's and the 1980's![11] Another remarks 'the term is both fashionable and elusive.'[12] A Christian commentator remarks 'if the use has mushroomed, its meaning is proportionately obscure.'[13] Another that it is a 'vague and ill-defined notion.'[14]

In general, 'modernism' seems identified with stronger belief in the truth of, and progress through, science and technology. The objective claims of Christianity are examined rationally - even if they are rejected as 'untrue'. 'Postmodernism' moved away from objectivity. It seems to have arisen through art, architecture and language rather than from science or

---

[10] See eg B Gower (1997); J Losee (1993); A Musgrave (1993); A O'Hear (1989); R Boyd et al (1991); and A F Chalmers (1982).
[11] Peter Brooker (1992) p.4.
[12] Madan Sarup (2nd Ed 1993) p. 129.
[13] Philip Sampson et al (1994) p 29.
[14] Alister McGrath (1996) p. 179.

philosophy. In art and architecture it came with a view that there was no 'pure' style and no 'true' art - so a plurality and mix of styles was acceptable. Language was seen as tied much less directly to external 'realities', and linguistic precision was unattainable. Recognising that different *perceptions* of reality could be equally valid, it may then have seemed a short step to recognising that there is actually a plurality of 'realities'. There is in postmodernism no 'God's eye view' (indeed no objectively observing God), so any human perspective is presumed equally 'valid'. Postmodernism (in the sense that we will take it) is a form of relativism, a thesis that what is 'true' or 'objectively real' is relative to different traditions, cultures or epochs, and there is nothing that is 'real' in an absolute sense. Contrast with the tenets of Descartes those of this kind of secular postmodernism:

- God (a personal powerful objective creator) does not exist.
- Human reason is unreliable (or perhaps just a facility for survival accidentally developed by our genes through Darwinian natural selection).
- 'Truth' is relative to a particular culture.
- The 'self' may be an illusion.
- 'Morality' is culturally related and without absolutes.

Now, of course, such relativism is actually self-defeating, contradictory and incoherent. To say 'there is no such thing as absolute truth' is itself a statement - apparently of absolute truth! A set of 'tenets' of 'postmodernism,' such as those suggested above is itself a contradiction, since any 'tenets' can (the postmodernist says) be 'true' only within a particular culture - so 'postmodernism' itself might validly mean the opposite to someone else!

If we think about it, a world of *complete* relativism or *complete* rejection of reason would be incoherent and impossible to live in. The postmodernist denies that there is any 'grand narrative' or overall unity of truth as taught eg by Christianity, Islam, Marxism or Humanism. Yet, as many have pointed out[15], postmodernism usually goes on to become itself a 'grand narrative'! *Pure* relativism is incoherent and unworkable.

---

[15] Eg Sarup (1993) p 154; Sampson (1994) p 46.

Even Plato pointed this out to his contemporaries[16] - but still the same old incoherent relativism keeps surfacing with new names!

So how widespread is a pure postmodernist viewpoint? In our view few hold either to complete postmodernism or (in the sense of believing there to be 'no limits' to the scope of science'[17]) to 'scientism'. Enthusiastic preachers (who have read a book on it!) sometimes exaggerate the extent of postmodernism in the thinking of young people.[18] In Autumn 1997, the founder/chair of the newly formed movement Christian Students in Science (backed by the main UK Christian youth organisations) presented to the Christians in Science conference. results of a survey of student views of science and faith.[19] In general, students believed that there *was* objective truth in science, and their relativism was limited to areas of religion/morality.

There are, however, two respects in which faith in science *has* declined markedly. Firstly, it is now seldom seen as the means of human salvation through bringing in an earthly paradise. Wars are now seen not just to arise out of poverty, but to devastate places like the relatively affluent Bosnia. Human propensity for cruelty, war and genocide seem unlikely to lessen with technological advances. Secondly, whilst science may concern 'truth', few are prepared simply to trust 'the experts' because experts are now generally recognised to be very fallible. Neither of these two points, however, lessens a general belief that there *is* a truth – at least in the area of science.

Where, however, 'postmodernism' or 'relativism' is rife is in the areas of 'religion' or 'morality'. This is common amongst those who have no particular religious belief or claim to being religious, but it also appears amongst those who are religious. So is it sensible to accept critical realism in (say) science, but be postmodernist in religion? Before looking at a few forms of religious postmodernism, we need first to look at Christian faith itself and how far it claims to be objectively true and rational.

---

[16] See Plato, *Thaetetus* 161 C-E.
[17] Tom Sorrel (1991) p. 25 makes this central to 'scientism'.
[18] This includes David Tomlinson (see below) in (1995).
[19] Justin Marston (1997).

The New Testament Views of Reason

The term 'Christian' first arose in Antioch as a nickname for followers of Jesus Christ, and it seems only sensible to define 'Christian' belief as an acceptance of the teachings of Christ.

We would then make four main contentions:

1. That Jesus is a historical person whose teachings are accurately presented in the New Testament.
2. That those who wrote the New Testament believed that their faith was reasonable and that reason was essential though insufficient for true Christianity.
3. That the historic church, and in particular the early Fathers and modern mainstream biblical Christianity, have been basically correct in their interpretation of the New Testament.
4. That this system of teachings makes the best overall sense of our human condition and experience (including both scientific and historical evidence).

Points (1) and (4) form the concern of a large part of this book, but some comments on the other two may be helpful here. Do the writers of the New Testament expect faith to make sense in a rational way? Is reason opposed to such faith? It must be emphasised, of course, that to them (as to us) Christian faith is a relationship of trust in God - not just a reasoned set of beliefs. God's kingdom is entered in a childlike way, through a response of the will to the message of the crucified Christ (Mt 18:3-4; Lk 18:17; Jn 1: 12; 1 Cor 1: 17). Neither reason, nor knowledge, nor intellectual belief in God can substitute for this kind of faith that involves response (1 Cor 8:l; Jas 2:18-23). Spiritual understanding and power, moreover, depend on the Holy Spirit - not merely on correct logic (Jn 16:13; 1 Cor 2:4). It is also obvious (and Christian philosophers recognise this) that sometimes people hold true beliefs without knowing the logic behind them, whilst others have apparently 'rational' beliefs which turn out to be wrong.[20]

Nevertheless, having said all this, it is clear that neither Jesus nor his apostles rejected knowledge or reason. They argued

---

[20] See eg Swinburne (1981) Ch. 2 etc. and see our Section 10.

logically about doctrines, expecting their teachings to make sense (eg Jesus in Mt 5:46, 6:30, 7:11, 16). Jesus appreciated the value of eyewitness accounts (Jn 15:27). It is, moreover, the non-intellectual fisherman Peter who instructs Christians to: 'Always be prepared to give an answer to everyone who asks you to give the reason for the hope that you have. But do this with gentleness and respect' (1 Pet 3:15).

Reading Paul's letters in the New Testament one is struck by the continual use of logical and rational argument. Paul's whole approach is structured and logical.[21]   In dealing with unbelievers, the apostles continually argued and disputed, starting from whatever assumptions their listeners shared. So we are told:

> As his custom was, Paul went into the synagogue, and for three Sabbath days he reasoned with them from the Scriptures, explaining and proving that the Christ had to suffer and rise from the dead (Acts 17:2 see also 9.22,29, 14.16-17).

> Every Sabbath, he reasoned in the synagogue, trying to persuade Jews and Greeks. (Acts 18:4 see also 19:28)

The second of these quotes relates to Corinth, of which in his letter he says that:

> My message and preaching were not with wise and persuasive words, but with a demonstration of the Spirit's power. (1 Cor 2:4).

Paul came to Corinth from his experience at Athens, where it seemed that intellectuals did nothing but talk about the latest ideas! His sermon/speech in Athens produced at least four converts including a philosopher, but the general 'worldly wisdom' with its focus on clever words simply laughed when Paul got to the bit about the resurrection of Jesus. Paul objected to the 'wisdom of this world' meaning not *reason* as such, but rather the *naturalistic assumption* that the supernatural was impossible. The Christian message of 'the cross' and its power must always remain 'foolishness' to those who begin with the naturalistic or physicalist *assumption* that there is no spiritual power, no supernatural, and no powerful creator God. The classical sense of 'physicalism' is to mean 'the view that the real

---

[21] See eg Rom 2:1; 1 Cor 6:2; Gal 2:14.

world is nothing more than the physical world.'[22] Paul argues that worldly wisdom, if it actually begins by ruling out the message of the Cross and Resurrection, is not true wisdom but folly, and is spiritually barren (1 Cor 2:6, 1 Cor 1:18-25). He continued to 'reason', however, with Jews and with non-Jews both in Corinth and beyond. His arguments eg in 1 Corinthians Ch. 15 about the resurrection are both logical and historical. Paul had very personal and powerful experience of God and wanted to see all Christians have the same, but as we pointed out in our earlier book *Christianity, Evidence and Truth*, he appealed to (i) *nature*, (ii) *experience*, and (iii) *historical evidence* as evidences for his faith.

New Testament Christian Faith claims to be both true and reasonable - although foolishness to those blinkered to a physicalist view of reality. Yet today there are some surprisingly diverse threats to the acceptance of this fact from those who claim the name of Christ.

Some (Theologically) Liberal Threats to Reason and Truth

Theological 'liberals' stay within the church but do not assume the whole Bible to be inspired by God. The 'traditional' liberal view has been 'modernist', holding that there *is* a unique truth but that the Bible often gets it wrong. There is, however, a new kind of *postmodernist* liberalism. In 1995 the Senior Anglican Chaplain at Loughborough University (Rev David Hart) wrote:

> 'Whereas the modernist project analysed the contents of the faiths in the detail of their stories and structures, and gave the liberal theologian a chance to 'compare and contrast' the different religions on the cosmic menu, the postmodern reality is a collection of *petites histoires* of the tribal deities that tell us little of the deities themselves, rather more of the cultures that formed them.'[23]

He gets, he says, the 'same sense of the holy' in a Pentecostal meeting, high mass, before a Sri Lankan Buddha and in a South India elephant festival. The God of 'fundamentalism' is (he says) a 'tribal god' and the 'supernaturalistic metaphysic is no

---

[22]Blackburn (1996) p. 287. Assertion by some including Christians in Brown (1998) of 'non-reductive physicalism' is linguistically confusing – and in our view is also philosophically untenable (see Section 3).

[23] Hart (1995) p. 1.

longer credible to the Western mind'.[24] There is, he thinks, no objectively real supernatural dimension. The focus of 'non-realism' (as Hart calls it) is not on a *really existing* God but on human religious experience - the 'sense of the holy'. Thus:

> ...in our contemporary pluralist world there are many choices available to us in the exercise of our spirituality... the new approach to religion has to be less on the divine figures than we have often found in the past and more on the individual's appreciation of the world of other people and the world of nature. In this case we could well speak of a new model for a non-realist Trinity - in which the focus ever shifts between the self, others and the world of nature.[25]

University chaplains, trying to stake a claim to serve the wider student body, sometimes prefer to speak vaguely about 'helping you explore your spirituality', rather than advance narrow and exclusivist claims like those of Jesus and St Paul. At first sight it does indeed sound all very inclusive and relativist - everyone is right after all! But is it? Compare the following two passages from David Hart:

> ...a non-realist spiritual growth means freedom.. to escape from religious dogmatism and exclusivism.... the new truth that will become apparent as this postmodern pilgrimage takes place will not be simply an amalgam of previous religious truths but will be a new and fuller truth...[26]

A *true* postmodernist relativism would reject all 'meta-narratives' or universal truth systems - making a total escape from dogmatism! But then we find that actually a new dogmatic truth *will* become apparent. Jesus and Paul with their foolish premodern belief in a 'supernaturalistic metaphysic' will turn out simply to be mistaken - all they got right was that human beings could have certain emotive experiences of 'spirituality' as they drank their warm cocoa together (or whatever). Having rejected all 'tribal deities', David Hart (and his mentor Rev Don Cupitt) will set up their own tribal deity and invite us to 'worship and serve the creature rather than the Creator' (Rom 1:25). These words of St Paul were applied to those of whom he said 'claiming to be wise they became fools' (Rom 1:22). It was

---

[24] Hart (1995) p. 50.
[25] Hart (1995) p. 149-151.
[26] Hart (1995) p. viii., p. 9.

his experience of those at Athens who rejected any dimension of the supernatural (as we shall see) which led him to speak witheringly to the Corinthians about the foolishness of worldly wisdom based on naturalism. (1 Cor 1:21-2).

Don Cupitt (and for all we know David Hart whom we have never met) seems a sincere though confused man. Their views are not *true* relativism (for true relativism is incoherent and impossible to live with), but simply a reassertion of old naturalistic assumptions attacked not only by Paul but by Jesus when he told a bunch of earlier theologians: 'You are wrong because you know neither the Scriptures nor the power of God.'(Mk 12:24). The God of Jesus is a creator God of power, not merely a human sense of the holy.

Hart is perfectly entitled to hold naturalistic views which amount (in any normal semantic sense) to a religious form of naturalistic atheism. It may be hard for some to understand how, with such views, he can assent to the Articles of his church, but we can see how it seems reasonable to someone in the fog of postmodernism floating on a sea of 'faithism' which focuses on the believer rather than what is believed.

In our view, however, his whole approach is both irrational and deceptive. It is irrational because there either is or is not a personal God who either approves of (say) worship of the elephant headed god Ganesha or not. It is deceptive because its claims to all-inclusive open-mindedness disguises a dogmatic naturalism. We ourselves are open in our claims that there *is* religious truth, and argue for both the rationality and the contemporary relevance of a belief in the objective reality of a supernatural dimension.

Perhaps there are few today who would *explicitly* follow Don Cupitt or David Hart. Yet their kind of assumptions (even amongst those who would not claim to be 'Christians') are fairly common. A late 1990's TV series and book *Lives of Jesus* emphasised the radically different "Jesus's" in different traditions. Its author tracks his move from a view that 'all that mattered was the Jesus of faith' to a conclusion that it is 'really' the power of the resurrection myth rather than what actually happened which is important.[27] Now in fact the Jesus of the New Testament taught that there actually *is* a being we call God, who exists independently of what we think, who created us all whether we believe it or not, and who will one day call us all to account in judgement whether we like it or not. We believe that this is either true or not, Jesus was either right or mistaken, and either rose again or didn't. But the kind of feeling many people have today is that religion is 'subjective', so all this may simply not be relevant to them. It is not that Jesus was mistaken, but that it somehow doesn't apply to them unless they relate to it.

We all, of course, accept that when there are debates between eg Christians and Jews there should be politeness and mutual respect; but postmodernist society *also* insists that no one is presumed to be 'right'. For an Evangelical Christian to attempt, for example, to persuade a Jew that Jesus was, *from God's objective viewpoint*, the Jewish Messiah, is considered cultural arrogance to be roundly condemned. This is itself ironical, since a condemnation of Evangelical Christians for *being* Evangelical (ie for wanting to evangelise) contravenes the central 'everyone is right' assumption of postmodernism!

It may, of course, be that the non-religious person simply assumes that there is *in fact* no God, so *any* moral or religious viewpoint which assumes God exists is suspect. This would actually be a dogmatic atheism disguised as broadmindedness. It may, perhaps more likely, be that people mistake a rightful toleration of alternative religious views in a pluralist society, for the acceptance that such alternatives are 'equally valid' in the sense of truth. Underlying this is the assumption that God is not a real person so 'equally valid' can be seen simply in terms of 'what it does for you'. This extends to moral issues. Since those with (say) active homosexual or promiscuous heterosexual lifestyles are rightly permitted in a pluralist society, and since some of them experience 'spirituality', anyone in the church who believes such a lifestyle is actually *wrong* is thought to be bigoted or homophobic. The church is urged to 'move with the times', and if 'the people' (most of whom never go to church) want to accept such lifestyles in ministers, the press are most put out when the Archbishop declines and mentions strange ideas

---

[27] Tully (1996) pp. 209-10.

like God's ideals in marriage. Oddly, *some* moral principles (eg anti-paedophilia, self-determination and tolerance) *are* taken by many ardent moral relativists as absolute. But they want to decide themselves which ones are absolute, not have God decide. How, anyway, could God decide if he is not there? The church is seen not a means and channel for proclaiming the will of God, but a kind of club where people can meet and experience 'spirituality' together.

We would not, of course, wish to deny the existence of genuine perspective in religion. Even in human terms, different people can perceive the same individual differently. But surely we have to use reason to decide whether any given two 'views' are really just views, or contradictory accounts at least one of which must therefore be wrong? If, for example, Muslims say that Jesus was not crucified, and Christians say that he was, surely one or other must be right? If (as Jews and Christians assume) there *is* a personal God who prophesied a coming Messiah, then either Jesus was the one God had in mind or not? The assumption that any and all religious viewpoints are 'equally valid' seems not only irrational but also incoherent. We believe that there *is* a unique religious reality, and reason plays a part in determining whether alternative claims to truth may just be perspectives or are in contradiction.[28]

Some Charismatic Threats to Reason and Truth

There are also challenges to rational Christianity made by enthusiasts in the church whose 'experientialism' is from a perspective entirely different from David Hart. In fact the problem is not new. John Wesley, the great 18th century founder of the Evangelical movement in our own land, argued for a 'middle course' in regard to reason:

> Amongst them that despise and vilify reason, you may always expect to find those enthusiasts who suppose the dreams of their own imagination to be revelations from God... When, therefore, you despise or depreciate reason, you must not imagine that you are doing God service: least of all, are you promoting the cause of God when you are endeavouring to exclude reason out of religion... it directs us in every point both of faith and practice: It guides us with

---

[28] See also Trigg (1998) ch. 3 for criticisms of religious relativism.

regard to every branch both of inward and outward holiness...
Permit me to add a few words to you. likewise, who overvalue
reason. Why should we run from one extreme to another?.. Let
reason do all that reason can: employ it as far as it will go. But, at
the same time, acknowledge that it is utterly incapable of giving
either faith, or hope, or love; and consequently of producing either
real virtue or substantial happiness. Expect these from a higher
source, even from the Father...[29]

Wesley, like St Paul, emphasised the insufficiency of reason and
the need for divine power to operate in the life of the believer.
We certainly believe that Christians need to be open to a power
or 'dynamic' of God which is not produced by reason or
argument but by God's Holy Spirit. But, in the tradition of St
Paul and John Wesley, we must oppose the 'enthusiasts' who
elevate some inner light or experience and denigrate reason and
evidence. Sadly, one Christian commentator laments:

> The postmodernist rejection of objectivity pervades the Evangelical
> church. "We have a generation that is less interested in cerebral
> arguments, linear thinking, theological systems," observes Leith
> Anderson, "and more interested in encountering the supernatural."[30]

Let's get the supernatural in perspective. The gospels record
an amazing promise of Jesus that miraculous signs would
accompany not just the apostles but 'those who believe' (Mark
16:17), and at the day of Pentecost in Acts 2, the disciples
experienced the coming of the Holy Spirit in power. Later, the
apostle Paul spoke of the Spirit-given *charismata* or gifts (*eg*
prophecy, speaking in tongues and healing) being exercised in
the early church (1 Cor 12:8-11). There seems no reason to
expect that either the promise of Jesus or the instruction of the
apostle was limited to some early phase of the church, and the
present authors share the viewpoint of those (sometimes called
'charismatics') that we should expect to see the Holy Spirit
move in power today. One comparatively recent impetus for this
has been the so-called 'Toronto blessing', which started in
Toronto in January 1994 and soon came to Britain. What many
saw as 'new' in this (eg sometimes the disconcerting occurrence
of hysterical laughter in previously sedate and 'respectable'

---

[29] John Wesley, *The Case of Reason Impartially Considered.*
[30] Veith, (1994) p.211 citing Leith Anderson (1992) p. 20.

Christians!) had in fact been noted amongst Pentecostals throughout the century, and, indeed, in earlier times.[31] The 'Toronto' thing has to be seen as part of a continuum of experiences of those open to the working of the Holy Spirit in power.

We know of many Christian meetings in which the power of the Holy Spirit, and human reactions to him, have been seen to operate in ways which we cannot fully understand. It would be silly to think that we could always understand the strategy of God, or what is the interplay of spiritual forces in some particular situations. This, however, is certainly not to say that our faith is irrational, or that some kind of inner light or feeling should replace intelligent understanding of the Bible. The reality of the *charismata* is no excuse for people who start out fairly orthodox and finish up weird, wacky, and morally wrong, because they ignored the fact that their 'inner revelations' led away from the teaching and standards of Jesus. The 'if it feels right it must be good' approach is postmodern, not Christian. Christianity is neither an alternative 'trip' nor a kind of 'do it yourself' objective truth.

But does such an attitude characterise charismatics generally? One recent book cites what it calls a 'prominent advocate' for the 'Toronto blessing' as saying:

> 'Feel, don't think', and 'If it makes sense it is not from God - if it is from God it doesn't make sense.' [32]

The author, a gracious man of God, obviously did not mean to mislead (he is positive about Roger Forster on p. 100 although recognising that he is 'on the charismatic side'!). Nevertheless, the quotation is not from a written source, but is taken from an unsympathetic journal quoting a peripheral figure. So we wrote to the following church leaders, known for sympathy to charismatic phenomena including the 'Toronto blessing':

Gerald Coates (Pioneer)
Colin Dye (Kensington Temple)
Lynn Green (YWAM)
R T Kendall (Westminster Chapel)
Jeff Lucas (Revelation Church)

---

[31] See Ken & Lois Gott (1995) appendix A.
[32] Oliver Barclay (1997) p. 117.

Sandy Millar (Holy Trinity Brompton)
John and Eleanor Mumford (Vineyard)
John Noble (Pioneer)
Dave Richards (Basingstoke Fellowship)
Wes Richards (Kings Church)
Martin Scott (Pioneer)
Terry Virgo (New Frontiers International)
All said they 'strongly disagreed' with it.

If the person concerned really did say this (and Roger Forster himself, has been accused on the internet, in writing, and from pulpits, of saying all kinds of things he hasn't!) it is most definitely not the view of any of the leading British charismatics we asked. They also strongly disagreed with equal unanimity with a view mentioned in the same book that "(Biblical) doctrine is the opponent of true spiritual experience." Holy Trinity Brompton, the cradle of the Toronto experience in the UK, is also renowned for initiating the Alpha courses which are very much to systematically teach basic doctrine. There is no perceived 'conflict' between God's truth and experience of God - how could there be?

What about biblical interpretation? Unfortunately, we *have* come across some 'charismatics' (though not leaders) who say: 'You don't need to study the Bible in context, all you need is the Holy Spirit to interpret it.' The Holy Spirit does, of course, illuminate the Bible to Christians, but the placing of inner feelings above making rational sense of the Bible is dangerous and at variance with New Testament Christianity. Charismatics, like any Christian group, have their share of mindless enthusiasts, but mainstream charismatic leaders and churches do not stand for this.

A "Post-evangelical" Threat to Reason and Truth

Nowadays it's pretty trendy to be 'post' things. We had thought of starting a 'post-everything' movement, so that no-one could be 'post' it! Anyway, David Tomlinson, who moved from the Brethren, through House Church leadership, now as an Anglican calls himself a 'post-evangelical', and Nick Mercer (who has moved from being a Baptist to an Anglican minister) seems to toy with applying the term to himself.[33]

Tomlinson's book contains some historical perspectives and various criticisms, many of them true, of Evangelicalism. But, as Nigel Wright says:

> the large majority of the points he has made had also been made from within evangelical ranks...[34]

On language, Tomlinson notes that Evangelicals are often naive about the use of metaphor. We agree; this is one reason why we write books like this one! On morality, he notes, as many have before him, that Evangelicals sometimes mistake western middle class culture for Christian morality. But are there, then, no *genuine* moral principles revealed to us by God? If there are any, don't *some* of them *coincide* with conventional middle class morality? That Evangelicals often confuse marriage with wedding was noted by one of us in 1981,[35] but the logical conclusion from this is certainly not simply that cohabiting is OK or is a 'purely private' affair as Tomlinson suggests.[36] Of course Evangelicals *are* often muddled, bigoted, or unthinking - but this does not show there is *no* consistent Evangelical view or that no Evangelicals have thought about it. So what is the particular contribution claimed for the *post*-evangelical? Tomlinson says:

> post-evangelicals tend to be people who identify culturally more with postmodernity.[37]

Postmodernism means a rejection of 'metanarratives',[38] and he sees this as an age of 'pluralism and relativism'. Confusingly, however, he then claims to espouse 'critical realism' - which is not postmodernism at all. Some statements seem contradictory, eg:

> I am not saying theology and doctrine are unimportant... Doctrinal correctness matters little to God.[39]

---

[33] Tomlinson (1995), and Mercer in Cray (1997).
[34] Wright in Cray et al (1997) p. 96.
[35] Paul Marston *The Biblical Family* (1981) in Ch. 4: 'Marriage and Wedding'.
[36] Cf eg 1 Cor 5:11.
[37] Tomlinson (1995) p. 76.
[38] Tomlinson (1995) p. 77.
[39] Tomlinson (1995) p. 41.

He parallels Jesus' story of the self-righteous Pharisee and the repentant sinner with one of a 'Spring Harvest leader' who thanks God for the Scriptures and pledges himself to proclaim them, and a bishop who draws his salary on the basis of being a believer and pastor but is not sure he can believe in miracles and isn't sure if he even believes God exists but is 'searching'. Apparently Tomlinson sees 'searching' (with the implication of agnosticism) as the modern equivalent of repentance. The problem with this is that, on any reading of the New Testament, Jesus did not praise uncertainty but repentance and faith. He did not commission his disciples to go out and lead interesting but forever inconclusive discussions but to be witnesses to his actual resurrection, to preach, teach, baptise and make disciples. If, in the philosophical sense, 'certainty' is impossible - we are happy to speak of 'conviction', but conviction there surely must be. David Tomlinson's post-Evangelicalism, moreover, seems not to be a product of charismatic 'experientialism'[40], but a reaction against the legalism and shallow thinking of some Evangelicals. It is a pity that his 'answers' are themselves so nebulous, seeming to lose sight of the evangelical baby in a desire to renew the bathwater.

Some 'Reformed' Threats to Reason and Truth

The term 'Reformed' refers to the teachings of the 16th century 'Reformers' (Luther, Calvin, Zwingli, *etc*). Their theology was based on some distinctive teachings of. Augustine. Augustine was a profound thinker, and we can admire much of what he had to say, particularly on science-faith issues. On some topics, however, it seems to us that when converted (c396 AD) he was fairly orthodox, but later introduced some ideas perhaps more related to his pre-conversion beliefs into Christian theology.[41] Two particular ideas which seem to us novel and unbiblical were his later views that:
1. 'nothing happens unless the omnipotent wills it to happen.'[42]
2. The state should use 'fear of punishment or pain' to force nonconformist Christians to accept his theology.[43]

---

[40] As Oliver Barclay suggests in (1997) p. 117.
[41] See our own (1973, 1989) which has an appendix on Augustine.
[42] Augustine, *Enchiridion* xxiv.

He linked the two. If God *forces* people to be converted so should we - and thousands of sincere Bible-believing Donatists perished through his influence. In the sixteenth century his disciples, the Reformers, likewise persecuted, imprisoned, and killed many faithful Bible-believing Anabaptists, as well as adopting his distinctive new ideas on the sovereignty of God.

Today, some of those who identify themselves as of a 'Reformed' viewpoint (many of whom, it must be said, are godly Christian people with holy lifestyles) are sometimes critical of the Charismatics for irrationality. But what of 'Reformed' theology itself? Is there not a contradiction between a God who 'can change the evil wills of men, whichever, whenever, and wherever he chooses and direct them to what is good', and the God who is Love and 'wants all men to be saved' but (according to Augustine) does nothing to save them? Surely there is contradiction in saying with Augustine: 'in the very fact that they acted in opposition to his will, his will concerning them was fulfilled.'[44] Surely there is contradiction in saying (as one modern theologian has said) 'while God ordains moral evil he is not the author of it', and 'Does not Scripture frequently say that God's will is changed... such changes are only apparent not real.'[45] No one denies, of course, that there *are* mysteries in dealing with God, but there is a difference between a mystery and a blatant contradiction. As already mentioned, the Augustinian doctrines of God have been linked throughout history to terrible practical 'contradictions' like the killing and persecuting in Jesus' name of other Christians for their beliefs. Whilst the Reformers were ruthlessly persecuting Anabaptists, those who advocated freedom of conscience (including great Christian scholars like Erasmus who extolled the piety of the Anabaptists, and the leading Anabaptist teachers themselves like Hubmaier and Denck[46]) also attacked as irrational and unbiblical the Reformed ideas of God's sovereignty. They all believed in a powerful God who acted in history and in individual lives, but it made no sense to believe that everything which happened was

---

[43] Augustine, *Corr Don.* xxiii.
[44] *Enchiridion* xxv, xxvi.
[45] Helm (1993) p. 196., p. 138. See also Sections 4 and 5 below.
[46] Cf Williams and Mergal (1957).

God's will when the Bible said it wasn't[47] and when there was evidently in the world moral evil which God says he hates.

We need to be clear on this. The Bible sometimes uses figurative/allegorical language, and there is bound to be mystery in theology (as, indeed, there is in understanding physics). But neither metaphor nor mystery changes the basic fact that Biblical Christianity is supposed to *make sense*. This is not to be negated either by those who rely just on feelings or by those who 'interpret' biblical texts to deny their obvious meaning. Mystery is not contradiction. The Bible may sometimes use symbolic language, but it does mean what it says.

Defining Mainstream Christian Orthodoxy

Our claim in this present volume, then, is that biblical or Bible-believing Christianity (ie Christianity which takes the Bible as authoritative) 'makes sense' and is consistent with modern science and historical study.

This issue, of course, may be of interest both to committed Christians and to those who are not yet believers but who wish to consider seriously whether or not Christianity is true. In either case it will obviously be necessary to ensure that what we are considering IS the Christianity of the Bible. Thus we will, without assuming that all our readers share our acceptance of the inspiration of the Bible, cite or quote the Bible as a definitive source for biblical Christianity. We generally use a modern translation of Bible, though we may sometimes refer to the Hebrew or Greek originals.

Now, if 'biblical Christianity' is, indeed, to be defined as the Christianity taught in the Bible, it must also be recognised that there may be variations in the way in which people interpret it, How, then, can one decide the true meaning? Can Christians simply reinterpret it to mean whatever they like? We would emphatically deny this. As Christians, of course, we seek the inner witness of the Holy Spirit that our understanding is correct. On an objective level, however, any interpretation of integrity should:

---

[47] Humans can choose not to do both God's will (eg Mt 23:37, 1 Jn 2:17) and his plan (Lk 7:30). Cf also Forster & Marston (1973, 1989).

1. Make sense of the actual text and fit the words used.
2. Be in line with its literary form (poetry, history, etc).
3. Be in harmony with other biblical passages.
4. Be in harmony with other known facts.
5. Take cognisance of the interpretation taken by spiritual Christians throughout history.

This last point is not to suggest any infallibility of the church, but that one should be suspicious of identifying as a valid Christian belief any novel modern theology or approach to biblical interpretation that has no support in previous Christian history. Thus, though this is very much a book about today's thinking on issues of faith, history and science, we often cite earlier Christian teaching - in particular from early church periods. References to the standard American edition of the *Writings of the Fathers,* edited by A Roberts and J Donaldson (1985 printing) are made as follows:

> The Ante-Nicene Fathers, vol ii, p 314 *(Ant Nic Fath,* ii, 314) The Nicene and Post-Nicene Fathers, series 2, vol iii, p 212 *(Nic & Pos Nic Fath,* **2,** iii, 212).

References to such teaching, and to other mainstream Christian views eg of 19th century Evangelicals or early Fundamentalists, do not, of course, presume that they are 'authoritative' - but are to show that as our interpretations of the Biblical text are the most reasonable they are the ones the church has most commonly taken.

Some readers may perhaps be surprised to find what *are* the mainstream Christian positions on some issues. Take literalism, for example. Early Jewish commentators, leaders in the early church, leading nineteenth century evangelicals *and* the scholarly founders of 'Fundamentalism', all clearly recognised that the Bible sometimes spoke in allegory. The non-literality, for example, of the 'days' in Genesis 1 is not a modern idea, but has been taught by important mainstream church leaders from the beginning. We stand in this same mainstream position and believe the modern 'young-earth creationists' (who have a package of beliefs including a world made in six literal days) are mistaken biblically as well as scientifically. Many individuals amongst them, of course, are godly Christian people whose lives commend their Lord. But we are concerned that neither unsuspecting Evangelicals (who may adopt their system) nor interested non-Christians (who may reject it and Christianity with it) should mistake young-earth creationism for orthodox historical Christianity. Actually, if pursued consistently, young-earthism can lead to some pretty unorthodox conclusions. This will become apparent when we look at issues of Creation in some detail later in this book.

God and the Honest Questioner

One final issue for this section concerns faith and questioning. Isn't 'faith' believing without asking questions? Well actually, the God of the Bible seems to like people who are prepared to be real and honest with him, Abraham, for example, is presented in the Bible as a friend of God (2 Chron 20:7, Is 41:8, Jas 2:23). Yet when God tells him about his intentions to judge Sodom, Abraham is far from unquestioning and subservient. He reminds God about aspects of divine character which are inconsistent with certain courses of action! (Gen 18:20-5) Again, the Bible shows Job as unable to understand his own suffering and convinced that there has been a slip-up in the divine administration; yet God commends him for 'speaking rightly', and his honesty leads him to an encounter with God (Job 8:20, 9:24, 13:15, 38:1, 42:7). The prophet Habakkuk is shown questioning God's providence, taking his stand on a watchtower to wait for God's answer - and he gets it! (Hab 1:2,5,2:1-2). To the self-righteous, inflated with their own importance in the order of things, God may say, 'Who are you to answer back to your maker?' (eg Rom 9:20). But the God of the Bible responds to the honest searcher after truth, for Jesus himself said, 'Seek and you will find' (Mt 7:7-8).

We believe in asking questions and in looking for answers. It is our hope that some may be helped in this by what we write in the rest of this book.

2
'Big Questions' God & Science

The Big Questions

One of the most extraordinary events in the closing years of the twentieth century must have been the outpouring of public grief in the UK (and elsewhere) over the death of Diana, Princess of Wales. There were hard-bitten men and cool businesswomen in tears, seas of flowers, and more shops shut than on Christmas day. Was it because, in her, people saw the paradoxes of themselves written large? She was a fairytale Cinderella princess, but she battled eating disorders, became a one-parent family, and had found no lasting relationship. She was a figure desperate for love and acceptance, yet one who affirmed human values against all odds and acted in warm selfless compassion. In a world dreary of mere technology and humdrum economics, she brought a whiff of glamour with a social conscience.

At the start of the twentieth century, who would have thought that a figure like Diana: beautiful, strong, fragile, lonely and vulnerable, would touch so many strings at its close? In the century's opening optimism, many might have thought that, by its end, technology would have removed want, medicine removed disease, psychology peoples' neuroses, counselling their marital problems, and sociology their difficulties of living in harmony? Sadly, this is not so. Diana lived, in the words of the CD, like a 'candle in the wind'. It was like the defiance in an earlier age of Blaise Pascal, who contrasted in his *Pensées* the fragility of mankind with the vast unthinking, uncaring universe, but said 'Mankind is just a reed, but a thinking reed.' Somehow, underneath it all, people feel that there is a worth to being human. Somehow, also, they feel that death should not be the end of what is worthwhile in humanity. Though already the effect is fading, even the non-religious flocked to express this in support for the memorial fund set up.

Throughout the past century, many works of art and literature, eg those of Gauguin, Kafka and Beckett, have reflected this search for meaning, portraying man as trying to make sense of a puzzling and pointless universe. In the late twentieth century, Damien Hirst (who brought the art world the delights of the half sheep and other sculptures) became obsessed with death in his works, though one searches them in vain for any meaningful answer to its challenge of nothingness. The collection of modern paintings in an exhibition in the Royal Academy in 1997 were described in the *Independent* as: 'ironic, post-modern and heartless'.

But questions about the meaning and fate of humankind are not just for artists and 'philosophers' for they affect us all - the meaning and destiny of the human species is reflected in each individual member of it. Does humanity have a design and purpose? Or are we all a kind of cosmic accident - with all human achievement, 'good' and 'evil', 'noble' and 'base' destined to an eventual oblivion of destruction in an unthinking universe? Do we as individuals have any meaning, or are we accidental little flickers of consciousness in an eternity of nothingness? More practically, can our lives have any real purpose? How can we manage our relationships in a culture in which, for example, that relationship of marriage, which should be the closest, so often ends in divorce?

Though for much of the time we are too busy living day to day to ask such questions, most of us are aware of them. There may be times - such as the death of a loved one or some personal crisis - when they are the most acute; but the questions are always there.

On an individual level, these questions of meaning and purpose are, of course, deep in the psychology of men and women as thinking beings. Nearly 3,000 years ago the writer of the biblical book of Ecclesiastes wrestled with them, and looked at many of the ways in which people try to avoid facing them. He tried living for pleasure (2:1), sex (2:8), or simply 'drowning his sorrows' with alcohol (2:3). He tried undertaking great building projects, doing on a grander scale what many of us do with our houses and gardens! (2:4-6). He tried amassing wealth (2:8). What was his final conclusion? 'Everything was meaningless, a chasing after wind' (2:11). How remarkably this prefigures the words of the twentieth century writer and broadcaster Malcolm Muggeridge. A former Utopian and agnostic, as a Christian he wrote:

> 'I never met a man made happy by worldly success or sensual indulgence, still less by the stupefaction of drugs or alcohol. Yet we all, in one way or another, pursue these ends, as the advertiser well knows.'[1]

Even worthy undertakings, such as the arts, knowledge, or justice, can enhance but not in themselves create a meaning for life. The writer of the Ecclesiastes also knew this. He tried the arts, focusing on choral work (2:8). He saw that 'wisdom is better than folly' and turned to the academic world for fulfillment (2:13). His conclusion could face many academics today as they throw themselves into the round of research, conferences, and published papers:

> "The fate of the fool will overtake me also. What then do I gain by being wise?" I said in my heart, "This too is meaningless." (2:15).

What, finally, about throwing oneself into a 'good cause'? Alas, he concludes that even this seems pointless if 'all share a common destiny - the righteous and the wicked, the good and the bad' (9:2).

On their own, none of these things found, in the words of Ecclesiastes, 'under the sun' can pretend to give us a purpose or meaning; without anything more, they act at best as sedatives or distractions to avoid facing the basic questions (2:17). If this life, and the realm of the purely physical, 'under the sun' is all there is, then the writer can see no meaning in it all.

Perhaps, though, he didn't look carefully enough. Perhaps he lacked the resources of modern science. So let us take a look at what modern scientific atheism has to offer.

'Scientific' Atheism

At the present time the 'popular science' sections of most 'serious' bookshops are almost dominated by a narrow coterie of expert self-publicists who praise each other's books on their respective dust covers. They include Peter Atkins, Richard Dawkins, Daniel Dennett, Steven Pinker and the journalist John Gribbin. Much of what they write is metaphysics not 'science'

---

[1] Muggeridge (1968), p 96.

popular or otherwise, and their books are full of extended analogy and parables (we might call them 'Penpops Fables' since Penguin 'popular science', books are especially full of them). We are going in this section to call their world 'Denkinsland' and explore what it is like.

The primary starting point is a ruthless rejection of any idea of the primacy of MIND or of conscious design in the structure of the world. Dennett totally rejects any form of what he calls 'skyhooks':

> 'a *skyhook* is a "mind-first" force or power or process, an exception to the principle that all design and apparent-design is ultimately the result of mindless, motiveless mechanicity.'

The universe began without mind or design. Earth resulted from blind purposeless forces. Several billion years ago there was a 'spontaneous arising of self-replicating, yet variable entities'[2] ie life. Chance mutations in this first replication system led (somehow) to a 'DNA/protein based information technology' which is:

> 'so sophisticated... that you can scarcely imagine it arising by luck, without some other self-replicating system as a forerunner'.[3]

Once established, random undesigned mutations in the DNA genetic sequences occasionally gave rise to features beneficial for survival in prevailing environment. Natural selection enabled these particular organisms to survive and reproduce where others failed, causing a diversification and development of organisms. In structural terms, various 'thresholds' were passed: multi-cell-systems, nervous-systems, consciousness, language, and technology.[4] However complex the structures, however, nothing has been planned or designed:

> 'Natural selection is the blind watchmaker, blind because it does not see ahead, does not plan consequences.'[5]

The survival 'unit' in this process is not the organism, but the 'gene'. The coding in the DNA (the 'genotype') causes particular features in the organism (the 'phenotype'). If the latter

---

[2] Dawkins (1995), p. 160
[3] Dawkins (1995) p. 175
[4] Dawkins (1995) pp. 180ff
[5] Dawkins (1986) p. 21.

are useful to ensure the survival of the genes, then those genes (and therefore those phenotypes) will persist. Our human bodies are nothing but huge lumbering robots that have evolved through blind natural selection as gene survival mechanisms. Genes unconsciously programme not only the development of our bodies (phenotypes) but behaviour leading to the building of external structures eg of birds in building nests (a kind of 'extended phenotype'). Individual organisms are simply part of a wider picture of gene survival. Natural selection, being blind, will avoid pain for organisms only if this enhances gene survival. So:

> 'The total amount of suffering per year in the natural world is beyond all decent contemplation... In a universe of blind physical forces and genetic replication, some people are going to get hurt, other people are going to get lucky, and you won't find any rhyme or reason in it, nor any justice. The universe we observe has precisely the properties we should expect if there is, as bottom, no design, no purpose, no evil and no good, nothing but blind, pitiless, indifference.'[6]

Consciousness, then, is nothing but an emergent property of matter operating blindly under natural selection on purposeless replicator systems. Dennett states:

> 'An impersonal, unreflective, robotic, mindless little scrap of molecular machinery is the ultimate basis for all the agency, and hence meaning, and hence consciousness in the universe.'[7]

Natural selection explains it all, there is no 'mystery' about us or our consciousness. Dawkins writes:

> 'in the conviction that our own existence once presented the greatest of all mysteries, but that it is a mystery no longer because it is solved.'[8]

In Denkinsland there is no 'progress' in any sense of the whole system moving towards a goal. As there is no design, no particular development can be said to be 'good' or 'fitting' (as God does in Genesis) as a stage towards achieving the designed ends. Some organisms are more complex than others, but from the perspective of genes and natural selection a simple survival

---

[6] Dawkins (1995) p. 155.
[7] Dennett (1995) p. 203.
[8] Dawkins (1986) p. xiii.

mechanism may be as effective and so as 'good' as a complex one. 'Good' just means successful.

At one very recent 'threshold' of development, 'culture' has emerged. Culture consists of transmission of ideas, which Dawkins has named 'memes',[9] which themselves compete for survival. Morality, ethics, religious beliefs, etc, are all (in Denkinsland) memes which have emerged and been transmitted because they have survival value. Memes, like genes, 'obey the laws of natural selection quite exactly.'[10] Thus successful memes:

> 'have in common the property of having phenotypic expressions that tend to make their own replication more likely by disabling or pre-empting the environmental forces that would tend to extinguish them.'[11]

Dawkins and Dennett, then, seem to regard memes as a kind of virus, a replicator with its own genetics preying on an independently produced organism (in this case the human brain). Like organic viruses, memes have their own ancestry and mechanisms for success with their hosts. The meme for 'faith', for example, contains within it (they say) the discouragement of any kind of critical judgement which would make its host brain reject it.

In a thorough Denkinsland, then, ethical values and feelings of purpose and meaning are nothing but memes. Their survival value (ie in infecting human minds) need have no reference to whether they are 'true' or relate to anything 'real'. They may *sometimes* have the functionalist effect of helping the infected organism to survive (as least until the meme can be passed on), but even this is not necessary. It is as fortuitous for memes that brains happen to have evolved open to meme-infection as it is for fleas that dogs happen to have evolved open to flea infestation.

'Consciousness', on this theory, has no particular meaning. We have noted Dawkins' assertion that natural selection now solves any supposed mystery of human existence. Dennett, ruthlessly denying any 'skyhooks' for the human mind, can see

---

[9] See eg Dennett (1995) p. 341 ff following Dawkins (1976).
[10] Dennett (1995) p. 345.
[11] Dennett (1995) p. 359.

it only as an accidental by-product of the physical process of natural selection of brains. Even if consciousness is regarded as a unity (which is doubtful for Dennett suggests it is more like a parallel processor[12]), it must certainly cease with death.

So what are we to make of these ideas (or we might say memes) of Denkinsland, with which they labour with evangelical ardour to infect the rest of us? Most of us, frankly find it all rather bleak. There is no way to *disprove* it of course. Dennett's *determination* to see reality in terms of unidimensional, non-dualist, skyhook-free, determinism will be impervious to any 'evidence'. But what we can note is some rather strange attempts of its progenitors (or one might say meme-parents) to special-plead away its implications.

Firstly, neither Dawkins nor Dennett are quite happy with the term 'reductionist', which in this context (sometimes called ontological reductionism) means that one thing is seen to be 'nothing but' something else (eg consciousness is nothing but an accidental by-product of brain mechanisms). Dawkins claims to be a 'hierarchical reductionist' (which means he reduces things in stages), whilst Dennett declaims against 'greedy reductionists' (which means he prefers to do it slowly).[13] Sometimes these terms are used strangely (eg Spencer is a 'greedy reductionist' because he wanted to derive 'ought' from 'is' too quickly).[14] Personally it is not the *stages* or *speed* of reduction we find unacceptable, but the notion that it makes sense at all.

There are, however, some more direct indications of discomfort at the logic of Denkinsland. Dennett speaks of:

> our transcendence, our capacity to 'rebel against the tyranny of the selfish replicators' as Dawkins says.'[15]

This is striking in Dawkins' book *The Selfish Gene*. After umpteen chapters telling us how over aeons of time genes have directed organic evolution through natural selection (including that of the brain) to act out their bidding, he suddenly tells us that we don't have to obey them. Why have they so badly

---

[12] Dennett (1991) has this as a main argument; see also Dennett (1996) Ch. 3.
[13] Dawkins (1986), Dennett (1995).
[14] Dennett (1995) p. 466.
[15] Dennett (1995) p. 471. Others (eg Leakey (1992)) make the same jump.

bodged it? Where did our amazing freedom of action come from? Not from skyhooks anyway according to Dennett. But what mechanisms *can* Denkinsland offer us? All Dennett offers us is 'cranes'.

> 'A *crane*...is a subprocess or special feature of a design process that can be demonstrated to permit the local speeding up of the basic slow process of natural selection.'[16]

Sex, apparently, is a crane, and so are lots of other things. Well, firstly, it is hard to see in what sense it can 'speed up' the process. On what scale can natural selection be measured? What is 'advanced' and what is 'lower'? Natural selection just concerns success in survival – there is no 'progress' *towards* anything, for the process is blind and directionless anyway. In any event, a 'crane' is merely something that increases a rate of change (assuming even that we can measure this) *under* natural selection. It accelerates changes in genes – but it does not cancel effects of selection to favour gene 'selfishness'. So how could it help us see where freedom from genetic determination came from? We can find no explanation in Denkinsland.

The next point concerns meaning. As human beings we always seem to ask not just 'how?' but 'why?' Now here Dawkins and Dennett seem to differ. Dawkins suggests that questions like 'Why is there anything rather than nothing' (asked since the middle ages) is one that it is not 'legitimate or sensible to ask.'[17] He claims science can answer some 'why' questions – but when one looks at his examples they are really all 'how' questions in disguise. Purpose is an illusion. Dennett, in contrast, accepts that a basic human characteristic is that *'we want to know why'*.[18] So let's go with Dennett, and ask some 'why' questions.

Is there anything special about humans? Interestingly, Dennett picks out various features seemingly unique to our species:

> They (ie ethical theorists) all agree in seeing morality to be, in one way or another, an emergent product of a major innovation in perspective that has been achieved by just one species Homo

---

[16] Dennett (1995) p. 78.
[17] Dawkins (1995) p. 113.
[18] Dennett (1995) p. 22.

Sapiens taking advantage of its unique extra medium of information transfer, language.[19]

Genesis 1-3, of course, identifies three characteristics that mark out humankind:

1. The use of humanly created language (Genesis 2:19,23).
2. The recognition of morality (Genesis 2:17).
3. The uniquely inter-personal relationship (supremely in the deep knowing within marriage) leading to culture (Genesis 2:18,22,24).

Dennett agrees that all these are distinctive, but wants them to have special meaning without the 'skyhooks' of intended design. So how does he go about it?

Let us focus on a more specific issue, the meaning of ethics. To Dennett (as to us) wrongdoings like 'murder' or 'rape' are uniquely human – the terms are not properly applied to animals. Dennett also recognises the potential of ethics based on revelation:

> if you believe that the Bible… is *literally* the word of God, and that human beings are put here on Earth by God in order to do God's bidding, so that the Bible is a sort of user's manual for God's tools, then you do indeed have grounds for believing that the ethical precepts found in the Bible have a special warrant that no other writings could have.[20]

Dennett (and Nietzsche whom he quotes at length, and others) raise the God issue to contrast it with their own ideas. Christian theology teaches that in the beginning there was God and God's self-expression which was also God (John 1.1). Between the persons of the Trinity existed language, relationship, and interpersonal reaction. God is Love, and the rightness of love relationship between persons is eternal. Humankind, created in the image of God (with male/female in marriage reflecting that unity but plurality of persons) was subject to moral law as revealed by God. The church has always, of course, taken elements of the Genesis account figuratively (of which more later), but it is not a fairy story and it presents the truth about the human origins and condition. The Bible, Christians believe, is a

---

[19] Dennett (1995) p. 456.
[20] Dennett (1995) p. 476.

record of humankind's encounters with that one God, and the divine revelations in it indicate what is right and wrong. Certainly millions of Christians so believe – whether or not Dennett is right to assert that the 'unchallenged view of philosophers who work in ethics today' differs.[21] Humankind is seen as having an 'essence' consisting in conformity to the divine image.

Dennett, in a rather muddled way, seems to be recognising the consistency of this view of human essence and morality. He rejects it, of course, because he believes there is no God and so no 'skyhook' type prior design for humankind. So how, then, *is* he to maintain meaning for human essences, and for meaning and morality, *without* any skyhooks?

First, he recognises the 'naturalistic fallacy', ie, that 'you can't derive "ought" from "is".[22] But he argues that it 'has to' be derived from something, and concludes:

> The most compelling answer is that ethics must *somehow* be based on an appreciation of human nature – on a sense of what a human being is or might be, and on what a human being might want to have or want to be. If that is naturalistic then naturalism is no fallacy.[23]

Dramatic, but not very logical. What *is* human nature? There are no skyhooks, remember, no externally defined 'essence' of true humanity. 'Human nature' can mean only what human beings actually *are*. If they *are*, in fact, capricious, cruel, uncaring, selfish, arrogant etc, then that *is* human nature. So how can an 'appreciation' of that nature define how we *ought* to act? The 'sense of what a human being is' can only tell us that human beings *ought* to behave as they in fact all do behave - which is not a lot of help..

What of what a human being *might be*? Well we have all kinds of potentials – eg more greed, more selfishness, more cruelty, genocide, sadism, pointless destructive acts etc. Who is to say which of these potentials we *ought* to choose? One cannot define what is 'right' according to human potentials, for the

---

[21] Obviously moral philosophers like Mary Midgely (sympathetic to the Christian viewpoint), do point out complexities in the issues (eg in Midgely (1994) p. 110), but Dennett exaggerates.

[22] Dennett (1995) p. 467.

[23] Dennett (1995) p. 468.

essence of what is 'right' is to tell us *which* particular human potential we ought to choose.

Likewise with what a human being might *want to* be. Some might want to be masters of the world, to enslave others etc. Ethics tell us which particular desires are 'right' to follow - so we cannot *define* what is right according to desires.

Trying to define ethics by looking at what human beings *are,* or *could be* or *want to be* is all equally circular and illogical. It is not so much using a skyhook as trying to haul oneself up by one's shoelaces. It is no use Dennett bandying about terms like 'greedy reductionist' in all directions, like a blind Cyclops with a club. The idea of deriving morality from *anything* when one denies any skyhooks is a nonsense – whether one's reductionism is slow, fast, hierarchical or otherwise. Dennett's criticisms of other 'naturalistic' ethics (including utilitarianism, Kantianism, and the new sociobiologists) are all true – but his own system does not work either.

Looked at another way, let us remember that morals are *nothing but* memes – a kind of intellectual virus that has infected human brains. But, says Dennett, we should not make the 'genetic fallacy', the 'mistake of inferring current function or meaning from ancestral function or meaning.' So Dennett goes on to quote Nietzsche saying:

> the origin of a thing and its eventual utility, its actual employment and place in a system of purposes, lie worlds apart; whatever exists, having somehow come into being, is again and again reinterpreted to new ends, taken over, transformed and redirected by some power superior to it; all events in the organic world are a subduing, a becoming master, and all subduing and becoming master involves a fresh interpretation, an adaptation through which any previous "meaning" and "purpose" are necessarily obscured or even abandoned.[24]

Our moral codes, then originated through a combination of :

i.   organic selfish genes which developed our brains through natural selection for survival.

ii. the infection of culturally transmitted memes.

---

[24] Dennett (1995) p. 465. Also quoted in part on p. 470, quoting from Nietzsche's Second Essay.

So what 'superior power' has adapted these, and who or what is to say that it *is* 'superior'? Apparently:

> Once memes are on the scene, they, and the *persons* they help create, are the potential beneficiaries.[25]

It is 'persons' then which are the 'higher entities' with their 'meme infested brains'. It is persons who (presumably) 'build a transcendent focus of meaning' on the base provided by genes.

Now if this is simply a description of the fact that there are loosely defined entities called 'persons' in Denkinsland, infected by memes of intention of moral feelings, this can hardly be denied. But the question is not whether or not different people have different *moral feelings*, but whether *morality* has any meaning. This distinction is crucial. As an analogy, consider the difference between studying what different cultures have *thought about* cosmology, and deciding which set of views corresponds with some kind of cosmological reality. There is, we note, a difference between a sociological study of beliefs and belief systems, and a question as to whether those beliefs relate to anything 'real' or 'true'. A sociological study of people infected with a meme of belief in a flat earth is interesting, but does not tell us if that belief is 'true' or relates to a physical reality. Now likewise, a sociological study of (say) groups who *believe* child rape is acceptable, is not the same as asking whether their ethical beliefs are 'true' or relate to any kind of ethical reality. The problem is that in Denkinsland ethics are *nothing but* memes, and there is no basis to decide which are 'better' or 'worse' memes – any more than one has (in Denkinsland) a better or worse virus. Memes are just self replicating virus-type ideas. The decision that one particular meme is 'better' comes as part of the meme package itself. In other words, any meme is as 'good' as any other, since it can be judged only by its own self valuation. Yet this is not how Dennett (or Dawkins) speaks. Thus, eg, he says the 'legion of devotees' of Nietzsche:

> has included a disreputable gaggle of unspeakable and uncomprehending Nazis and other such fans whose perversions of

---

[25] Dennett (1995) p. 470.

his memes make Spencer's perversions of Darwin's seem almost innocent.[26]

Now hang on a minute. We thought that the whole point was that memes evolve, have their own inbuilt survival value, and are adapted by superior powers? There have been a lot more Nazis than 'true Nietzscheans' – so why (in his view) is it a 'perversion'?

Then again, Dennett informs us that the Hutterite society (who resemble the Amish):

> achieve impressive success, but only at the cost of prohibiting the free exchange of ideas and discouraging thinking for oneself... That is why (their) solution is a nonsolution to the problems of human society.[27]

What does a 'nonsolution' mean? Nothing, surely, more than that the meme which has infected Dennett's brain differs from the memes in their brains – which we knew already.

There was a school of ethicists called 'ethical intuitionism', centred around G E Moore (1873-1958), who claimed to be able to 'intuit' ethics directly. Strangely enough, the ethics they intuited turned out to tally remarkably well with those that happened to prevail in their particular intellectual Cambridge/Bloomsbury set. Likewise here. The supreme memes (mysteriously identified by Dennett without skyhooks), turn out to value above all the kind of freedom of ideas so precious to wealthy, intellectual Professors in institutions of high privilege. What a coincidence!

The inventors of Denkinsland don't really *live* there. Their logical conclusion would be not only that personal identity (if it exists at all as a unity) ceases with death, that there is no purpose to the whole evolutionary process including us, no meaning to our lives (other than mere *feelings* of intention), and no way to decide whether one ethical meme is 'better' than another. They could not live with this, so they only go on package tours to Denkinsland.

Dawkins, in his 1998 *Unweaving the Rainbow,* begins by noting the depression of a foreign publisher of his first book at

---

[26] Dennett (1995) p. 464.
[27] Dennet (1995) pp. 474-5.

his 'cold bleak message', and the effect on a young girl that 'it had persuaded her that life was empty and purposeless'. With extraordinary arrogance Dawkins associates this with accusations of arid joylessness 'flung at science in general' – as though his own philosophy and 'science in general' were somehow equivalent. The book reminded us of a comment made the previous summer by the Starbridge Lecturer in Science and Religion at Cambridge (a former President of the British Psychological Society):

> (Dawkins) purports to be speaking for the whole of science as though all scientists think what he thinks, but they don't... I think there is undoubtedly truth in Darwin's theory of evolution, but it is not a complete explanation of everything as Dawkins makes out – and he muddles up what is validly established science and the ideas he had in the bath last night, and he presents this as though is it a seemless robe and it is actually quite misleading.[28]

Dawkins speaks of the 'very proper purging of saccharine false promises'[29] – though he does not tell us why it is 'very proper' given that his actions are nothing but the result of a particular meme. As we read on, we sense his bitter disappointment on leaving a credulous childhood in which father Christmas descended chimneys and there was a tooth fairy and a heaven[30] though this hardly makes it imperative for him to crusade for the enlightenment of other misled souls. Apart from the odd reference to 'the sense of wonder in science', we search the book in vain for any kind of *rationale* for optimism, commitment to truth, or any other positive message. Its forays into theology are crude and he persists in the delusion that the Genesis creation accounts were intended as 'scientific' in the same sense as present DNA theories.[31] He loses no opportunity to have a crack at his arch rival and fellow atheist Stephen Jay Gould.[32] Ironically, Sir Anthony Hewish, whose sense of

---

[28] Fraser Watts (1998) in an interview in Cambridge included in the Christian Students in Science (CSIS) video *Encounter* (1999) – for copies see www.csis.org.uk

[29] Dawkins (1998) p. ix.

[30] Dawkins (1998) p. 139.

[31] Dawkins (1998) p. 183 etc

[32] Dawkins (1998) pp. 195-209 - though as Michael Ruse has pointed out to us, Gould is both more tolerant and less 'religious' in his brand of atheism.

wonder at the discovery of pulsars (in 1967) is a main instance cited by Dawkins,[33] is actually a Christian who thinks Dawkins fails to understand the mysteries of modern scientific reality.[34] In general, Dawkins' book mixes up his 'bath-thoughts' with true enough bits about DNA fingerprinting, and junk DNA, and with many useful anecdotes.[35] But where in it is any answer to the rational despair in his readers that he cited in his preface? So it's a bit of a surprise that it all turns out to be rather complicated as well as meaningless and purposeless! So if you are lucky enough to catch an Oxford meme you may be able to wax lyrical in and about poetry! But what is all this but an upmarket rendition of the irrational leap to singing the Monty Python 'Always look on the bright side of life'?

The kinds of thoroughgoing atheism presented by Dawkins and Dennett are not, in fact, new. Dennett quotes much from the nineteenth century philosopher Nietzsche, who understood well the connection between meaninglessness and the fading of God from our beliefs. Nietzsche could not stand the idea of God always watching him and loving him even in his evil; he determined therefore, that God had to die.[36] Man was then supposed to laugh in the face of the emptiness of the universe, and rise above it to become superman. Zarathustra says to the Higher Man: 'He who sees the abyss, but with an eagle's eyes - he who grasps the abyss with an eagle's claws; he possesses courage.' [37] Nietzsche himself, however, was unable to do this; his mind snapped under the strain (we say this with compassion) and for the last years of his life he was insane.

How does all this compare with old fashioned 'humanism'? 'Humanism', in its original sense, meant the assertion of human values in a Christian framework.[38] It was entirely rational to

---

[33] Dawkins (1998) p. 34.

[34] CSIS also interviewed Hewish in August 1998. Hewish's research assistant (also mentioned by Dawkins) was Jocelyn Bell Burnell – a devout Quaker.

[35] Did you know that 'an elephant's penis swings at a frequency much slower than sound' (p.74)?

[36] See for example, Nietzsche (1884) in the words of the Ugliest Man, p 278.

[37] Nietzsche (1884) p 298, We are, of course, aware of the difficulty of being certain of Nietzsche's exact meaning, caused by his comparatively unsystematic approach.

[38] This refers, for example, to followers of Desiderius Erasmus (1467-1536),

assert such values for a being designed and made in the image of a personal Creator. In the modern atheistic and negative sense, however, the term 'humanism' means an attempt to assert similar values for a mankind viewed as a result of chance material forces. But why should human actions, if there were no design or purpose behind being human, have any more significance than those of apes or ants? Modern humanism's values are 'borrowed' from Christianity without the philosophical basis that gave them validity.

A French philosopher who called himself a 'humanist' was the existentialist Jean-Paul Sartre. He wrote in 1946: 'The existentialist finds it extremely embarrassing that God does not exist, for there disappears with him all possibility of finding values in an intelligible heaven.'[39] Sartre's plays, above all, show what a great understanding he had at that time of the significance of disbelief in God's existence. He was wrestling with the problem that if (as his atheism implied) mankind is a product of chance, then there is no 'truly human nature' or 'human essence' which defines for us how we should live. Neither human purpose nor morality has any logical basis. Nevertheless, at that time Sartre was hopeful that man could create meanings for himself. Writing later about that earlier part of his life, he was less optimistic; comparing himself to a traveller without any meaning or vocation, he lamented: 'Atheism is a cruel long-term business.'[40] He then tried to solve his problem by plunging into a commitment to a cause: the communist philosophy of Karl Marx.

Ironically, however, Marx's own thought showed Sartre's problem even more clearly. Marx's *1844 Manuscripts and The German Ideology* (written 1845-6) set the framework for all his thinking, and introduced the idea of a 'truly human essence' from which man was alienated. Later notebooks (1857-8) mention also alienation. In his last works like *Das Kapital* (1867) the concern has become narrowly technical – but the same assumption of 'alienation' underlies them. Yet Marx claimed that man was simply a product of material forces. Who or what, therefore, determined this 'truly human essence'? Marx

---

[39] Jean-Paul Sartre (1946) p 33.
[40] Sartre (1964), p 157.

claimed that the fundamental 'realities' were material and economic, and that moral codes were just a kind of side product 'projection' of these realities; they were a part of the 'ideologies' used by the dominant classes in societies. But we might then ask Marx in what sense of the word his promised classless society would be 'better'. And if it is not 'better', then why should we work for it? Marxism really had no answers to the problems of human identity, morality and meaning which Sartre had asked. Where did Sartre himself finally arrive in his quest for meaning. The philosopher Jean Guitton cites a report that, right at the end of his life, Sartre admitted in an interview that he had finally come to want to testify to the existence of God – but his companion Simone de Beauvoir suppressed the interview.[41] Perhaps this is only rumour, but whether or not he himself found an answer, he had clearly laid out the issues.

The simple truth is that naturalistic systems ('science' based or not) may *describe* organisms which *feel* they have meaning, purpose or ethics - but cannot provide any logic for such things to have any basis in reality.

We might have come to writers like Dawkins and Dennett, the doyens of late 20th century Penguin popular science, expecting that some wonderful new answers to questions of meaning would come from their science. Instead, as noted, one finds only marginally updated references back to the same old tried and failed atheism of earlier philosophers like Hobbes[42], Hume and Nietzsche. Their works are full of word pictures and parables (which we earlier dubbed 'Penpops fables') some of which are to 'prove' obscure distinctions reminiscent of scholastic philosophy. They seem to contain very little actual science and no research – they are essentially homespun philosophy. But Dawkins, for example holds an Oxford Professorship (specially endowed by Microsoft) for the 'Public Understanding of Science'. His militant atheism is presented as though a part of science. So we might ask: 'can science *as science* really answer questions of meaning and purpose?' Many eminent scientists, who have published real scientific results, seem not to think so.

---

[41] *Paris Match*, 12th December 1986.
[42] If Hobbes was not actually an atheist God is excluded from his natural world.

Albert Einstein, probably the most revered scientist of the twentieth century, wrote:

> The scientific method can teach us nothing else beyond how facts are related to, and conditioned by, each other. The aspiration toward such objective knowledge belongs to the highest of which man is capable, and you will certainly not suspect me of wishing to belittle the achievements and heroic efforts of man in this sphere. Yet it is equally clear that knowledge of what *is* does not open the door directly to what *should be*. One can have the clearest and most complete knowledge of what *is*, and yet not be able to deduce from that what should be the *goal* of our human aspirations ... the ultimate goal itself and the longing to reach it must come from another source."[43]

Professor Stephen Hawking, who has become a living icon for modern science, wrote:

> ...even if there is only one unique set of possible laws, it is only a set of equations. What is it that breathes fire into the equations and makes a universe for them to govern?... Although science may solve the problem of how the universe began, it cannot answer the question why does the universe bother to exist? I don't know the answer to that.[44]

Famously, this is put that *science answers questions of 'how?',* *but not the more crucial ones of 'why'.* Dawkins scoffs at this, but does not refute it - and his supposed 'why?' answers are really only 'how?' ones. Science is just the study of nature - even if that includes the human brain and psychology. The natural space-time world itself - that which is 'under the sun' in the words of Ecclesiastes - cannot provide meaning.

There are, then, two possibilities. One would be a totally bleak version of Denkinsland, where there is in fact no meaning, purpose or morality. The other possibility is that these things can be found by looking outside nature, to metaphysics.

Ludwig Wittgenstein (1889-1951), in his acclaimed 1921 work *Tractatus,* concluded that 'the solution of the riddle of space and time lies *outside* space and time', but went on to argue that actually 'the riddle [of life] does not exist' - or at least

---

[43] Albert Einstein (1954), p 41.
[44] Hawking (1993) p 90.

cannot be expressed and answered in language.[45] This made him paradoxically a father-figure both to logical empiricists (who denied meaning to metaphysics) and to some existentialists (who thought metaphysical phenomena real but incommunicable). Both these two great systems of atheistic twentieth century philosophy ran into blind alleys, and are now largely dead. Wittgenstein himself moved away from the *Tractatus,* and in his *Lectures on Religious Belief* a few years later found a place for religious language. Such language still seems, however, to refer to a life-directing frame of reference rather than allowing us to ask whether or not God really exists - reflecting the insistence in his later works that language is used differently in different spheres.

To most of us, in any event, simple denial that there *is* a 'riddle' is a hollow 'solution'.[46] If we cannot find a meaning within the purely physical space-time, then it makes sense to see if it can be found on another level - through a different but related reality in the realm of 'metaphysics'.

Science, Metaphysics and Religion

'Metaphysics' is defined thus by dictionaries of philosophy:

'the questions of metaphysics arise out of, but go beyond, factual or scientific questions about the world.'[47]

'questions about reality that lie beyond or behind those capable of being tackled by the methods of science.'[48]

Science enables us to construct generalisations as part of a description of natural processes, and to use these to successfully predict future natural events. Metaphysics asks questions about persons, consciousness, meaning, and morality.

There is a tradition that claims that the questions of metaphysics are *meaningless*. This starts with the eighteenth century philosopher Hume and he was looked to by the Logical Empiricists or Positivists (cf below Section 10) who claimed that anything that was not verifiable by observation was

---

[45] Wittgenstein (1921) 6.521.
[46] Derek Stanesby (1985), chap 3, gives a Christian view of Wittgenstein and his followers.
[47] Lacey (1996) p. 205.
[48] Blackburn (1994) p. 241.

meaningless. Associated with these was Quine, the man to whom Dennett dedicated his book. Inevitably, of course, they *do* in practice raise metaphysical questions. They then attempt to answer these naturalistically - an attempt which is doomed as we have shown. A scientific description of what *is* cannot include evaluations or analysis of purpose – the argument inevitably becomes circular.

The Christian claim is that the other 'reality' spoken of by Wittgenstein is a religious reality. It can be recognised, can be described in language (at least to no *less* an extent than we can describe, eg fundamental physical realities in the light of modem physics) and *is* both described and experienced in Christianity. Christianity claims to give men and women a real meaning and purpose for the fullest development of their beings in all their potentialities: mental, spiritual and aesthetic. It presents mankind, male and female, as a product of divine design, made in the image of a personal God, and capable of receiving eternal life becoming God's children through faith. In this way, mankind may find its true place in the universe, beginning to live in God's way in his world, relating to others as God intended. Christianity claims, moreover, to solve mankind's universal problem of death (which seems to deny any meaning to the individual), for in the historical Resurrection of the man Jesus Christ, death has been both defeated and shown to be defeated. Now, all this may be mistaken, it may be a lie, it may be raising false hopes, it may be a wishful dream; but the one thing which it certainly is *not* is irrelevant to contemporary mankind. If we are talking about the authentic message of Jesus, and not some anaemic version of Christianity, then it is certainly worth bothering to find out what it says and whether or not it is true. We will begin, however, with more general issues of personal identity and theism, to which we turn in the next two sections.

3
Personal Identity

The "I" Data and Science

As we have already noticed, the apostle Paul appeals to evidences from nature, from history, and from personal experience to establish the truth of Christianity. Noticeably, in approaching those with no established belief in a creator God, he begins from nature (eg Acts 17). This is logical, because the idea of a personal creator has to make sense to someone before they can understand and accept that Jesus was sent by him. In a sense, though, it is even more basic that we understand something of what we mean by a 'person'. This is central both to our understanding of ourselves and to the assessment of whether belief in a personal God makes sense. This section has, inevitably then, to be rather more 'philosophical' than much of this book, so we hope that readers will bear with this.

So first let us think about the basic experiences which each individual person throughout history has had to interpret. This is couched in the first person, though obviously we tend to infer that there are others with similar reflections.

1. **Experiences:** I am aware/conscious of having experiences.
2. **Existence:** As Descartes famously wrote: 'I think therefore I am'. What he called our 'intuition', a felt ability to perceive some things very clearly, leads me to conclude that *if* I am experiencing then *I* must exist to be having the experiences. The experiences themselves could be hallucinations, dreams, or of some external reality. But, whatever they are, I am experiencing them and so I must exist.
3. **Sensory experience/qualia:** I am aware that I do not usually control what I experience. My sensory experiences are largely 'given' to me and include a variety eg visual and tactile experiences. *Qualia* are qualities of immediate experiences presented to consciousness, eg of 'red' or 'headache' or 'taste of bananas'.
4. **Volition/Intentionality:** I seem to feel that 'I' am making decisions. 'I' decide to raise 'my arm' and my arm raises.

5. **Freedom:** I seem to feel that I have a 'freedom' in making my decisions. I choose to do certain things when I 'could have done' other things.

6. **Thought:** I am aware of several kinds of internal intentional 'thinking' which are different from perception, including:

    a. imagining visual images: these can be particular, although putting in detail is not easy

    b. thinking of universal concepts eg 'a dog' 'a triangle' – which may or may not have particular images associated with them, ie they may be abstract with no particular 'kind' of dog or triangle.

    c. reflection, using language, on propositions and their relationships, which may involve using logic.

    d. me: I come to think of 'me' as including the part of what I perceive as my body. In some ways I experience my 'mind' or 'consciousness' as being 'inside' my body and experiencing and acting 'through' it – but the I-body relationship is much more intimate than this.

These kinds of 'internal' immediate experiences have been shared by humans throughout history. But there is also an amount of data generated by reflection and more recently science which is 'external' but relates to our minds and brains:

A. **Reality:** Most of us tend to assume that there is some kind of 'external reality' which is physical. Some experiences are interpreted as 'perception' ie of what is 'real'.

B. **Dreams:**. Some experiences (my 'waking experiences') seem to make some kind of coherent sense – I conclude that these relate to an external 'reality', others (my 'dreams') are less coherent and I come to believe that they do not relate to any external reality. This is, of course, quite an elaborate inference – though we make it very early in life.

C. **Brain Complexity:** The brain contains billions of cells (neurons or neurones). Each neuron can communicate with between 2,000-200,000 others, and many experiences set up a wave of reactions firing across numerous cells. Some cells (eg in the retina of the human eye) act as very sensitive particle detectors.

D. **Brain-Mind:** It is found that different parts of human experience are associated with molecular (chemical and electronic) changes in the brain cells. In some cases of damage, however, an undamaged part can sometimes be adapted to take over a task it does not normally do. Though reducible to parts, the brain is a complex system that sometimes reacts holistically – ie on a wider basis.

Two obvious questions arise. Firstly, how can we relate and reconcile our personal experiences (the 'I-story' and qualia) with the objective ideas of observation and science (the 'O-story')? Secondly, if we find a way to link the I-story and O-story, will this also be in line with concepts of personal identity, 'soul' and eternal life as taught in Christianity? Readers for whom (1) to (6) above seem obvious and for whom reconciling to (A) to (D) is simply not a problem can skip the rest of this section! **Feel free to go straight to the conclusions!** Others will have to persevere with some fairly tricky stuff – though much of it is getting used to the long words philosophers enjoy. First, then, we consider the meanings of the term 'reductionism'.

Reductionism

The essence of 'reductionism' is that one system of ideas can be 'reduced', to another. Within science itself, for example, it may be claimed that biology can be 'reduced' to chemistry, that descriptions in terms of organisms are just a shorthand way of 'really' saying things about molecules. Some have suggested that statements about 'mind' are 'really' just other ways of saying things about brain patterns.

We need, however, to make careful distinctions between types of 'reductionism'. Though some of us may not like the long words, it is helpful to note the distinction elaborated by Arthur Peacocke and others[1] between 'methodological reductionism', 'ontological reductionism' and 'epistemological reductionism'. Methodological reductionism is:

> the necessity the practical scientist finds of studying problems that are presented to him at a given level of complexity, and particularly with respect to the living world, by breaking down both the problem and the entities studied into pieces and proceeding by exploring the lower as well as the higher levels of organisation.[2]

---

[1] eg Barbour (1998).
[2] Peacocke (1985) p.9.

This, he rightly argues, is an inevitable part of the process of scientific progress. But the danger is that this process of *methodological* reductionism can slide into a belief that the essential nature or being involved in the higher order system *is* nothing more than the sum of the beings of its constituent parts. This view, that the whole is nothing more than the parts, is called 'ontological reductionism' (from *ontology* the Greek word for being). Thus he says:

> The procedure of analysis which is required by their own discipline becomes almost unconsciously a philosophical belief about biological organisms being 'nothing but', the bits into which they have analysed them... Biological systems, on this view, are 'nothing but', complex patterns of atoms and molecules.

It is the 'nothing but' which is the key. None of us would, for example, deny that brains are composed of molecules - and that for certain purposes (e.g. to study brain chemistry) this is the best way to regard them. But this does not mean that brains are 'nothing but' collections of molecules, or that mental experiences are 'really' just neurological patterns.

In a sense methodological reductionism means that a reductionist *model* is being used – without assuming that the reality corresponds in all respects to the model. Studying the brain, for example, as *though it is* deterministic is a similar (and valid) methodological tool. The Christian Professor of Psychology Malcolm Jeeves explains:

> working psychologists adopt a strategy of methodological determinism, but the extent to which this becomes a metaphysical determinism varies between one psychologist and another.[3]

To use a study approach as a model does not *have* to imply that the reality (the 'ontology' the actual being of the thing) conforms to that model in all respects. To treat the brain as, in some respects, *like* a machine (methodological reduction), does not have to imply that it *is* 'nothing but' but a machine (ontological reduction).

Ontological reductionism has a further implication. If the higher order system is actually 'nothing but' the lower order

---

[3] Jeeves (1983) p. 18. In Jeeves (1998) p. 213 a similar distinction is made for 'methodological determinism'.

one, then any language used to describe the higher order system means exactly the same as (and no more than) the language used to describe the lower order system. It simply says exactly the same thing in a more 'shorthand' way, a kind of 'translation'. If, for example, emotions are 'nothing but' patterns of brain cells, then 'I love you' means *exactly the same thing as* 'My brain cells have a particular configuration'. This Arthur Peacocke calls 'epistemological reductionism' (from *episteme*, the Greek word for knowledge of truth). *Ontological* and *epistemological* reductionism are, therefore, bound up together, but both are a radical step from the *methodological* reductionism which may be proper to science.

Ontological reductionism is not new, and there seems little to support either the view that it is a recent problem of 'bourgeois science'[4] or the view that it is a recent aberration of a godless Darwinism. In the ancient stoicism of Zeno (c 300 years BC), everything in the universe (including time and thought) was supposedly reducible to some kind of bodily substance - a kind of ultimate materialism. The apostle Paul met stoic philosophers in Athens and actually quoted from a stoic source (probably Cleanthes) though his own philosophy was very different. Later, reductionism ran rife in the morose stoicism of the second century Roman Emperor Marcus Aurelius, who persecuted the church. His *Meditations* assert:

> You can become indifferent to the seductions of song or dance or athletic displays if you resolve the melody into its several notes, and ask yourself of each one in turn, "Is it this that I cannot resist?"... In short, save in the case of virtue and its implications, always remember to go straight for the parts themselves, and by dissecting these achieve your disenchantment. And now, transfer this method to life as a whole ...

The idea that the aesthetic enjoyment of music in human consciousness is 'nothing but' the sum of hearing a series of individual notes is, to most of us, patently absurd. Both the present authors can play all the notes in the *Appasionata Sonata*. It is our inability to play them in the right order and relationship that makes us unlikely to win the Tchaikovsky prize!

---

[4] As in Rose (1985) p. 29.

In the eighteenth century, the writings of atheist philosopher David Hume abound in the phrase 'nothing but'. Hume began by assuming that 'all our ideas are derived from impressions and are nothing but copies and representations of them', and impressions:

> may be divided into two kinds, those of sensation and those of reflection... posterior to those of sensation and derived from them.[5]

Having assumed that the only kind of admissible realities were sensorially based 'perceptions', he was forced to explain consciousness (which, ironically, is implied in his continual use of the word 'I' throughout his treatise) as a kind of bundle of perceptions:

> ...what we call a mind is nothing but a heap or collection of different perceptions, united together by certain relations, and supposed, though falsely, to be endowed with a perfect simplicity and identity.[6]

With disarming candour Hume admits a year or so later:

> of the section concerning personal identity.... I neither know how to correct my former opinions, nor how to render them consistent ... all my hopes vanish when I come to explain the principles that unite our successive perceptions in our thought or consciousness. I cannot discover any theory which gives me satisfaction on this head.[7]

Hume is a kind of patron saint of modern atheists, and the failure of his reductionist programme of mind to matter might well have served as a warning.

From the examples already cited it may be obvious that ontological reductionism can occur at various levels. Within science, for example, the behaviour of gases in the general gas law (PV=nRT) can be explained by reduction to the kinetic behaviour of their individual molecules. This is the 'reduction' of one physical system to another. In similar vein, but greatly differing in scope, is the idea that the functioning of the brain is nothing more than the behaviour of its constituent atoms. This, however, is still reducing the physical to the physical. It is along lines of Francis Crick, famous in the discovery of DNA, who

---

[5] Hume (1739) bk 1.
[6] Hume (1739) bk1 ch iv.
[7] Hume (1740) *Appendix.*

said that the ultimate aim in modern biology is 'to explain all biology in terms of physics and chemistry'.[8]

Of a rather different order altogether is a claim that consciousness is 'nothing but' patterns of brain cells, and that justice, beauty, and morality are in turn 'nothing but' manifestations of social consciousness. 'Consciousness' and 'morality' are *not* self-evidently physical, and to reduce them to the physical is a very different exercise than simple 'physical to physical' reduction. Crick himself makes the 'astonishing hypothesis' that:

> You, your joys and your sorrows, your memories and your ambitions, your sense of personal identity and free will are in fact no more than the behaviour of a vast assembly of nerve cells and their associated molecules.[9]

After repeatedly making statements like 'you are *nothing but* a pack of neurons' he eventually lamely remarks that

> The words *nothing but* in our hypothesis can be misleading if understood in too naïve a way.[10]

He does not tell us how to take it in a non-naïve way.

Likewise on a social level. E O Wilson, in his 1975 book *Sociobiology*, looked for the social sciences to be 'biologicized'. Wilson is a religious atheist anxious to win converts to his atheistic creed, seeking to replace Christian belief with an artificially created myth of science - though it remains rather obscure just what is the object of it all! Another atheist with a zeal to make converts is the physical chemist Peter Atkins, an ultimate reductionist who wrote:

> the motivation of all change is the natural dispersal of energy, its spontaneous collapse into chaos. The richness of the world, the emergence into it of art and artifacts, of opinions and theories, can be traced down to the level where it can be merely the gearing together of the steps to dispersal.[11]

Atkins has suggested that all knowledge may one day in principle be translatable into mathematics.

---

[8] Crick (1966) p. 10.
[9] Crick (1994) p. 3.
[10] Crick (1994) p. 261.
[11] Atkins (1981) p. 41.

Evangelical scientists, such as D M MacKay (who popularised the term 'nothing buttery' for those who keep saying something is 'nothing but' something else!), have made penetrating criticisms of reductionism. They have been, however, far from alone in their criticisms and in fact ontological reductionism (though still infecting bookshop shelves of so called 'popular science') finishes the century (indeed the millennium) largely as a spent force in the intellectual community – its surviving advocates shiftily inventing adjectives for it like 'hierarchical' or 'intertheoretic' to make it sound respectable.

Mind and Brain

As we look specifically at mind-brain issues, we will need to establish some terms. First three basic ones:

i   **Idealism:**   In the philosophical sense absolute idealism holds that all reality is fundamentally mental and 'matter' has no existence independent of some mind's perception of it.

ii **Materialism[12]/Physicalism:**   Absolute physicalism holds that only the physical is 'real', and all phenomena will ultimately be describable in terms of physics.[13] Mental descriptions, if they have any meaning, are 'reducible' to physical ones.

iii **Dualism:**   This is a view that mental and physical are two fundamental kinds of reality. These two kinds of reality can be seen either as separate altogether (substance dualism) or as radically different and irreducible properties of a single reality (property dualism).

In their crudest forms, idealism believes only in mind, materialism only in matter, and dualism in both. Inevitably, though, views tend to be more complex than this, so here are some further terms:

iv **Dualistic Interactionism/Cartesian Dualism:**   This is the view that mind and brain are distinct realities which interact

---

[12] 'Materialism' is the older word, eg in Armstrong (1968) 'Materialist theories try to reduce mind to body'. We prefer the term 'physicalism'.

[13] See eg *The Concise Oxford Dictionary* (1995). We consider so-called 'non-reductive physicalism' later in this section.

causally with each other. It is the 'common sense' view – the view that we all tend unreflectively to take. It is called 'Cartesian dualism' after Descartes.

v   **Epiphenomenalism:** This is a view that holds mental phenomena to be accidental by-products of the brain, which have no effect on actions.

vi **Behaviourism:** Behaviourism advocates study of actual behaviour rather than of mental processes which are not 'real' in any full sense. One variant is that distinctions between brain and mind are purely grammatical, and so all language about mental phenomena are 'reducible' to statements about actual and possible behaviour.

vii **Identity Theory:** A form of physicalism which holds that conscious phenomena are identical with brain states. *Token identity theory* (or *token physicalism*) claims that *every* mental event is identical with *some* physical event. *Type identity theory* makes the stronger assumption that every psychological *type* of mental event is identical with a particular *type* of physical event – thus the psychological character of any mental event is an aspect of its intrinsic physical character.

viii **Perspectivalism:** A kind of property dualism which holds that both mental and physical phenomena are equally 'real' but are different perspectives or dimensions of the same event. Some recent works seem to mean the same by 'dual aspect monism'[14] though we shall not use this term.

ix **Functionalism:** Mental states are seen primarily in terms of *function*, in the same way in which computer programs function to move from input into output. In strict functionalism mental events have no meaning other than in terms of the process of getting from input to output. This implies, however, that some such function might be attainable through other media than organic ones. Most usually functionalists seem to be physicalists, though it may not be essential.

---

[14] Eg Jeeves (1997) p. 223; Polkinghorne (1998) p. 54.

Cartesian Dualism and Reactions Against It

As noted in points (1) to (6) above, our human experience of mental phenomena is direct and obvious, the existence of some externally real 'matter' is an inference. So are only mind and ideas 'real' and matter 'not real'? Idealism says 'yes'. It was put forward forcibly by the philosopher Bishop Berkeley (1710) and has always had some following - sometimes actually amongst physicists like Mach and Eddington!

To most people, however, it seemed logical to suppose that both mind and physical matter were real. Rene Descartes (1637) accepted this, and put forward a dualist-interactionist scheme (called Cartesian dualism after him). He assumed that in the unity of the human individual the mind was an immaterial substance which acted *causally* in making the body act, and in turn was acted on by the body in receiving sensations etc. This means that his form of dualism is 'interactionist'. Descartes has been criticised, even ridiculed, for a suggestion that the mind 'controls' the body through the pineal gland, but actually he was much less naive about this than is often supposed:

> I am not only lodged in my body as a pilot in a vessel, but that I am besides so intimately conjoined, and as it were intermixed with it, that my mind and body compose a certain unity. For if this were not the case, I should not feel pain when my body is hurt, seeing I am merely a thinking thing, but should perceive the wound by the understanding alone, just as a pilot perceives by sight when any part of his vessel is damaged...[15]

Leaving aside the obvious fact that *details* of his schema may need amending (eg we dislike the term 'mind substance') some kind of Cartesian dualism seems so 'obvious' as to be almost self-evident, and alternative schemas (especially any which actually rejected the reality of mind) faced great problems. This basic point was recognised by modern philosopher John Searle who (though no follower of Descartes), wrote in his 1984 Reith Lectures:

> I'm conscious, I AM conscious. We could discover all kinds of startling things about ourselves and our behaviour; but we cannot discover that we do not have minds, that they do not contain conscious, subjective, intentionalistic mental states; nor could we

[15] Descartes (1637) pt iv.

discover that we do not at least try to engage in voluntary, free, intentional actions.

Our natural tendency to interpret these experiences in a dualistic way *could* perhaps be mistaken. Such a mistake would, however (as John Searle also points out on his p.97) be of a different order from a mistake such as believing the world to be flat It would concern the whole basis on which we conceive of a reality at all.

There were dissenters from Cartesian dualism. For example, Darwin's friend T H Huxley suggested that

Consciousness... would appear to be related to the mechanism of the body, simply as a ...[side] product of its working, and to be... completely without any power of modifying that working.[16]

This is *epiphenomenalism:* the view of mental phenomena as having no causal effect but as being simply an accidental by-product of physical processes. It has two major problems. Firstly, the powerlessness of mind to alter the train of pure physical causation would call into question the meaningfulness of morality. Not only the insane, but everyone else would be 'unable to help' the way they acted or thought - which would raise big questions about what it would mean to say that they 'ought' to have done otherwise. Moral codes could still be studied as ideas correlating with brain states which affect behaviour, or as ideas associated with brain states which increase probabilities of genetic survival - but morality itself would appear to have no meaning. This does not, of course, disprove epiphenomenalism - but it does imply that the majority of epiphenomenalists (as people keeping a sense of right or wrong) are inconsistent. The other major problem with it is that it seems to fail to do justice to our actual experience of acts of the will.

In the 1920's-30's, however, 'behaviourism' offered a more serious challenge to Cartesian dualism. Behaviourism advocates study of actual behaviour rather than of mental processes. The philosophical behaviourism of J B Watson (1919) all but denied reality to the mental. It suggested that thinking was reducible to

---

[16] Huxley (1898) vol 1 p.240.

sub-vocal responses and intentional acts to muscular contraction.

The foolishness of the attempt to convince people (effectively) that they don't really exist, was matched only by the silliness of the Logical positivism rife in analytic philosophy of that time. Logical positivism said that anything not directly verifiable by empirical observation was meaningless. Apart from the fact that the principle itself was not verifiable, this was so full of holes that by 1978 even its leading advocate A J Ayer admitted in an interview in *The Listener* (2nd March) it was almost wholly false. On the mind issue, John Searle, writing more recently, remains amazed that for over fifty years:

> in the philosophy of mind, obvious facts about the mental, such as that we all really do have subjective conscious mental states and that these are not eliminable in favor of anything else, are routinely denied by many.[17]

Figures like the influential Quine who speak of 'repudiating' mental phenomena altogether,[18] sound to most of us just like pretending something isn't there which we all know is. Daniel Dennett's 1995 book is dedicated to Quine.

Also rather inexplicable was the influence of Gilbert Ryle's famous attack on his own 'straw man' version of Cartesian dualism in *The Concept of Mind* (1949). Ryle felt that with his book the 'Gordian knot' of the mind problem had now, at last, been cut! He claimed the basic mistake of Descartes and his Cartesian followers (made, we are solemnly assured, because Descartes' religious scruples were in revolt against the rising mechanical determinism in science!) was a category mistake. Such a mistake is one such as when having noted on the cricket field the bowler, batsman etc, a foreigner asks where on the field is the 'esprit de corps' of which he has heard. Ryle argued that when we say that both mental and physical exist', it does not simply mean a different 'kind' of existence; rather, the word is being used in an entirely different way - to suppose otherwise is a category mistake. Ryle suggested that distinctions between brain and mind were purely grammatical, and so all language about mental phenomena are reducible to statements about

---

[17] Searle in Warner & Szubka (1994) p.279.
[18] In Quine (1960).

actual and possible behaviour. This epistemological reductionism, of course, implies ontological reductionism. It means the same because it is the same thing.

Now obviously we must concede that Cartesian dualists, like anyone, might have made such category mistakes. But what Ryle actually does is to produce a series of special pleadings which supposedly show illogical implications of Cartesianism. We will briefly look at one example, which concerns our common experience that we may plan an action in our minds before we attempt to put it into practice. This experience is, in fact, the basis of our idea of design. Ryle asks, then, whether we can take as a mark of rationality the planning of actions before they are taken. In analysing this, however, he seems to be taking this to mean that we assent to abstract principles of rational action before doing something. But, he says, 'It is perfectly possible to plan shrewdly and perform stupidly'. Actually this statement itself seems a 'category mistake' on his own principles, as it mixes two levels of meaning, and he is confusing here various things. Firstly, no one seriously means by 'shrewd' merely an assent to some rational principles. A person can be 'rational' without being 'shrewd' for the latter implies a perception of practicalities (which is still a mental capacity) as well as rationality. Ryle also confuses 'ontology' (what is) with 'epistemology' (how we know it). A mind IS 'shrewd' if it can plan practically. We KNOW that it is shrewd because we see the evidence of this capacity in the resulting actions. Finally, Ryle argues that if rationality consists in 'prior, planning of actions' then should there not also be 'prior planning of the planning' and so on in infinite regress? This is a category mistake. If the mark of a rational action is prior rational thought, it does not follow that the mark of a rational thought is more prior rational thought for this would be to assume that action and thought are on similar levels of being - which they clearly are not. He also seems to focus on the priority in time of the thought, whereas any sensible Cartesian dualist would accept that the rational thought can go on interactively with the action it 'plans'.

Although he does not accept its mechanistic views, Ryle sympathizes with behaviourism. We should note in passing that in fact extreme behaviourism was quite mistaken in supposing that physical science concentrates only on what is observable. Throughout history, scientific advance has involved creation of 'unobservable' concepts like atoms, charge, genes, microbes, quarks etc. Physicists today hypothesize the 'existence' of non-observable sub-atomic particles, in order to explain what they do observe. Of course, in a sense (as Eddington and others pointed out) electrons 'exist' in a different sense from elephants - just as 'mind' exists in a different sense from 'body'. There has also, in recent years, been the new critical realist movement in which the meaning of 'observable' has been questioned and extended, But the logical positivist attempt to suppose that atoms were 'really' oblique ways of speaking about large scale phenomena has now been recognised even by Ayer (1978) as absurd. In a similar way, Cartesians hypothesize the existence of other minds to 'explain' observed behaviour. of course, both physicists and Cartesians might be wrong in their respective hypotheses. In specific instances a Cartesian might mistakenly believe that a mind was directly involved in a body, when in fact the body was a robot into which a mind had 'preprogrammed' particular actions; but then physicists also sometimes make mistakes and this does not make their theories meaningless. We cannot, of course, even be certain that there are other minds at all - any more than that there are 'really' electrons. The only difference is that we are sure that our own mind 'exists' - whatever arguments philosophers like Ryle may construct which effectively deny their own reality. The trend in thinking about these issues over the last couple of decades encourages us to believe that in time Ryle's ideas on mind will be classed along with the already discredited notions of the logical positivists - both are magnificent attempts to discount as 'pseudo-questions' some basic issues concerning reality, and to disprove (mainly by sounding confident) the patently obvious.

One commentator remarks:

> The next stage beyond Ryle is dominated by the writings, during the 1950's and 1960's of J J C Smart and David Armstrong, the most prominent of the so called 'central-state identity theorists.[19]

---

[19] Rorty in Warner & Szubka (1994) p. 122.

Both those named tried to develop Ryle's ideas to make them sound more plausible. J J C Smart remarks:

> Radical behaviourism has always worn an air of paradox... Ever since Gilbert Ryle at Oxford persuaded me to reject the last vestiges of Cartesian dualism, I had been a materialist about the mind. Admittedly the philosophy of mind to which Ryle attracted me was a sort of behaviourism, which I later came to reject...'[20]

Armstrong boasts a similar lineage.[21] The basic tenet of their theory is that mental events, states and processes are identical with neurophysiological events in the brain, and the property of being in certain mental state (such as having a headache or believing it will snow) is identical with the property of being in a certain neurophysiological state. Thus Smart recently reiterated:

> I assert that beliefs and desires are physical states of the brain.[22]

They claim, then, that their ideas solve the problem of how mental intentions (eg I want to raise my hand) can 'cause' physical events (my hand rises). It is, they say, because the mental intention is identical with a pattern of neurons, and this latter pattern given rise physically to the muscle contraction etc. But what is consciousness on this view?

> Consciousness is a self-scanning mechanism in the central nervous system.[23]

The difficulties of determining exactly what identity theorists are saying has been emphasised by Sir Karl Popper, one of the best known philosophers of science in the twentieth century.[24] Taken in any obvious sense, however, their approach has some very basic problems not so much in explaining action but in explaining the experiences of consciousness. Briefly these are:

- **'Qualia':** consciousness involves our experience of qualities of experience. I can *experience* 'red' or the 'taste of bananas'. All the information about my brain patterns (or

---

[20] Smart in Warner & Szubka (1994) p. 20.

[21] See Armstrong (1968) chs 5 & 6, also Armstrong (1980).

[22] Smart in Warner & Szubka (1994) p. 21.

[23] Armstrong (1980) p. 199.

[24] See eg Popper & Eccles (1977) p. 81.

someone else's brain patterns) would not convey to me the actual *experience*.[25]

* **Felt Intentionality:** consciousness involves intention – *felt* as well as expressed.[26]

* **Emergent social properties:** which are on a social level, eg loyalty to a moral ideal or recognition of betrayal.[27]

* **Freedom:** if physical events are deterministic, can there be any meaningful human freewill?[28]

The first of these is particularly telling, yet what seems obvious to some of us seems to be a blind spot with others. It is obvious eg to moral philosopher Mary Midgely, to theologian Keith Ward to philosopher/lawyer Thomas Nagel and to many others that the first hand *experiences* of consciousness are different *in kind* from normal physical 'facts'.[29] Yet the Churchlands, for example, having listed such problems identified for identity theory, go on to compare their reduction of mind to brain with that eg of chemistry to physics.[30] Daniel Dennett, in spite of his prominence in Penguin so-called 'popular science', seems like some kind of Canute, waiting for the waves pounding against reductionism to recede. He tells us 'in crashing obviousness lies objectivity'.[31] Yet 99.9% of people feel themselves to be a sentient subject (which he wishes to replace with a parallel processor) and experience qualia (which he 'disqualifies').[32] His fundamental tenet is 'dualism is to be avoided at all costs' (p. 37). He can, of course, easily knock down the 'straw man' version of dualism he puts up – eg he seems to identify 'real' with 'spacial' (eg p. 130) so if there is a Cartesian subject it must be 'some place' in the brain (p. 39). Basically he asserts 'Somehow the brain must be the mind' (p. 41) – he simply seems unable to grasp what is self evident to most of us that consciousness and qualia are of a different kind of reality from

---

[25] See eg Jackson (1982); Nagel (1974), and in Warner & Szubka (1994) Ch. 5.
[26] See eg Popper (1978); Searle (1990).
[27] See eg Taylor (1987).
[28] See eg Popper & Eccles (1978).
[29] Midgely (1994); Ward (1996) Ch.7; Nagel in Warner & Szubka (1994) Ch. 5.
[30] Churchlands in Warner & Szubka (1994) Ch. 3.
[31] Dennett (1991) p. 80.
[32] Dennett (1991) chs 2 & 12.

brain state descriptions.[33] Identity theory in this form is fundamentally incoherent. British philosopher Roger Trigg has shown that Dennett's approach undermines both rationality and any sense in which knowledge or belief is possible.[34] Dennett studied under Ryle and admired Quine, and Searle plausibly suggests that Dennett's work 'is in the tradition of behaviourism... and verificationism.'[35] Dennett suggests:

> Human consciousness is itself a huge collection of memes (or more exactly meme-effects in brains)...[36]

'Consciousness' as a bundle of memes being parallel processed sounds like a materialist version of Hume's 'bundle of perceptions' – though it is, if anything, even less rational. Why not call his book *Consciousness Denied!* rather than *Consciousness Explained* ?

Rescue Attempts for Physicalism

As the problems of identity theory became more obvious, most physicalists in recent years seem to have espoused 'functionalism' advocated by Sellars (1963) and later Putnam. Functionalist Jerry Fodor explains:

> Functionalism construes the concept of causal role in such a way that a mental state can be defined by its causal relations to other mental states. In this respect functionalism is completely different from logical behaviourism... functionalism is not a reductionist thesis. It does not forsee, even in principle, the elimination of mentalistic concepts from the explanatory apparatus of psychological theories.[37]

All that functionalism says is that states have to be causally related to later states – and that this applies to mental as well as physical ones. It shifts focus rather from forms of type-physicalism which insist that particular types of mental state have *inevitably* to be associated with certain types of neurobiology. Fodor states:

---

[33] Searle (1997) p. 99 is as amazed as we are that Dennett simply fails to see this basic point.

[34] Trigg (1993) pp. 202-9.

[35] Searle (1997) p. 97.

[36] Dennett (1991) p. 210.

[37] Fodor in Warner & Szubka (1994) p. 31.

In the functionalist view the psychology of a system depends not on the stuff it is made of (living cells, mental or spiritual energy) but on how the stuff is put together.[38]

In computing terms the essence is in the software not the hardware, and it could in principle be realised in other media (eg silicon rather than carbon based life etc) – even though Fodor says in practice that physicalists expect it to be linked just with life forms as we know them. Actually Fodor seems to think functionalism is compatible with everything from interactive dualism to token physicalism. This adaptability encourages some to imagine that functionalism can somehow square the circle:

A materialist can (by accepting functionalism) agree with the Cartesian intuition that a person or the mind of a person *qua* subject of that person's mental states is not identical to the body or any part of it.[39]

Others try to rescue physicalism by emphasising that in 'two absolutely physically identical universes' all the events and mental processes would be identical.[40] This might have worked in nineteenth century physics. With modern uncertainty physics two universes could not *be* exactly the same for longer than a fraction of a fraction of a nano-second anyway, which is insufficient for any mental events to register – so we're not sure that this 'thought experiment' with identical universes has any meaning at all!

Anyway, functionalism really doesn't answer any basic mind-body questions, as Fodor admits:

Most psychologists who are inclined to accept the functionalist framework are nonetheless worried about the failure of functionalism to reveal much about the nature of consciousness... the problem of qualitative content proves a serious threat to the assertion that functionalism can provide a general theory of the mental.[41]

Treating the 'mind' as functional, if this is linked with some kind of physicalist identity theory (token or otherwise), does not

---

[38] Fodor in Warner & Szubka (1994) p. 5.
[39] Shoemaker in Warner & Szubka (1994) p.56.
[40] Horgan in Warner & Szubka (1994) p. 239.
[41] Fodor in Warner & Szubka (1994) p.37.

account for qualia. It does not explain or describe our subjective experience of (say) red. John Searle concludes:

> Functionalism can't account for qualia because it was designed around a different subject matter.[42]

Actually, the major problem here is not with analysis. Artificial intelligence, ie computers, can analyse. The computer Deep Blue beat Kasparov in a famous chess match, but there is no evidence that it enjoyed doing so! It is *possible* that computers may become self aware – the difficulty is how we can ever know that they are. If, as Thomas Nagel explored in a key paper, we struggle to imagine what it is like to 'be' a bat,[43] how will we ever manage to imagine 'being' a super computer? Nagel's own conclusions on functionalism are telling:

> functionalism, though part of the truth, is not an adequate theory of mind... the complete truth is much more complicated and more resistant to understanding... a theory which succeeded in explaining the relation between behaviour, consciousness, and the brain would have to be of a fundamentally different kind from theories about other things: it cannot be generated by the application of already existing methods of explanation.[44]

David Chalmers suggests that 'consciousness arises in virtue of the functional organisation of the brain.'[45] We could, however, imagine a world functionally identical to ours but where there was actually *no* consciousness. Thus, Chalmers asserts, he was forced to accept that 'consciousness is a nonphysical feature of the world.'[46] Chalmers' functionalism is therefore 'non-reductive', and he finishes up with a property dualism in which 'consciousness' is structurally parallel to the physical but not logically implied by it.

A central problem is that, with or without functionalism, any real physicalism seems to relapse into reductionism. Kaegwon Kim has argued that nonreductive physicalism is inherently

---

[42] Searle in Warner & Szubka (1994) p 291.
[43] See Nagel (1974).
[44] Nagel in Warner & Szubka (1994) p.64-5.
[45] Chalmers (1996) p. 248.
[46] In Searle (1997) p. 164.

unstable. Either 'you have espoused eliminativsm or you are moving further in the direction of dualism'.[47]

Freewill and Determinism

Before making a Christian assessment, we need to raise in more detail one issue previously just touched on. In point 5 above it was noted that I seem to feel that I have a 'freedom' in making my decisions. I choose to do certain things when I 'could have done' other things. Let us look at a suggested line of reasoning with six propositions:

P1 All particular 'decisions' are associated with particular brain cell patterns.

P2 Brain cell patterns form part of a sequence of purely physical processes.

P3 Physical processes are 'deterministic' in the sense that the pattern at time t determines with certainty what the pattern will be at time t+1.

P4 This means that any decision is pre-determined by existing brain cell patterns and is completely predictable.

P5 This implies that my sense of 'choice', that I 'could have' chosen otherwise is an illusion, ie *I have no 'freewill'*.

P6 If my freewill is an illusion and my actions were predetermined then I have no moral responsibility for my acts.

'Hard determinists' may accept all six. Determinists Michael Ruse and E O Wilson, for example, state:

> In an important sense ethics, as we understand it is an illusion fobbed off on us by our genes.[48]

At a 1998 conference in Oxford, Ruse presented the total failure of his system to provide a 'meta-ethic' (ie any but a sociological meaning for 'ethics') as though it was the answer to the problem!

Many, however, reject various of the six propositions. A J Ayer (1954), for example, questions whether our 'feelings' of freewill prove we have it, and in any case redefines freewill as meaning an absence of *external* constraint: 'To say that I could

---

[47] Kim in Warner & Szubka (1994) p. 257
[48] Ruse and Wilson (1993) p. 310.

have acted otherwise is to say that I could have acted otherwise if I had so chosen.' This view is sometimes called 'compatibilism'. But what does 'I could have done otherwise if I had so chosen' really mean? Presumably it means: *"My actions were entirely determined by the deterministic physical reactions of my neurons. IF these HAD started with a different pattern then my actions would have been different."* Either (i) this is a tautology or (ii) (on an assumption that the whole universe is predetermined) it has no assignable meaning since the 'if' is an empty set always predictably destined to be empty. We might not go quite as far as those who have argued that 'mechanism (ie physical determinism) is incompatible with the existence of any intentional behaviour.'[49] Compatibilism does seem to us, however, to be a non-answer. A more detailed analysis on this is given by Peter van Inwagen.[50] It should just be noted that when we say 'freewill' we do not mean a 'compatibilist' version, but what is sometimes called a 'libertarian' view.[51] This is that some human decisions are made with a genuine choice the results of which are not predictable with certainty. We are unconvinced by statements like 'We can be both determined and free at the same time'[52] – to which adding that the self is located in 'the metaxy, the tensive relationship between soil and spirit' does nothing to square the circle.

We will come back later in this section to consider whether strict determinism is compatible with moral responsibility and with Christian belief. At this point, however, we would like to explore P3 and P4 – determinism.

Around the seventeenth century developed 'the mechanical philosophy' - associated with two very committed Catholics Mersenne and Descartes and with the devout Anglican Boyle, and the Royal Society. Reality was defined in terms of particles in motion, and animals were machines. Determinism ruled and a more empirical base was given to an idea inherent in ancient atomism. This mechanistic view developed throughout the 18th

---

[49] Malcolm (1968).

[50] Van Inwagen (1983).

[51] These are sometimes called freedom of 'spontaneity' and of 'indifference' but we believe these terms are misleading and avoid them.

[52] Ted Peters (1997) p. 160. Many of Peters' comments are helpful, a few look syntactical but we can assign no meaning to them.

and 19th centuries (eg by Laplace), the brain being regarded by the deistic/phrenology circles as nothing but a machine. In physics there was a 'Newtonian world' of particles in motion. Given total knowledge of all particles at time **t** one could (in theory) predict their position and motion at time **(t+n)** - ie the future was totally deterministic and predictable. In summary:

19th Century World

- reality = particles in motion.
- state at time {**t**} determines state at {**t+n**} - everything is in principle predictable.
- mechanical models are central - phenomena (even sub atomic) are picturable.
- observer is 'external' - a spectator not a participant.
- often tended to reductionism - nothing buttery.

But anomalies were building up. Einstein publicised the fact that light photons had both wave and particle characteristics and in the 1920's this extended to electrons. In 1927-8 came Heisenberg's uncertainty principle. This says we can measure the *position* of an electron *or* its *momentum* with any degree of accuracy - but *not* both at once. This is *not* simply due to practical problems of measurement - it is because both are not defined simultaneously within the system. In summary:

20th Century World

- reality = wave-particle duality at sub atomic level - position and motion not simultaneously definable.
- indeterminacy - the path taken by individual particles after collision is *in principle* unpredictable - we can predict macro events only on a statistical basis.
- reality is ultimately unpicturable - Bohr introduced the idea of complementarity - apparently incompatible pictures each 'true' in its own framework.
- the observer was not external - the act of observing fixed a particle at the moment of observation at a particular location (cf Schrodinger's cat paradox in physics literature).
- holistic approach (Bohr again) - particles could not be seen in isolation as information about locations of one after collision bore on what could be determined about others.

Leaders in this movement were Max Planck (a church warden), Werner Heisenberg, Neils Bohr, Edwin Schrodinger, and Arthur Eddington (a committed Quaker). Some physicists didn't like it. Einstein (who was a pantheist) objected to the notion of God 'playing dice'. It has, however, become the view accepted by virtually all mainstream physicists. A further relevant development has occurred since the 1960's with ideas of chaos theory. In some systems, very small changes in initial conditions can lead to great changes in macro events. A butterfly flapping its wings could 'cause' a storm 100 miles away! So could parts of our brain be like this? Could our brains be 'chaotic systems', tipped in key decisions by a very few particles? If so, then they may be unpredictable on some issues *even in principle*. In this case, then one of three things could apply:

1. Our decisions might in fact all be determined by God - though humanly unpredictable.
2. Our decisions might be determined by 'chance', ie by no conscious agent at all.
3. Our decisions (or some of them) might be determined by our own freewill a primary concept with no further level of explanation.

From the very inception of the uncertainty theory, Eddington advocated the third option. Other physicists have also been interested. Stephen Hawking, for example, has also raised the determinism/freewill issue noting that:

> It doesn't make much difference whether this determinism is due to an omnipotent God or to the laws of science. Indeed, one could always say that the laws of science were an expression of the will of God.[53]

Hawking's own 'solution' is that since anyway the brain is too complex to analyse and demonstrate to be deterministic, we'd best just get on with an 'effective theory' which includes freewill and moral responsibility.

Physicist Roger Penrose, has written extensively on 'mind' issues. He has noted, for example that light sensitive cells in our retina can respond to very small numbers of photons, and that 'there might be neurons in the brain proper, that are essentially

---

[53] Hawking (1993) p. 124.

quantum detection devices'.[54] This, incidentally, answers Jeeves' point that brain cells are large compared with the levels at which indeterminacy occurs.[55]   It is not the size of the *detection device* but the size of *stimulus* which is important. Penrose then raises the point of whether quantum indeterminacy could parallel freewill choice. He notes that the indeterminacy:

> is something that 'takes place' only when sufficient amounts of the environment become entangled with the quantum event... One would have to contend that the 'mind-stuff' somehow influences the system only at this indeterminate stage.

He then does not rule it out but remains unenthusiastic. It seems to us unfortunate that the picture he gives is of looking to see how a (logically) 'external "mind" might have an influence on physical behaviour.' He doubts this because then

> why is an experimenter not able by the action of "will power" to influence the results of a quantum experiment?

Two points arise here. Firstly, it is illogical to suggest that if quantum results inside my brain are associated with my acts of will then I should be able to influence quantum events outside. One might as well argue that if I can raise my arm by a conscious decision then I ought to be able to raise anyone else's arm in the same way. More fundamentally, however, as *modern* neo-Cartesian dualists we are unhappy both with the term 'mind stuff' and with its assignation, even logically, as 'external'. With such an image he can, of course, ask at exactly what point the external mind 'intervenes' in quantum processes. But if the quantum processes are themselves the expressions of and encapsulation of that mind, the system can be holistic and the question has limited meaning. Penrose's own formulation actually seems rather less far from our own views than it might appear at first sight.

Current Options

Even in the secular world, reductionism and monistic materialism are in decline. In the mid-1980's Christian social psychologist Mary Stewart Van Leeuwen stated:

---

[54] Penrose (1987) and (1995) p. 349.
[55] Eg in Brown (1998) p. 94.

It is safe to say that almost all Anglo-American psychologists are becoming 'token' perspectivalists, inasmuch as they are beginning to acknowledge that science cannot give a complete account of personhood...[56]

This trend has continued. Some kind of 'property dualism' or perspectivalism seems most common. There is also a continuing presence of some kind of dualistic interactionism or Cartesian dualism. John J Haldane has written:

Quite recently, and rather against the tendencies of the 1960's and 1970's there has been something of a revival of realist versions of dualism.[57]

Amongst experts in the field of mind, a modern revival of this classic view of Descartes was heralded by the 1933 Rede Lecture and 1937-8 Gifford Lectures of Nobel prizewinning neuro-scientist C S Sherrington.[58] An interesting 'convert' was neurosurgeon Wilder Penfield, whose startling conclusion after a distinguished career of brain studies as a monistic materialist was:

it is easier to rationalise man's being on the basis of two elements than on the basis of one.[59]

In 1978 a massive volume arguing for dualist interactionism was issued by the Nobel Prize winning neurophysiologist Sir John Eccles FRS, and renowned philosopher of science Karl Popper: *The Self and Its Brain*. In it they have also given much useful criticism of the alternative views described above.

Popper and Eccles's form of interactionism asserts the unity of consciousness both on philosophical grounds and on the grounds of evidence from empirical studies by Sperry.[60] But within consciousness two worlds, may be distinguished, making three in all including the physical as shown overleaf.

Eccles has repeated this schema more recently.[61] Animals exhibit conscious behaviour, but Eccles quotes Sperry with approval:

---

[56] Van Leuwen (1985) p. 68.
[57] Haldane in Warner & Szubka (1994) p. 196.
[58] Sherrington (1933), (1938) & in Laslett (1950).
[59] Penfield (1975) pp. 113-4.
[60] Sperry (1977).
[61] In Templeton (1994).

Self-consciousness appears to be almost strictly a human attribute according to present evidence ... It seems not to be found in animals below the primates, and only to a limited extent in the great apes.[62]

The World-3 of Popper is exclusively human - for it consists of human created mental products.

World 1	World 2	World 3
PHYSICAL OBJECTS AND STATES	STATES OF CONSCIOUSNESS	KNOWLEDGE IN OBJECTIVE SENSE
1 INORGANIC Matter and energy of cosmos	Subjective knowledge	Cultural heritage coded on material substrates
2 BIOLOGY Structure and actions of all living beings – human brain	Experience of: perception thinking emotions dispositional intentions memories dreams creative imagination	philosophical theological scientific historical literary artistic technological
3 ARTEFACTS Material substrates Of human creativity Of tools Of machines Of books Of works of art Of music		Theoretical systems scientific problems critical arguments

Dualist interactionism may leave the human mind or 'psyche', the self-conscious 'observer' in a somewhat privileged position – 'interacting' with the physical realm (through the brain) in a unique way. Interestingly (though in a different context) such a privileged position for the observer is also given in various mainstream versions of the uncertainty principle already outlined. In them it is the act of observing which 'collapses' the various potential positions of a particle into one actual one; observer interaction is essential to determination of what becomes physical reality. It is, of course, possible that physics may one day abandon this idea - but at our present state of knowledge it offers powerful analogical support to the suggestion that human minds (and any other similar minds God may have created elsewhere in the universe) are special.

---

[62] Eccles (1980) p. 6 quoting Sperry (1977).

Amongst other dualist interactionists, one of the most interesting is John Foster who approaches the issue from the standpoint of an Oxford analytic philosopher. As such he gives trenchant critique of behaviourism, token and type identity theories. Though he emphasises 'degrees' of dualism, his approach seems to exclude mere property dualism (or perspectivalism) from the term. He is robust in defending as coherent the idea of mental causes of physical events:

> Why should the fact that mind and body are so different in nature make it difficult to understand how there could be causal relations between them?[63]

He defends this mental-physical causation, the reality of a 'Cartesian subject' (ie a unified 'me' which is having the experiences), and libertarian rather than compatibilist freewill. All, he claims, are not merely 'common sense' realities, but are the most logical on a philosophical level.

Christian Responses

The Greek word 'soul' (*psyche*) had a variety of meanings. Much of the 1994 book by Francis Crick (a man admittedly not much known for theology) assumes that Christians believe we *possess* an immortal soul. There may have sometimes been careless theologians, but the biblical use of either the Hebrew *nephesh* or the Greek *psyche* does *not* imply that 'the soul' is some kind of substance distinct from the body. Thus, eg, Genesis 2:7 says that man '*became* a living soul', not that he *got* one. Verses traditionally taken as implying some kind of separate 'soul' are based on dubious translations. In the Bible, humans definitely do *not* 'have an *immortal* soul'. Only God is immortal (1 Tim 6:16) and humans '*seek for* glory and honour and immortality' (Rom 2:7) receiving eternal life as a gift (Romans 3.21). Some of the expressions used by Cartesians like 'mind-stuff' or 'mental substance' are not particularly biblical. What does seem essential is that human beings are responsible to make moral choices, and that their 'selves' are open to reconstitution through a divine act of resurrection. So how have recent Christians seen these issues?

---

[63] Foster (1991) p. 159.

(i) Perspectivalism/Property Dualism

Some kind of perspectivalism has been popular with many Evangelicals in the last few decades. An undoubted leader in this was Professor of Communications (and neuroscientist) D M MacKay. He speaks in terms of an 'I-story' (an inside view of events) and an '0-story' (an observer view of events). Seen thus man is:

> a unity with many complementary aspects, each needing to be reckoned with at a different logical level, and all interdependent.[64]

By 'interdependent' however, he does not mean that interaction takes place - a thing he specifically denies. MacKay states that he finds 'something to agree with' in both dualism and monism. He states that mental and physical phenomena are both 'real', but that they do not 'interact':

> It seems to me sufficient rather to describe mental events and their correlated brain events as the 'inside' and 'outside', aspects of one and the same sequence of events, which in their full nature are richer - have more to them - than can be expressed in either mental or physical categories alone.[65]

His references to the inside view ('I-story') and observer view ('0-story') as perspectives on the same events sound like a version of identity theory, though MacKay himself (when one of us asked him at a conference in 1985) appeared not to associate his own ideas either with Eccles or with identity theorists.

MacKay and his followers then, no less than Eccles, rejects the idea that the mental can be 'reduced' to the physical, or is just another way of saying the same thing. In some sense, then, both are 'dualists'. So where is the point of difference?

Before exploring this, a brief aside on brain manipulation. Some have thought that the possibility of surgical division of the brain is threatening to the Christian idea of mind. Both Eccles and MacKay, however, see the effects of such division (commissurotomy - the severing of nerve fibres joining the two brain halves) simply as dividing off a part of conscious mind, whilst leaving an intact self-conscious mind and its associated

---

[64] MacKay (1980) p 80.
[64] MacKay (1980) p 14.
[65] MacKay (1980) p. 14 etc.

personhood.[66] The possibility of chemical manipulation, of the brain and hence the mind is no more inherently mysterious than any of the daily experiences we all have of the physical world 'affecting' our consciousness through sensory experience. Yet this can continue to be presented as though a problem for 'strict dualists' even by so thoughtful a book as that by Christian social psychologist Mary Stewart Van Leeuwen.[67] Cartesian dualists have surely never claimed that mind is *independent* of body - that is the whole point of 'dualist *interactionism*'. What they do assert is that mind is a causal agent in physical brain processes which are not strictly deterministic.

This marks the difference between MacKay and Eccles. Is a completely deterministic view of the brain either plausible or compatible with Christian belief? Eccles states strongly:

> If physical determinism is true, then that is the end of all discussion or argument; everything is finished. There is no philosophy. All human persons are caught up in this inexorable web of circumstances and cannot break out of it. Everything we think we are doing is an illusion...[68]

MacKay, in contrast, argues that it would be unproblematic for the Christian if it turned out that:

> ... knowledge of our brain mechanisms and the forces acting on and in them were sufficient to allow our actions to be predicted (secretly) by a detached observer.[69]

So who is right? Actually we can ask several distinct questions about this (some of which we already asked above):

1. Would strict determinism mean that our 'feeling' of making decisions was in fact illusory?
2. Would it mean that we were right to be 'fatalistic' in the sense that if someone predicted our actions with certainty and told us, then we would 'have no choice', but to follow the predictions?
3. Would it make moral responsibility void?

---

[66] Eccles (1980) and MacKay (1980).
[67] Van Leuwen (1985) p. 89.
[68] Eccles (1980) p. 546.
[69] Mackay (1974) p. 78.

4. Would it not imply a strange behaviour on God's part to create a world which had a humankind deterministically programmed to sin?

Question (1) is not really a problem, for in MacKay's terms it confuses the 'I-story' with the 'O-story'. What is referred to as 'I' is still making the decision - even if on the level of the 'O-story' that decision is entirely predictable and inevitable.

To answer (2) MacKay took two lines of approach. The first was a development of an argument first put forward by the outstanding twentieth century physicist Max Planck (who was also religious). Planck took as starting point that: 'an event which can be foretold with certainty is in some way causally determined.'[70] Suppose, then, that it turns out that the human will is also causally determined, in the sense that if a man makes a decision then an observer if sufficiently intelligent, and if he remained perfectly passive would be in a position to foretell the behaviour of the man in question (p.89). The point here is that if the observer communicates his prediction to the man who is in the process of deliberating then he has ceased to be passive, the man actually faces a new situation (he now knows more of his motives, he knows what he *would* have decided if the observer had not spoken to him, etc). This new situation, then, may change his decision. But if the new situation is similarly analysed by the observer, and similarly communicated, then the situation is changed yet again - and so on ad infinitum. Put another way Planck asks:

> Can we, at least in theory, understand our own motives so exactly and so completely that we are able to foretell accurately the decisions necessarily arising from their interplay?

His answer is that our conclusions as observers (as it were) of our own brains, if communicated to the decision making 'participant' side of us, change the situation - again leading to an infinite regression. In a sense then, says Planck:

> A man's own will... can be causally understood only as far as his past actions are concerned...[71]

---

[70] Planck (1937) p. 88.
[71] Planck (1937) p. 105.

This whole idea was later termed by MacKay 'logical indeterminacy' and worked out in detail in several books.

We accept that logical indeterminacy does succeed in answering the objection: 'Surely if a super-intelligence predicts for me what I will decide then I have no choice but to believe him or her?' In other words it answers the classic problem of 'fatalism'.

Rather more questionable is whether it answers objection (3) - the question of 'sin' and moral responsibility. MacKay argues:

> There is no logical way in which I could pass from the data of the O-story to a valid conclusion, from my standpoint, that 'I didn't do it: it was inevitable-for-me'. The logical answer would be 'You did, and it was not inevitable-for-you, even though your brain went through physically determinate motions'.[72]

The view that sin is 'reduced to the category of mechanical malfunctioning' is therefore wrong because it:

> disastrously confuses the categories and standpoints of the I-story and the O-story. 'Mechanical malfunctioning' is an O-story concept, 'Sin' is something I commit. The one does not necessarily exclude the other: they might even be complementary correlates.[73]

Morality is an I-story concept, and cannot be negated by an O-story concept like physical determinism - for they are complementary perspectives. To negate it would require a concept on its own I-story level. A fatalism would be such a concept for it convinces the I at its own level of I-story that no decision is to be made. Since, in MacKay's view, logical indeterminacy makes fatalism impossible, morality is in no danger.

MacKay seems, however, inconsistent, for on the same page he states:

> Obviously there will be special cases of brain malfunction in which responsibility is diminished or abolished because the normal link between rational decision and action is weakened or overridden.

Unfortunately 'brain malfunction' is an O-story concept, whilst 'rational decision' is an I-story one - and by MacKay's own rules they cannot be mixed like this. If the mind were (as

---

[72] MacKay (1980) p. 96.
[73] MacKay (1980) p. 97.

dualist-interactionists suppose) interacting with the brain, then one could see how it might be possible to argue that the mind was not wholly responsible for actions resulting from faulty brain mechanism. But according to MacKay the mind is simply a different dimension or perspective on the same events described in brain mechanism terms - there can be no interaction. Both a 'normal' deterministic brain, and an 'abnormal' deterministic brain, have an 'I-story' dimension, and neither can (according to logical indeterminacy) be subject to fatalism. Both types of person, therefore, must logically remain equally culpable for their actions.

MacKay goes on to argue that it would be as fallacious to reduce sin to a mechanical malfunction as to imagine that a programming fault in computer software must imply a mechanical failure. But this analogy is even more confusing - for in his system the mind does not *use* the brain (as software uses a computer), but describes from a different perspective exactly the same thing. MacKay's form of compatibilism, like the secular ones, simply appears to us to be unsustainable.

When we turn to point (4) above, the problems get worse. Perhaps logical indeterminacy might, as MacKay claims[74] help us understand divine foreknowledge. But it does not explain why a good God would want to create and sustain a world in which human wills were causally determined to sin. A suitable adjustment of the physical starting conditions would have meant a sinless world. This argument has nothing to do with the individual human's 'I-story', it concerns God as creator and observer.

MacKay himself responded to this question (actually asked him by one of the present authors both as a student in the late '60's and for the last time in 1985) in terms of Mackay's own Calvinist tradition. In this, in the final analysis man cannot question God who is viewed as literally incomprehensible. The present authors, however, do not share that tradition, nor believe that this is a proper use of Romans 9,20 (see our *God's Strategy in Human History* (1973, 1989) on this issue). It is our present belief, therefore, that physical determinism (in the sense of P1-

---

[74] Eg in MacKay (1974)

P6 above) is not logically reconcilable either with meaningful morality or with biblical belief in God - though we recognise that many fine Christian people would not agree with us.

Those who take MacKay's approach include the evangelical Professor D Gareth Jones.[75] Another Evangelical, the distinguished Professor of Psychology Malcolm Jeeves, is sympathetic to Eccles' position but comes down on the side of a MacKay type perspectivalism.[76] In a later book he seems a little more cautious, though points out that MacKay's determinist-compatibilist view of human freedom is more compatible with *theological determinism*.[77] This is hardly an advantage, since it is precisely the concept of a total theological determinism which (given the pain and suffering in the world) makes MacKay's system incoherent. If God really determines everything why would he determine it like this?

Physicist/theologian Professor John Polkinghorne rejects reductionism and epiphenomenalism – but also rejects Cartesian dualism because in it:

> matter and mind fail to coalesce into the one world of our psychosomatic experience. The only possibility appears to be a complementary world of mind/matter in which these polar opposites cohere as contrasting aspects of the world stuff...[78]

This sounds like perspectivalism, but does he think our brains are deterministic? Polkinghorne insists that 'the denial of human freedom is incoherent',[79] but rejects the idea that quantum uncertainty provides a basis for that freedom (p.28). His own suggestion is that 'openness' emerges from complex dynamic systems – going on to describe the impossibility of predicting in chaotic systems.[80] But suppose we imagine our brain is such a system, surely:

> either: A: It is only *unpredictable in practice* as we cannot know the starting conditions in enough detail

---

[75] Jones (1981) p. 118.
[76] Jeeves (1995).
[77] Jeeves (1997) p. 223
[78] Polkinghorne (1980) p.71.
[79] Polkinghorne (1989) p.10.
[80] A view repeated in Polkinghorne (1998) ch. 3.

> or: B: It is *unpredictable in principle* because of effects
> of quantum uncertainty (individual or holistic)
> or of the maths of non-linear dynamic systems.

It seems to us that A is inconsistent with morality and B seems
entirely consistent with our own view of interactionism (though
probably not with the usual 'straw man' version of it attacked by
critics). Polkinghorne joins the now ritual condemnation of 'god
of the gaps theology'. (The 'god of the gaps' approach restricts
God to working *only* in the 'gaps' in physical process sequences
– its denial seems often to lead today to a denial there even
could be any such gaps). Then, puzzlingly, he concludes:

> There is a sense in which all free action, ours or God's, depends
> upon 'gaps', the inherent incompleteness which makes openness
> possible.[81]

Perhaps Polkinhorne belongs in our view (iii) below – we're not
sure.

(ii) Non-Reductive Physicalism

Fuller's interesting book[82] advocates a 'Christian, non-
reductionist materialism' which rejects dualism. He gives,
however, no details of how the circle is to be squared to achieve
this. What does seem apparent is his debt to the liberal Anglican
scientist/theologian Arthur Peacocke. Peacocke is an avowed
physicalist, but insists:

> There are systems, at every level of complexity, whose future
> development is unpredictable.[83]

These include non-linear dynamical systems as well as quantum
uncertainty. In an earlier work Peacocke claimed that dualism
'cannot be made coherent'[84] and espoused functionalism:

> human actions can properly be described as transcendence-in-
> immanence, the functional intending 'I' transcends the
> physiological-physical sequence which yet, as it unfolds, is the same
> 'I' in action.[85]

---

[81] Polkinghorne (1989) p. 34.
[82] Fuller (1995) p.47; the book does contain some other more helpful ideas too.
[83] Peacocke (1993), p. 152.
[84] Peacocke (1979) p. 133.
[85] Peacocke (1979) p. 131.

Well... yes. We are unconvinced, however, that his form of functionalism solves the problems left for physicalism by others, and cannot accept a form of theism which denies the possibility of God acting other than in natural processes and negates any point in intercessory prayer.

Christopher Kaiser spoke of the 'relative autonomy' of nature, ie:

> the self-sufficiency nature possesses by virtue of the fact that God has granted it laws of operation.'[86]

Van Till amended this to 'functional integrity' of nature.[87] In the basic sense that nature has to be rational and predictable this is fine – but there is a danger that it can come to imply physicalism, in which case how can God *act* in any special sense in the world?

Warren Brown's book tries explicitly to formulate an evangelical version of 'non-reductive physicalism'.[88] To invent a phrase like eg 'square circle' does not, of course, ensure that it has meaning, and we have already given some reasons for believing that all forms of physicalism either transmute to perspectivalism or collapse into reductionism. Brown's book has some useful material[89] but what *is* non-reductive physicalism? Malcolm Jeeves (adding nothing to his other more detailed books) is clear that by it he means a MacKay- type property dualism.[90] Nancey Murphy, however, defines it as:

> The acceptance of ontological reductionism, but the rejection of causal reductionism and reductive materialism.[91]

Now Peacocke (who has co-edited with Murphy and is later cited by her) defined 'ontological reductionism' in similar terms, but whether and in what sense he himself accepts it seems unclear.[92] Soon after he writes of:

---

[86] Kaiser (1991) p. 15.

[87] Van Till (1996). See also our comments in Section 4.

[88] Brown (1998) came out after contributors had presented papers on similar themes to the summer 1998 CiS/ASA Oxford conference.

[89] Eg we found helpful Nancey Murphy's exploration of the diversity in Greek and early Christian views of 'soul' – especially Aquinas.

[90] Brown (1998) p. 89 etc. Others also refer to MacKay. (pp. 118, 220).

[91] Brown (1998) p. 130.

[92] Peacocke (1985) p. 11.

Concepts not even 'in principle', conceptually reducible to those of the physics and chemistry we have hitherto known... genuine 'theory autonomy', that is, non-reducibility of higher level concepts.[93]

Peacocke's more recent book continues to speak of :

A complex hierarchy of levels, with a science appropriate to each level... Very often these concepts cannot be envisaged or translated into those appropriate at lower levels of organization... terms such as 'consciousness', 'person', 'social fact', and, in general, the languages of the humanities, ethics, the arts and theology... a strong case can be made for the distinctiveness and non-reducibility of the concepts they deploy.[94]

This does not seem to be ontological reductionism, so what does Murphy mean by it?

No new kind of metaphysical ingredients need to be added to produce higher level-entities from lower. No "vital force"...[95]

Well, of course, even dualist interactionists like John Eccles (let alone property dualists) did not suggest there was a 'vital force' added in this crude kind of way. Peacocke noted in the first passage cited above that biology generally had abandoned such notions. But is this all that is mean by 'ontological reductionism'? Or is she really accepting (what most of us surely mean by the term) that the higher structure *is,* in its essence or being, 'nothing but' the sum of its parts? How could this be compatible with any form of Christian belief?

Murphy also (rightly) defines epiphenominalism as:

the theory that conscious mental life is a causally inconsequential by-product of physical processes in the brain.[96]

Yet on a later page she makes two statements:

{1} Consciousness and religious awareness are convergent properties and they have top-down causal influences on the body... {2} mental events can be reduced to brain events and the brain events are governed by the laws of neurology...mental events are simply the product of neurological causes...[97]

---

[93] Peacocke (1986) p. 61.
[94] Peacocke (1996) p. 41.
[95] Brown (1998) p. 129
[96] Brown (1998) p. 9.
[97] Brown (1998) p. 131.

How can *both* be true and how is the second not epiphenominalism?[98] In this context Murphy emphasises 'top down causation' which means to:

> take account of the causal influences of the whole on the part, as well as of the part on the whole.[99]

We don't really know what this can mean to an ontological reductionist. Surely to her the whole is *nothing but* a collection of brain cells acting deterministically in mutual interaction? If the reaction of each individually can be described in deterministic terms of stimulus (ie input) and output, then at what point in the process does 'the whole' have an input? One can invent a term like 'top down causality' but this does not ensure that it has any special meaning. Moreover, when we are then told that 'consciousness and religious awareness' have this top-down causal influence this is even stranger. Even if one could somehow conceive that the higher order *physical system* had such an influence (which, as we just said, is dubious), the higher order *physical system* is surely not the same as *'consciousness'*? Murphy then actually says on the same page that 'consciousness' is 'the *product* of neurological causes'. How can it be the product of that for which it is also the cause? Her more specialist concepts (like 'supervenience') we will discuss on our internet site,[100] but in any event they do not solve the above problems. An emphasis on the *complexity* of interaction with the environment is no substitute for genuine *openness* of response. Indeed, on human freewill, the contributors to Brown's book offer us only compatibilism and logical indeterminacy - answering none of Peter van Inwagen's (or our) objections as cited above. Murphy also raises the obvious question of how God can *act* in a physicalist world, but seems to offer only an abandonment of what she calls the 'common view of divine action in conservative Christian circles' for the views of 'liberal theologians' like Arthur Peacocke and Maurice Wiles.[101]

---

[98] A view rejected clearly by Flanagan (in Block (1997) whom she cites.

[99] Brown (1998) p. 130.

[100] See www.reason-science-and-faith.com

[101] Brown (1998) pp. 147-8. We consider Peacocke on this in section 5.

We agree, of course, with the book's rejection of crude ideas that a human 'has' an 'immortal soul', and that words like 'soul' and 'spirit' do not have a consistent technical meaning in Scripture. But how is it useful, eg, to tell us that in Mt 10:28 parallels show the word '*psyche* would refer not to "soul" but to "vitality"?[102] If the word 'soul' carries too much baggage let's use 'self' – not a word that re-invites vitalism.

Not only do we think the book fails to solve the philosophical (let alone theological) problems, but we reject its assumptions of trends in current philosophy. Murphy states:

> Philosophers see dualism as no longer tenable, the neurosciences have completed the Darwinian revolution, bringing the entire human being under the purview of natural selection.[103]

In the heyday of behaviourism and positivism one might have expected to see this kind of triumphalist statement. But, as we have shown, behaviourism retreated to identity theory which in turn retreated to functionalism. Philosophers like A J Ayer and Hilary Putnam have moved away from positivism, whilst Anthony O'Hear, Roger Trigg, David Sorrel, Fraser Watts, and many others would deny this kind of Denkinsland 'Darwinism explains everything' mentality.[104] The situation clarifies when we find that Murphy 'follows' the Churchlands as her guide and wants to take a 'middle position' between Daniel Dennett and Thomas Nagel.[105] The problem is that there *is* no such position. The Churchlands and Dennett effectively *deny* qualia, and deny consciousness itself in any meaningful sense.[106] They simply do not understand that consciousness (even in the sense that MacKay called the 'I story') is different in kind from physical events. Even a 1997 book co-edited by Flanagan (whom Murphy cites approvingly) refers in the introduction to Dennett and the Churchlands as the most extreme of the 'naturalists' who 'have been charged with trying to do away with consciousness for the sake of explaining it.'[107] They do not, it

---

[102] Green in Brown (1998) p. 162.

[103] Brown (1998) p. 24.

[104] Eg O'Hear (1997), Trigg (1993) Ch 9, Sorrel (1991), Watts (above).

[105] Brown (1998) p. 140 also p. 16; p. 18.

[106] See eg Churchland (1980), Dennett in Marcel & Bisiach (1988) reprinted in Block etc al (1997), and see above.

[107] Block (1997) p. 5.

infers, represent 'the general sentiment of those who work on consciousness'.[108] We agree with Searle, Dennett is a throwback to positivist behaviourism, not the shape of the future. We should not hitch the Christian wagon to such ideas.

(iii) Non-Determinist Non-Physicalist

So what of non-physicalists? Amongst the philosopher/ theologians, we referred already to the defence of 'libertarian' dualistic freewill by Peter van Inwagen. Richard Swinburne, the Nolloth Professor of the Philosophy of the Christian Religion at Oxford, actually argues for a 'substance dualism'.[109] Keith Ward, Regius Professor of Divinity at Oxford, also decisively rejects determinism in favour of libertarian freewill:

> ...some processes actually rule out determinism. If human acts are really free...[110]

Some scientists also seem sympathetic. The Catholic scientist and historian of science Stanley Jaki espouses dualism.[111] Rodney D Holder, an evangelical physicist now ordained, shares our support for the Eccles viewpoint.[112] John Wright is another scientist with similar views.[113]

The present writers believe in a dualist mind-brain interaction and that the brain is not wholly deterministic or predictable. But let us reiterate a few things we do *not* believe:

- *We do not believe in an inherently immortal soul.* At the resurrection God will reconstitute our *psyches* (or 'selves') to be 'embodied' in 'spiritual bodies'. St Paul is very wary (cf 1 Corinthians 15) of speculating on their nature.

- *We do not believe the mind rides in the body like a dalek (or ghost) in a machine.* The relationship is much more intimate than this in the mind-body unity that makes up a human.

---

[108] Block (1997) p. 3.
[109] Swinburne (1980) & (1994).
[110] Ward (1998) p. 73.
[111] Jaki (1970) & (1978).
[112] Holder (1993)
[113] Wright (1994) ch. 6.

- *We do not conceptualise the mind as a 'substance', nor as somehow 'external' to the body.* The mind is inherent *in* the brain processes, not added or external.

- *We do not believe that 'mental decision' has to be prior in time to the resulting act.* 'My' decision can be concurrent with and interactive with the act it concerns.

- *We do not believe that mind 'interferes' or 'intervenes' in brain processes.* It does not 'interfere' in the processes for the processes are its own self expression.

- *We do not see the mind as 'spatial', and the question 'at what point in the brain does it intervene?' has no meaning for us.* We conceptualise brain patterns holistically.

The problem is that many of the perspectivalist criticisms of dualistic-interactionism seem to assume that it involves believing one or other of the above. We clearly believe that the brain is not deterministic in the sense that (even in principle) its state at time **t** enables total prediction of its state at time **t+1**. So would a perspectivalist who shared our views of a degree of brain indeterminism ascribe it to 'chance' rather than 'mind'? If so, we might ask what is to be gained by this? Behaviourism and epiphenomenalism are clear forms of determinism – though both systems are logically incoherent. MacKay's logical indeterminism is physically deterministic and (in our view) inconsistent with human moral responsibility and divine goodness. But when many modern versions of Christian dualistic-interactionism and Christian perspectivalism have made all necessary caveats and modifications to try to match reality, we wonder how much gap there really is between them.

Questions Arising from Personal Identity

Current thinking, then, makes it very difficult to ignore or 'reduce away' the existence of the self-conscious 'self'. Where such 'selves' came from is part of the greater mystery of the source and purpose (if any) of the universe as a whole. Our contention is that belief in a personal creator God (or more particularly the Christian God) makes the most sense of both. If we are personal 'selves', is there some greater personal 'self' who stands as a Creator to our universe? This is the subject of the next section.

4
Nature & Theism

The Meaning of God

Our overall aim is to explore the rationality of Christian belief. Now that we have investigated something of what being a 'person' means, we can ask whether the belief that there is a *personal* creator God makes best sense of us and our universe.

The technical term for such a belief is 'theism'. The Christian philosopher Richard Swinburne defines *theism* as a belief that there is a God, by which is meant:

> "something like a 'person without a body (ie a spirit) who is eternal, free, able to do anything, knows everything, is perfectly good, is the proper object of human worship and obedience, the creator and sustainer of the universe".[1]

A theistic God is both 'transcendent' (exists separate from the universes) and 'immanent' (exists in the universe). Theism differs therefore from 'pantheism' which sees God as co-extensive with the physical universe (immanent) but not in any way above or separate from it (transcendent). Theism also differs from 'deism' which holds that God created the universe to be independent of himself and remains outside it. A variation of this is 'semi-deism' in which God remains outside the universe but occasionally 'interferes' in its processes which are independent of him. We consider these further in Section 5.

Theists believe that God is a 'person'. As human beings we can understand what this means only because we ourselves are 'persons' and experience personhood *from the inside*. But exactly how far should theists parallel divine and human characteristics? Obviously when anyone speaks of the 'arm of the Lord' they do not really believe that he has a body – this is 'anthropomorphism', ie it means using human characteristics metaphorically. Religious language involves the use of model and metaphor – just as scientific language does.[2] But if we speak

---

[1] Swinburne (1993) p. 1.
[2] See eg Barbour (1998) ch. 5, Jeeves and Berry (1998) pp. 104ff.

of God eg having emotion or changing his mind, is this also 'anthropomorphic' or metaphorical?

There are divergent views amongst theists on these issues. Our own view is that the church historically has been too much influenced by Greek ideas of God which present him as unmoveable, impassive, and inscrutable. This is true whether it comes in the Plato-influenced Augustine or the Aristotle-influenced Aquinas. The biblical God chose Abraham and the Jews, not Plato and Aristotle[3], as a preparation for the coming of his Son Jesus the Messiah. The Hebrew understanding of God did see him as 'other', but took seriously personal characteristics which Greek abstract philosophers abhorred. A Greek philosophical approach might be to take some abstract point as a lens through which to read everything else.[4] Hebrews did not do this, but encountered God as he revealed himself to them. We are going to look, then, at various similarities and divergences in theism, with particular concern to establish what is the theism of the Bible. This is because it is the latter, and not theism in general, which we believe makes best sense of our universe.

1. *Creator:* 'In the beginning God created heaven and earth...' Our own human experience of creation means that we have something 'in mind' before it comes to exist 'in reality'. The process can sometimes, of course, be pretty well instantaneous, though at other times the idea comes long before the reality. God's creativity is the first thing the Bible says about him, and is a general feature of theism.

2. *Sustainer:* God not only made everything, but (in theism) everything owes its continued existence to him. He 'upholds' the universe (Heb 1:3) for it has no existence independent of his continuing will to keep it in existence. To use an analogy suggested by D M MacKay: on a TV screen one can observe various characters, laws etc, and from sequences can imply 'causality'.[5] The cause, however, of the

---

[3] To Plato perfection is total changelessness, whilst Aristotle's god is an 'unmoved prime mover' hardly even aware that he is driving the universe.

[4] Paul Helm (1993) illustrates this today in taking his fear of a 'risky' universe as the touchstone through which all else must be viewed.

[5] MacKay (1963).

picture being there at all is a different level of causality. God is *the* reason the universe continues to be there at all.

3. *Relational:* It is increasingly recognised that part of the essence of personhood is to relate to other persons. Relationality not rationality is central to personhood. If 'God' were a singular consciousness then he could relate to no one and would not be personal. The word for God used in Genesis 1 is *Elohim*, which is plural. In Genesis 1 it says 'Let *us* make man in *our* own image.' Christian theology understands this as a trinity of persons. Thus in Genesis Ch. 1 there is God, there is the word of God which is spoken, and there is the Spirit of God who hovers creatively over the face of the waters.

4. *Emotional:* The Biblical God experiences anger (eg Ex 32:10), pleasure (eg Mt 3:17), displeasure (eg Is 65:12, 66:4), sadness (eg Gen 6:6) and divine love (eg Jn 3:16). These imply, of course, particular attitudes and behaviour patterns, but must surely involve more than that. A human 'deep love' for someone implies not only behaviour patterns designed to please her or him, but also a deep emotion. Surely theism should not regard God as less than human but more than human? If God reacts to millions simultaneously, then he must have 'mixed feelings' in a way almost unimaginable. But to suggest that he has no emotion at all would be to depersonalise him.

5. *Reactional:* Part of personal relationship is *reaction* to what the other person does. The Old Testament is adamant that God 'changes his mind'. To Jonah, for example, God simply says that he will destroy Nineveh in judgement. But Jonah, like all Hebrews (and even like the Ninevites) knew very well that this was conditional (Jonah 3:9, 4:2). When the Ninevites repented the Bible says 'God changed his mind' (*wayinahem*). Some versions put 'relented' or 'had compassion', but the word just means 'changed his mind'. Thus in setting out the general principle in Jeremiah 18.9 and 11 it is used for a change in either direction – not just 'compassion'. Theologians who follow Augustine (eg Paul Helm[6] – on which see also our comments in Section 1)

---

[6] Helm (1993) p. 52 etc.

suggest that this is a 'metaphor', and God never really changes his mind at all. This is misleading. The words 'the Lord has bared his mighty arm' have a clear metaphorical meaning – they mean exerted his strength. But what is 'God changed his mind' a metaphor *for*? In the Augustine/Helm theology it means: 'At this point God reveals what he had really intended to do all along even though he previously said he meant to do something else'. Surely God is not a liar, and if he says he will destroy, then he means it 'at the time' – though his people understand what Jeremiah explicitly teaches, that he can change his mind *according to their actions*. The Aramaic versions of the Old Testament which would have been read in first century synagogues are called the *Targums*.[7] Generally these removed any anthropomorphisms[8] but there was never any question of removing the concept of God changing his mind – it was central to Jewish understanding that God *reacts*. So what about the 'changelessness' of God? Ironically, the Greek word for this comes only in Hebrews 6:17-18, where the emphasis is on the fact that God gave an oath to assure them that he wouldn't change his mind (cf Gen 16:22, Psalm 110:4). In the Old Testament, in the very chapter which says that God 'is not human that he should change his mind' (1 Sam 15.29) it *twice* says (vs 11, 35) that he *has* changed his mind over Saul. The meaning is clearly that God does *not* change his mind *like a man* (ie capriciously or through lack of faithfulness), but *does* change his mind in response to human choice. God is never shown in the Bible as *capricious*. 'He who promised is faithful' (Heb 10:23). His character, motivations, reactions, etc are changeless in the sense of being always consistent with his divine love and faithfulness. Jeremiah 18 does not say God is capricious, it says that he changes his mind *according to human action and reaction*. This is an essential part of being *personal*. Helm, in a chapter on 'Eternity and Personality' argues that his timeless divinity can 'act' but seems to have no idea that

---

[7] Final redactions were later, but most scholars accept their material as early.

[8] Grossfield (1988) pp. 19-20.

being a person is communal and involves *reaction*.[9] It is, to us, a sad irony that in a well meant effort to *exalt* God, Augustinian theologians have actually *depersonalised* him. When we say someone is 'constant' and 'faithful' we do not mean to deprive him or her of the capacity to *react* in personal relationships. From a biblical standpoint a God who was immutable, impassible, emotionless, and unchanging, would be locked in his own timeless bondage - less than a person. The biblical God is one who both acts and reacts – and this is not just a matter of isolated verses but the whole feeling of the Old Testament account. The God of our theism is the one of the Bible not a reconstructed depersonalised God in the name of sophistication.

6. *Time and Sequence:* The first century Jewish writer Philo reasoned that since time is measured according to spacial movement, therefore time itself must have been created at the same moment as the universe.[10] Variations of this were repeated by Augustine, Boethius, and many other Christian theologians. With the special relativity of Einstein in the twentieth century, physics finally caught up with the religious notion that time is a property of space. Physics also shows that 'time' is not the constantly flowing uniform thing that had been thought, but varies according to how things move within its frame of reference – it can slow up or speed up!   So how does God relate to time? If God is uniquely inherently 'eternal' then he must in some sense be outside time, which is his creation. However, if he is also able to 'change his mind' as biblical theism insists, he cannot also be outside of *sequence*. There evidently is to him a present, past, and future sequence, though in this he is omni-temporal (ie present to all time-frames) just as he is omni-present. God also, of course, enters into our time just as he acts in our space. God is the 'I AM' of Exodus 3.14, but the Jewish people to whom this was sent never took it to deprive God of sequence and reaction. We broadly agree (though with some reservations) with some of the current

---

[9] Helm (1988) ch. 4.
[10] Philo (Tr 1929)

ideas on this put forward eg by Polkinghorne, Swinburne, Ward and to some extent with Pinnock.[11]

7. *Omniscience:* Persons are distinguished by cognitive knowledge, and God is no exception. In fact, the God of theism knows *all that there is to know*. In recent years, however, along with a more biblical view of a God who reacts, has come a realisation that there are genuine aspects of 'openness' in the future. God could, for all we know, have chosen to make a strictly deterministic 'block' universe in which nothing ever happened which was not predetermined. But this universe isn't such a place. God has not denied himself the excitement of surprise – although sometimes the surprise is unwelcome! Having said this, plainly the Christian God does know a great deal about the future – and this indeed makes him stand out from false gods (Is 41:22). He prophesied, for example, even from Eden that he would send one who would 'crush the head' of the serpent. If God has a set intention he can presumably predict what he will do. He also knows that there will be a new heaven and a new earth - because that is what he has decided to do and it does not depend on individual human reaction. Perhaps there are other elements which he knows through some mystery of time – certain verses seem to indicate this (eg Isaiah 53 prophesying details of Jesus' death). But this need not negate the concept of elements of openness – and that when God knows *all that there is to know* this need not include parts of the future which are still open and so are not part of 'what there is to know'.

8. *Sovereignty:* All theists believe that God is in some sense 'sovereign' over the universe he has created and sustains. So does this mean that he wills everything which happens? St Augustine believed so. He taught that God 'wills nothing he cannot do' and 'nothing, therefore, happens, unless the Omnipotent wills it to happen' (*Enchridion* 24). Some have seen similar ideas reflected in the Islamic Qur'an which

---

[11]   Polkinghorne (1989) ch.7, Swinburne (1986) ch.4, Ward (1996) ch.11 Pinnock (1994). Roger Forster shared the platform in a late 1997 conference with Pinnock – one which produced a plethora of misrepresentation in a certain section of the British Christian press.

repeatedly asserts that Allah 'sends whom he will astray and guides whom he will.'[12] The Bible, in contrast, assumes that God has allowed mankind freedom to choose to do things which God does not want (see eg Is 65:12). Jesus, in a moving lament over Jerusalem, said: 'How often *would* I have gathered you under my wings as a hen her chicks, and yet you would not.' (Mt 23.37).[13] Not only can God's *will* be resisted, but Luke 7.30 tells us that some people' rejected the *plan* of God for them'. This does not mean, of course, that God's ultimate plans for a new heaven and a new earth could be thwarted. One way to think of this is by analogy to certain physical systems. In these it is impossible to predict even in principle what any given individual particle will do – but the *overall* pattern which will emerge is perfectly predictable. The people mentioned in Luke 7.30 have rejected God's plans *for them*, but the overall final pattern is still predictable. Though the final pattern has been determined by God, the details are open and affected by human choice. Biblical books like Daniel and Revelation which are most concerned for the sovereignty of God are also the clearest in portraying the conflict between God and the forces of evil operating through humans and their choices. For this reason Jesus taught us to pray that God's will be done on earth as it is in heaven.

9. *Morality:*   Major theistic religions assume that morality applies to persons – both human persons and the person of God. For Hebrew-Christian theism, the moral term 'righteous' has a legal connotation, and for God to be 'righteous' means he judges justly whilst for us it means that we are 'acquitted' in his court.[14]

So is there in fact such a God? On this there have *always* been two views – atheism is not merely a modern phenomenon. The Epicureans, who disputed with Paul in Athens (Acts 17:18), did not believe in a creator God, nor that the universe was designed.

---

[12] Cf eg the Qu'ran *Surah* 35.8 and Copleston (1989) ch 3.

[13] Augustine has to 'interpret' this to mean 'despite her [ie Israel's] unwillingness, God did indeed gather together those children of hers whom he would' which makes nonsense of the whole thing!

[14] See Wright (1997) ch. 6.

They claimed all was due to a fortuitous or chance association of atoms following physical laws. Speaking of such, Minucius Felix, an early third century Christian, wrote:

> I feel the more convinced that people who hold this universe of consummate artistic beauty to be not the work of divine planning, but a conglomeration of some kind of fragments clinging together by chance, are themselves devoid of reason and perception.[15]

As science developed, the same basic choice remained - is the physical world planned or accidental? Robert Boyle, key early scientist and a founder of the Royal Society, wrote of:

> some, whose partiality for chance makes them willing to ascribe the structures of animals to that, rather than to a designing cause.[16]

Was the universe designed or was it accidental and purposeless? The choice between 'design' and 'chance' has always been there, and modern atheists who believe it is purposeless are unoriginal.

Design and Chance

We need here to establish what are the meanings of 'design' and 'chance'. As we have said, the word 'design' implies the presence of a personal agent (human or divine) in the mind of whom there is an intention prior to something happening. But this intentionality may not be the only level of valid explanation.

To spell this out further, consider how a person could say:

i.   'John intentionally smashed the window.'
ii. 'The stone John threw smashed the window.'
iii. 'No-one smashed the window, it was the wind.'

The first of these concerns an act of design – it is an explanation at the personal 'I-story' level. The second could also be true but 'explains' the event on a purely physical level. It is about mechanisms, not intentions. But what about the third? The term 'no-one' operates as an alternative on the level of *intentions* not on the mechanical level – in a sense it is an alternative to 'John' not to 'the stone'. But it is not an alternative personal agent – rather it is an assertion that there is no personal

---

[15] Minucius Felix: *Octavius* (*Ant Nic Fath*, iv, 182).
[16] Boyle (1688) p. 525.

agent at all. The word 'chance' is also sometimes used like this. 'The window broke by chance' is like saying 'no-one broke the window' – it asserts that *no* personal agent was involved.

There are, however, three[17] very distinct senses in which the word 'chance' is used:

1. **Chance$_1$:** This is the sense used in the theory of probability. Probability can be variously defined in terms of ratios of equally likely events, limiting ratios, or degrees of subjective belief. All basically see probability as a feature of human ignorance - none deny the essential determinism of events.

2. **Chance$_2$:** This is the sense already mentioned in the Uncertainty Principle in physics. The mainstream interpretation of it is that 'particles' such as electrons cannot be seen wholly as particles, but as waves of 'potential'[18] or 'probability waves'.[19] The position of an electron can be determined at the instant of its observation, but its path between two successive observations is not only unknown but undefined. It can be ascribed either a velocity or a position, but not both at once. After an impact with another particle, its position when next observed cannot in principle be predicted. This is not just because there are hidden variables which we don't know, but it is an essential part of the system itself. Particle paths after impact are unpredictable *in principle.*

3. **Chance$_3$:** This is in a sense of lack of design as already described above. 'John met Mary by chance' implies that there was no design on either part. In this sense the word must imply the absence of any personal agent (whether human, demonic or divine) who has an intention that something should happen. Chance$_3$, then, is a purely negative term: it asserts the non-presence of a personal causal agent. Thus 'The window broke by chance$_3$' means the same as 'No one broke the window' as given earlier.

---

[17] Some also define a 'logical probability', though in our view it is meaningless unless it reduces to one of these others.

[18] Werner Heisenberg (1971) – deliberately using an Aristotelian term!

[19] Max Born (1949).

We might note that another sense of chance is sometimes presented as 'the interaction of two totally independent chains of events', eg 'John met Ann by chance', where the chain of events which led to John being there was quite 'independent' of the chain which led to Ann's presence. It is not really clear what this means, however, since 'chains of events' are abstractions we pick out from a world in which cause-effect is simply one continuum. Unless this is $chance_3$ in the sense of there being no design or intention for it to happen, it has no meaning at all.

So what about the above three senses of chance? It must be noted that both $chance_1$ and $chance_2$ are terms descriptive of processes in the physical world, whereas $chance_3$ tells us about intentionality (or rather lack of it) behind such processes. $Chance_1$ and $chance_2$ tell us about predictability in physical processes: $chance_1$ in practice (because of human ignorance) and $chance_2$ in principle (because of uncertainty physics). Neither imply that $chance_3$ (lack of intentionality) is present.

To illustrate this for $chance_1$: a familiarity with Ann's habits may enable us to say 'There is a 60% $chance_1$ that Ann will go out tomorrow.' Yet this does not imply $chance_3$ (that there is no design involved) for it is her decision whether or not to go out. As a second example: statisticians know that numbers of suicides fit a probability pattern known as the 'Poisson distribution'. But this is not to deny that each individual act of suicide involved someone in what was very much a personal act of decision. Suicide is a '$chance_1$' event but certainly not in any $chance_3$ sense of unintended.

What about $chance_2$? It might be that we could find that within Ann's brain uncertainty physics ($chance_2$) governed the particle movements associated with her decision. Would this also imply $chance_3$, that her sense of volition was illusion? Christians have sometimes become confused on this. One writes:

> to the physicist, the outcome among quantum probabilities is strictly a matter of chance. The electron's behaviour shows randomness, not freedom... in physics the only alternatives are determinate cause and indeterminate chance, and freedom cannot be equated with either.

But physicists *as physicists* are simply asserting in principle unpredictability (ie $chance_2$). They cannot as part of physics decide whether the unpredictability is to be ascribed to a volition

(Ann's mind) or to no volition (ie chance$_3$). Such a decision is metaphysics, not physics. Presumably some physicists may deny that human volition could be associated with this unpredictability just as others (like Eddington in 1928) asserted its likelihood.

The non-existence of a personal agent (chance$_3$) is a hard thing to be sure of. Thus we may think, for example, that 'John met Mary by chance$_3$' (ie there was no personal causal agent) when, in fact, Sue had been planning for weeks to contrive this 'chance meeting'. In 1 Kings 22:34 a soldier 'drew his bow at random', and shot the disguised King Ahab. The soldier had no design to shoot the king, but perhaps a providential God had contrived it. 'It happened by chance$_3$' is, we must remember, a statement that something (ie an intention) does *not* exist. Whilst positive evidence for something's existence may be presented, it is hard to present positive evidence for something's non-existence - and so it is hard actually to present any evidence that chance$_3$ applies to a particular set of events.

If we believe in the reality (in any sense) of the *human* mind, we believe that human intentionality lies *behind* physical processes – not that it is an alternative explanation to them. Similarly, the theist (whether Christian or otherwise) believes that divine intentionality lies behind physical processes – not that it is an alternative explanation to them. God 'creates the winds' (Amos 4.13) – but this is not a 'scientific' explanation in competition with one based on rising air currents caused by the sun. God 'clothes the lilies' (Mt 6:38), but this is not a 'scientific' explanation in competition with one based on the triggering by the lily DNA of pigment production.

If this applies to predictable processes, surely it must also apply to unpredictable ones? What about, for example, the processes of mutation, which (according to the neo-Darwinian synthesis) cause the differences on which natural selection works? Suppose that scientists are right in their descriptions of such processes. These may be unpredictable in practice because of human ignorance of causes (chance$_1$) or possibly (if the mutation processes turn out to be triggered by particle reactions subject to the uncertainty principle) unpredictable in principle (chance$_2$). But purely physical descriptions of processes cannot tell us whether there is or is not intentionality behind them (ie is it God or chance$_3$). Some believe there is no purpose behind them, though some key early Darwinians like Asa Gray, and some founding neo-Darwinians like R A Fisher, thought that behind the processes was a creator-God. R A Fisher, incidentally, was rightly described by Richard Dawkins as:

> The formidable English geneticist and mathematician, who could be regarded as Darwin's greatest twentieth century successor as well as the father of modern statistics.'[20]

Fisher knew a thing or three about both genetics and chance$_1$! What Dawkins neglects to mention is that, as a much venerated scientific figure at Cambridge, Fisher:

> attended Chapel regularly (reputedly wearing the hood of a different honorary degree each Sunday) and even on occasion preached in his own characteristic style. His scriptural knowledge was as extensive and accurate as his erudition in many fields.[21]

With Fisher's dislike of 'abstract dogmatic assertions' not 'derived from the teaching of Jesus', and his emphasis on religious humility,[22] one wonders what he would make of Dawkins' own dogmatically atheistic version of the neo-Darwinism Fisher himself did so much to establish.

It is, though, most unfortunate that the word 'chance' has three so very different meanings, because people keep muddling them up. Atheists do it regularly. Jacques Monod (1970) for example, defines 'design' much as we have and discusses various ways in which designed structures might be recognised. He describes the sequences of biological physical cause-effect phenomena which constitute genetic change, and which involve processes to which chance$_1$ descriptions apply. But then he suddenly announces:

> We say that these events are accidental, due to chance...Pure chance, absolutely free but blind, at the very root of the stupendous edifice of evolution... It is today the sole conceivable hypothesis.[23]

---

[20] Dawkins (1995) p. 43.
[21] F Yates & K Mather in *Collected papers of R A Fisher* (Ed Bennett, 1971) Vol 1 p. 29.
[22] Cf his 1955 broadcast on Science and Christianity, cited in Bennett (1971) p. 28.
[23] J Monod (1970) p 110.

For so influential a book, this is astonishingly confused. After a similar description of genetic phenomena a Christian geneticist could presumably equally suddenly announce, 'We say that these events are designed, owing to God.' Neither would relate immediately to any part of the physical observation: both are metaphysical statements. For Monod to go on to say that his particular metaphysics is the 'sole conceivable' one is absurd.

Monod's switch to using 'chance' as a causative agent rather than a process description has often been noted.[24] More significantly, however, Monod seems to go on to confuse unpredictability with lack of design. Yet, ironically, if events were totally predictable, then presumably sceptics could argue that there were no room left for any purpose or design to operate! If everything is law-like, then sceptics argue that there is no room for God to exercise volition, but if it isn't, then it must be chance and not God!

Richard Dawkins seems to exhibit a similar confusion in statements like:

'The "watchmaker", that is cumulative natural selection, is blind to the future and has no long-term goal.' [25]

Natural selection is the term used to describe a physical process - of course, it can have 'no long-term aim'. The question, however, of whether or not there is any volition behind that process is a quite different one, a metaphysical question which Dawkins seems to assume he has answered, but never actually addresses in this or later books. Most of his book *The Blind Watchmaker* attempts nothing beyond a demonstration that, given the existence of chemical and physical laws, no break in natural processes is necessary to explain organic life. How could this (even assuming that he could actually demonstrate it) show that a God did not intend evolutionary processes to happen?

Sadly, there are Christians who copy the confusions of atheists − often actually quoting the atheists to 'prove' their own confusion makes sense. Philip Johnson is a Christian lawyer with no expertise in either science or metaphysics, whose confusion of the two has been widely influential. According to

[24] eg Peacocke (1979), Bartholomew (1984).
[25] Dawkins (1986) p. 21.

the Concise Oxford Dictionary the word 'evolution' means 'a process by which species develop from earlier forms'. If we add to it the term 'neo-Darwinian' this implies that the particular main mechanisms involved are genetic mutation and natural selection. It is just a purported description of physical processes; there is nothing there about whether it is purposeless or not. Johnson, however, claims that 'modern science educators':

> Are absolutely insistent that evolution is an *unguided* and mindless process and that our existence is therefore a fluke rather than a planned outcome.[26]

Defined like this, of course, *no* theist could believe in 'evolution'. We are not, at this point, considering whether the specific words in the Hebrew-Christian Bible are consistent with organic evolution (we consider this later), but whether evolution as such rules out *theism*. Johnson asserts that 'modern science educators' insist it does ie that evolution is inherently atheistic.

Ironically, however, Johnson gives in the same book figures showing that, of Americans who believe in evolution, most believe it was a God-guided method of creation and under one in five evolutionists (which is under 1 in 10 in the whole population) believe it was godless. Neither the dictionary definition, nor the way the majority of Americans (or British) use the word, would back up Johnson's claims. He makes much, however, of the (American) National Association of Biology Teachers definition:

> The diversity of life on earth is the outcome of evolution on unsupervised, impersonal, unpredictable and natural process of temporal descent...[27]

Actually, in the year his book was published the NABT agreed (after representation from Alvin Plantinga and Huston Smith) to remove the words unsupervised etc from its definition, in rightful recognition that the theory of evolution is purely a description of physical processes and should not include metaphysics.[28] Unabashed, Johnson continues to quote a few vociferous atheists to try to 'prove' his point in defiance of all dictionary definition, NABT definition, philosophy and popular

---

[26] Johnson (1997) p. 15.

[27] Johnson (1997) p. 15.

[28] Reported in *Christian Century* Nov 12 1997.

language usage. He insists that a physical process description (evolution) carries the metaphysical assertion that there is no design and that 'modern science' is inherently materialistic and atheistic. We have to reject this, and insist that both 'natural' origins for winds and 'natural' origins for species are compatible with the metaphysical claim that the processes involved were and are designed and sustained by a Creator. If some individuals (like Dawkins) choose to associate lack of design with evolution, this is part of their metaphysics, not their science.

Physical processes are, we insist, distinct from the question of whether there is any purpose behind them. There are, however, circumstances in which it seems logical to conclude that there probably is.[29] Here is a demonstration done for students by one of us (guess which one!): Three packs of cards were produced, each one containing two blanks, three O's, and one each of the letters D, E, G, L, S, U, V and Y. Each pack was shuffled by a different student, and taken back by the lecturer who laid each pack out by turning over each card in turn on a table. The three packs looked like this:

Pack 1:	E	D	G	V	O	O		L	S	O		U	Y
Pack 2:	S	D	U	G	V	L	E		O	Y		O	O
Pack 3:	G	O	D		L	O	V	E	S		Y	O	U

Now there are actually 518,918,400 distinct possible orders these cards could come up in. The first two patterns passed without comment, but the third brought howls of disbelief! All three *might*, of course, have been deliberately engineered by the lecturer - but in any event the students were sure about the third one. The $chance_1$ of getting a meaningful pattern by unplanned $chance_3$ would be remote. Conclusion: someone planned it!

Science and Our Universe

So does our universe look as though it was designed? To think about this we first have to explore what kind of universe it is. One of the present authors works in a university science faculty,

---

[29] In Section 10 we consider the 'Design Theory' of Moreland and Dembski.

and, like any other in the land, the picture taught there (by Christians and non-Christians) is roughly as follows:

1. About 10-13 billion years ago our universe (including its time and space) began with a 'big bang' - giving rise to a universe which has been expanding ever since.
2. From the big bang began a complex system in which stars and galaxies form and develop in predictable ways.
3. Our solar system formed some 4-5 billion years ago, by mechanisms still under dispute.
4. Life began with tiny micro-organisms around 2-3 billion years ago (within about 300 million or so years from the cooling of the crust), with sexual reproduction of cells by 1 billion and the first visible creatures 700 million years ago.
5. Life evolved by a series of mutations in the genetic code (DNA), each change which had survival value being preserved by natural selection, and each mutation which did not being eliminated. The broad record of this process is reflected in fossils in the geological strata.
6. Modern humankind (and self consciousness) emerged, probably coming through a fairly narrow 'bottleneck' in geologically very recent time, perhaps 100,000 years ago.

There are, of course, some Christians who would question not merely details of this mainstream science schema (nor even just aspects of 5 and 6) but virtually the whole thing. In their view the descriptions in Genesis indicate a young-earth and seven literal days of creation, and nature has somehow to fit into such a schema. Though we believe their view mistaken theologically no less than scientifically, we take their arguments seriously and will look at them in detail later. At this point, however, whilst recognising the fallibility of science, we note that a view something like that of 1-6 above is virtually universal amongst serious scientists, and evidence for much of it grows steadily. Suggestions put about by some well meaning religious amateurs that it is all about to collapse are fantasy. Puzzles remain, and amendments and changes of emphases are likely, but the *general* picture is based on overwhelming evidence. What we wish to do here, then, is to explore what it means for theistic belief in a creator-God.

Weighing the Evidence: the Improbable Universe

What might indicate design?[30] The first thing might be some surprising structure within natural law and processes– it may 'look as though' life and consciousness were 'intended to' emerge. The second is that there may be points within natural processes where events occurred which were either very unlikely or even impossible under normal natural law. In the light of this let us ask three basic questions:

1. Why does the structure of matter enable inhabitable universes and ultimately life to form ?
2. Why is this universe inhabitable ?
3. How did life actually originate ?

Of these, (1) concerns fundamental physical constants, where there are amazing 'coincidences' that enable the conditions to be formed for life. Regarding (2) and (3), let's consider the implications of two possibilities:

Suppose that it were possible to show that (given suitable basic physical constants), there would be good 'chances' {$chance_1$ = probability) of getting first an inhabitable universe and then the formation of life. This would not necessarily imply that these events were 'chance' {$chance_3$ = undesigned}. As already indicated, we believe that God works 'through' natural processes, and they are not independent of him. He could well have set natural physical constants which led 'naturally' to life.

Suppose, on the other hand, it turns out that (even given suitable basic physical constants as in (1) the 'chances' {$chance_1$ = probability) of getting first an inhabitable universe and then a formation of life are actually pretty remote. This would then give much stronger evidence that it was not {$chance_3$ = undesigned} but someone planned it.

There is a direct parallel here with the card demonstration above. The first two sequences of letters might have been planned by the lecturer, whereas the students were sure that the third had been planned. The 'improbable' pattern in the third made much stronger the evidence that it had been planned.

---

[30] We wrote this section before reading Dembski's work, with which there are obvious parallels as we explore in Section 10.

With this in mind we may now ask some 'why?'questions:

(1) Why does the structure of matter enable inhabitable universes to form?

Various fundamental physical constants seem to be very 'fine tuned' to allow the formation of chemical elements as we know them. Elements essential to life - like carbon - are manufactured inside stars from lighter elements. Very, very, precise 'coincidences' of energy levels in Helium-4. Beryllium-8, Carbon-12, and Oxygen-16 are needed for Carbon to form without it all turning into oxygen. Cambridge Professor of Astronomy Martin Rees, and popular science writer John Gribbin state:

> This combination of coincidences, just right for resonance in carbon-12, just wrong in oxygen-16, is indeed remarkable. There is no better evidence to support the argument that the Universe has been designed for our benefit - tailor made for man.[31]

Though they themselves reject the conclusion that there was a creator, Rees and Gribbin go on to mention that there are: 'at least two other striking coincidences that help to make the Universe a fit place for life.' Thus e.g. if one of the four fundamental forces in nature (weak interaction) had been very very slightly different, then the stellar production and distribution of essential heavier elements could not have taken place. In this case we could not have been here. Such instances have multiplied in recent years.

(2) Why is this universe inhabitable?

Even given suitable fundamental constants, a 'big bang' along the lines of present scientific theory could have produced a great number of different universes. The vastly overwhelming proportion of these would be (in crude terms) either a series of black holes or have matter spread out thinly and evenly. In none of these could life exist. What kind of figures are we talking about? Professor Paul Davies is a cosmologist/ physicist, a popular writer on both sides of the Atlantic, and has no Christian axe to grind. He once estimated that for every time a big bang produced a universe in which life could exist there would be one

---

[31] Gribbin & Rees (1990) p. 247.

followed by at least a thousand billion billion billion zeros of universes where life was impossible.[32]   There would be astronomical odds against getting a universe where life were possible. He also notes numbers of 'improbable' design features in a later book.[33] Stephen Hawking once stated:

> The odds against a universe like ours emerging out of something like the big Bang are enormous. I think there are clearly religious implications.[34]

How then should we explain the fact that we *are* in a universe where life is possible? One obvious answer would be 'someone planned it' – like the card example above. But suppose, for the moment, we try to find an answer which leaves it unplanned and accidental – what are the options? Some try to argue like this:

> "Since it is inhabitable, it must have happened. However improbable it seems, now that we know that it is inhabitable we have to accept that the unlikely odd did in fact come up."

This is not very plausible. It was tried with the students in the card experiment without success. "Look," the lecturer argued, 'since you now know that it did in fact happen to come up, you have to accept that it did happen by 'chance' {chance$_3$ = undesigned} whatever the odds against." They were not convinced. The issue was not whether or not the cards came up meaningfully, but whether or not someone planned it. The cosmology question is not 'Did the universe turn out to be inhabitable?' but 'Given that it is inhabitable what is the most plausible explanation for this?' Now if 'chance$_3$' (implying a very low chance$_1$) were the *only* possible explanation, then we would have to accept that the unlikely event had come up. But it isn't the only possible explanation. We actually have two possibilities:

1 < There is a designer-God who intended it to be inhabitable>

2 < It was accidental that it turned out to be inhabitable>

If the first was actually *impossible*, then the second would have to be true. But suppose that, rather, we just assign a very low *a priori* probability to the first – say one in a million? In other words, without knowing any specific physical features of our

[32] Davies (1980) p. 168; see also David Wilkinson (1993).

[33] Davies (1992).

[34] Quoted in Boslough (1985) p. 121.

universe we would say there is only one in a million (0.000001) chance it was intended by a God, and 0.999999 chance it wasn't. We can then also find, in probability terms, two further figures:

Pr [Universe is inhabitable IF God designed it] = 1

Pr [Universe is inhabitable IF it is undesigned] = p

Where p, according to Davies is 0.00 (a billion billion billion zeros) 1, ie an almost inconceivably unlikely figure.

In scientific terms we can then apply Bayes theorem:[35]

Prob [God exists GIVEN universe is inhabitable] =

$$\frac{\text{Prob [universe inhabitable IF God designed it] x Prob\{God exists\}}}{\left\{\begin{array}{l}\text{Prob[universe inhabitable IF God exists] x Prob [God exists] +}\\ \text{Prob[universe inhabitable IF undesigned] x Prob[no God exists]}\end{array}\right\}}$$

ie

$$\frac{1 \times 0.000001}{1 \times 0.000001 + 0.999999 \times p}$$

which is as near to one (or certainty) as makes no odds. As Bartholomew writes:

> It is clear that the prior odds against God's existence would have to be absurdly small before atheism would have any credibility whatsoever.[36]

We share some of his reservations about this, and don't see it as a 'knock down proof' for God's existence. Nevertheless, its general import does seem to us valid, and in strict terms of logic atheism is irrational.

Another attempt to avoid a divine planner for the universe runs like this.

> "Suppose that there are actually an enormous number of universes. all started by unplanned big bangs. Just occasionally one will arise in which life is possible. Obviously, it is that one in which we would evolve and be here to ask questions about origins! So here we are!"

This argument sort of works, but what evidence is there for multiple universes?

One of its chief protagonists, Max Tegmark of Princeton, was featured in an article in New Scientist on 6th June 1998. The article noted the undoubted *possibility* within quantum physics of multiple universes and then admitted:

---

[35] We return to Bayes theorem in Section 10.

[36] Bartholomew (1984) p, 57.

But the main reason for believing in an ensemble of universes is that it could explain why the laws governing our universe appear to be so finely tuned for our existence... this fine tuning has two possible explanations. Either the universe was designed specifically for us by a creator or there is a multitude of universes: a multiverse.

Tegmark's idea, first suggested as a joke, was that all mathematically possible universes must exist. "Why should only one mathematical structure out of all the countless mathematical structures be endowed with physical existence?" asks Tegmark. Well, why shouldn't it? What's the evidence it isn't? According to Tegmark, we can plot various ranges of the basic physical constants within which a universe will be inhabitable. If it turns out that ours is fairly near the centre of the range for each constant then this (he thinks) 'proves' we are just one of a multiple set. But why on earth (if we pardon the phrase) should we assume that *if* there are multiple universes then ours has to be 'typical'? Couldn't he just as well argue that if it was *not* central on some constants then it could not have been designed as God would have put it central? The whole argument is a nonsense one, based on gratuitous assumptions – and no amount of complex mathematics can alter its faulty logic.[37] No one is denying the quantum *possibility* of parallel universes, but neither Red Dwarf nor Starship Enterprise will ever be able to visit or count them – and (apart from some arguments based on complicated mathematics but spurious logic) the only basis for accepting them seems to be faith.

An interesting section comes in the book-video series by Russell Stannard[38] aimed particularly at Religious Education in the UK. All the fine tuning aspects are pointed out. Then we get three short reactions on why *our* universe is so 'fine tuned':

i.   Nancey Murphy (Christian philosopher-theologian) believes God designed it.

ii. Alan Guth[39] (atheist cosmologist) accepts science cannot presently find reasons but has the faith that one day it will.

---

[37] See also the http//www.csis.org.uk editorial 'Quick, think of Something!'
[38] Stannard (1997).
[39] Guth's 'inflationary theory' (on which in Guth (1997) p. 15 he says 'the verdict is not yet in') suggests how, given a small initial 'seed', matter could be generated in the early stages of the big bang. This has no theological significance. Guth and others give short interviews in Heeren (1998).

iii. Peter Atkins (atheist chemist) believes that there are innumerable universes that can never be visited or checked, and we are in the one that happens to be inhabitable.

Who exhibits the greatest blind faith we wonder?

(3) How did life originate?

Supposing that a big bang produced a universe in which life were possible. Suppose also that, amongst the myriads of planets which we presume (although we cannot check) are scattered throughout it, a few happened to have the very very narrow conditions needed for life to exist. What would be needed for life to begin, and how often would it come about by 'chance' {chance$_1$ = probability} if it were not somehow rigged?

Life implies reproduction. This must involve genetic information being used (with a suitable energy source) to build living structures from basic chemical building blocks and also pass on its own genetic or replication code.

Let's look at the basic building blocks for life, and some points about numbers and complexity. The blocks are:

- amino-acids to build proteins
- nucleotides for nucleic acids (RNA or DNA)
- monosaccharides (single sugars) and lipids

Vast numbers of 'building blocks' are involved. Each human cell, for example, contains 46 chromosomes (molecules of DNA) totalling some 6 billion bonded pairs of nucleotide bases (adenine-thymine, and guanine-cytosine pairings) the order of which contains the human genetic code. The simple E. coli bacterium (living in our gut!) is a prokaryotic single cell (ie has no nucleus), but has a wound up DNA strand which is 1000 times its own length and has 3,000 genes made of some 4 million base pairs. RNA is a shorter, single stranded molecule, but still with large numbers of nucleotide bases. Even proteins may have molecular weights of 50,000.

The whole is part of a complex, interdependent cycle. All living cells today are either eukaryotic or prokaryotic. The eukaryotes contain DNA strands in a nucleus, the simpler prokaryotes (bacteria), contain DNA strands but have no nucleus. In both types part of the DNA information is copied onto smaller transient messenger RNA (mRNA) molecules. These then (having, in eukaryotic cells, passed through pores in the nuclear envelope into the cytoplasm) interact with the transfer RNA (tRNA) molecules and with ribosomes to translate the information in the mRNA and form long chains of correctly sequenced amino acids to make proteins. During all of this the cell has to perform many other metabolic processes (eg respiration) requiring gene expression. The DNA also replicates itself by unwinding, splitting along its 'ladder-like' helical structure of bonded pairs of nucleotides along each half attracting and bonding with an appropriate available nucleotide (synthesised by the cell itself) to form two new DNA strands.

DNA therefore has two fundamental properties which are required by any genetic material: it can self-replicate and it can direct a chain of syntheses which produce the proteins required for all cellular properties, including the nucleotide building blocks needed for replication. Note that there's a 'chicken and egg' problem here. Proteins cannot be synthesised without DNA (or RNA), but you cannot make DNA without proteins to act as catalysts to synthesize the building blocks of DNA.

So is it possible to find a model in terms of 'natural processes' alone, which could explain how this horrendously complex interdependent system originated? Such a model is not inherently 'naturalistic' (in the sense of excluding the idea of divine design behind such natural processes), and it would not be 'anti-Christian' for a scientist to search for one. On the other hand, 'naturalism' will need some such model, and it is interesting to consider the current situation regarding any. There are three possible lines of approach on it.

The first is the idea that at some particular moment in the primeval soup a system suddenly came together. Actually, even the most ardent atheist recognises that the chances of getting just one DNA molecule (let alone an ongoing system) merely by random movements of atoms, are much less than the chance of getting a jumbo jet from an explosion in a parts factory! If earliest life systems were (as many now suggest) based on the simpler RNA rather than DNA, the problems are only slightly reduced, such systems would still be very very complex. Any spontaneous formation would have been wildly and inconceivably improbable.

The second model for life origins which involves purely natural processes is based on the idea of a nucleic acid molecule (presumably RNA) 'evolving' rather than spontaneously forming. Such a model must explain:

1. How did the basic organic building blocks originate in adequate quantities and proportions?

2. How did some of these come together to form more complex organic molecules which 'locked on' rather than simply fall apart again or be broken down by other chemical agents present ?

3. How did they survive and begin to replicate, with all the complex interdependence of even the simplest system ?

Hearing some enthusiastic popular scientists one might think that such a process of molecular evolution was unproblematic Actually there are massive problems at every major stage. Experiments (begun in the 1950's) with electrical discharge in gaseous soup produce only minute and unconcentrated organic building blocks. How and where could they become concentrated in the early earth? How could they eventually build into ongoing 'simple' life systems with all their complexities?

One might expect scepticism from some of the Christian biologists and geologists not committed to the inevitability of a purely natural process explanation.[40] But, perhaps more notably, in a chapter on 'origins of cellular life', S L Wolfe's standard advanced textbook states that once the basic building blocks :

> ... formed in sufficient quantities. they presumably assembled spontaneously into macromolecules such as proteins and nucleic acids. A major problem presented by such assembly reaction is that they primarily involve chemical condensations... it is not clear how condensations became predominant in the primitive environment.[41]

Formation in the sea, underwater volcanoes, and hot clays (the current hot favourite!) have all been suggested - and all have problems. Wolfe goes on to admit:

---

[40] Eg. Croft (1988) or Brooks (1985).
[41] Wolfe (1993) p. 1127.

... the specific reactions accomplishing the transformation of non-living to living matter have proved to be the most difficult to imagine and test...

The text is littered with 'may haves' and 'presumablys', but offers very little suggested detailed mechanism. Another standard (undergraduate) text admits:

> The origin of life remains a matter of scientific speculation, and there are alternative views of how several key processes occurred... Whatever way prebiotic chemicals accumulated, polymerized, and eventually reproduced, the leap from an aggregate of molecules that reproduces to even the simplest prokaryotic cell is immense and must have been taken in many smaller evolutionary steps...[42]

Detailed natural biochemical mechanisms for these steps (which must have taken less than 1 billion years after the earth formed, 300 million years after it cooled) are not forthcoming.

There is also a third approach, that taken by advocates of a 'complexity theory' which involves purely natural processes but is anti-reductionist. Biologist Brian Goodwin speaks of how the:

> sciences of complexity lead to the construction of a dynamic theory of organisms as the primary source of the emergent properties of life that have been revealed in evolution.[43]

His emphasis is on the organism and its interaction with environment, not as a paradigm to replace the idea of the 'selfish gene', but as a kind of postmodern alternative truth.[44]

Goodwin's 'close friend' Stuart Kauffman is highly critical of the possibilities of life 'being slapped together piece by piece by evolution' and says baldly:

> Anyone who tells you that he or she knows how life started on the earth some 3.45 billion years ago is a fool or a knave. Nobody knows.[45]

He points out the enormous biochemical problems of developing any such model, including one starting with an 'RNA world' which:

> ...offers no deep account of the observed minimal complexity of all free living cells.[46]

---

[42] Campbell (1993) p. 511.
[43] Goodwin (1994) p. xii.
[44] Goodwin (1994) p. 33.
[45] Kauffman (1995) p. 31.

His own central theory is that:

> When the number of different kinds of molecules in a chemical soup passes a certain threshold, a self sustaining network of reactions – an autocatalytic metabolism – will suddenly appear.[47]

'Careful theoretical work', he claims 'strongly supports the possibility', however, 'scant experimental work supports this view as yet', and, indeed, we don't in general even know 'which molecules catalyse which reactions'. In his view, though, life emerged 'whole not piecemeal' and its emergence was virtually inevitable. Like many Penguin 'popular science' books, it is fairly religious in a secular kind of way. Kauffman is specifically critical of what he calls evolutionary 'just so stories', but much of what follows seems to be extended analogy based on nodal systems and Boolean algebra. Parts of it seem again to be like the 'Penpops fables' with which 'Penguin popular science' is replete. It contains striking metaphor and analogy, but lacks any detailed application. His book is not reductionist, and *could* prove to be a right approach, but at present seems to have little evidence for it and even less in the way of any detailed biochemical model.

Even the journal *Nature* itself, pursuing what it calls its "reductionists' agenda" of removing purpose from explanation, admits that after an extensive post-war search for possible 'natural' mechanisms for life origins:

> "Unfortunately, there is as yet not much that is tangible to report ... there have been many pointed investigations... but there is not yet an unambiguous pointer to the mechanisms that may have led to the emergence of living organisms..."[48]

Some suitable 'natural process' explanation for life's origins may, of course, one day be forthcoming. Perhaps some kind of evolutionary 'locking on' model, or a holistic complexity model might actually work. But within actual present science (rather than wishful thinking or scientific 'triumphalism') it has to be said that there is nothing at present which even gets close.

---

[46] Kauffman (1995) p. 43.

[47] Kauffman (1995) p. 47.

[48] *Nature*, 3rd Nov 1994.

Design and God

There can never be any design evidences that are 'knock down proofs' of theism. Evidence for the existence of some specific physical entity (eg the 'abominable snowman') within a recognised class of such entities (eg organic creatures) may follow accepted lines. Evidences for the purported source and ground of *all* being is either all around you or not there at all – it depends if you 'see' it. There are, however, two basic distinct aspects of apparent design in our universe:

[1] Properties:
   a) Properties of basic matter which are incredibly 'fine tuned' to make it possible for a big bang to generate elements (rather than just have particles or the lightest element).
   b) Extraordinary properties of those elements which make possible the emergence of life systems given the elements.
   c) Properties of matter and life systems which apparently enable them to support the existence of centres of 'consciousness.

[2] Improbabilities:
   a) The extreme improbability, even given the right physical constants, that a big bang world produce an inhabitable universe rather than black holes or a thin atomic mist.
   b) The apparent improbability that life systems would form on earth given the presence of all the needed atoms.

The second category, the 'improbabilities', may involve 'gaps' which at present seem to have no 'natural' explanations (or at the least none not involving wildly improbable events). We will return to the 'gap;' concept at the beginning of the next section, but just raise the point here. Though it is, of course, conceivable that eventually all such gaps will be filled, the present prospect looks bleak. Theists sometimes seem nervous of suggesting any metaphysical 'explanation' for such improbable events: 'Does this not risk losing God as the gaps inevitably disappear?' There are two fallacies here.

The first is that, actually, over the last half of the twentieth century, the gaps seem to have widened not decreased. It is not, of course, that we know less – scientific knowledge is increasing at an incredible pace. It is rather that as we climb (as it were) to one peak, we then find that there are further peaks which look even further off than the one we have just scaled. Who, in 1950, would have dreamed that life would be so *extraordinarily* complex or that the big bang was so *extraordinarily* fine tuned?

The second is that, for the theist, even if all the 'improbabilities' were explained in terms of normal and likely natural processes, the underlying properties would still require explanation. Science can never 'explain' ultimate properties, but only show some to be consequences of more basic but still unexplained constants. The ultimate 'why' questions are 'Why is there anything rather than nothing?' and 'Why does it look so much as though the properties of matter were expecting someone?'

To many of us, the universe 'looks like' a theatre designed for life. Freeman Dyson once famously remarked:

> The more I examine the universe and the details of its architecture, the more evidence I find that the universe in some sense must have known that we were coming.[49]

Not only does it look as though the universe is intended for life, but it looks as though *conscious* life were intended. Theism, a belief in a personal designer, seems logical.

We are not, of course, pretending that there are no problems in theism. The problem of suffering, in particular, is one that has always troubled those with faith – and is explored in the Bible eg by Job and Habakkuk. But we do believe that the universe looks like a result of design. Science has not removed the mystery and wonder of the universe in which we find ourselves. Rather it has increased it.

---

[49] Dyson (1979) p. 250.

5

Divine Acts & Miracles

Introduction

Theists, as we have seen, believe that God is not merely *a* cause alongside other causes but at a different level of causality is *the* cause of everything continuing to exist. New Testament Christianity reflects this in teaching that God 'holds together the universe by his word of power' (Heb 1:3 RSV see also Col 1:17), that is, anything exists only because of his continued will that it should. In this section we will explore further this Christian theism and its view of God acting in his world.

In our culture we believe the operations of nature follow regular sequences. The analysis and description of these regular sequences is the work of science, and we use terms like 'cause and effect' and 'laws of nature' as part of our framework for this. The question 'Do all events happen according to scientific law?' is really asking 'Would it, *in principle,* be possible for us to construct laws which explain and predict all physical events?' This is not, of course, the same as asking whether our present laws/theories can do this. When people ask whether or not there are 'gaps' in natural causal sequences, they don't mean 'gaps' in our present knowledge, but events which no such laws (even given unlimited facts and intelligence) could be constructed to predict. When people ask, then, whether or not everything happens according to 'natural processes', or whether there are 'gaps' in 'natural processes', we think that this is what they mean to ask. To the theist, of course, if God chooses to do something which is not reducible to or predictable by 'scientific law', then there is, in one sense nothing 'unnatural' about it. Everything which God does is, by definition, 'natural' as it is in line with his own nature. But we think that it is still a useful term by 'natural processes' to mean events which happen according to 'laws of nature'. Whether these are complete, whether they are dependent on, or independent of, a God, is a separate question. Whilst, however, 'natural processes' is a theologically neutral term, the term 'naturalism' implies 'a theory of the world that excludes the supernatural or spiritual'.[1] This is not theologically neutral, but implies the non-existence of both God and (in any real sense) the human psyche.

As theists in a scientific age two lots of interrelated questions arise over this. The first concerns how God can *act* in the world, and the second whether or not it is rational to believe that 'gaps' in natural processes occur. On the actions of God we may ask:

1. Is *everything* which occurs to be seen as a direct act of God?
2. If not, then how are events which are *specific* acts of God different from the *general* process by which he maintains physical reality?
3. Are specific acts of God
   a) Restricted to gaps or breaks in regular natural processes?
   b) Restricted to operating within regular natural processes?
   c) Sometimes occurring in gaps or breaks in the regular natural processes, and sometimes operating according to regular natural processes?

Let us recap on divergent views of God:

i. **The Deist:** Believes God made the world and leaves it running independently of him/herself. God does not 'act' in it at all, and there are no 'gaps' in the regularity of natural processes.

ii. **The Pantheist:** Believes God *is* immanent in but not outside or transcendent from the world ie that nature is God. The absolute regularity of natural processes (or laws of nature) reflects the character of God, and there are no 'gaps' in this regularity as this would mean God denying himself.

iii. **The Semi-deist:** Believes that God made the world independent from him/herself, and can act *only* by 'interfering' in the regular processes under which it runs – ie by making gaps in these regular natural processes.

iv. **The Theist:** Believes that God made the world, but continues to uphold it otherwise it would have no existence. God may operate *through* natural processes (eg in feeding the sparrows and 'clothing' the lilies), but as they are not independent of him he can vary from the regularity of his

---

[1] *Concise Oxford Dictionary* (1995).

actions if he wishes. To us, the regularity of his actions are what we call 'natural processes', and departure from these would appear as 'gaps' in the regularity of such processes.

Thus to the *deist* and *pantheist* there cannot be gaps in the regularity of natural processes. To the *semi-deist* there has to be gaps. To the *theist* there may or may not be – we have to find out empirically (whether by revelation or by direct observation or both). A theist's recognition that God is sustainer and upholder of reality should leave it open to *possibility* that such 'gaps' exist. Their existence or non-existence cannot be determined *a priori*, but only by experience and observation.

A semi-deist approach is sometimes called a 'god-of-the-gaps' theology – God works *only* in the gaps in natural processes. Not only is this a denial of true theism, but there is a danger that as 'gaps' are filled by further scientific explanation there will be no room left for God at all. Some forms of 'creationism' do seem to concentrate on 'gaps' virtually to the exclusion of discerning God throughout nature. This is not exalting but diminishing God, and it is not biblical theology however sincere its advocates may be. On the other hand, it does seem to us that, in their anxiety to avoid restricting God to a 'god-of-the-gaps', some modern Evangelicals almost seem to deny the possibility that there *could* be 'gaps' at all in a total regularity of nature. Thus Howard van Till writes of creation's 'functional integrity', and Denis Alexander that the gaps in our knowledge 'will inevitably shrink'.[2] Neither (as we understand them from public and personal communications) would apply this to biblical miracles such as the resurrection of Jesus. Both are Christian theists and acccept that the God of the Bible has the option of varying his activity in nature as and when he chooses. The debate is not about what God *could* do, but about whether (at the present moment in time) we are entitled to assume that he has *in fact* gone for a 'functional integrity' (ie unvarying regularity?) in nature. We will return near the end of section 10 to the 'god-of-the-gaps' debate on issues of nature in general.

At this point it may be useful to identify three kinds of 'gap' which *could* exist in the regularity of natural processes:

---

[2] Van Till (1996), Alexander (1998). p.18.

1. Gaps in 'determinism' associated with human volition (as previous section).
2. Gaps in regular natural processes associated with eg origins of life or development of consciousness.
3. Gaps in regular natural processes associated with biblical (or modern day) miracles, eg turning water into wine or the resurrection of Jesus.

In one sense, the first of these is hardly a 'gap' in the regularity of natural processes but rather a recognition that natural processes are indeterminate. Given that this is so, some might wish to suggest that at most (2) could turn out to involve something wildly improbable as at low enough odds 'anything could happen'. We see something in this argument, though it seems a bit far fetched. A second point is whether we should regard (2) and (3) in a radically different light. Presumably an event like the resurrection is a specifically 'one-off' or singular event, whereas it might turn out that (say) a natural process origin of life is (in terms of the universe) unexceptional. But suppose we compare, for example, the origins of the first life with the plagues sent on Egypt. Both are past events. Both, in the Bible, are seen as happening according to the intentions of God. In neither instance does the Bible writer specifically assert that a 'break in the regularity of nature was involved' – partly because they simply did not think in those terms. In neither case does it seem to us 'sacrilegious' or 'impious' for scientists to look for natural process explanations of what occurred – but in neither case can theists be sure *a priori* that such explanations will necessarily (even in principle) be forthcoming. If they turn out not to be, then perhaps this may be thought to indicate more strongly some involvement of divine choice and volition. But recognition of God's involvement does not *depend* on such 'gaps'. God's dealings with Moses and Pharaoh (Ex 1-14 and cf. Rom 9:17) involved 'mighty works' to 'make his power known in all the earth'. Paul also says that since the creation of the world God's invisible qualities, his eternal power and divine nature, have been clearly seen, being understood from what has been made (Rom 1:20). But discerning such intentionality behind natural structures and events is not dependent on noting departures from regularity in nature.

From a modern 'scientific' standpoint, where regularity in natural processes is described by scientific law, one may usefully distinguish two 'kinds' of miracle:

* **Type-i:** Those which involve no alteration in the regular physical cause-effect sequences, but involve 'coincidences, to such a degree that participants see them as divinely provident.

* **Type-ii:** Those which appear to have no possible way to explain them without suggesting an alteration in the usual physical cause-effect sequences.

Several points about this distinction may be made.

Firstly, it is by no means a new distinction. In the early fifth century, Augustine distinguished between miracles which are the outcome of inherent causes (*semina occulta*) introduced by God at the first creation, and those which result from God's intrusion into the natural order when he alters something to a 'wholly different nature.[3] Augustine, of course, is also insistent that *anything* God does is not 'against nature', since for God 'nature' is whatever he has made, whether by inherent cause or by miracle.[4] Nevertheless, he thought (and we agree with him) that the distinction was a useful one. A similar distinction has been taken up in one way or another by many writers who have analysed the question of miracles.[5]

Secondly, we must re-emphasise that, although the distinction is ancient, the Hebrew Bible writers themselves did not make it since they had no strong idea of 'scientific law'. When something remarkable or unusual happened the Hebrew writers might note that such an event was unusual or even 'unique' and that God had done it for some purpose. What they lacked was the purely intellectual curiosity as to whether it involved movements of matter within or outside what we would now call normal scientific laws which describe regularity in nature. They simply did not think in those terms.

---

[3] Augustine, *City of God*, Bk 21 sec viii,,(*Nic,& Pos.Nic,Fath.*, 1. i,460). See also *Contra Faust. Manichaeum*, xxvi.3. (*Nic. & Pos. Nic. Fath.*, l, iv, 322).

[4] see eg *The Literal Meaning of Genesis*, vi, 12.

[5] See e.g. R F Holland (1965) pp.. 43-51; Colin Brown (1984) p.174 etc, (1985) p.65 etc.

Now this is not to say either that they were naively credulous or that they were unaware of the normal patterns of physical sequence. Mary, for example, knew very well that babies are not conceived without sexual intercourse - and her reaction reflected this (Lk 1:34)[6] The newly healed man born blind knew that what had happened was unusual - in fact he proclaimed that it had never before happened in the history of the world (Jn 9:32). But what we are saying is that their prime interest was on the meaning and origin of a remarkable event - not its relationship with what we call 'laws of science'.

A third point, which is connected to this, is that if in the light of our present knowledge a biblical 'miracle, is seen to come into the type-i rather than the type-ii category then this does not cast doubt on the biblical record. To take up our earlier example, a programme on British TV in August 1998 analysed how the plagues in Egypt described in Exodus may be 'explained' by 'natural' causes - but this in no way challenged (or meant to challenge) the Bible assertion that God sent them. God is as much the author of natural causal sequences as of the type-ii miracles, It is GOD, in fact who (according to Jesus in Mt 6:26) feeds the birds - but he does it through natural causal sequences.

This leads to some basic questions about type-ii miracles which relate to the more general ones noted earlier about God's purported action in the world:

1. Are type-ii miracles logically possible, and if so is there sufficient evidence to believe that they have occurred?

2. In what relationship do these type-ii miracles stand to faith? In what way can type-i miracles be ascribed to a 'personal involvement' of God?

3. Why, if type-ii miracles occur, do they occur only in some instances and not in others with apparently similar circumstances?

Theistic Belief and the Possibility of Miracles

Are type-ii miracles rationally possible? That is, can events occur which differ from the usual sequences of 'natural law'

---

[6] See also C S Lewis (1947) ch.7.

which we observe? This depends on one's assumptions. Let us recap on the following three belief systems:

Deterministic Naturalism (which implies atheism)
- Physical nature is all that there is, a 'closed system.
- Physical phenomena follow invariant patterns of cause effect.

Deism
- God has created physical nature to function independently of him and to have invariant patters of cause-effect.
- God has left this as a 'closed system' and has no further involvement or interaction with it.

Theistic Supernaturalism
- God exists separately from physical nature which is only a part of total reality.
- Physical nature does not function independently of God, but depends for its continuing existence on his will and power.
- The laws of science represent our generalisations about God's usual patterns of working in physical cause-effect sequences.

Each of these has a kind of self-consistency, but none of them is obviously and self-evidently true. *If* physical nature were a closed system following invariant laws (as either of the first two would imply) then clearly type-ii miracles would be impossible. But *if* a creator-God exists, then there is clearly no reason why he should not periodically vary his pattern of working - i.e. produce a type-ii miracle. His existence would imply that type-ii miracles would be possible - the only question being whether and when they had actually happened.

It may just first be worth noting that both Christian theologians and leaders in the field of science have held just the kind of view of theism related in the first paragraph of this chapter. Thus, e.g., Jean Buridan (c1295-1366) followed early church figures in writing:

> One could say, in fact, that God, when he created the universe, set each of the celestial spheres in motion as it pleased him, impressing on each of them an impetus which has moved it ever since. God has, therefore, no longer to move these spheres, except in exerting a general influence similar to that by which he gives his concurrence

to all phenomena. Thus he could rest on the seventh day from the work he had achieved, confiding to created things their mutual causes and effects.[7]

This refers back to early church teaching eg that of Chrysostom on Jn 5:17 that Jesus reveals his unceasing care for us:

> he calls "Work" the maintenance of created things, bestowal of permanence on them, and governance of them through all time...[8]

Later, in the Reformation, Calvin's Genesis commentary also speaks of God sustaining the world, and that:

> if God should but withdraw his hand a little, all things would immediately perish and dissolve into nothing.[9]

Amongst founders of modern scientific thinking, the chemist Robert Boyle, one of the great early luminaries of the Royal Society, wrote in 1685 that it must produce adoration of God to know that all the complex machinery of animal organisms:

> ... as well as the rest of the mundane matter are every moment sustained, guided, and governed, according to their respective natures and with an exact regard to the catholic laws of the universe; to know, I say, that there is a Being that does this everywhere and every moment, and that manages all things without aberration or intermission.[10]

Boyle's later *The Christian Virtuoso* (1690) expanded on this theme. Now Boyle was probably the leading figure in what is called the 'mechanical philosophy', which arose at this time. This is the belief that the physical cause-effect sequence is unbroken and totally predictable. Yet, because he believed that this whole chain was only there because God was continually sustaining it, Boyle had no trouble in accepting the biblical miracles. R S Westfall though he outlines well Boyle's whole views on this seems not really to grasp the consistency of Boyle's position - and sees his acceptance of miracles as a 'contradiction' to his general views.[11] Yet Boyle even gives an

---

[7] Jean Buridan, *Quaestiones Super Octo Physicorum*, Bk.8.
[8] *The Fathers of the Church*, Vol 74, p. 140 (Tr R C Hill).
[9] Calvin (Tr 1965) p. 103.
[10] Boyle (1685) p.140-1.
[11] Westfall, (1973).

analogy of a quill pen writing which is a kind of seventeenth century equivalent to our one of the television screen.[12]

Many other scientists could be used to illustrate this view. The following is taken from the great early 19th century geologist William Buckland, who says that many people maintain:

> that the system of the Universe is carried on by the force of the laws originally impressed on matter, without the necessity of fresh interference or continued supervision on the part of the Creator, Such an opinion is indeed founded only on a verbal fallacy; for 'laws impressed on matter" is an expression which can only denote the continued exertion of the will of the Lawgiver...[13]

Buckland too has been misunderstood. Hooykaas, for example, correctly ascribes the 'biblical' view to Newton, but mistakenly describes Buckland as a 'semi-deist'.[14] Three further points need to be made. The first is the role of science. Suppose that we take, eg, Boyle's law in physics that: 'The volume of a given mass of gas is inversely proportional to the pressure upon it if the temperature remains constant.' This law describes what is normally observed, but it does not say why it happens nor why it always should. As science progresses we may break down existing laws into more basic units: in this case we may explain Boyle's law in terms of the movements of molecules of gas. Yet this does not explain why molecules act in this way nor why they always should. As we progress further we may talk in sub-atomic terms. Yet no matter how far we reduce the phenomena to more and more basic laws we will never be able to say why they behave as they do nor why they always should. Moreover to say something like 'because it is in their nature to do so' really adds little more. Scientific laws may be valid or invalid, useful or useless, but ultimately are no more than detailed descriptions of how things normally behave which enables us to predict future behaviour. They answer the 'how' not the 'why' of physical existence. The Christian theist believes that this ultimate 'why' is because of the will and volition of God.

The second point concerns terms like 'breaking' laws, or God's 'intervention' in 'natural law'. To the Christian theist, the

---

[12] Boyle, *Works*, 2, 48.
[13] Buckland (1820). p,18.
[14] Hooykaas (1959) p. 170 etc. Cf Paul Marston (1984) Section 5.5.

laws of nature' have no existence independent of God. If we talk at all of God 'breaking' them then we must be careful what exactly we mean. You may speak of 'breaking, a habit of early rising on a particular occasion - but that habit does not somehow exist independently of you. To say 'I intervened this morning in my habit of early rising by lying longer in bed' would be rather strange, Yet, to the Christian, laws of nature can be perceived as habits of God. We may doubt, then, whether terms like 'God's intervention', are really appropriate - and scientists such as those cited above actually tend to avoid them in their writings.

The third point is to note again the issue of miracles in creation. We have noted those Christians who imply that creation *must have* involved type-ii miracles if it were really him doing it. We rejected this because God is not restricted to 'gaps' in natural processes but also works through them. On the other hand we also noted the Christians today who seem so nervous of a 'god-of-the-gaps' theology that they attack anyone who suggests that there might be some. True theism recognises that God can work both through natural processes and through type-ii miracles, and the Bible language often leaves it open to an empirical study to discern which - because the writers were not really interested in the question.

An acceptance, then, of the possibility of miracles (type-i and type-ii), is a rational part of any Christian theism - i.e. a belief in a personal God who both created and sustains the universe by his word of power. The two types are distinguished from our standpoint – whether they 'feel' any different for God is beyond our human scope to guess.

Attacks on Miracles

If, then, miracles are so obviously a rational part of a Christian worldview, how did there come to be thought to be any particular problem with them?

We have seen how the Christian view sees God both as separate from and yet continually maintaining the physical world. Augustine, as we have seen, distinguished type-i and type-ii miracles. Unfortunately, however, his analysis of the type-ii spoke in terms of God 'changing the nature of what he has created'. This could very easily be seen as God intervening in something to which he had given some kind of independent existence. To those philosophers whose experience of God is not that of the living personal God of the New Testament, but a rationally derived God from pure intellectual discussion, this smacked of inconsistency.

Perhaps one of the first was the Jewish pantheist Spinoza. As a pantheist he believed that God was in everything but had no separate existence from the physical world. In other words, the physical world (even if embodying God) was a closed system. On these assumptions, as Colin Brown put it in his study:

> ...to Spinoza laws of nature were divine decrees. they were perfect and simply could not be broken. To suggest that God broke his own decrees from time to time was unthinkable. It would be like suggesting that God was acting against his own nature, or that his wisdom needed correction.[15]

Naturally, however, one could very much question the basis on which he assumed his pantheism to be true. Yet this was also a kind of basis for the later deist movement. From around 1624[16] began a tradition which 'rationally deduced' from experience and nature (with no reference to Jesus or the Bible) the idea of a God who created but then took little further interest in the world. With such a God miracles would, of course, never occur.

We must note the origins of this. The pantheist or deist believed that God had simply created perfect laws - and it would be against his nature to 'violate' them. But we note:

i.   These were usually philosophers, not scientists' in our sense.

ii. They did not begin either from observation as a base for inviolable law, nor from the God of the Bible, but from a God deduced from pure Reason.

David Hume, in his influential *An Enquiry Concerning Human Understanding* (1748), argued rather differently. Both the pantheist Spinoza and the deists had emphasised Reason rather than experience. 'Rationally' they believed that Deity must be 'self consistent' which (in their minds) ruled out

---

[15] Brown, (1985), p. 8; see also (1984), Ch. 2, and Geisler, (1979) p. 15 etc,
[16] Ideas of Lord Herbert (1624) were continued by Toland (1696), Tindale (1730) and Woolston (1720).

miracles. But David Hume, was not only a sceptical agnostic but also an avowed 'empiricist', i.e., he believed that all knowledge came from experience. Thus his belief in the inviolability of natural law could be based only on experience.

Hume's basic argument, then, was:

1. Assessing the truth of any reported event is a balance of probabilities.
2. The a priori improbability of anything 'violating the laws of nature' is so great that overwhelming human testimony" would be necessary in order to make us accept it.
3. The right kind of human testimony (reliable, sophisticated, first hand witness, of incontrovertible miracle) is lacking. Also, there is a natural human tendency to exaggerate, and miracles are usually more reported amongst what he called 'ignorant and barbarous nations'.

Hume concluded that miracles have not happened and do not happen.

This is riddled with contradiction. Firstly, it is hard to see how anything for a real empiricist can be so *a priori* improbable. If all knowledge comes from experience then we have to wait and see. Secondly, as Colin Brown points out, Hume refused to accept in his own day the testimony of doctors and men of repute in Paris who had examined and accepted miracles. He replied only that 'the absolute impossibility' of such events must be sufficient refutation 'in the eyes of all reasonable people.'[17] In other words, having begun solely by appeal to the evidence, he finished by refusing to look at it.

In brief, the problem with his argument is that:

i.   He begins from the firm and unalterable experience' that laws are inviolable.
ii.   But this is true only if he assumes that this experience must exclude the many claims throughout history to have witnessed them.
iii. On such a basis - having ruled them out it is not surprising that he concludes them to be impossible.
iv.   It is all a classic case of assuming what you want to prove.

---

[17] Colin Brown (1985) p.22.

Hume's Philosophical Offspring

Who, in the main, carried on the Humean position? Ironically, one group was that of those in various schools of 'Radical Theology' which began in the nineteenth century, One of the twin pillars of assumption made by such theologians was the impossibility of miracles. Thus one of its great early figures, D F Strauss, wrote in his *Life of Jesus* (1835-6, Tr 1846) that any narration must be presumed to be myth if it is:

> Irreconcilable with the known and universal laws ... according to these laws, agreeing with all just philosophical conceptions and all credible experience, the absolute never disturbs the chain of secondary causes by single arbitrary acts of interposition...[18]

Which are these 'all just philosophical conceptions'? Are they those 'rationally deduced' from the character of God by the deists, or 'derived from experience' by Hume? In neither case are they much of an alternative to looking at actual human testimony. Yet these shaky foundations led to all kinds of supposedly rational emasculation of real Christianity. One famous early follower was J E Renan who began by assuming: 'Miracles are things which never happen; only credulous people believe they have seen them...'[19] Many other theologians followed, and some even today have made little philosophical progress. One of the great 'heros' taken up by 1980's T.V. theologian Don Cupitt was that very same D F Strauss.

A second group of heirs of Hume and Strauss are a small group of anti-supernaturalist philosophers. Apart from a suspicion that the strength of feeling exhibited by such atheists goes deeper than mere intellectual difficulty, the actual arguments seem either to be linguistic tricks or a kind of deification of science, and Christians have made detailed criticisms of them.[20]

A third group who might go along with the impossibility of miracles are some artists, In D H Lawrence's controversial book *The Rainbow* (1915), Brangwen thinks about the water being changed into wine:

---

[18] D F Strauss, (Tr 1846, 2nd Edn 1892) vol 1 p. 88.
[19] Renan (1863).
[20] See Geisler (1979) p. 48 etc.

so much rain-water - look at it - can it become grape juice, wine? For an instant he saw with the clear eyes of the mind and said No... Water, natural water, could it suddenly and unnaturally turn into wine, depart from its being and at haphazard take on another being? Ah no, he knew it was wrong...

Artists, presumably, rely on gut reaction rather than rational thought. The 'clear eyes of the mind' should have said 'yes'. Obviously the miraculous MUST be the 'out of the ordinary' - otherwise it would not be miraculous. But there seems not any rational reason to rule out, before actual examination, the possibility of type-ii miracles occurring.

The one group which, on the whole, seem to have had little trouble about the possibility of miracle is mainstream British scientists. As we have seen, this includes even those (like Boyle) who supported most strongly a 'mechanical philosophy' of cause and effect. Even T H Huxley, one of the most famous agnostic scientists of the age of Darwin said that 'the so-called a-priori arguments against Theism, and, given a Deity, against the possibility of creative acts, appeared to him 'to be devoid of reasonable foundation.'[21] Neither special creation nor miracle were *a priori* impossible. Today, alas, a tiny group of vociferous atheists seem to be seen by British media as representing 'science'. Professor Lewis Wolpert, chair of a committee for the Public understanding of Science, and regular writer in the *Independent on Sunday*, stunned a 1996 conference at Kings College London with the repeated assertion that he was a follower of Hume - whose notions on idea-based empiricism make even less sense in the light of modern physics than they did in Hume's own time. Daniel Dennett, whose Denkinsland we visited in Section 2, begins his work with a rejection of any kind of supernaturalism – though on what basis he makes his assumption we are not told. It clearly cannot be empirical, as it is an assumption impervious, it seems, to any kind of evidence.

The final group who reject type-ii miracles are those who seemingly do so for theological reasons. David Jenkins, for example, a former Bishop of Durham (and anathema to British Evangelicals) seems to accept that God *could* do type-ii miracles (which he mocked as 'divine laser beam type of miracle'), but

---

[21] Huxley (1898) p. 167.

adds that this 'would not seem to be a choice which he cared or would care to use.'[22] Another liberal Anglican theologian, Arthur Peacocke, quotes Jenkins with approval but also adds:

> One has to recognise, with Hume, that adequate historical evidence for such a contravention of the originally divinely established laws of nature could never, in practice, be forthcoming.[23]

Why one 'has to recognise' a gratuitous assumption which rejects empiricism and is impervious to any testing is not made clear. Such theologians seem to decide *a priori* that nature must be uniform irrespective of any actual physical evidence, and decide *a priori* that God 'would not care to do' type-ii miracles irrespective of the testimony of the gospels and the life of Christ. Empiricism is effectively rejected both in nature and in theology. To be fair to Peacocke, he later (p.183) expresses uncertainty about his rejection of type-ii miracles, but it does seem a strange view for an avowed theist to take.

Faith and Type-ii Miracles

Are miracles for the Christian a 'proof' of faith, or are they only accepted because of faith? In fact the relationship is complex.

Three main words are used for some sense of 'miracles' in the New Testament: *semeia* (signs*)*, *terata* (wonders) and *dynameis* (mighty works). All go back to Old Testament ideas and words.

A number of things must be remembered about this. Firstly, in the biblical context believers were not arguing for the possibility of the supernatural. Even when Paul was arguing his case before the sophisticated Greeks (including Epicurean sceptics) his sermon simply begins with the assertion of who God is, appealing to their own deeper consciousness and religious roots. He does not argue that Jesus' resurrection proves the supernatural, His argument is rather that the resurrection affirms God's approval of Jesus as the man by whom the world will be judged (Acts 17:31). Even this, in itself, is not absolute 'proof', for Paul is well aware that there may be false 'signs and wonders' (2 Thess 2:9).

---

[22] Jenkins (1987) p. 4.
[23] Peacocke (1993) p. 142.

The pattern goes back right to Israel's beginning. God is to be distinguished from other gods in that he acted in bringing out their nation for himself by 'signs and wonders... and a mighty hand' in actions never seen before or since' (Deut 4:4). Yet, on the other hand, if a prophet gives a sign or wonder which takes place and he says "let us go after other gods" then 'The Lord your God is testing you to find out whether you love him with all your heart' and that false prophet must be rejected (Deut 13:1-4.). The basic point is that whilst signs and wonders may be expected to accompany the activity of a 'supernatural' God, they are not in themselves a *proof.* The genuineness of the true God and faith in him is attested by a wider range of human experience.

This pattern is followed in the New Testament where Jesus also recognises that false prophets may do signs and wonders, whether type-i or type-ii miracles (Mt 24:24, Mk 13:22). Matthew 12 is very interesting. Jesus performs a miraculous healing (v.22-3), but his opponents put it down to evil arts. Jesus indicates that they should discern his genuineness from the wider moral context. Asked (v.38) for a sign, his reply indicates that they should look to the example of those who repented (like the people of Ninevah and the Queen of Sheba) at the preaching of the word. It is the response of the will rather than the unwilling conviction of the intellect which is the key to faith (Jn 7:15.). He even obliquely acknowledges that a resurrection will not convict a person who refuses to repent at the message of the Law and the Prophets (Lk 16:29-31). The miracles which he did were 'signs' of his messiahship - for they were also parables of his Kingdom. The driving out of Satan and the miraculous provision recalling God's manna in the wilderness were both things which one might only expect from God's Messiah - yet some saw these miracles and missed their significance by immediately afterwards asking for a sign (Mt 12:38, 16:1).

None of the biblical words used for 'miracle' have as primary meaning any kind of suspension of 'laws of nature', A 'sign' is something by which one recognises a particular person or thing, a confirmatory, corroborative, authenticating mark or token.'[24]

---

[24] See the *The New International Dictionary* (Ed, Colin Brown), vol ii, p. 626. Colin Brown refers to all three words in (1985) p. 74 etc.

They are extraordinary but not necessarily type-ii miracles. Their significance is in that in their wider context they point to God and his activity. A 'wonder' (which in the New Testament is used only together with 'sign') means a kind of portent. It is something that brings a person up sharply and seems to demand an interpretation.[25] Finally, Jesus' miracles are called 'mighty works, because 'in them God's rule on earth begins to have a powerful effect' and the fight against evil is carried out on the level of human existence.'[26] The work is paramount, the power is because God is involved.

Type-ii miracles, then, do occur, and their very unexpectedness may pull people up sharply and raise questions in their minds. But such miracles are not intended as magic tricks to convince unwilling atheists. Rather they are the natural expectation when God is at work in the Messiah (Jesus) or his followers (Mk 16:17-28). As such they are further confirmatory signs to those who discern the work of God going on.

Christians have, in the main, recognised that miracles are 'proofs' only in this kind of context. Origen, for example, the great early Greek Christian, wrote:

> Without miracles and wonders [the apostles] would not have persuaded those who heard new doctrines and new teachings to leave their traditional religion...[27]

He asserts that miracles are still being done in his day. Yet he admits that in and by themselves the miracles are no infallible proof of divinity. The real tests are the purity of life of the miracle-worker and the betterment of mankind by their results.[28]

Great early scientists such as Robert Boyle (whose views we already mentioned), and philosophers of science like Bacon were just as clear. Boyle cites with approval:

> one of the first and greatest experimental philosophers of our age, Sir Francis Bacon, that God never wrought a miracle to convince atheists.[29]

---

[25] See *The New International Dictionary*, vol ii, p. 632 etc.

[26] See *The New International Dictionary*, vol ii, p. 603.

[27] See Colin Brown (1984), (1985) Also Origen in iv, 397,491.) *Against Celsus* I:ii,III:lxviii (Ant.Nic.Fath, iv 397, 491).

[28] Origen in *Against Celsus* II:xlviii (Ant.Nic,Fath, iv.450 etc).

[29] Boyle (1690), p. 41.

Bacon and Boyle believed in miracles, but not as self-standing 'proofs' of the truth of any system of Christian doctrine.

Even where miracles have been presented as 'proofs', they are usually thought to be part of a wider picture of prophecy and moral content. Wesley, for example, who led the evangelical revival in Britain in the eighteenth century, appealed to the classic proofs or miracles, prophecies and the moral character of its writings as proof of biblical authority.[30] These points were later repeated by such as William Paley, and early nineteenth century evangelical leaders like Simeon and Chalmers.[31] Colin Brown cites several more recent leaders who have claimed to see miracles as 'proofs', showing that in no instance are they actually thought to be self-sufficient as proofs.[32]

Sometimes, of course, Christian apologists may have objectives which differ from those of the early church because they speak to people of different viewpoints, C S Lewis, in perhaps one of the most widely known books on miracles, followed earlier writers like Paley in arguing against anti-supernaturalists that miraculous occurrences would be only to be expected if the Christian world view were correct, He was aiming at those who doubted the possibility of miracles rather than those who doubted their significance. Earlier parts of the present chapter have had the same objective.

In what relation, then, do miracles, particularly type-ii miracles, stand to faith? Firstly, Jesus taught that miracles come in response to faith. Their actual occurrence, then, is largely dependent on faith. To onlookers, it is not in any way irrational to believe in the possibility of miracles - even though there may be scepticism in particular cases. Yet the miracle will never be an absolute 'proof' of the truth of Christianity. The miracle should be seen in its real context as a natural part of what may be expected if the Christian world-view is true, and to come in a context of 'making whole' which is central to the Christian religion. In such a context miracles do then point as signs, to the

---

[30] Wesley, *A Clear and Concise Demonstration of the Divine Inspiration of the Holy Scriptures* in (1872 Ed) vol xi.
[31] Paley, (1794) p. 7 etc; Simeon , *Works,* 14, p.351; Chalmers, (1814), p. 253.
[32] Colin Brown, (1984) Ch..8.

spiritually discerning, confirming the truth and authority of Jesus.

The Actions of God

All the main theistic religions (in particular Judaism, Christianity and Islam) picture a God who 'acts' in the world. In type-ii miracles this 'action' is fairly obvious. It must, of course, be noted that it is impossible absolutely to prove that a particular miracle is in one or other category. With our modern views that all scientific discoveries may be superceded later by further discovery, we cannot rule out the possibility that later discoveries will enable a type-ii miracle to be reassigned as type-i.[33] On the other hand, it is impossible to tell whether, in an individual incident, what we thought was a 'natural' causal sequence did involve some change. Thus, e.g., when Jesus calmed the storm, it might turn out that there was some suspension of usual physical laws - we cannot have the data to determine this.

But what of the type-i events themselves – whether we designate them specifically as 'miracles' or just as God 'acting' in the world? Can we say that prayer, for example, has been answered *only* if a type-ii miracle occurs? Surely not.

But if events occur within natural law (even assuming that natural law has no existence independent of God) how can God be said to 'act' in any specific way in some but not all events which occur within those laws? Various different approaches to this are summarised in several recent books, including those by Barbour (who is sympathetic to Process theology[34]) and some whose views are more similar to ours - like Polkinghorne and Jeeves & Berry.[35]

In Augustinian theology, of course, the question has no real meaning – for *everything* happens according to the will and plan of God, so *everything* is a Divine act. To us this is not only incoherent, but does not reflect the God of biblical theism.

---

[33] See also eg Ninian Smart (1986).
[34] For an outline of what this is see below.
[35] Barbour (1998) Ch. 12; Polkinghorne (1998) ch. 5; Jeeves & Berry (1998) Ch. 5.

A second approach comes in the work of liberal Anglican Arthur Peacocke, whose rejection of type-ii miracles was noted earlier. He bases his answer to how God 'acts' in the world mostly on the concept of 'top down' causality. In some systems the whole system 'causes' changes in its constituent parts, and he pictures God as influencing individual lives on a 'whole system' basis. We have serious problems with this. The first is that he links it to an 'identity-theory' model of human nature[36] that (as we argued in the last chapter) is both dated and untenable. The second is that, having described it, he admits

there is still a lacuna in our explication of the God/world 'causal joint' [37]

Though he pictures God's input as 'information' rather than 'energy', he then admits that information input implies energy input and is unable to answer the question as to where in the system this happens.

The third is that (taken with a rejection of type-ii miracles) it seems to endanger the real transcendence of God and risk lapsing into pantheism (although Peacocke is certainly an avowed theist). It is hard to see this as consistent with any *Christian* theism, where 'signs and wonders' are a part of the messianic identity for Jesus, and were promised to his followers.

Interestingly, though Peacocke (like many moderns) makes the ritual denunciation of 'god-of-the-gaps' theology, he then asks whether, recognising quantum uncertainty, we might:

propose a 'God of the unpredictable gaps'? There would then be no fear of such a God being squeezed out by increases in scientific knowledge'.[38]

We made just such a suggestion in our (1989) *Reason and Faith,* and were interested to see why Peacocke rejects it. His argument seems to be that such a view is 'grounded on the assumption that God *does* know the outcome of natural situations which are unpredictable to us'. If God does not know the outcomes of quantum events, then Peacocke argues that God cannot decide to direct any of them. Though (as already indicated) we share his

---

[36] Peacocke (1993) p. 160.
[37] Peacocke (1993) p. 163.
[38] Peacocke (1993) p. 153.

view that quantum events may normally be unpredictable to God (ie the future is genuinely open), we cannot fathom why this should mean that God cannot decide to control some of them if he so chooses.[39] We are not, necessarily, saying that this is the *only* way in which we can picture God's general action in the world. Whatever conceptual models we use we are unlikely to capture all of the way in which God relates to our world (a point well made by Barbour[40]) but this at least helps.

Chance$_2$ and Chance$_3$

We distinguished difference senses of the word 'chance' in the previous section. It is worth, at this point, pulling together ideas which relate chance$_2$ (quantum indeterminacy) with chance$_3$ (lack of any intention of purpose behind events). Put simply: are all, none or some of the chance$_2$ inherently unpredictable quantum events also chance$_3$ ie lacking any intention, purpose or direction? There are several alternative answers.

D M MacKay (1978), takes the view that everything is divinely determined. The corner-stone of his approach is a universal extension of Proverbs 16:33: 'The lot is cast into the lap, but its every decision is from the Lord.' This, says MacKay, shows that God is the author not only of space-time but of all the events in it.

Chance, on this basis, is a property in human relationships; it does not apply to God's authorship of the events in the world which are strictly directed and willed. To MacKay, all chance$_2$ (uncertainty) is simply chance$_1$ (human ignorance), but none is chance$_3$ since God determines all. It seems extraordinary to use one verse in Proverbs to derive this kind of universal. Of this verse Derek Kidner wisely remarks:

> The Old Testament use of the word 'lot' shows that this proverb (and 18:18) is not about God's control of all random occurrences, but about his settling of matters properly referred to him. Land was 'allotted' (Josh 14:1, 2), likewise Temple service (1 Chron 25:8).[41]

---

[39] Cf Clayton (1997) who holds our view on foreknowledge, but thinks it 'easier to make the case for divine action today than at any time since Newton.' (p. 173).

[40] Barbour (1998) p. 322.

[41] Kidner (1964) p. 122.

It seems extraordinary to conclude from God's control of lots during matters specifically and prayerfully referred to him, that he determines *all* details of *all* events. It is made the more so as MacKay himself asserts that the 'doctrine of divine sovereignty over "chance" events ... says nothing to warrant the idea that all or indeed any such events are intended to offer divine guidance to men.' MacKay universalises the control, but not the guidance. In reality, of course, his view of chance depends on his view of God who, he claims, is 'one who ordains all events according to his determinate counsel and foreknowledge'. As we have already given reasons to reject this theology, we must also reject his objections to chance$_3$. W G Pollard's book (1958) was an earlier one which similarly saw God's decision as behind all apparently chance$_2$ uncertainty events.

Arthur Peacocke gives chance a more independent role. Implicit in the initial conditions set by God, was a vast range of potential universes - the chance sorting of possibilities is the means for potential to become actual. God sets up the system and leaves it to 'chance' for the 'gamut' of 'potentialities' to be explored. Specific chance$_2$ (uncertainty) events are also chance$_3$, (lacking intentionality) – though the *whole system* is (Peacocke says) intended. The basic idea of chance$_3$ being deliberately *used* by God creatively seems to us a good one, but in universalising it Peacocke leaves no room for meaningful human or divine agency. Elements in writers like Mackay, Peacocke, Pollard, Geach, and Bartholomew are useful, but any acceptable form of theism needs to leave room for such agency.

We have already argued that uncertainty physics leaves openness in the universe. We have no problem in conceiving that different uncertainty events may be 'determined' by human volition, divine volition, or be chance$_3$ (ie no volition). In our earlier book we made this point, and it seems accepted also by Polkinghorne.[42] It should also be noted (as we argued in Section 3 above) that this does *not* involve 'intervention' from outside physical processes. 'I' am not 'outside' but internal to the physical processes in my own brain. God is not 'outside' but immanent in the physical processes which he chooses to determine. My and his will are integral to physical processes

---

[42] Forster & Marston (1989) p. 409; Polkinghorne (1998) p. 90.

though logically distinct from them because they refer to a different order of reality.

What objections can be made to this approach and model? D J Bartholomew objects that to get a sequence which appeared random would place a lot of restriction on God.[43] We do not understand this comment, even allowing the paradoxical 'test for randomness' to be valid. For one thing, it begins from the wrong end. Surely no one is suggesting that God faced an *a-priori* requirement that his series of choices must look random? Rather, we are looking after the event at a series of choices which do, in fact, look random, and asking whether or not they are consistent with a hypothesis that divine volition was involved. Certainly, if a sequence were actually caused by interacting volitions, there is no reason why it should not look random. Suicide statistics are random, but each is the result of an act of volition.

What other objections have been made to such ideas? There are, of course, the by now expected ritual mutterings of 'god-of-the-gaps' – though Peacocke has now at least recognised that these 'gaps' are inherent and irreducible according to the physical system itself, not just gaps in knowledge likely to be filled in. Another refers to it as implying a 'hole-and-corner deity, fiddling around at the rickety roots of the cosmos'. This is just purely emotive. God *declares* that he acts through revelation, and it is through spiritual discernment that events are seen as 'signs'. If God chooses to leave openness for human and divine 'action' at the very heart of every single part of the physical creation (ie at particle level), then it is hardly 'hole in the corner' – nothing could be more central to physical reality.

The theism which we believe makes most sense of reality involves an 'internal-to-matter' role for human acts of volition, and an 'internal-to-matter' role for divine acts. Both can occur 'within' the openness of natural processes, though God can also act in abrogation of these in type-ii miracles. Viewed thus, there is a spiritual dimension behind physical reality, throughout it and interacting with it. The question which this raises is whether there are other spiritual beings. The sacred writings of all main

---

[43] Bartholomew (1984) p 128.

theistic religions (Jews, Christians and Muslims) seem to assume that there are, but we will discuss this on our website rather than here, as it does not affect the main issues of theism.

Process Theology

A point we have consistently insisted on is that there is openness in the universe, and that *reaction* is an essential part of the personal nature of the biblical God. Some hostile critics have suggested that this is 'really' Process theology. Therefore, although many readers may not even have heard of Process theology, we need to briefly address this issue. The founder of Process philosophy was A N Whitehead.[44] Later Process theologians have adapted and extended this philosophy.[45] Some have doubted whether Process theology really has a transcendent God at all, though Barbour insists that it does.[46] The real problem, however, is that although the Process God does *react*, it is unclear how he *acts*. Even Barbour admits some problems on this score, and Polkinghorne (whose openness theology stands closer to our own) is much more critical.[47] We must insist that the biblical God *acts*, through creation *ex nihilo* and through both type-i and type-ii miracles. He acts through nature and in history – supremely, of course, in the incarnation. Our own openness theology arises out of Wesleyanism, the Radical Reformation, elements of the early church – and above all the Bible. It owes nothing to Process theology, and it would be foolish to reject biblical truths simply because some of them may be reflected in its doctrines.

Design Theory

A rather different movement which has been much in the news at the end of the 90's is loosely called 'design theory' or 'intelligent design'. Two leading figures in it are the biochemist Michael Behe and the lawyer Phillip Johnson. What they are saying is relevant to our present topic, and we will look again at the broader movement and some others in it in Section 10.

---

[44] Whitehead: *Process and Reality* (1929).
[45] See eg Hartshorne (1948); Griffin (1975).
[46] Barbour (1998) p. 326.
[47] Barbour (1998) p. 327; Polkinghorne (1998) p. 87.

Michael Behe is a Catholic biochemist whose book *Darwin's Black Box* suggests that there are systems which (analogously to a mousetrap) are 'irreducibly complex systems'. These are systems in which each part is essential for the whole thing to work, and if any one part is missing the whole is useless. It is difficult (he says) to see how these types of systems could evolve on a stepwise basis - all the elements are either there (in which case it works) or not (in which case it doesn't). He also argues that few if any explanations of supposed evolutionary processes have been worked out in any detail at the biochemical level. Writers like Dawkins ignore the difficulties of describing any biochemical level sequence that would explain organic developments in terms of purely natural physical cause-effect sequences. Behe's central point is that scientists are like those who have not noticed an elephant in the room - the elephant is 'Design'. Whilst everything *might* have been designed, for some parts of nature it seems the only possible explanation.

There are various different versions of Behe seen in different reviews. Jerry Coyne sees Behe as 'a new more sophisticated version of scientific creationism' (ie young-earthism).[48] Coyne finds 'ample evidence' for evolution from palaeontology, embryology, biogeography and vestigial organs' and, although 'there is no doubt that the pathways described by Behe are dauntingly complex', he has a touching faith in natural process evolution and simply adds 'their evolution will be hard to unravel'. Coyne also repeats the evidence for 'molecular evolution' dismissed as circumstantial in Behe's book (pseudogenes etc). To Coyne, Behe is a thinly disguised 'scientific creationist', whose tactic of labelling as 'God' what we don't understand dooms God to disappear as our knowledge inexorably increases. Behe's 'folksy us and them style' apparently reflects his 'creationist roots' - Coyne does not tell us what roots Dawkins' equally folksy style indicates!

Tom Cavalier-Smith's review is entitled 'the Blind Biochemist'.[49] Cavalier-Smith admits that Behe's book contains 'relatively few factual errors', and that 'For none of the cases mentioned by Behe is there yet a comprehensive and detailed

---

[48] Coyne in *Nature*, Sept 19th 1996.
[49] Cavalier Smith in *TREE*, 4 April 1997.

explanation of the probable steps in the evolution of the observed complexity.' The review contains various bits of nit picking about which articles Behe hasn't read (he apparently missed one of Cavalier-Smith's own which appeared in a book edited by someone else!). It also attacks Behe for criticising the non-quantitative nature of evolutionary explanation and failing to give any quantitative version of creative design himself. Behe's book is 'antiscientific', 'intellectually shallow and unoriginal', 'worthless', 'ignorant', 'deceitful', 'blissfully unaware', etc. Cavalier-Smith finishes:

> Are these various omissions merely through ignorance or by deliberate intent because as a Catholic, Behe prefers the illusion of an intelligent biochemist creator to mutations and the blind gropings of macro-molecules?

The 'blind groping' here is, of course, just as metaphysical a phrase as 'intelligent biochemist' - though Cavalier-Smith may, in his own words, be 'blissfully unaware' of this. Where does the review leave us? Whether Behe is mistaken in any of his particular examples, it leaves us with the admission that few or no detailed biochemical models for evolutionary change exist, and with no answers on the more general issue of whether there are indeed 'irreducibly complex systems'. Does Cavalier-Smith concede that there *might* be such a system? If so, at what point should we conclude that we have found one?

Michael Roberts' review in *Science and Belief*[50] says: 'Behe has put the God-of-the-gaps argument in clever guise...' Roberts portrays Behe as suggesting we 'place our faith in a vulnerable position' because:

> it is a faith of a God only in the gaps, and should biochemistry one day fill the gaps then our faith would collapse.

Roberts portrays a vulnerable semi-deist, whose position he admits difficulty in distinguishing from a young-earth one. He also wrongly ascribes to Behe the view that only some biological structures are designed.[51] The journal Editor Denis Alexander himself wrote a review seeing Behe as adopting Thomist objections to evolution.[52] Both Roberts and Alexander

---

[50] Roberts (1997) pp. 191-2.
[51] Repeated Roberts (1998) – Behe's point is about what we *know* is designed.
[52] Alexander's review was in *Triple Helix* Winter Edition 1997/8 p.21.

are friends of one of the present authors, and would not dream of intentionally misrepresenting anyone. To some extent the ambiguities in Behe's book invite it, but nevertheless these seem to be misunderstandings of him.

We wrote to Behe to clarify some ambiguities and can state:

1. He is a Christian theist who sees God's activity in all of nature - he is not a semi-deist.

2. He does not hold a 'young earth' position - but accepts the established scientific timescales.

3. He is not *inherently* anti-evolution, and does not see evolution in itself as anti-Christian.

Our own view of Behe is critically sympathetic. He is right to point out that a lot of Dawkins, Dennett and other Penguin 'Popular Science' just contains what we call 'Penpops fables' - intuitive allegories and models with no biochemical detail. He is right to point out that the gaps in natural-process explanation have (in one sense) widened not diminished in the last half century. He is right to raise the issue of the possibility of 'irreducibly complex systems' - indeed Stuart Kauffman's ideas of complexity in life in some senses raise similar issues.

Before we look at our central point of divergence from Behe it may be useful to illustrate some of our own views on miracles. We believe type-ii miracles happen today (we listed some in our *Reason and Faith*). More recently, a friend had amiloidosis. This is an apparently incurable condition for which no mechanism of 'spontaneous remission' is known. Medical tests were definitely and conclusively positive. She was prayed over by the elders of the church (as enjoined by James). When she went back to the hospital there was no trace of the condition. The hospital were so surprised they retested the original samples and found the condition still there in them. Now of course one cannot 'prove' a type-ii miracle has occurred, for someone can always think up some non-miraculous explanation (eg the specimens were switched, the doctor lied, or the woman was unknowingly transported and operated on by aliens). But it looks pretty much like a type-ii miracle to those of us prepared to accept them. In a sense the details of science seem to make the diagnosis more certain, and so increase the evidence that a type-ii miracle has occurred. But we do not see the conclusion that it was a miracle as a 'scientific' explanation. It is rather an admission that no scientific explanation is presently possible - and that is how most normal people who believe in miracles would put it. Since science is (at least as we understand it) *by definition* a search for natural-process explanations, medics may continue to look for a 'scientifc' explanation of the recovery. Science *as such* cannot 'accept' type-ii miraculous explanations of events - though scientists as people may and should do.

Suppose, however, that someone suggested the invention of a new *scientific* term 'healing' in situations where no natural explanation applies. They might then add:

> If an explanation for a biological recovery phenomenon could be found that only required general natural laws, then *'healing in the scientific sense'* (HITSS) would be falsified.

In this sense 'HITSS' would then be a *scientific explanation* for our friend's recovery, rather than a conclusion that no scientific explanation existed. HITSS is a *perfect* scientific explanation, it leaves no aspect of the event unexplained. But let us spell out how this differs from our own view:

1. **Our View:** A type-ii miracle seems to have occurred and *no scientific explanation is possible*, though scientists may still seek one.

2. **The HITSS View:** No natural processes can account for this but it is fully *scientifically* explained by HITSS and so no better scientific explanation is possible.

The second of these, we believe, simply misunderstands the nature of science. Science, by definition, looks for explanations in terms of natural processes. It cannot, of course, prove there are no gaps in these where type-ii miracles operate, but had it stuck with 'explain all' concepts like HITSS it would never have developed in the first place. A type-ii miracle is a gap in scientific explanation, not a part of it.

Now on p.238 of *Darwin's Black Box* Behe attacks Dr Richard Dickerson, an evangelical Christian and a scientist, for suggesting that science is a 'game' in which we try to see 'how far and to what extent we can explain the behaviour of the physical and material universe in terms of purely physical and material causes, without invoking the supernatural.' Leaving aside Behe's apparent misunderstanding of 'game' to mean a bit of fun rather than its established serious philosophical sense, this attack is misguided. Had science accepted supernatural causes as part of scientific explanation, it would never have developed. Why look for explanation, for example, of sickness in terms of microbes if a simple 'God did it' will explain it perfectly?

Behe's central confusion is analogous to HITSS. He accepts that 'Design is simply the *purposeful arrangement of parts.*' (p. 193) Design, thus, is a metaphysical term - it implies *purpose* not causal mechanism. But then he seems to want to introduce a new term 'Design' which is not metaphysical but has a 'scientific' sense. He states:

> There is an elephant in the roomful of scientists who are trying to explain the development of life. The elephant is labelled 'intelligent design.[53]

So exactly what kind of elephant is this? The scientists, quite properly, are seeking for a sequence of natural processes which would 'explain' the origins of life - that is what the word 'explain' means in a scientific context. So what could Behe be saying about the design elephant?

EITHER: (i) They miss the fact that, whatever the sequence, the whole structure of reality evidences Design.

OR: (ii) They miss the obvious fact that any natural-process explanation would imply so improbable a set of starting conditions that it looks like it was 'fixed'.

OR: (iii) No such sequence is possible (even allowing, say, for life to evolve first elsewhere and 'seed' our planet) and a type-ii miracle must have happened.

If the design elephant is (i) no theist would disagree with him. It may be that *American* theists (because of their peculiar civil laws) can't mention the elephant in schools because it's a religious elephant - but that is a legal not a philosophical problem. If his design elephant is, in fact, (ii), we would have no philosophical problem with that either. Actually, though, his ensuing description of 'irreducible systems' seems to be suggesting (iii). The whole point about an irreducible system is

---

[53] Behe (1996) p. 193.

that because each part is essential it *cannot* evolve piecemeal and *no* natural sequence can be imagined to develop it.

So is this really what he means and does this mean that 'design' becomes a part of science? When we asked him his response seemed unclear. Firstly he asserted:

If an explanation for a complex biological phenomenon could be found that only required general natural laws, then 'design' in the scientific sense would be falsified.

This *seems* clear. The design elephant is present *only* if no natural sequence is possible, and so a break in natural sequences (which is what we call a type-ii miracle) *must have* occurred. But Behe also gives in his book the example of a bacterium developed by a possible but highly improbable bombardment by cosmic rays on successive days, which in responding to us he confirmed would be a type-i miracle but 'clearly a detectable instance of design'. But this *would* have a 'natural' explanation and so not be 'scientific design' in his sense. So are we now to have *three* types of design:

1. **Purely metaphysical design** (either a metaphysical elephant or not an elephant at all, in any event not present at scientific discussions).

2. **Detectable but not scientific design** (a small elephant? not an elephant? present/not present at scientific discussions?).

3. **'Design in the scientific sense'** (a large elephant? definitely present at scientific discussions?).

Not only is this confusing but 'design in the scientific sense' (DITSS) is a dubious notion. If it is a *scientific* concept then is it a scientific *alternative* to a natural-process description? If it is, then presumably it *perfectly* explains the phenomena, and no alternative scientific explanation (eg one in terms of natural processes) could better it. It is hard to see how a concept which stops us looking for natural process explanations is good science. On the other hand, if it is not an *alternative* to natural process description, but *as well as*, this sounds like a metaphysical rather than a scientific concept.

Suppose that (say) DNA life turns out to be a irreducibly complex system, and no one can find a natural-process to reasonably account for it. We would have no problem in supposing that a type-ii miracle had occurred - or at the least a type-i miracle of such unlikelihood as to make it obvious it was rigged. But this would be a gap in scientific explanation, not a part of it. Behe's 'design in the scientific sense' (DITSS) seems exactly analogous to 'healing in the scientific sense' (HITSS) above. It would be - for anything for which he invoked it - a *perfect* scientific explanation. It would not relate to other scientific laws and processes of course, but would explain phenomena 'perfectly'. If such 'explanations' had been accepted as a valid part of science, then frankly science would never have developed.

Michael Behe is saying some important things, but should drop the idea that 'design' is a scientific concept. His motive may, perhaps, (as we already hinted) partly be because in America 'religion' cannot be taught in government run schools, and perhaps a recognition of 'design' can be made only if it is a scientific rather than a metaphysical term. One is reminded of the American lawyers in a famous 1980 hearing who for similar reasons argued that 'God' is not necessarily a religious term.[54] One cannot, however, reformulate truth and philosophy because of peculiarities in the American legal system. The design elephant is metaphysical; if this means she is excluded from American schools, then so be it.

Behe is a Christian theist who has no philosophical objection to God using a process of evolution to create. In this he differs from that other leading figure in the 'Design Theory' movement, the lawyer Phillip Johnson. We briefly considered in our last section Johnson's confusion of science and metaphysics, which effectively bans God from natural processes and (of course unintentionally) undermines Christian theism. We note here that if we are right in picturing divine and human volition operating within the 'natural' phenomena of uncertainty, some direction might be given to evolution by a God mainly operating in type-i directive processes. To reiterate, science as such cannot infer either intention or lack of it. Any such inference is metaphysics, going beyond physics. If apparent 'gaps' or improbabilities in natural processes seem sometimes to point to miraculous divine activity, our faith should not depend on such gaps. God *is* the God of nature.

---

[54] Repeated by Moreland in (1989) p. 221, cf Section 10 below.

Omnipotence, Impossibility and Christian Theism

We turn finally in this section to briefly consider why certain features of the created universe may be as they are. The biblical God is omniscient (knows all that is knowable) and omnipotent (can do anything possible). There are, of course, many things which are impossible with us but possible with God (cf Mk 10:27). In the face of Mary's incredulity at the human impossibility of a virgin birth, the angel points out that 'with God nothing is impossible' (Lk 1:37). But this has to be read in context. Elsewhere we are told that it *is* impossible for God to lie, ie to act against his nature (Heb 6:18). It is also impossible for him to 'do' something which is effectively a contradiction in words, eg to give a human freewill and then determine the results of her choices. There is no point in putting 'God can' in front of nonsense and pretending it is meaningful. Two 'restrictions' on omnipotence, then, are the divine nature itself and the restriction of non-contradiction. One interesting feature of the theology-science dialogue on theism is speculation about exactly how much 'freedom' God had in creating a world. God could, presumably, have decided to create nothing. But if he decided to create a world in which there were moral beings with free choice, then some non-contradiction conditions must surely apply. There has to be a general regularity – even though the universe may be dependent on God for its moment by moment existence. If results of free-being decisions were totally unpredictable, then no inter-being communication would be possible. On the other hand, if everything were totally deterministic there would be no room for free choice and so no morality. A universe is needed, therefore, which is generally predictable but has elements of openness. Perhaps something like a quantum based universe would do.

Actually, it is possible that science can further elucidate some of the constraints involved. Stephen Hawking concluded in *A Brief History of Time:*

> [God] would, of course, still have had the freedom to choose the laws that the universe obeyed. This, however, may not really have been that much of a choice; there may well be only one, or a small number, of complete unified theories, such as the heterotic string theories that are self-consistent and allow the resistance of structures

as complicated as human beings who can investigate the laws of the universe and ask about the nature of God.

Even if there is only one possible unified theory, it is just a set of rules and equations. What is it that breathes fire into the equations and makes a universe for them to describe? The usual approach of science of constructing a mathematical model cannot answer the questions of why there should be a universe to describe.[55]

Given that God decided to create something rather than nothing, and given a desire for self-conscious moral beings like us to exist, there are non-contradiction constraints.

There is a further point. People sometimes ask why would a God have made such a gigantic universe or kept it empty for so long before creating mankind. Gribbin and Rees (who are atheists) actually make the point that, in order for stars to generate the elements needed for us, both the size and time were needed:

Given the laws of physics that operate in our universe, all those billions of stars and billions of light years are necessary for our existence.[56]

If, to God, there is sequence but not time as we know it, then not just a thousand but a million years is as one day. The choice of law-like preparation for us (and for any other sentient beings created in this universe in his image) carried the decision of a particular time-frame in our reference.

It may be that there are similar constraints operating, for example, on the age-old issue of the problem of pain. At one level pain is useful in directing action and the relationship between pain and consciousness is itself mysterious (as phenomena like hypnosis show). How can we know what non-contradiction constraints operated?

Our concept of a God who acts within and without natural processes, which have no existence independent of him, still leaves other mysteries, eg:

- What kind of 'experience' of volition does God have?
- What is it 'like' to have sequence but be multi-temporal?

---

[55] Hawking (1988) p. 174.
[56] Gribbin & Rees (1990) p. 14.

- What are the relative roles of divine volition, human volition, and chance$_3$ in any given event?
- Why are there not more or less type-ii miracles?

There are, however, also many mysteries in modern scientific views of matter. In physics too, time is mysterious and has paradoxical properties. In physics the human observer is 'privileged' – fixing one particular line of quantum probability by observation. Total reality cannot be expected to be simpler than physical reality. Mystery remains, but our contention is that a suitable form of theism makes best sense of our human experiences of consciousness and nature.

We have made no secret of the fact that we regard *Christian* theism as the most rational form of theism. This is for several main reasons:

1. A Trinitarian view of God maintains interpersonal communication and reaction as central to personhood.
2. A view that parallels human and divine freewill, volition and action, is faithful to our inner experiences.
3. Christian theism makes the best sense of the life of Jesus of Nazareth, a figure who needs consideration in respect to all main religious forms of theism.

This last point we will turn now to consider.

6

God & Jesus

Has God Communicated?

Suppose that theism is correct, and there really is a personal God with characteristics something like our own. Would such a personal God who made a universe, life, and people, wish to communicate with them?' Surely the answer is yes? So are there any serious claims to be communications from him?

Actually, there aren't many. Religions like Animism concern the day by day placating of innumerable spirits and, although they may somewhere have a 'high god' or 'great spirit', offer little information about him.

Other major religions are what we call 'religions of the way'. There are, of course, great differences between the respective 'Ways' of Hinduism (Dharma), Buddhism (the eightfold path) and Taoism (Tao). In Hinduism, for example, the Bhadavad-Gita emphasises devotion to deities in a way foreign to the others. What they share is a lack of emphasis on the personhood of the individual - and parallel to this a lack of strong identity of a personal creator-God. The individual seeks not rightstanding before a personal and righteous God, but 'enlightenment' implying either personal extinction or absorption into some kind of universal. None of them contains a claim to communication from a personal creator-God.

The three major theistic faiths are Judaism, Christianity and Islam. So what do they claim about whether or not God has communicated with us? Remarkably, the three main faiths in a creator-God all agree:

1. That he communicated with the Old Testament Hebrew prophets. According to the Muslim holy *Qur'ân*, God inspired Noah and the Jewish Old Testament prophets, 'spoke directly unto Moses' and 'imparted unto David the Psalms'. Jews and Christians will clearly agree with this.

2. All three faiths, moreover, agree that God made the promise that a 'Messiah' would come to Israel.

The Christian *New Testament*, the traditions of non-Christian Jews handed down and embodied in the written *Talmud*, and the Islamic *Qur'ân*, also all refer to Jesus of Nazareth. A central question, therefore, concerns the nature of the expected Jewish 'Messiah' and whether Jesus was that Messiah.

To Christians, Jesus was indeed that Messiah, not just a prophet but the expression of God himself, who fulfilled the messianic prophecies by dying for our sins and rising again.

The non-Christian Jewish view is recorded in the written *Talmud* which includes the *Mishnah* (compiled 100-200 AD) and the later *Gemera* commentaries written on this. They are legal rather than historical, but one passage reads:

> Jesus was hanged on the Passover Eve. Forty days previously the herald had cried, 'He is being led out for stoning, because he practised sorcery and led Israel astray and enticed them into apostasy. Whoever has anything to say in his defence, let him come and declare it.' As nothing was brought forward in his defence he was hanged on Passover Eve.[1]

This recognises that although as a Jew he might have been expected to be stoned to death, he was actually 'hanged' on Passover Eve - as John 19.14 states. Acts 5:30 and 10:39 shown that 'hanged' was a natural Jewish way to refer to Crucifixion. The sorcery charge presumably relates to his miracles and was made in his lifetime (Matthew 9:34, Mark 3:22). Other passing references are made in the Talmud to his followers performing miracles.[2]

To Muslims, Jesus was born to the virgin Mary (3:42-51), was a prophet who spoke from God (2:87, 3:48 etc), was one who (unlike Mohammed himself) performed miracles (5:110) and was the Jewish Messiah (3:45). The *Qur'ân* rejects the trinity and the idea of Jesus as 'God's Son' – though it seems to be reacting to crudely literalistic versions of these ideas (eg 25:2). Though the *Qur'ân* speaks of the:

> day that I (Jesus) die and the day that I shall be raised up to life again' (19:33 and 19:15)

it also says explicitly:

---

[1] *Babylonian Sanhedrin* 43a.
[2] See eg F F Bruce (1974) Ch 4.

They killed him (Jesus) not, nor crucified him, but so it was made to appear to them... of a surety they killed him not. (*Qu'ran* 4:157)[3]

The *Qur'ân* claims that Christians have forgotten much of the true message of Jesus which the *Qur'ân* itself restores (5:14).

Let us, then, summarise the views of Jesus taken by the three main monotheistic religions:

1. **The Son of God:** The New Testament presents Jesus as the 'Son of God', a human embodiment of the divine, who, in being crucified took on him all human sin, and was resurrected to give us eternal life.

2. **A Human Prophet:** The Islamic Qu'ran sees Jesus as an important prophet, not divine, who did not die but was taken up by God. As he did not die there could be no resurrection.

3. **A Jewish Magician:** The Jewish Talmud presents Jesus as an executed 'sorcerer'. Some modern books also present him as basically a Jewish wonder-worker, misunderstood and deified by later followers.

Although, of course, Christianity, Islam and non-Christian Judaism have much in common, they are irreconcilable on the key question 'Who was Jesus?' To Christians, the deity and death/resurrection of Christ are central to their faith, whilst Judaism denies the deity and Islam denies both deity and death. How can we assess the rival views? We will suggest three ways to consider this:

i. **Coherence:**   Is the Christian version of Christ a logical fulfilment of the Old Testament and its prophecy? Does it form part of a pattern which makes sense?"

ii. **Historical Sources:** Which is most likely to be a good historical source of information about Jesus: the Christian New Testament, the Mishnah/Talmud of Judaism, or the Muslim holy Qu'ran?

iii. **The Gospel Accounts:** Do the accounts – in particular of the death and resurrection of Jesus – bear the hallmarks of being historical accounts of independent origins?

---

[3] See also Deedat (1987).

Looking for a Coherent Pattern

Christians, Jews and Muslims agree that God spoke to the Jews through the Law, the Psalms and the Prophets as already indicated. Much of the Old Testament concerns universal issues of right and wrong, justice, and individual relationship with God. But three things stand out:

1. Through the Law, God established that human sin was a serious affair, that it could not just be forgiven but needed sacrifice (pictured in animal sacrifice) to put it right.

2. From the very first, there was indication that God's special relationship with the Jews would one day be a means to reach all nations.

3. Early hints at a coming 'Messiah', focused later into one who suffered sacrificially, even died, but was victorious.

Let's look at these three. Concerning sin and sacrifice, from the very beginning the God of the Bible is seen to be interested in right and wrong. In Genesis we find the account of Adam and Eve and the primary sin - a story repeated in the holy *Qur'ân*. Soon after, a link is made between sacrifice and being accepted by God. The story of Noah is about judgement on sin and immediately afterwards is linked to sacrifice. Abraham, founder and forefather of the Jewish nation, offered sacrifice. The sacrifice of the Passover lamb, begun when Israel was born as a nation, was made to turn away the divine judgement on sin. With Moses, the first national Jewish leader, came a codifying of the moral law - including the 'ten commandments' - but also clear links of sacrifice to forgiveness of sin. The *Qur'ân* shares the Jewish and Christian view that God revealed these things to Moses. The *Qur'ân* says both that Moses was given 'the Scripture' (2:53; 2:82) and the 'Law' (5:44; 7:145). These links between sacrifice and sin were repeated throughout the history of the Jewish people, and were still there in the time of Jesus.[4] The *Qur'ân* (like the New Testament) says Jesus came to 'confirm that Law' though was also given 'the Gospel' (5:46).

---

[4] Actually, the *Qur'ân* says that 'To every people did We (ie God) appoint rites (of sacrifice)' (22:34).

So what is it about? Can sacrificing animals really, in themselves, make a difference to God's forgiveness of human sin, or is it rather a picture of something deeper?

From the very beginning, there are growing hints that God has a plan to deal with sin - and that this centres on a coming 'Messiah' figure. A human figure who will crush the head of evil is first prophesied in Eden. Later, Abraham promises: 'God will provide himself the lamb for the sacrifice' (Gen 22:8). In this Abraham surely prophesies beyond the immediate situation of God's provision of a ram instead of Isaac and looks ahead to a much later and more momentous divine provision of a sacrifice. The *Qur'ân,* incidentally, describes this whole incident and has God add 'This was obviously a trial and we ransomed him with a momentous sacrifice.' (37:106-7). In the Bible God soon after promises: 'through your offspring all nations on earth will be blessed, because you have obeyed me.' In one sense, the Old Testament pictures the nation of Israel as God's chosen servant, but in another sense there is a growing recognition that a Messiah will come to Israel.

The book of Isaiah, coming from some 4-5 centuries before Christ, powerfully develops this theme. The birth of a royal child, whose titles include 'Mighty God, Everlasting Father, Prince of Peace' is prophesied in Isaiah 9.6. The servanthood of the nation of Israel later focuses (from Ch. 42) on a coming individual. Ch. 53 is worth reading entire, but here is an extract:

"... to whom has the arm of the Lord been revealed ?... He was despised and rejected by men, a man of sorrows and familiar with suffering. Like one from whom men hide their faces, he was despised and we esteemed him not. Surely he took up our infirmities and carried our sorrows, yet we considered him stricken by God, smitten by him and afflicted. But he was pierced for our transgressions, he was crushed for our iniquities; the punishment which brought us peace was upon him, and by his wounds we are healed. We all like sheep have gone astray, each of us has turned to his own way, and the Lord has laid on him the iniquity of us all... He was assigned to a grave with the wicked, and with the rich in his death, though he had done no violence, nor was any deceit in his mouth. Yet it was the Lord's will to crush him and cause him to suffer, and though the Lord makes his life a guilt offering, he will see his offspring and prolong his days...

Who is this figure? It sounds like some kind of expected Messiah, but what kind exactly? We should note:

- He is to be rejected by his fellows who will believe him judged by God (v. 3, 4).
- He will be 'pierced' (v. 5) and die (v. 9).
- His death will be a sacrifice to bear others' sins and bring them forgiveness (v. 4, 5, 10, 11).
- Although he will die, he will afterwards see results and live long (v. 10-12).

So who is it? Muslims, Messianic Jews and other Christians, all claim that Jesus was the Jewish Messiah.

If this is true much becomes clear. The sacrifice of animals was 'an annual reminder of sins, because it is impossible for the blood of bulls and goats to take away sins... we have been made holy through the sacrifice of the body of Jesus Christ, once for all.'(Heb 10:3-4). The prophecy in Eden that evil would 'crush the heel' of the human who himself crushed evil, was fulfilled literally as well as in a spiritual sense as a nail was driven into the heel of Jesus. Abraham's prophecy that 'God will provide himself the sacrificial lamb' was fulfilled in Jesus in the very area (Moriah) where the prophecy was made. Jesus was executed according to both Jews and Christians, on the eve of the Passover. At the very time he was on the cross, the Passover lambs were being killed in the nearby Temple. The 'picture' and the 'reality' were side by side. The prophecies of Isaiah were fulfilled in the crucifixion and resurrection of Jesus. How, indeed, could anyone live after being pierced and dying but through resurrection?

There is another amazing thing. Psalm 22 seems to almost perfectly describe a crucifixion but was written over 900 years BC. Its writer David had no such experience, and crucifixion was unknown to his people at that time. Its meaning becomes clear when Jesus himself uses on the cross its first words: "My God, my God, why have you forsaken me." When God, in the words of the *Qur'ân*, 'gave the psalms to David', he gave one psalm prophetic of the Messiah who was David's descendant.

The Muslim teaching that Jesus was the Messiah but did *not* die would wreck the whole pattern of sacrifice and prophecy built, by God over centuries of teaching and prophecies to the Jewish nation about the coming Messiah. Moreover, both Jews and Muslims accept that this pattern did come from God. But could it be that the books, for example of Isaiah, have been tampered with? Did, for example, enthusiastic early Christians somehow get at them? This has always seemed very unlikely because the Jews themselves have kept the text of Isaiah, meticulously recopying it throughout generations. Then, in 1947, an Arab shepherd discovered the 'Dead Sea Scrolls' in a cave in Israel. Amongst multiple copies of Old Testament books was a near perfect scroll of Isaiah, reliably dated by scholars as before the time of Christ. This copy (a thousand years older than the previous oldest copy!) had the same text, with all the same prophecies. So now we know that the books at the time of Jesus, those which would have been accepted by Jesus himself, *are no different from later versions.* Our present book of Isaiah, with its remarkable prophecies, is the one the Jews had before and during the lifetime of Jesus. To anyone who has studied the Old Testament the crucifixion of Jesus is an obvious fulfilment of a whole pattern laid down for the coming Messiah. Neither the Muslim rejection of his death, not the non-Christian Jewish rejection of his Messiahship *make sense.*

Assessing the History

The second major approach is to consider scientific or rational approaches to history. Why should we believe that the Jesus of the four Gospels is the historical Jesus - rather than (say) the one in the *Qur'ân* or the latest bizarre book on him in the high street shops? Are the Gospels really 'history'? Various aspects of this can be considered.

1. History in what sense?

We believe that the Gospels *are* 'history'. But first we must ask what does this mean? Gospel writer Luke (1:1-4) tells us how he set out to compile a reliable account of the important events of Jesus' life much as any historian would - using proper sources and eye-witness accounts. Christians may believe his account is 'inspired' - but this does not imply that he wrote it in some kind of trance or visionary experience. This is in contrast to

Mohammed (for example) who was illiterate, made no pretence to have examined any historical documents or sources, but wrote his accounts of Jesus 600 years later from a visionary religious experience. The Gospel writers compiled their accounts from contemporary materials - as *history*.

No good historian makes up bits to fit his or her theories, but *all* historians *select* their material in order to bring out a particular *perspective*. Any modern book about history recognises this.[5] Thus when John's Gospel (20:30-31) is open about the perspective and purpose for which its material was selected, it is none the less 'history'. There is no reason to suppose that the writer made it up.

The four Gospels are historical compilations. They are *not* independently written down memoirs of four eyewitnesses. There are sections common (word-perfect) to Matthew, Mark and Luke, and each pair of these three share passages not in the other one. It is clear that the first three included in their accounts material selected from some in common circulation. This material may have been written (scholars have nicknamed it 'Q') or oral[6]. Historical writers in those days were not expected to use quotation marks, so they did not indicate sources or quotations.

On another aspect of the 'literary conventions' of the Gospel writers, it is no problem that some of the events in them are given in different orders. The writers were concerned with the reality of events, not the order. One of the earliest sources says that Mark 'the interpreter of Peter, wrote down accurately, though not in order, whatever he remembered of the things said or done by Christ.'[7]

This brings us to the question of 'who wrote them ?' Actually, although 'Luke' seems to have a single author (who also wrote 'Acts' and was a friend of Paul)[8], most are best regarded as compilations edited within particular church traditions, rather than as works of specific authors. We personally accept as

---

[5]   See eg secular writers Tosh (1991), Carr (1990) and Christians eg Brown (1987) and Bebbington (1990).

[6]   See Wenham (1991).

[7]   Eusebius: *Ecclesiastical History* iii 39.

[8]   See eg I Howard Marshall (1988)

probable the 'traditional' associations of the other three Gospels (see below), but they are not essential, and the gospels themselves carry no such claims. The real questions are about the accuracy of the Gospels and early sources they used.

2. The Manuscript Sources.

Various museums today have the actual physical copies of the New Testament books which are in common Greek. Experts can accurately determine the dates at which those copies were made. This can be done by comparing them with styles of handwriting and production known from archaeology to have existed at particular times. Expert Bruce Metzger estimated there were 5,366 such manuscripts, more recently Graham Stanton stated 5,487.[9] Most of the earliest papyri have been found only this century. The King James (or 'Authorised) translation of the Gospels (1611) was based on a Greek text reconstructed to that standardised in the fifth century.[10]   By the mid nineteenth century, the Gospels in available Bible versions could also use the ancient Greek copies called the *Codex Vaticanus* and *Codex Sinaiticus* (found 1844). The term 'codex' means a book, a format the early church pioneered. These two, though then the oldest, still dated from the 4th century and archaeology had not yet examined evidence for the accuracy of their contents. It was, therefore, just about plausible at that time to suggest that the Gospels were late and inaccurate compilations. This century, a number of earlier copies written on papyrus have been found. These include the 3rd century Chester Beatty papyrus 1 (found 1931), the late second century Bodmer Papyrus P66 and P75 (found 1956) and the *early second century* Pap457 fragment of John (found 1935). The Rylands fragment of John is the oldest definite fragment of a copy, and Paul Marston has actually seen it in Manchester where it is held. Written on both sides, it enables us even to calculate the size and number of the pages which went to make up the Gospel. Carsten Thiede has argued that a papyrus fragment found in a cave near the Dead Sea, and dated to pre-50 AD, is a fragment of Mark 6.[11] We would like to believe it but find the evidence unconvincing. What does

---

[9] Metzger (1981); Stanton (1997) p. 37.
[10] The 'Received Text' and 'Stephanos' are just different versions of this.
[11] Thiede (1992) and Thiede and D'Ancona (1996).

seem likely is that the church was putting together the four gospels into a single 'codex' or book by about 150 AD.[12]

If recognition of these four was early, did the church somehow artificially select them from lots of others? We do have copies of some apocryphal 'gospels' today. They are mostly collections of supposed teachings of Jesus with no evidence of first-hand knowledge of the real background in which the Jesus of history actually lived.[13] E P Sanders, an eminent but certainly not theologically conservative scholar, has written:

> I share the general scholarly view that very, very little in the apocryphal gospels could conceivable go back to the time of Jesus. They are legendary and mythological.[14]

Some Muslims have suggested that the so called 'Gospel of Barnabas' is more authentic than the four in the Bible. Since there is no copy earlier than a sixteenth century copy in Italian, and since it contains demonstrable geographical and historical blunders, this is a particularly odd claim and cannot be taken seriously.[15]

For the four authentic Gospels the early Greek manuscripts are backed up by early translations into Latin, Syriac and other languages, and also by copious quotes of most of them in the writings of early Christians.[16] Graham Stanton concludes:

> In comparison with many classical writings, students of the New Testament are indeed fortunate. There is a gap of over 1,000 years between the date of the original writings and the earliest manuscripts of Euripides, Sophocles, Aeschylus, Aristophanes, Thucydides, Plato and Demosthenes...There is rarely doubt about the words the evangelists wrote; most of the variations are minor and the original wording can be reconstructed without difficulty.[17]

3. What can archaeology tell us?

What relevance has the science of archaeology to the authenticity/accuracy of the Gospels? We are unlikely to find inscriptions relating to the specific claims of the Gospels about

---

[12] Stanton (1997) p. 203.
[13] See Bruce (1988), also Walker (1983).
[14] Sanders (1995) p. 64; see also Stanton (1997) p. 95 and Bruce (1988).
[15] See Anderson (1990) pp. 223-34
[16] More detailed reference was given in our *Reason and Faith* (1989).
[17] Stanton (1997) pp. 40-42.

Jesus – who would have made them? To the Romans Jesus was an obscure criminal in a superstitious race, and to the Jewish authorities in Palestine an executed troublemaker. What we can look for is:

1. To check if the Gospels give any descriptions not in keeping with known features of life in that period.
2. To see if the Gospels mention facts which could not have been known at a later date.

The answer to the first is simply 'no'. At one time, for example, it was claimed that those crucified were tied and not nailed to the *staurus* (cross or stake).[18] Then in 1968 the bones of a first century young man were found in Jerusalem with a large metal nail driven through the heels – obviously having been nailed in crucifixion.[19] All the general descriptions – boats, burial practices, tombs etc, are in accord with archaeology.[20]

In answer to the second question, it began to be established early in this century that the author of Acts (who also wrote 'Luke') gets right geographical points and titles of governors throughout Asia minor which would have been very difficult for a later writer to discover.[21] John's Gospel also seems to show familiarity with the terrain of Israel – a country changed radically by the destruction of Jerusalem in 70 AD.[22]

4. Accuracy and dating.

The evidence is very strong that the Gospels were all written in the first century, and that the copies we now have are accurate. We deduce this for the following reasons:

1. Their detailed local knowledge would not be available to writers in later centuries.
2. There had to be time, for example, for papyrus copies of John to circulate by the early second century to Egypt where was found the Rylands fragment mentioned above.

---

[18] Hewitt (1932).
[19] See eg Millard (1990) p. 132.
[20] See eg Millard (1990).
[21] See Ramsay (1895) and (1915), also Bruce (1961) ch 7, Barnett (1986) pp. 159-63.
[22] Robinson (1985).

3. The New Testament is quoted so extensively by early Christian writers from the first century onwards, that virtually all of it would be recoverable from these quotations alone.

4. By the third century, translations of the New Testament had been made into Latin, Coptic and Syriac.

At one time many argued that the Gospels were written hundreds of years after Jesus lived. The wild speculative late dates (eg end of second century) made by philosophers in the nineteenth century are simply untenable both from archaeology and because we have a part of an actual copy of John made early in the second century Scholarly consensus from all shades of opinion now favours a first century date. Bruce long ago concluded:

> A first century date for most of the New Testament writings cannot reasonably be denied.[23]

Stanton more recently stated:

> Most scholars believe that Mark's gospel was written between AD 65 and 75.[24]

Some have argued for earlier dates. Bishop John A T Robinson wrote some controversial theology[25], and was certainly not conservative. Yet he wrote:

> The time span over which the New testament Documents have been held to come into being.. having been stretched to its greatest lengths by the extremer German critics of the nineteenth century, has been contracting fairly steadily ever since. At the turn of this century, the span extended from about AD 50 to about AD 150 – and that was a good deal shorter than it had been on some reckonings. By the middle of this century, about AD 50 to about AD 100. I am personally of the opinion that it should be halves, or more than halved, again, from about AD 47 to just before AD 70... the first draft of Mark's gospel could be as early as 45 AD.[26]

As already noted, Robinson presented very powerful and detailed evidence for the early writing of the Gospel of John,

---

[23] Bruce (1961) p. 12.
[24] Stanton (1997) p. 23.
[25] Robinson (1961).
[26] Robinson (1977) pp. 53, 73.

based on the writer's knowledge of the terrain. Interestingly, N T Wright recently commented:

> John A T Robinson argued twenty years ago that the whole New Testament was written before 70 AD; the rest of the scholarly world has, by and large, ignored him rather than refuting him.[27]

Whether Robinson was right or not, the Gospels seem almost certainly to date from the first century.

5. What about the Dead Sea Scrolls?

The media really love 'conspiracy theories' and startling pronouncements and a lot of bunkum has been written and broadcast about these scrolls. Found in 1947 near the Dead Sea, they give a picture of the life of a community based there between about 170 BC and 70 AD. Gospel critics have claimed that they throw doubt on the Gospels either because the ideas in them are very similar to those in the Gospels and so Jesus was not unique, or because the ideas in them are very different so Jesus couldn't have been a real first century Jew! That about covers every possibility.

In fact, whilst some of the religious language used is (hardly surprisingly!) similar to that in the Gospels, there are (as one might) expect both similarities and important differences.[28] Apart from various flights of scholarly fancy in interpreting vague bits in strange ways, there is nothing in the scrolls to cast any doubt on the accuracy of the Gospels.[29]

6. Is Jesus mentioned elsewhere?

Surviving works from first and second century Greek, Roman or Jewish writers are few - but those there are refer to Christ and Christians much as we would expect.

The Jewish historian known as Flavius Josephus was born around 37 AD and wrote *The Antiquities of the Jews* in Greek around 93 AD. There is, of course, no reason to take him as more accurate than the earlier Gospels. He does, however, give useful background to characters such as Pilate, Herod, Caiaphas,

---

[27] Wright (1996a) p. 127.
[28] See eg Millard (1991) pp. 99-116.
[29] This was kindly confirmed to us by the Professor of Hebrew at Oxford, Hugh Williamson - with an explicitness unusual in academic circles!

John the Baptist and even Jesus' brother James.[30]   Pilate, for example, appears with a combination of pig headedness, ruthlessness, and hesitation one might expect of the figure in the gospels. Some have suggested that the picture of him 'washing his hands' is a later Christian attempt at propaganda to 'reduce the conflict between the Christian movement and Roman authority.'[31]   This seems to us a very strange suggestion. The portrayal of a weak prevaricating and manipulated ruler who eventually crucifies a man he believes innocent was hardly likely to endear Christians to the Romans. Sanders' whole approach to sorting out which bits he likes to take as 'historical' and which 'propaganda' seems to us fraught with difficulties – and is more likely to lead (as was once said of similar approaches by nineteenth century liberals) to the eventual contemplation of a 'Jesus' who is just one's own reflection at the bottom of a deep well! In our view all the characters in the Gospels (with the evidence of later writers like Josephus) are totally consistent with the application of even elementary psychology. Probably Pilate was approached by Caiaphas the night before, after Caiaphas' snap decision to move against a Jesus whom Judas reported to be unresisting. In the night, Pilate had misgivings (perhaps reinforced by his wife's reaction – maybe she had heard Jesus preach). From their reaction, Jesus' accusers were not expecting to be asked what the charges were when they brought him to Pilate. The picture of a man torn between superstition and expediency is vivid, and fully in accord with the Pilate of Josephus. There is nothing strange in a normally ruthless man being unnerved by superstition in dealing with an 'other worldly' figure like Jesus.

The current Greek versions of Josephus contain a passage referring to Jesus in terms that would imply a belief in his actual resurrection. This passage is that cited by Eusebius in 325 AD, and is textually uniform with the rest of the work. However, Origen (writing in AD 230 and 250) refers to Josephus' passage on James and adds:

---

[30] *Antiquities* xviii.5.2, xx.9.1.
[31] Sanders (1993) p. 274.

it is wonderful that, while he did not receive Jesus as the Christ, he did nevertheless bear witness that James was so righteous a man.[32]

In 1971 there was published a version of the passage preserved in the writings of Agapius, a tenth century Bishop of Hieropolis.

> At this time there was a wise man called Jesus, and his conduct was good, and he was known to be virtuous. Any many people from among the Jews and the other nations became his disciples. Pilate ordered him to be crucified and to die. And those who had become his disciples did not abandon their discipleship. They reported that he had appeared to them three days after his crucifixion and that he was alive. Accordingly, he was thought to be the Messiah about whom the prophets have recounted wonders.[33]

The finding of this was really a confirmation of what scholars had previously thought. It would be odd for Josephus not to mention Jesus at all, but as a non-Christian he would not have believed the resurrection really happened. Some time in the late 3rd century an over enthusiastic Christian scribe subtly changed this original text to give us the Greek versions which give the resurrections not as a claim made by the disciples but as a fact.

The other main Jewish source, the Talmud, has already been quoted above. It confirms that Jesus was crucified on the Passover eve, as the Gospels report.

Turning to the Romans, Pliny the Younger was a Roman Governor who wrote to the Emperor Trajan around AD 110-113. He wrote of the Christians that they met on a certain day very early 'when they sang in alternate verses a hymn to Christ as to a god' and bound themselves to a high moral conduct.[34]

The Roman historian Tacitus, writing shortly after, described how Nero tried to shift the blame for the great fire in Rome onto a group of people 'known as Christians'. He adds:

> 'They got their name from Christ, who was executed by sentence of the procurator Pontius Pilate in the reign of Tiberius.'[35]

This ploy of Nero was also mentioned by Suetonius, writing around 120 AD. Suetonius elsewhere mentions that around 49

---

[32] Origen: *Commentary on Matthew 17* (*Ant Nic Fath* x.424 and *Against Celsus* (*Ant Nic Fath* iv.416).

[33] See eg Bruce (1984) p. 49, Blaiklock (1983) pp. 27-31.

[34] Pliny: *Epistles* x 96-7.

[35] Tacitus: *Annals* xv p.44.

AD (as we would reckon it) Emperor Claudius 'expelled the Jews from Rome on account of the riots in which they were constantly engaging at the instigation of Chrestus.'[36] There were often Jewish riots when Jesus was preached (Acts 14;1-6) and a later pagan historian could easily think that 'Chrestus' himself had been present. This seems likely since 'Christ' is a title not a name, and it is one not many Jews would claim. Luke (Acts 18.2) also refers to this act of Claudius.

The non Christian sources, then, refer to Jesus and Christians exactly as we would expect. They confirm that Jesus lived in Judaea (Tacitus, Josephus and the Jewish *Talmud*); he kept and taught high moral standards (Pliny and Josephus); miracles were ascribed to him and his followers (the *Talmud*), who saw him as a Messiah and divine figure (Pliny and Josephus). He was put to death under Pilate (Tacitus and Josephus), by crucifixion (Josephus and the *Talmud*). By AD 64 Jesus' followers were numerous enough in Rome to be blamed by Nero for a great fire for which they were persecuted (Suetonius and Tacitus).

7. Conclusion

The Gospels themselves are early and authentic, the text of the copies we now have is accurate, and the most important details of Jesus' life, death, and claimed resurrection are reflected in early non-Christian sources. The evidence is that the 'historical' Jesus was essentially the one described in the four Gospels. *All* historical evidence, without exception, indicates that Jesus was indeed crucified (contrary to what the *Qur'ân* claims). Roman and Jewish sources confirm that his disciples claimed from the first that he rose again.

The Resurrection: Alternatives

As we have seen, everyone assesses the evidence for miracle according to his or her world view. "You're out of your mind Paul - your great learning has finally made you flip!" That was the reaction of the Roman governor Festus when St Paul spoke of the resurrection of Jesus (Acts 24:26). He (like those who laughed in Acts 17) recognised that Paul was not talking about some 'super spiritual' resurrection or a temporary restarting of

---

[36] Suetonius: *Life of Claudius* xv.

bodily functions, but a new kind of quality of eternal life. As we noted, Paul was critical of *a priori* naturalistic world-views. The death and resurrection of Jesus 'makes sense' because it is a part of a whole plan of a personal creator-God to deal with the problem of human sin and to offer us eternal spiritual life. This, in itself, does not prove it is 'true', but it means that we need to take seriously the historical evidence for it.

So what is the evidence? A group of Jesus' close friends and followers, dispirited after his execution, claimed to have seen and spoken to him over a period of about six weeks after that death. These were otherwise apparently honest and normal people, of all kinds of characters and backgrounds. They were prepared to die for their claims and many did. Their beliefs were reflected in early church teaching, and in the Gospel accounts compiled around 15-50 years after Jesus' death.

Let's consider the various alternative explanations to actual resurrection.

Alternative 1: A hidden meaning

The extreme versions of this suggest that 'really' the gospel accounts are in a secret code. Bookshops more interested in controversy (= profit) than truth, carry books by eccentrics who adapt respectable scholarly words like 'pesher' or 'midrash' (to the astonishment of scholars of all beliefs who know what the words really mean) to imply secret codes only they can crack.[37] Jesus was 'really' married once or twice, had children, lived to a ripe old age (and, one might almost add without much more fantasy, was occasionally seen sipping lager in Texas - or was that Elvis?). In such flights of unreality the resurrection accounts might mean anything.

To be taken rather more seriously are those who suggest that 'really' the earliest Christians believed in a 'spiritual' resurrection. 'The missing body story', they say, 'was added later on. Perhaps the people then were too dim to understand a spiritual resurrection, so the writers made it easy for them!' There are three big problems with this:

---

[37] Barbara Thiering (1992); John Shelby Spong (1994)

1. The writer of John's gospel uses quite complex language - one would have thought he, or Luke the educated Greek, could manage to explain a 'spiritual' resurrection. In fact Luke explicitly emphasises that the resurrected 'body' had physical properties (Luke 24.37-43).
2. The apostle Paul, as we noted at the start of this chapter, was thought insane for preaching an actual resurrection, not for preaching about getting a kind of warm feeling when he thought about Jesus.
3. The gospel accounts give far too much detail - appearances first to women etc - one would expect just a kind of campfire scene where they were suddenly all struck with Jesus' memory and had a 'spiritual' experience.

The accounts seem to refer to a supposed literal event - we have to look for some explanation other than 'spiritualising'.

Alternative 2: Mistake

The accounts record Jesus being taken hurriedly after his death to a nearby family tomb (Matt 27:57-61; Mark 15:42-47; Luke 23:50-55; John 19:38-42). Could it just be that Mary Magdalene and the others went to the wrong tomb early on the first Easter Sunday, and the story got out of hand before anyone could correct it?

The problem with this theory is that the tomb belonged to a man of some importance in the community: Joseph of Arimathea. Also present at the entombment was a Jewish council member: Nicodemus. Such men of standing and integrity would surely have denied any untrue rumours and simply produced the body? The authorities, moreover, would surely have known the location of the Jerusalem family tomb of a council member, and would have produced both tomb and body to scotch the rumours ?

The same objections apply to the suggestion in a more recent book widely on sale in high street bookshops. This suggests that people mistook James, Jesus' brother, for a resurrected Jesus.[38] Since, however, James himself became an early church leader (did he make the same mistake when he looked in the mirror?),

---

[38] A. N. Wilson (1992) p. 243 see also Wright (1997) for a trenchant critique.

and there is evidence that other early disciples were related to Jesus, the suggestion seems breathtakingly unlikely.

Finally, could it just have been that grave robbers stole the body, and so, although at the right tomb, Jesus' followers reached the wrong conclusions? The problem with this is that there was not much of a market for corpses in first century Jerusalem. Any commercially orientated grave robber who braved an armed guard to steal a body and leave the grave clothes behind would have to be very seriously deranged. In any case, it would not explain the actual resurrection appearances to Jesus' disciples.

Alternative 3: Fraud

There are various fraud suggestions. The simplest is just that Jesus' disciples stole his body - perhaps as a kind of afterthought. This was actually the earliest counter-theory put about by the authorities (Matthew 28:13). It was still apparently a view accepted by non-Christian Jews when the Christian philosopher Justin had a debate around the mid second century.[39] We might call this the 'opportunist' theory.

There are other more elaborate 'fraud theories'. These involve a supposed prior plot between Jesus and a small central group of followers (perhaps including Joseph of Arimathea and Nicodemus) to 'fake' his death and then resuscitate him afterwards.[40] We might call these the 'plot' theories. If, as most of them assume, Jesus actually died by mistake, then there has to be also an element of 'opportunist' cover up - ie the body was stolen to start the resurrection legend.

There are three very obvious problems with these theories:

1. Jesus and his followers taught a very high moral code - would fraud and deception really be at the centre of their message?
2. The claims to have seen Jesus by significant numbers of people mean that (unless they were exceptionally easily fooled) a large number must have been involved in the cover up if not in the plot.

---

[39] Justin Martyr, *Dialogue with Trypho*, ch. cviii.
[40] One such is the classic Schonfield (1965).

3. If it were a fake, how can we explain the boldness of the small group of demoralised disciples so soon after Jesus' death? How can we explain their readiness to die?

The versions which have Jesus himself involved in a supposed 'plot' have even more problems. Would it really be sensible - even if one plotted (say) to be drugged on the cross to look as though dead - to expect to survive a Roman flogging and crucifixion? What would be the point of faking a 'resurrection' if he could simply be recaptured and then be really killed? If Jesus made the kinds of claim he made about himself he either believed them (in which case he would not feel a need to fake a resurrection) or not (in which case he was a charlatan and/or a madman). Would a charlatan really be prepared to go to such risks and lengths for a dubious advantage (after all he already had lots of followers)? On the other hand, do his words read like those of a madman? They hardly seem so, even to many who are not Christians. But if he was not bad, and not mad, what is there left of this suggestion?

Alternative 4: Hallucination

Did all those who saw Jesus simply hallucinate? Again, there are three main problems:

1. There were apparently lots of different types of people involved, with very different characters, and at different times of day.
2. They actually did not seem to expect a resurrection to happen. The women went to the tomb to anoint the body - not to see if Jesus had risen (Mark 16:1, Luke 24:1). The first accounts of the women were received with disbelief (Luke 24:11).
3. Why didn't the authorities produce the body? Why invent the story that it was stolen?

Hallucination is not very plausible.

Alternative 5: Legend

Legends often spring up about remarkable individuals: Ulysses supposedly killed a Cyclops, St George killed a dragon, and King Arthur pulled a sword out of a stone block. If the Gospels were written down long after Jesus' death, couldn't they be full of legends?

There are four main problems here:

1. The gospels were not actually written all that long after Jesus' death - the first perhaps as soon as fifteen years after. Paul in a letter written about 20 years after Jesus' death reports that he was told about the resurrection only three years after the actual events (1 Cor 15:1).
2. All the very earliest references, including early Christian writings from the late first and early second century, refer to Jesus' death and resurrection.[41]
3. The actual accounts seem to contain a lot of detail and incidental corroboration (on which see below).
4. Anyone making up legend would surely have invented an 'eyewitness' version of Jesus emerging triumphantly from the tomb, or a dramatic first meeting with Peter. The gospels record neither.

Conclusion

No one can 'prove' that Jesus rose again - at least, not to the satisfaction of anyone who begins by assuming that anything 'supernatural' is impossible and inconceivable. What we *can* do is to show that:

1. The accounts of the resurrection date from soon after Jesus' death.
2. They were written by honest people preaching a high moral code and who were prepared to die for their beliefs.
3. The various 'alternative' explanations are not plausible.

The Resurrection: Reconstruction

Any detective knows that six honest and genuine eyewitness accounts of any lengthy event will all differ. People can be in different places and so see different aspects of an overall pattern. Different people can record different perspectives - noticing different details or skipping for dramatic effect over boring or irrelevant bits.

Do the four gospel resurrection passages read essentially like accounts based ultimately on different eyewitnesses? Or are

---

[41] Eg. 1 Clement xxiv (c 96 AD), Ignatius to Ephesus xx (c 110 AD), also Polycarp and Justin Martyr in mid 2nd century.

those sceptics and 'theologians' right who argue that the accounts are hopelessly contradictory? The renegade bishop of Newark, John Shelby Spong, sees the New Testament as written in a secret code (Midrash) which apparently he alone can crack, and has his own version of 'faith' which describes as legend the basic historical points of the creed he is supposed to avow. He casually remarks:

> The resurrection narratives of the Gospels agree on little if one looks for literal facts...[42]

The sceptical New Testament scholar E P Sanders remarks:

> Faced with accounts of this nature – sharply diverging stories of where and to whom Jesus appeared, lack of agreement and clarity on what he was like (except agreement on negatives) – we cannot reconstruct what really happened.[43]

Now no historian would suggest that we could reconstruct 'what really happened' for *any* event. What we are going to assert is that, based on reasonable assumptions, a model can be found for events which makes good sense of all the accounts we have and explains any apparent differences as due to perspective.

The Gospels: Origins and Nature

There are five basic accounts: the four Gospels and 1 Cor 15. Our model makes some reasonable assumptions about them:

1.   The four Gospels, although they have some other parts in common, contain four accounts of the resurrection which differ because they draw on different main sources.

2.   Each Gospel was an anonymous compilation edited in a different church tradition, but there is truth in the early church view that:
     * *Matthew* reflects some input from the disciple Matthew.[44]
     * *Mark* reflects Peter's preaching and viewpoint.[45]
     * *Luke* contains a more general compounded account.
     * *John* reflects input from the disciple John Zebedee.[46]

---

[42]   John Shelby Spong (1994) p. 235.
[43]   Sanders (1993) p. 278.
[44]   See eg R T France (1985) pp. 30-34 for some support for this.
[45]   See early church figures Irenaeus (*Adv. Haer* 3.1.2) and Eusebius quoting Papias (*HE* 3.39.14 ff).

3. Each account reflects the viewpoint of its main source, and therefore the geographical place each had in the story. Matthew, at Bethany, experienced events differently from (say) John in Jerusalem.

4. Each account (like all historical accounts) *selects* what to include, and describes events differently. Even in the same Gospel, Luke, for example, describes 'men in white' (Lk 24:4) but angels in Lk 24:23); he describes just Peter running to the tomb (Lk24:12) but later speaks of 'some of our companions' going (Lk 24:24).

5. Some accounts 'telescope' events. Thus in Luke's Gospel the ascension sounds as though it takes place on the same day as the resurrection – but in Acts (universally regarded as having the same author) it is six week later. We think Matthew similarly 'telescopes' events in Matt 28:4-5 putting together later accounts of the guards and the women's direct reports.

People

Though not essential, we follow John Wenham in most of his arguments for various blood relations between some of the main characters.[47] In particular (apart from the obvious ones):

- **Salome** was sister to Jesus' mother Mary, and also the wife of Zebedee and the mother of James and John
- **John** was therefore Jesus' cousin and 'the beloved disciple'.
- **Cleopas** (also called 'Clopas' or 'Alpheus' was brother of Joseph and so Jesus' legal uncle).
- **Mary** (also called 'the other Mary') wife of Cleopas (so aunt to Jesus and sister-in-law to his mother and Salome)
- **Mary Magdelene** (probably to be identified with Mary the sister of Martha and Lazarus who lived in Bethany).
- **Joanna** was the wife of Herod Antipas' steward Chuza.

Events

After Jesus' arrest in Gethsemane, most of the disciples fled in the opposite direction to Jerusalem, going to Bethany which is

---

[46] See eg John A T Robinson (1985) for comment.
[47] For more detail see Wenham (1993), Forster & Marston (1989) or on www.reason-science-and-faith.com

about a mile and a half the other way over the Mount of Olives. There they stayed during Jesus' trials and crucifixion.

Jesus' burial was just before the start of the Sabbath which by Jewish reckoning began at sunset. Various friends and relatives of Jesus stayed together that Sabbath in what we will call 'John's house' in Jerusalem. Around sunset the next day, two of these friends and relatives, Mary Magdalene and Mary the wife of Clopas (or Cleopas), went the mile and a half over the mount of Olives to Bethany to exchange news. This was natural enough as one had a brother and sister and the other a son there. The trip could be done by doing the first mile (a 'Sabbath day's journey) at the end of the Sabbath and the last half mile going downhill towards the village lights after the Sabbath ended at sunset and by the light of the Passover full moon.

Early next morning, Matt 28:1 (reflecting Matthew who was at Bethany) records how the two Mary's set out 'towards dawn'. Probably they had a prior arrangement to meet up with the others and go to anoint the body of Jesus which had been hurriedly laid in the tomb.

They went back to Jerusalem, to John's house, where were waiting, amongst others, John, Peter, Mary the mother of Jesus (see John 19:27) and Salome her sister. Salome joined the two Marys as (according to Mark 16:1 which reflects Peter's view) they went on to the tomb 'as the sun was risen'. Luke, with his more global picture, implies that they were joined en route by Joanna who, as the wife of Herod's steward, would have been staying at the nearby palace (perhaps with the Susannah of Lk 8:3?).

Meanwhile, Matthew implies, the guards at the tomb understandably fainted at sight of a shining angel, who rolled back the stone. They then recovered and ran off before the women arrived. *No one* saw the actual resurrection.

When the women did arrive at the edge of the garden, Mark makes it clear that they were some way off when they saw that the stone 'which was very large' had been rolled back. What did they conclude? John 20:2-3 tells us that Mary Magdalene concluded the body had been taken, and at that point ran back.

We should note two things about this. Firstly, the complex way things fit together. It is John who tells us that *just from seeing the stone* Mary Magdalene jumped to her conclusion, and Mark who tells us that they saw it some way off 'because it was very large'. Together this explains why Mary Magdalene did not see the angels at this point. By this time (as Mark and Luke say) the angels were inside the tomb, and Mary jumped to her conclusion and ran back before actually reaching it.

Secondly, note that John (unlike the other Gospels) has only mentioned Mary Magdalene. But note what she says after running back to his house: 'They have taken the Lord out of the tomb and **WE** do not know where they have laid him.'(20:2). This contrasts with 20:13 where she has by then lost contact with the other women and so says 'I do not know where they have laid him.' John 20:2 recorded the plural 'we' because that is actually what she said - and it was seared on John's memory.

Now two things happened at once. The other women went on (recorded by Matthew, Mark and Luke) to have a conversation with two angels who were by now inside the tomb. Angels, of course, have wings only in Christmas cards and stained glass windows - in the Bible they simply look like men. Luke refers to them as 'men' (24:4), but later as 'a vision of angels' (24:13). There is no contradiction. Likewise Matthew and Mark mention only one angel, whilst Luke mentions two. Perhaps only one speaks, and Matthew and Mark don't think it necessary to mention his companion.

Meantime, Mary Magdalene delivered her message to Peter and John who rushed off to the tomb (missing the other women in the maze of Jerusalem streets) and found it empty. The other women returned to John's house where they waited for Peter and John to get back, and then told their story about the angels. Amongst the hearers were Cleopas and his friend, who set off to Emmaus - as recorded by Luke. Their conversation on the road (Luke 24:13-33) shows that they knew exactly what the women, Peter and John would have told them.

The women had been given by the angels a message for the disciples. Having given the message to Peter and John back at John's house, they were running towards Bethany to tell the rest of the disciples when Jesus himself met them (Matthew 28:9). Matthew's Gospel records the meeting with Jesus immediately after the meeting with the angels - just as Matthew himself heard it recounted at Bethany. One can imagine the breathless haste with which the women tumbled out there their stories of meeting angels and then Jesus – Matthew's Gospel reflects just this.

The final appearances that evening, with them all back in Jerusalem, bring the day to a close. Matthew and John's later account of meetings in Galilee is in harmony with Luke's note in Acts 1:3 that Jesus appeared for 40 days before his ascension.

Conclusion

Where, then, are all the supposed contradictions? If the accounts fitted together any easier or if they all included exactly the same details, then we might suspect collusion. As it is, they do indeed look like accounts based on different eyewitness sources. They certainly do not look like legend or fantasy. Either an ancient Agatha Christie has cleverly constructed the four separate accounts or else they are independently compiled records of genuine events. Note in particular:

1. The incidental corroboration – eg:
    (i)   The use of 'we' by Mary to John makes sense only in the light of the other accounts.
    (ii) Only John and Mark together explain that Mary saw the large stone some distance off and ran back without entering the tomb

2. The unlikely features – eg:
    (i)   What Jew would make up an account in which the first to see Jesus was a woman, and angels gave women a key message to take to the male disciples?
    (ii) Why is there no account of anyone actually seeing Jesus rise? Surely a dramatic account of, say, Peter seeing this, would be an obvious thing to make up?

We cannot say that 'this is what happened'. What we can say is that this model makes good sense of all the data, and explains all the supposed 'contradictions'. In a wider context, the crucifixion and resurrection of Jesus can be seen as the key focal point of the dealings of God with humanity in history. He was 'Jesus Christ' which means 'Jesus the Messiah' – with prophecy, teaching, history and personal religious experience pointing to his uniqueness and significance to God's communication and action in human history.

7
Genesis Through History

Jesus and the Bible

If Jesus was really, as Christians believe, the incarnation of God, we obviously have to take seriously what he said. Assuming that the Gospels are at all accurate, it is obvious that Jesus believed that the Old Testament was in some sense inspired by God[1] and as *Christian* theists we accept that this is true. A consistent Christian theist, then, has not only to consider philosophical questions about God's relation to the world, but also the meaning of specific biblical teaching on nature and creation. So how should we understand these, and how do they relate to the scientific picture?

There are two opposite categories of people who feel that Christians really ought to 'take the Bible literally' on issues like the Genesis account of creation. Firstly, there are unbelievers who are impatient with what they regard as modern attempts to 'reinterpret' a Christianity which they believe, in the words of C S Lewis: 'implies a local "Heaven", a flat earth and a God who can have children.'[2] "If," they say, "Christians were really honest then they would take the Bible literally and admit that it is based on primitive superstition.'

Taking a similar view, but with quite different motives, are the dedicated and sincere Christians who believe that it is 'honouring God's Word' and 'giving God the glory' to take the Bible literally in all its apparent statements. As leading moderns revered by such people we shall take theologian E J Young, key young-earth creationist Henry Morris, and British scientist Prof E H Andrews. Thus Young, in rightly criticising the use of the term 'myth' for the Genesis accounts, then swings to the other extreme by arguing that it is 'straightforward trustworthy history'.[3] Likewise Morris begins with the bold assertion:

---

[1] See John Wenham (1993).
[2] C S Lewis (1960) p. 73.
[3] E J Young (1964) p. 105.

The Scriptures, in fact, do not need to be "interpreted" at all, for God is well able to say exactly what he means... Jesus Christ himself, accepted the Genesis record as literal history. There are no allegories in Genesis unless the dreams of Joseph are so described.[4] 'The Biblical record of origins was written to be understood, and therefore is to be taken literally rather than mystically or parabolically.[5]

There is, of course, some truth in both these viewpoints. The unbeliever is right to be sceptical of those who find, Einstein's laws of Relativity implied in obscure poetic verses of the Psalms, and the ardent 'literalist' is right to object to those who view the New Testament account of Jesus as some kind of 'cunningly devised myth' (2 Pet 1:16). Yet both are also mistaken, for they encourage an approach to the Bible with preconceived human ideas of what kind of literature 'it must be', rather than seeking to understand the evidence of Jesus and his culture on how God intended it to be understood. To argue, as does Morris, that it was written to be understood and 'therefore must be literal' is to arrogantly read a modern engineer's culture into a setting to which it is entirely foreign. It is also to deny the obvious fact that the most profound truths about *neither* the physical *nor* the spiritual can be conveyed or understood in this way. Neither physicists nor prophets are under the delusions that engineering with its 'literal' language deals with profound truths. Perhaps, before we go further in this we should avow that, whilst we believe Morris, Young, and Andrews to be confused and mistaken in their approach to the Bible, we recognise all three as fine and courteous Christian gentlemen - it is their exegesis not their spirituality we find defective. We might also mention those who make statements like:

> For most of its history, the creation account in Genesis 1 and 2 was understood as a literal depiction of God's work in the past.[6]

The writer is obviously sincere, but his statement is (in any normal sense of language) simply untrue – as we shall see.

We want, now, to do two main things. One is to look at the Jewish background, culture, and literary assumptions within

---

[4] Morris (1976) p. 31.
[5] Morris (1977) p. 55.
[6] Sailhamer (1996) p. 229.

which the creation passages were understood by the Jewish people, amongst whom were Jesus and Paul. The other is to look at subsequent Christian interpretations, to see if (say) a strictly literal interpretation was taken until recently. This will form a background to our later consideration of Genesis 1-3 for today.

Jesus and Paul in Jewish Context

As we have already seen, the Christian view of Jesus is that he came as part of a whole plan. God's special choice of Abraham and the nation of Israel was looking forward to the coming of a Messiah. The word 'Christ' is just the Greek translation of 'Messiah'. Jesus was recognised as 'the Christ' (eg Lk 9:20, Jn 4:25, Lk 22:67, Mt 26:63). We can see how Jesus as 'the Christ' was shortened to 'Christ Jesus' (cf Acts 2:31, 36, 38 and Acts 3:10, 3:20). Preaching 'the Christ Jesus' (Acts 5:42) and proving Jesus was 'the Christ' (Acts 9:22) mean the same thing. It could even be argued that 'Christ Jesus' in Paul's writings would better convey the sense if rendered 'Messiah Jesus' – to a 'Hebrew of the Hebrews' like Paul the Greek term surely never lost its underlying meaning.[7] Humankind were meant to act for God in his world and failed. The Jewish nation was appointed as God's 'chosen son', and 'suffering servant' (Ex 4:22; Is 41:8) in the world, but could not fulfil all that was needed. Jesus the Messiah was both representative human *and* representative Jew. The various works of N T (Tom) Wright are bringing this whole truth to us with new force. Human relationship with God is salvaged through the faithfulness of Jesus Christ or *faithfulness of Jesus the Messiah*.[8]

The incarnation did not happen in modern London or Texas but in first century Israel. The language and thought forms used by Jesus and Paul were the language and thought forms of first century Israel and its synagogues. Both were, of course, critical of aspects of religion amongst some of their fellow Jews. But Jesus often entered into dialogue with Rabbis and Pharisees, and Paul's letters contain many passages in which he is arguing his

[7] See also N T Wright (1991) Chs 2-3, and (1996b) p. 486.
[8] N T Wright (1997) p.106 (cf also (1996b) and (1992)). We argued for this rendering of Rom 3:22 in our (1973) – it is the most obvious in all its occurrences in the New Testament.

case from the Old Testament in a Rabbinical way with an obvious eye to convincing Jewish hearers. As we saw in Section 1 above, throughout Acts the apostles argued and disputed in the synagogues. As they did so they would have used the language, thought forms, and styles of exegesis which were common in synagogues. Let us, then, look carefully at the early Jewish approach, and then see whether the New Testament evidences a similar approach and in what ways Jesus and Paul may differ from Jewish contemporaries.

In broad terms, we can divide the available literature into:

- 'Philosophical' (eg Philo)
- 'Exegetical' (the Targumists and Rabbinic commentators)
- 'Mystical' & 'Apocalyptic' (eg the Jubilees, and Pseudographia)[9]

Two features are common to all of these. The first is a belief that the inspired biblical text contains layers of meaning. Often the spiritual meaning was seen as more important than the literal – even though the literal meaning was not denied. Paul, in a way entirely consistent for a Jewish Rabbi, referred to Genesis 2:24 but added 'This is a great mystery and I take it to mean Christ and the Church' (Eph 5:32). Like Philo and the Rabbis, Paul takes the Patriarchal stories as literal, but like a true Rabbi adds: 'Now this is an allegory...' (Gal 4:24).

The second feature is the common Hebrew use of Language purely figuratively and apocalyptically. Wright makes the same point about the Qumran community:

> They speak of the sun and moon being darkened, the stars falling from heaven and so on. When they do this, they aren't giving a primitive sort of weather forecast. They don't expect their readers or hearers to imagine that the space-time universe is literally going to come to a full stop, with a Big Crunch... (they) intend it to refer to events *within* what we call the space-time world, particularly the world of large scale international events and politics.[10]

Jesus, clearly, used language in the same way in speaking of his second coming (eg Matt 24:29). The event he prophesied will be

---

[9] A fascinating full study of this was presented by Justin Marston (Chair of CSIS) to the summer CiS/ASA conference at Oxford [Justin Marston (1998)]. Some of our present section is indebted to this.

[10] N T Wright (1996b) p. 116.

a real event, but the language he used was apocalyptic and figurative - it would be absurd to suggest that he somehow 'meant it literally' in defiance of all we know about how his hearers would have taken him at the time.

This, then, forms a background to understanding both early Jewish and early Christian teachers. What we want to know is not merely did they see an allegorical layer to the Genesis 1-3 passages, but whether *at the literal level* they believed that some parts of the passage were to be taken purely symbolically or metaphorically. The answer, as we shall see, is that they did.

Jewish Exegesis of Genesis 1-3.

Philo is of especial interest to the general Jewish understanding of Genesis 1-3 because, like Paul, he was a first century Jew who wrote in Greek. Sometimes he is referred to as a 'Hellenistic Jew' or a 'philosopher' as though this must make him a bit 'unsound'. We should, however, be clear that Philo has a very high regard for the Jewish Torah (ie Genesis-Deuteronomy), ascribes it to Moses, and most definitely shares the view of Jesus and Paul that it is inspired by God.[11] He is committed to the historicity of the biblical narrative (all the events, for example concerning the Patriarchs), and 'On occasion Philo even declared his admiration for the literal narrative' though in some passages 'he expresses the view that the literal interpretation is for those who are unable to see an underlying deeper meaning.'[12] Philo was no Pharisee, but he *practised* his Jewish faith (keeping the written law) as well as trying to harmonise its ideas with the 'science' and secular learning of his day. Philo begins his exegesis of 'Moses':

> He says that in six days the world was created, not that its Maker required a length of time for His work, for we must think of God as doing all things simultaneously, remembering that "all" includes with the commands which He issues the thought behind them. Six days are mentioned because for the things coming into existence there was a need of order... For it was requisite that the world, being most perfect of all things that have come into existence,

---

[11] See eg O'Fearghail in Finan and Twomey (1995) ch 3.
[12] O'Fearghail in Finan and Twomey (1995) pp. 46-7.

should be constituted in accordance with a perfect number, namely six. [13]

Philo does not believe that the inspired author intended us to take the 'days' either literally or chronologically. On humankind being made in God's image he says:

> Let no one represent the likeness as one to a bodily form; for neither is God in human form, nor is the human body God-like. No, it is in respect of the Mind, the sovereign element of the soul, that the word "image" is used; for after the pattern of a single Mind, even the Mind of the Universe as an archetype, the mind of each of those who successively came into being was moulded.[14]

He assumes that there really was a first and perfectly made man, from whom we descend, but the Garden of Eden is, he asserts, 'intended symbolically', as are the 'tree of life', the making of Eve from Adam's 'side' and other features. So does he think it is all 'myth'? No!

> Now these are no mythical fictions, such as poets and sophists delight in, but modes of making ideas visible, bidding us resort to allegorical interpretation guided in our renderings by what lies beneath the surface.

Philo is quite explicit. Genesis 1-3 is about real events, not myths, but God has chosen through Moses to use figurative or 'allegorical' language to speak to us.

Philo's philosophy of nature and time was profound: time is a property of space:

> Time began either simultaneously with the world or after it. For since time is a measured space determined by the world's movement, and since movement could not be prior to the object moving, but must of necessity arise either after it or simultaneously with it, it follows of necessity that time also is either coeval with or later born than the world.[16]

A number of Philo's key ideas (that the days were not meant literally but creation was instantaneous, and that time began with creation) were adopted by many later Christian writers, and

---

[13] Philo *On the Creation* 13-14.
[14] Philo *On the Creation* 69.
[15] Philo *On the Creation* 157.
[16] Philo *On the Creation* 26.

he influenced such diverse Christian teachers as Clement, Origen, Gregory of Nyssa and Ambrose.[17]

One very interesting point to note is that, although Philo is very clear that much of Genesis 1-3 was not meant to be taken literally, at times he writes as though it was. It is easy to mistake an assumption that the text is inspired and meant to teach us something with a belief that it was meant literally.

The Rabbinical writings were broadly similar in approach. The Targums (though put in their final versions later) were Aramaic paraphrases of the Hebrew text which were commonly used in 1st century Synagogue worship. Jesus, the disciples and Paul would all have heard Targumic interpretations regularly in their synagogues. Some Targumic language is clearly reflected in the New Testament - for example the 'Memra' (Word) is used as an alternative name for God. Thus eg:

> Before the creation of the world a garden had been planted by the Memra of the Lord God from Eden for the righteous, and he made Adam dwell there when he created him.[18]

This is reflected in John 1 and perhaps in Colossians 1:16. The Targums cite various things which God is said to have made 'before' the creation, add various numbers and some stories (eg on a dispute between the sun and the moon) which must surely be intended allegorically. *Targum Neofiti* has God putting 'the first Adam' into the garden, and adds that 'the Law is a tree of life for everyone who toils in it'. The later great Jewish exegetes followed this kind of line. Rashi, for example, argues that:

> The text does not intend to point out the order of the acts of Creation – to state that these (heaven and earth) were created first.[19]

He then goes on to argue that had this been intended the Hebrew word used would have been quite different. This whole tradition represented by Rashi, Ibn Ezra, Maimonides and Gersonides (some of which influenced key Christian scholars like Nicholas of Lyra) – consistently holds a high view of Scripture and the Pentateuch, but consistently specifically rejects overly literal

---

[17] See eg O'Fearghail in Finan and Twomey (1995) ch 3.

[18] *Targum Pseudo-Jonathan to Genesis* 2:8.

[19] See Hailperin (1960) p. 44.

understandings of Genesis 1-3.[20]   Maimonides, for example, probably the greatest Jewish exegete after Rashi, is quite explicit that parts of Genesis 1-3 cannot be taken literally. In, eg, the context of the snake, Eve and the tree of life, Maimonides has:

> The following is also a remarkable passage, most absurd in its literal sense; but as an allegory it contains wonderful wisdom, and fully agrees with the real facts, as will be found by those who understand all the chapters of this treatise.[21]

Gersonides similarly is quite clear that the order of things in Genesis 1 is to indicate priority, not chronology.[22]

It is not that it is *impossible* to find more literally minded Jewish commentators – just that the earliest and greatest by most judgements simply do not read the language of the text like this even when dealing with the 'literal' level of interpretation. But, some may think, we know of course that these later rabbis did not accept Jesus as the Messiah. Perhaps, then, figurative rather than literal understandings of words were a part of a Jewish apostasy of which Jesus (and Paul) were critical? Actually, the very reverse is the case. Right throughout the Gospel of John in particular, Jesus is continually critical of disciple, opponent, and the uncommitted for their failure to understand that he is speaking figuratively and *not* literally. In John 3 he speaks of being born again and pokes gentle fun at Nicodemus for being a teacher and not understanding that spiritual meaning is conveyed by figurative language. Perhaps Nicodemus was thinking that if Jesus 'meant to be understood' then 'he was therefore to be taken literally rather than mystically or parabolically'. In John 4 Jesus promises a Samaritan woman 'living water' and tells his friends that he has 'meat and drink' they don't know about - in both cases they mistake him to speak literally when he is speaking symbolically. In John 6 he tells people that they have to eat his body and drink his blood - and they are most confused. In synoptic passages like Matt 16:11 he also berates his disciples for not understanding that he speaks figuratively/allegorically and not literally. It is *not* a sign of spirituality nor is it to 'honour God' to take as much literally as

---

[20] For details see Justin Marston (1998).

[21] Maimonides *The Guide to the Perplexed* II.XXX (On Genesis 1-4).

[22] See eg Pearl (1971) p. 51 or Staub (1982) p. 100.

possible. Jesus' own preferred style was metaphorical/figurative, and he saw people's failure to understand this as due to lack of spiritual discernment (cf 'Oh you of little faith' - Matt 16:8).

The Christian believes that right from the beginning God chose to communicate with mankind through language: 'And the Lord God commanded the man....' Later he chose to use language again in communicating through the Bible. But the Hebrew and Greek languages, like our own, are used in a whole spectrum of ways. Metaphor comes constantly into language all the time. We just used, for example, the expression 'spectrum of ways'. But it would not be very sensible for someone to proclaim: "If Forster and Marston do not mean by 'spectrum of ways' that language contains a whole lot of literal colours then how can we trust what they say elsewhere?' Scientists, incidentally, use language just as metaphorically as anyone else. When physicists speak of 'waves' or 'electron spin' they are introducing terms used in other contexts but if pressed will soon affirm that (say) light 'waves' have properties quite different from the 'waves' from which the term was taken, and electrons do not spin literally like tops. They may, of course, be misunderstood. People may even say 'If we can't take Professor Andrews literally when he speaks of metal being 'fatigued' then how can we believe him when he says that the number 7 bus leaves at 6.45?' Foolish though this would be, some of the supposed literalist arguments about parts of Genesis are not greatly different.

We need to be clear on some basic points on how words are used - both in religious and in other contexts such as everyday or scientific ones. It is difficult if not impossible simply to remove metaphor altogether and 'speak plainly'. In Scientific thinking there was one school of thought which saw 'models' as optional extras - but a more profound analysis realises that part of the whole dynamic of science involves metaphorical images of thinking.[23] In theology, C S Lewis, who was of course a Professor in a field of languages, referred to those who ask:

"...would it not be better to get rid of the mental pictures, and of the language which suggests them altogether ?" But this is impossible.

---

[23] See eg Hesse (1966), Barbour (1974) and (1998) ch 5.

> The people who recommend it have not noticed that when they try
> to get rid of man-like, or, as they are called, anthropomorphic,
> images, they merely succeed in substituting images of some other
> kind.[24]

Our images of God and of many spiritual things are inevitably in
pictures, or words that derive their richness from quite other
contexts. This is true both of such Biblical images as of
'fatherhood', 'spiritual power', 'ascending to heaven' etc, and of
ones of human making like 'ground of our being' or 'universal
substance'. Jesus' teaching is full not only of specific 'parables'
but a whole range of metaphorical language. In such contexts
Jesus did not preface his words with the warning: 'What I am
about to say is metaphorical' - he simply assumed that those
who were spiritually discerning would realise this. If Jesus, as
Christians believe, shows us the Father, then we will expect God
to speak to us in metaphor without any explicit warning, and
God will expect us to be spiritually discerning in interpreting
His words. It is not honouring to Jesus' chosen means of
communication for someone to speak, as does eg E J Young,
about 'mere symbols'[25] as though there was something inferior
about this kind of language.

The kind of factual statements God makes about creation are
reliable where they touch on history and on the nature of the
physical world. But God's concern is neither that of the secular
historian nor that of the physicist. On a historical level, a
statement may have genuine historical content but be figurative
in form. This is quite different from a 'myth' in any usual sense
of the word (which is taken by Andrews, for example, simply to
mean a 'fairy story'[26]). None of the early Jewish or Christian
commentators thought Genesis 1-3 a 'myth' in the sense of fairy
story - we have already seen that eg Philo is adamant about this.
Only to those who think it was *meant* literally does it look like a
fairy story.[27]

This may be illustrated again from the words of Jesus himself.
Once he said: 'I sent you to reap what you have not worked for.

---

[24] C.S.Lewis (1960) p. 78.
[25] Young (1966) p. 8.
[26] Andrews (1978) p. 5.
[27] Cf Luther's comments later in this section.

Others have done the hard work and you have reaped the benefits of their labour.' Now this is a historical statement - it is not 'myth' or 'legend' which would be a false claim to literal history. It is not a 'fable' or 'parable' like e.g. that of the 'Prodigal Son' the point of which is unaffected if it has no connection with particular historical events. It is metaphorical history. Young, notably, ignores this category of language altogether, writing as though our choice were between on the one hand myth, fable, and legend, and on the other pedantic 'hansard-reporting' history. But here, although Jesus refers to an actual historical commission which he had given them, his language is figurative or metaphorical - his commission concerned souls not agriculture. He could, presumably, have 'explained himself more clearly', but he chose not to do so. If Jesus 'showed us the Father, then it would be no surprise if we found that God had used language similarly. The story of the 'snake' may be no more meant to teach us about reptiles than Jesus meant to tell us something about agriculture. It is not 'myth' it is 'history' - but its form is metaphorical. A point similar to this has been made by Spanner.[28]

Early Christian Views on Creation

It is a general principle to us that words inspired by the Holy Spirit are not 'of private interpretation' (1 Pet 1:20). It is, therefore, important for us to seek to understand passages like Genesis 1-3 in a way broadly in harmony with the way in which Bible-based Christians have always understood it.

There is, unfortunately, a common misconception that Christians all used to take it fairly literally, and that in a post-Copernican and Darwinian age some of us are now trying to cobble together some kind of non-literal understanding. This is simply not true. At *no* stage in the history of Christian interpretation of Genesis 1-3 has there been a 'purely literal' understanding. Here we are going to put forward and illustrate the following basic theses:

---

[28] Douglas Spanner (1987) with a new edition on the internet from 1999 on www.csis.org.uk

1. Only various Gnostics (including Marcionites, Valentinians and Manichaeans) saw the passages as *purely* allegorical. They held that the world was created not by God but by an inferior being, and matter was basically corrupt and evil.

2. All mainstream Christians (and Jews) therefore held that there *was* a literal interpretation of Genesis.

3. All mainstream Christians (and Jews) also held that there was *also* an allegorical interpretation (and perhaps also other levels such as moral etc).

4. All mainstream Christians (and Jews) agreed that certain parts of the *literal* meaning were metaphorically or figuratively expressed. Take, for example 'And God *said* let there be light...' God could not have used a physical voice before there was any air to speak in. Indeed, Jews and Christians generally agreed that God had no bodily parts.

5. Christian teachers when preaching *pastorally* from Genesis 1-3 spoke as though it was literal even when (as with Origen) they clearly did not think it was.

Where there was *disagreement* was:

i.   *How far* the literal meaning of Genesis was expressed metaphorically. Were the 'days' for example, periods of time or not? Were the events intended to be taken as being described chronologically nor not?

ii. How should those details taken literally within the literal meaning be reconciled with prevailing scientific ideas?

In general we would make some further generalisation about this.

1. **Earlier and Later Teaching:** The earliest teaching was that of the 'Greek Fathers' in the two centuries after Christ. Men like Justin, Clement, Theophilus and Origen, spoke the Greek language of the New Testament. Justin had close links and friendly debates with Jewish thinkers and so knew their approach. Clement knew the thought and school of Philo in his native Alexandria, and both he and Theophilus have interpretations of Genesis bearing marks of Jewish influence.[29] Origen studied Hebrew deeply with the help of

---

[29] Baker (1964) pp. 107ff.

his Rabbinic friends. In these, who stood closest to the thought and language of the apostles and the New Testament, there is, then, little hint of any crude literalism. Justin (cf below) does not *argue* that a 'day' can be a thousand years, he simply assumes it (as did the Rabbis). Origen does not *argue* that eg the 'days' were not meant to be literal and chronological, he simply gives a withering retort to hostile pagan critics on the *assumption* that no intelligent Christian takes them as intended to be literal and chronological. Methodius then comes in a generation after Origen, and it is a full century later that writers like Basil, Ambrose, Augustine etc write with no native Greek and (excepting Jerome who said very little about it) no understanding of Hebrew. Only then do we start to get discussion about how the sun could be literally made two days after 'day and night' or why the water above the firmament does not run off the roof.

2. **Plain Meaning?** For those today, like Henry Morris, who want a 'plain meaning', the past experience of literalists is not encouraging. Poor Basil, who was at least aware that *some* expressions were metaphor, finishes up in places seeming to imply a hard roof which is concave on the outer surface to collect the water; and even then contradicting himself in various ways.[30] The 5th century monk Cosmas Indicopleustes went the whole hog and finished up with a rectangular universe on the model of the Tabernacle. Mercifully, *Britannica* tells us:

> his idiosyncratic work is not representative of the general state of cosmographic theory among Christian philosophers of his day and had small influence on later writers.

3. **Tensions:** Even throughout the later periods (ie 4th century onwards), literalism was not dominant. On the 'days', for example, commentators tended to favour either Basil or Augustine. Basil was rather more 'literal' – though not entirely so, whilst Augustine believed that creation had been simultaneous and the days a logical device. As far as we know, no one suggested that divergent opinions on this were heresy. Augustine (who on other issues had no scruple to

---

[30] Jaki (1998) notes numbers of these difficulties for Basil and others.

imprison or banish Christians for theological divergence) was markedly tolerant – repeatedly recognising that any conclusions had to be tentative.

Let us, then, look at some of the teaching on issues like eg the 'days' or the creation of Eve from Adam's side. Ps 90:4 and 2 Pet 3:8 led many early teachers to see in the 'days' at one level an allegorical meaning of seven millenia as the supposed seven ages of world history. But what about the level of its 'literal meaning'? As we consider this it should be emphasised, of course, that it is not their *particular* ideas but their *approach* to Scripture in which we are interested.

One of the earliest relevant passages is in Justin Martyr (c109-165):

> For as Adam was told that in the day he ate of the tree he would die, we know that he did not complete a thousand years. We have perceived, moreover, that the expression. 'The day of the Lord is as a thousand years' is connected with this subject.[31]

The implication is that each day was a thousand years – a kind of early 'age-day' theory.

Theophilus of Antioch (c115-181) speaks at some length about the days of creation. His actual picture of the cosmos (oh dear!) is of heaven as a dome, and the earth as a kind of clod.[32] He notes that the plants came before the sun on day four, to confound the 'vain philosophers' who 'say that the things which grow on the earth are produced from the heavenly bodies, so as to exclude God.' So does he believe the order and timescale to be literal? If he does, it is certainly not the main point to him, for he immediately goes on to say:

> And these contain the pattern and type of a great mystery. For the sun is a type of God and the moon of man...

He proceeds to expand on this and it shows the tenor of most of his comments. It is the type and the spiritual significance which interest him. On the 'tree' he says 'it was not the tree, as some think, but the disobedience which had the death in it.' The 'rib' story is recounted, but Theophilus is again more interested in the

---

[31] Justin *Dialogue* 82 (*Ant Nic Fath* 1 p. 240). This is also in the Talmud *Genesis Rabbah* 19:8.
[32] *Theophilus to Autolucus* 13.

spiritual truths this implies. As for the 'serpent', he assumes that the voice which spoke through it was that of 'Satan' a fallen angel. There is no need to discuss the linguistic or vocal abilities of snakes. The strong influence of Jewish and Jewish Christian sources is shown in an exegesis 'which is both literal and speculative'.[33] By our standards today it is actually highly allegorical in its understanding.

From the second century onwards, the Gnostic heresy was a major force, and Christian orthodoxy was formulated in contention against it. Gnostics, as already noted, held that the physical world was inferior, made by an inferior god, whilst the true spiritual God was to be found not by faith but by the impartation of a secret knowledge (*gnosis*) through the cult. Second century Gnostics used the biblical creation passages, employing allegorical methods to draw out of them fanciful Gnostic meanings. Much of what early Christian leaders said was directed not so much against the ancient versions of physicalists like Daniel Dennett (of which there were some) but ancient versions of Barbara Thiering (cf. last section n37) who read Genesis as an elaborate code and denied that it implied God created in any sense the physical world (which was evil). Mainstream Christians were affirming that the passages really were about the creation of the world, not denying that their descriptions were couched in figurative language and images.

Clement of Alexandria (c155-220) was *the* great defender of mainstream faith as the way to true 'knowledge' in opposition to Gnostic teaching. He adamantly rejected their fanciful teachings, though respected Philo and the true place of non-literality in understanding Scripture. He seldom expounds Genesis 1, but in one place writes:

> That, then, we may be taught that the world was originated, and not suppose that God made it in time, prophecy adds: "This is the book of the generation; also of the things in them, when they were created in the day that God made heaven and earth" (Gen 2:4). For the expression "when they were created" intimates an indefinite and dateless production. But the expression "in the day that God made", that is, in and by which God made "all things," and "without which not even one thing was made," points out the activity exerted by the

---

[33] Baker (1964) pp. 110ff.

Son. As David says, "This is the day which the Lord has made... for the Word that throws light on things hidden, and by whom each created thing came into life and being, is called day.'[34]

The first sections of Clement's *Eclogae Propheticae* are largely devoted to Genesis. It is highly allegorical, eg the 'water which is above the heavens, because it is spiritual and invisible, signifies the Holy Spirit, the purifier of invisible things.'[35]

Tertullian (c160-220) wrote (in Latin) about the creation, but his main point was that matter was not eternal and it is not clear how literally he took the days etc.

The saintly and scholarly Origen (c185-254), a man who suffered torture for his faith, is described in *Britannica* as the 'most important theologian and biblical scholar of the early Greek Church'. Origen was, as we noted, fluent in Greek and Hebrew. His *Homilies on Genesis* contain the following:

> The text said that "there was evening and there was morning," it did not say "the first day," but said "one day." It is because there was not yet time before the world existed. But time begins to exist with the following days. For the second day and the third and fourth and all the rest being to designate time.[36]

The 'one day' repeats Philo's point, and might hint at a simultaneous creation view. The *Homilies*, however, are not dissimilar in tenor to those of Theophilus. Compare:

> Just as the sun and the moon are said to be the great lights in the firmament of heaven, so also are Christ and the church to us...

Origen takes there, however, to be two or more levels of meaning, thus on Gen 1:24-5:

> There is certainly no question about the literal meaning. For they are clearly said to have been created by God, whether animals or four footed creatures of beasts or serpents upon the earth. But it is not unprofitable to relate these words to those which we explained above in a spiritual sense.

We are mystified by the suggestion sometimes made that Origen 'sacrificed the literal meaning entirely for the mystic'. This is simply not true. Modern studies have emphasised that:

---

[34] Clement *Miscellenies* vi.16 (*Ant Nic Fath* 2.514).

[35] Clement *Eclogae Propheticae* viii, 1-2.

[36] Origen *Homily 1* (Tr Heine).

When the Bible speaks, as it frequently does, in a figurative or parabolic language: the modern exegete will call 'literal' what the sacred writer meant to express by the figure or parable, but for Origen that would be the 'spiritual' meaning... Origen in fact believed in the historicity of the Bible much more than the most traditionalist of our exegetes do today.[37]

He brought all available linguistic, literary genre, geographic and all other resources to bear to 'contribute to the interpretation of the literal meaning'.

In the *Homilies*, Origen expounds Genesis 1-3 pastorally, and, indeed, had we no other source we would have suspected Origen to take the 'days' literally, whilst emphasising also the spiritual meaning. However, he wrote around 231 AD:

What man of intelligence, I ask, will consider a reasonable statement that the first and the second and the third day, in which there are said to be both morning and evening, existed without sun and moon and stars, while the first day was even without a heaven? And who could be found so silly as to believe that God, after the manner of a farmer, 'planted trees in a paradise eastward in Eden' ... And... when God is said to 'walk in the paradise in the evening ... I do not think anyone will doubt that these are figurative expressions which indicate certain mysteries through a semblance of history...[38]

This forcefully indicates the dangers of reading 'literality' into sermons or homilies on Genesis 1-3. Origen believes that this physical world is 'literally' a creation of God (he adamantly rejects Gnosticism). But he (like Philo) does not take the chronology or the days as 'literal' – even when dealing with the literal rather than allegorical level of interpretation he believes that elements were meant figuratively or metaphorically. His work, then, is not filled with speculation about how light existed without the sun etc, but concentrates on the spiritual meaning.

This completes a survey of what might be called 'early' Christian teaching. Theophilus, Clement, and Origen all take approaches which emphasise the figurative and spiritual meanings of the creation passages – though all believe that God really did create the physical world and that Genesis 1-3 speaks (though sometimes using metaphor) about this.

---

[37] Crouzel (1989) p. 62-3, see also De Lange (1976) p. 106.
[38] Origen *First Principles* Bk 4 ch 3.

Later but Pre-Geology Views

We move now beyond what could be called 'early' Christian teaching, but stay in the ages before geology began.

There seems little to tell us what was generally thought about the 'days' in the century after Origen. Methodius (c260-312) was a bishop ostensibly highly critical of 'Origen'. A recent study shows, however, that Methodius was largely criticising positions which Origen had never held.[39] Interestingly, though, in reference to Gen 2:22-3 Methodius upbraids his correspondent for 'explaining the passage in too natural a sense' and points out that that Paul guided us 'to allegorise the history of Adam and Eve as having reference to Christ and the Church.' He gives the balance:

> It is a dangerous thing wholly to despise the literal meaning... Paul is not to be despised when he passes over the literal meaning...[40]

Much of his teaching seems not much different in tenor from Origen himself. In a large fragment of his teaching on the 'days', the catena begins with a citation of Psalm 90:2-4 which is 'to establish the familiar point that the days of creation are a thousand years.'[41] There are six of these before Adam, and six from Adam until the present (the seventh day being the day of judgement), making thirteen millennia in all. With this, far from what we today would call a 'literal' interpretation, we may leave Methodius.

The next group of known Christian teachers are a lot later, being born some three centuries after Christ's death. Hilary of Poitiers (c315-368) in *On The Trinity* is mainly concerned with the eternal nature of Christ, but adds that 'the creation of heaven and earth and other elements is not separated by the slightest interval in God's working.'

Basil (c329-379) was well educated and aware of Greek secular learning. His famous *Homilies* on Genesis, however, were not philosophical treatises but *sermons* given before a

---

[39] Patterson (1997) p. 204.
[40] Methodius *The Banquet of the Ten Virgins* Discourse III (*Ant Nic Fath* vi, p. 317).
[41] Patterson (1997) p. 206.

group including workmen and artisans. *Homily 1* includes much discussion of 'beginning', and suggests that:

> Perhaps the words 'In the beginning he created,' were used because of the instantaneous and timeless act of creation, since the beginning is something immeasurable and indivisible.'

He asserts that the main point about the earth is that 'all things are kept under control by the power of the Creator' – the form of it is unimportant. Actually, he thinks it spherical, small, and holds the middle place of the universe but adds:

> Our amazement at the greatest phenomena is not lessened because we have discovered the manner in which a certain one of the marvels occurred. (*Homily 1*)

Quite so. Basil insists that 'water means water' and not some fanciful meaning, but his target seems to be the various forms of Gnosticism (Marcionites, Valentinians and Manichaeans are mentioned) rather than the Alexandrian schools of Philo, Clement and Origen. Basil himself is clear that:

> When we speak of a voice and a word and a command with reference to God, we mean the divine word, not a sound sent out through phonetic organs.. the bent of his will is presented in the form of a command, because it is easily comprehended by those who are being instructed. (*Homily 2*)

Quite so. Basil does, however, want to take rather more literally than (say) Origen *some* of the details. As already noted, the tangles into which this leads him are cold comfort to moderns who suggest we can derive high level science from Genesis. Presumably none of them believes the sky is a solid dome with concave tanks on top of it for water.

It is hard to see how far Basil takes the 'days' literally – like Origen's *Homilies* the sermon is not an ideal place to explore this. In a passage which speaks of 24 hours, Basil continues:

> It is also characteristic of eternity to turn back upon itself and never to be brought to an end. Therefore he called the beginning of time not a 'first day' but 'one day'; in order that from the name it might have kinship with eternity.. For, Scripture knows as a day without evening, without succession, and without end, that day which the psalmist called the eighth, because it lies outside the week of time. Therefore, whether you say 'day' or 'age' you will express the same idea... (*Homily 2*)

The whole passage is no less complex than this extract, and hardly indicates a simplistic view of 'days'. He does seem to take the order literally, and rather unconvincingly gets around the creation of the sun on the fourth day by portraying the sun as a 'receptacle' of light – drawing analogies with the moon even though he later shows understanding of lunar eclipses. He repeats the earlier suggestion that the sun comes on the fourth day to show that it is not the source of life. Interestingly, he takes the words 'let the waters bring forth' and 'let the earth bring forth' to indicate a kind of divinely ordained spontaneous generation (*Homilies 7 and 8*); 'since God is enduing it with the power of active force.' Such ideas enable the modern evolutionary creationist Howard van Till to claim Basil as a kind of precursor – though only in a very oblique sense.[42]

Ambrose of Milan (c339-392) gives in his own *Homilies on Genesis* a rather verbose free interpretation of Basil's work. Ambrose repeats, eg that God's 'voice' is not literal, has a version of the complex passages about the meaning of 'day' etc. In an added section on *Paradise*, Ambrose adds that 'in the figure of the serpent we see the Devil'. He also, however, gives an interpretation of Eve and the temptation which is a copy of a highly allegorical one by Philo: the serpent stands for enjoyment, the woman the emotions of the mind and heart, etc.[43]

John Chrysostom (c334-407) was a great preacher whose overwhelming concern in his *Homilies* was pastoral. He appears to take the days 'literally' but in truth is totally unconcerned with scientific issues, and also repeatedly emphasises that ideas are being given 'concreteness of expression' in Genesis 1-3 to help our 'limited human understanding'. Man is not, he emphasises, in any physical sense in God's image, and when God 'planted a garden' his should clearly not be taken 'in human fashion' (*Homily 13*). On the 'side' used to form Eve he writes:

> Don't take the words in human fashion; rather, interpret the concreteness of the expressions from the viewpoint of human limitations. You see, if he had not used these words, how would we

---

[42] Van Till (1996).
[43] Cf translation by John Savage (1961).

have been able to gain knowledge of these mysteries which defy description ? (*Homily 15*)

Amongst Latin Fathers, *Britannica* calls Augustine of Hippo (c354-430) the 'greatest thinker of Christian antiquity'. Even those who, like ourselves, are unsympathetic to parts of his theology and novel reinterpretations of predestination, accept that he was a deep thinker and a key figure in much both of Catholic and Reformation theology. On creation his views were orthodox and undogmatic, following closely those of Philo and other Jewish thinkers and reflecting earlier church thinking. In his book *Genesis in the Literal Sense* he recognises that it is valid for Christians to see an 'allegorical' level of interpretation in Genesis 1-3, which is distinct from its 'literal meaning'.[44] His book is, however, *specifically* about this 'literal' or historical level of understanding (in parts of which the language should be taken figuratively) *not* the allegorical level In the introduction, translator J H Taylor pertinently remarks that a reader:

> may be puzzled by the fact that he has called it a literal commentary. The days of creation, he suggests, are not periods of time but rather categories in which creatures are arranged by the author for didactic reasons to describe all the works of creation, which in reality were created simultaneously. Light is not the visible light of this world but the illumination of intellectual creatures (the angels). Morning refers to the angels' knowledge of creatures which they enjoy in the vision of God, evening refers to the angels' knowledge of creatures as they exist in their own created natures. Can this sort of exegesis be literal interpretation?[45]

The point, says Taylor, is that the use of figures of speech or metaphor in a narrative about actual historical events does not mean that it is an 'allegorical narrative'. Augustine is insisting that Genesis 1-3 really *is* about the creation of physical things – not *merely* some kind of coded reference to the spiritual (as taught by some forms of Gnosticism in his own day[46]). It is about real events, and he seeks to understand it in the sense the author intended, but this does not mean that he 'takes it literally' in the modern sense. He had declared in his *City of God* that:

---

[44] Augustine *The Literal Meaning of Genesis* i.1.

[45] J H Taylor (1982) p. 9.

[46] The Manichees, he claims, deride it altogether.

of what fashion those days were, it is either very hard or altogether impossible to think, much more to speak. As for ordinary days, we see that they have neither morning nor evening but as the sun rises and sets. But the first three days of all had no sun, for that was made the fourth day...[47]

This is a theme constantly repeated in *The Literal Meaning of Genesis*. He suggests (like Philo) that in fact everything was created at once, and the days have a time-based or temporal character not physical but ideal. Thus he writes:

> God created all things simultaneously at the beginning of the ages, creating some in their substance and others in pre-existing causes.[48]

He returns repeatedly to the 'days'. Thus eg:

> Thus in all the days of creation there is one day, and it is not to be taken in the sense of our day, which we reckon by the course of the sun; but it must have another meaning, applicable to the three days mentioned before the creation of the heavenly bodies. This special meaning of "day" must not be maintained just for the first three days, with the understanding that after the third day we take the word "day" in its ordinary sense. But we must keep the same meaning even to the sixth and seventh days. Hence "day" and "night" which God divided, must be interpreted quite differently from the familiar "day" and "night", which God decreed that the lights he created in the firmament should divide...
>
> We took evening to mean the limit of a created nature, and the following morning the beginning another to be created... Whatever evening and morning were in those days of creation, it is quite impossible to suppose that on the morning following the evening of the sixth day God's rest began. We cannot be so foolish...
>
> That day in the account of creation, or those days that are numbers according to its recurrence, are beyond the experience and knowledge of us mortal earthbound men. And if we are able to make any effort towards an understanding of those days, we ought not to rush forward with an ill considered opinion, as if no other reasonable and plausible interpretation could be offered.[49]

Augustine immediately goes on to reassert that he is not taking an 'allegorical' but a 'literal' view here – it was about real historical events. He confirms that he takes the days 'literally' –

---

[47] Augustine *City of God* vol 1 (*Nic & Post Nic Fath* ii. 208).

[48] Augustine *The Literal Meaning of Genesis* vii.42.

[49] Augustine *The Literal Meaning of Genesis* iv.26, 32-34, 44.

but what he means by 'literally' is very different from what modern 'literalists' mean. Day, evening and morning did *not* (he says) all occur simultaneously at the time of creation. They came 'separately and in the order set forth in Sacred Scripture' – but the Genesis language reflected the angelic perspective, which could know something either directly in God (morning knowledge') or in its later actual being (evening knowledge').[50]

The 'Paradise' of Genesis 2-3 he interpreted 'in both senses, sometimes corporeally and at other times spiritually'.[51] On what we would term 'scientific' aspects of Genesis 1-3 Augustine's approach and treatment is consistently and commendably non-dogmatic, thoughtful, and rational. Later he says:

> It is in a figurative sense that the serpent is called "the most subtle"... because of another spirit – that of the Devil – dwelling in it... What is said to the serpent, therefore, and is intended for him who worked through the serpent, is undoubtedly to be understood in a figurative sense.[52]

Remember that all this is in a book called *Genesis in the Literal Sense*. Even to the later Fathers, the 'literal sense' did *not* exclude the use of symbolic or figurative language. Taylor remarks how widely read this work was in the Middle Ages,[53] and we shall see how widespread in the church was acceptance of his non-dogmatic non literalistic approach.

It is worth here mentioning a 'refutation' in a recent book by Malcolm Bowden of our briefer outline in *Reason and Faith* of early Christian views on the 'days'. Though we are flattered to be 'refuted' in a book which also 'refutes' the motion of the earth, geology, radiometric dating, the big bang cosmology, quantum theory, relativity, and many of the major theories of modern mainstream science, the accuracy of the author is not recommended by the fact that we are transmuted after the first few mentions from 'Forster and Marston' to 'Forster and Marsden' under which we appear in the index. But what does he say? He argues firstly that Basil was a 'sensible literalist'. Well what we said was:

---

[50] Augustine *The Literal Meaning of Genesis* iv.29-33.
[51] Augustine *The Literal Meaning of Genesis* viii.1.1.
[52] Augustine *The Literal Meaning of Genesis* ix.2,36.
[53] Taylor (1982) p. 12.

Basil, for example, who specifically claims to take it all literally specifically refers to 24 hour periods. Yet later he adds, 'Whether you call is "day" or whether you call is "eternity" you express the same idea,' and in fact adopts a complex interpretation.[54]

Bowden's quotation of a passage from Basil (which is evidently aimed at Gnostic heresy) casts no doubt on our assertion. On Augustine, Bowden ignores the clear passages which show a non-literal and non-chronological view of the days, and says he 'only has to quote one passage' to 'demolish' our argument.[55] In this passage Augustine speaks of human 'conjectures' of great antiquity for mankind, and says 'reckoning by the sacred writings, we find that not 6,000 years have yet passed.' Augustine, like most Christians of his era, thought that the origins of humankind (ie Adam) dated around 5,600 BC (not 4004 because they used the LXX). There was, of course, no empirical evidence to the contrary, and in any case we would think that his date for Adam and Eve was not far out – as we shall see. The passage is nothing whatsoever to do with the literality of the 'days'. Only one other early figure is mentioned by Bowden – without any quotation at all:

> An examination of the works of Origen, Calvin and others who are quoted as open to a non-literal view will refute this claim.

On Origen (the only really *early* figure mentioned), this is just factually untrue. Origen (like ourselves) was in one sense a 'sensible literalist' – but part of the 'sensibleness' was a clear recognition (in a passage we quoted above) that the 'days' were *not* intended as literal and chronological. We agree with Bowden that 'to allegorise a passage is not to deny that it was a historical event'. But the point is that the sections we quote from eg Philo, Origen and Augustine are not 'allegorising' the passage. Rather, they are specifically about the literal and historical level of interpretation of Genesis 1 – and it is on *this* that they assert some of the language (eg the 'days') to be metaphorical. There was, they thought, *also* a totally allegorical interpretation of the passage (as Paul also gave for the story of Abraham, Isaac and Ishmael) – but this was a separate issue.

---

[54] Forster and Marston (1989) p. 205.
[55] Bowden (1998) p. 39.

Over the next millennia, Christian teachers differed in their degree of literality. Those more influenced by Basil tended to be rather more literal, those by Augustine rather more figurative. More details of this are given in the book by Jaki[56] - we can here only give a few snapshots.

In the sixth century the Alexandrian tradition was upheld by John Philoponus. Philoponus emphasised that Moses was chosen by God 'to lead men to knowledge of God and to a way of life appropriate to it.'[57] The universe was neither a result of 'chance' nor was it eternal, but was created by a personal God. Details of science, moreover, should not be looked for in Scripture.

Moving to the seventh century, there is today in the Western Church a lot of interest in 'Celtic' Christianity. In Britain, beautiful places like Iona and Lindisfarne are recognised as centres of an early Christ-centred gospel and commitment to Scripture and service. A recent scholarly work on the seventh century (Irish) Celtic church asserts:

> The scheme of creation… is essentially that of Saint Augustine: the whole of creation took place simultaneously in a single creating act beyond time, and the sequence of days in the Genesis account is a logical not a temporal distinction.[58]

Amongst Saxons, Bede (673-735) in his *Hexameron* cites Augustine copiously, though does not always follow him. However, one recent study states:

> The English monk, Bede of Jarrow (673-735) usually adopted an allegorical interpretation of Scripture. Yet Bede's extensive study of astronomy led him to justify and employ that discipline when discussing the literal meaning of astronomical allusions in Scripture.[59]

The Saxons, however, were more interested in the pastoral (or perhaps also the 'saga') aspects. Bede influenced figures associated with the famous emperor Charlemagne (768-814) and his son Louis the Pious, for example Claudius of Turin.

---

[56] Jaki (1998).
[57] Jaki (1998) p. 94.
[58] Smyth (1996) p. 39.
[59] McCluskey (1998) p. 34.

Claudius' commentary on Genesis is 'largely drawn from Augustine's *The Literal Meaning of Genesis.* [60]

Moving to the scholastic period, Paris and Oxford were the main centres of learning. A study of the views of contemporaries of the Bishop of Paris, Peter Lombard (1100-1160), shows eg that Roland of Bologna, Honorius Augustodeunensis, Hugh St Victor, Robert of Melun and others all adopted Augustine's figurative view of the days.[61] Adelard mainly quoted Augustine but was disinterested in this question. Peter Lombard himself, apparently motivated by a dislike of Origen's ideas, insisted on literal 24 hour days – though in this was therefore unusual amongst his peers.

At Oxford the massive learning of Robert Grosseteste (c1175-1253) came to dominate. Grosseteste's *Hexameron* has a tiered interpretation which includes literal and allegorical meanings. On the literal level, Grosseteste summarises the views of Augustine, Basil, and numerous others on the 'days' – but feels no need to reach a conclusion himself, believing several are legitimate. Some of his disciples were less reticent. Richard Rufus, for example, whilst showing an interest *only* in the 'literal' level – clearly plumps for Augustine's metaphorical view of the days.[62]

Thomas Aquinas (1224-1274) made this proviso about his comments on the creation issues:

> Two rules are to be observed, as Augustine teaches (*Gen. ad. lit. i*) The first is, to hold the truth of Scripture without wavering. The second is that since Holy Scripture can be explained in a multiplicity of senses, one should not adhere to a particular explanation, only in such measure as to be ready to abandon it if it be proved with certainty to be false; lest holy Scripture be exposed to the ridicule of unbelievers, and obstacles be placed to their believing.[63]

This is adequate answer for those who criticise the scholastics for harmonising their theology with Aristotelian physics. Aquinas was perfectly clear that if one day his physics proved

---

[60] Gorman (1997) p. 313.
[61] Colish (1994) ch. 6.
[62] Raedts (1987) p.189.
[63] Aquinas *Question lxviii.*

defective then Scripture could as well be explained on that level in other ways. We may also note that he then says, after noting some chronological problems:

> If, however, we take these days to denote merely sequence in the natural order, as Augustine holds (*Gen. ad. lit. iv*) and not succession in time, there is nothing to prevent our saying... that the substantial formation of the firmament belongs to the second day.

A fairly clear acceptance of possible non-literality on the days, then, from the 'Angelic Doctor' of scholasticism.

Perhaps the most influential commentator in the next period was Nicolas of Lyra (c1270-1349) who was greatly indebted to the Jewish commentator Rashi. *Britannica* describes him as: 'one of the foremost Franciscan theologians and influential biblical interpreters of the Middle Ages'. Jaki is highly critical of Nicolas[64] though another more specialist assessment says that:

> Like Rashi, Lyra was not an extreme literalist in interpretation.[65]

This seems to us a more balanced assessment of Nicolas. Needless to say, contemporaries of Nicolas (like the Mystic Meister Eckhart) were even less literal in their understanding.

We have now surveyed something of the first thirteen centuries of the church after the death of Christ. We have shown that, whilst exegetes differed in their degree of allegory, simple literalism was not orthodoxy and large groups of Bible-believing Christians thought eg the 'days' were not literal.

By the end of the fifteenth century a new situation was arising. It was an age where sterile scholastic logic chopping, genuine personal mystic piety, and abuses in the church, all competed. Luther's effectual starting of the Reformation around 1517 needs to be seen against its background. The 'greatest European scholar of the 16th century' Desiderius Erasmus (1469-1536) advocated study of the Christian fathers instead of sterile scholasticism, was *highly* critical of abuses in the Catholic Church, edited a new Greek New Testament, and so 'encouraged the growing urge for reform, which found expression both in the Protestant Reformation and in the

---

[64] Jaki (1998) pp. 127ff; to be honest, Jaki is very critical of virtually everyone.
[65] Hailperin (1963) p. 141.

Catholic Counter-Reformation.'[66] His views on faith were not very different from Luther's, but unlike Luther he did *not* believe in state persecution to enforce theology and he *did* believe in the need for holy living - his background was from the group who gave us Thomas A Kempis' *The Imitation of Christ* in 1441 (the Brethren of the Common Life). In these two aspects (state persecution and holy living) he differed from the Lutherans, but agreed with the Anabaptists (whom he admired). Some of these - like Balthasar Hubmaier (1485-1528), Hans Denck (1495-1527) and Menno Simons (1496-1561) - were scholars, and many were persecuted both by Catholics and Reformers for their plain New Testament beliefs.[67] We say this to avoid, as we consider the great Reformers Luther and Calvin, the common myth that Luther was either the first or most radical critic of wrong Catholic popular practices and doctrines.

Certainly, however, Luther begins his *Commentary on Genesis* by saying that before he himself attempted it:

> there has not been anyone in the church who has explained everything in the chapter with adequate skill.[68]

Fortunately, although he thought Augustine and Ambrose had 'childish ideas', Origen talked 'twaddle', Averoes was 'silly' and 'stupid' etc, his own views are now available. His usual main authorities, Augustine, Hilary and Lyra, are all proclaimed not literal enough – and in particular Luther advocates six literal days of creation about 6000 years ago. He claims: 'Moses wrote that uneducated men might have clear accounts of creation'. In some ways one may sympathise. Some of the wilder flights of allegory are far fetched, and we ourselves believe that the account is fundamentally about the creation of the world. But Luther's approach contains two basic problems. The first is that the 'uneducated man' in the Genesis writer's mind was a Jew saturated in the Jewish language and culture and reading Hebrew, not a German peasant listening to a translation. The second is that Luther himself cannot possibly do this consistently.

---

[66] See *Britannica* for these and other comments in this section.
[67] See eg the classic Broadbent (1931).
[68] Luther, Martin (Tr J Pelikan, 1959-86) p. 3.

Take, for example, the serpent. Luther says:

> Moses makes mention of the serpent only and not of Satan. Although these statements are ever so veiled, nevertheless, through the enlightenment of the Holy Spirit, the holy fathers and prophets readily saw that this was no an affair of the serpent, but that in the serpent there was that spirit, the enemy of innocent natures.....

Aha! Apparently the uneducated man needs the holy Fathers to grasp this bit. However:

> Although I said.. that God is speaking with the serpent in a way that is specifically aimed at Satan... yet I do not agree that, like Augustine whom Lyra follows, we should apply allegorically to Satan those statements which fit well with the nature of the Serpent.

The uneducated man *also* needs Luther to help him know *which* bits of the Early Fathers to believe and which not. God speaks to the serpent who does not understand him, and (says Luther) 'the serpent was punished because of the sin of the devil who had misused the serpent' – which is a bit like punishing a victim of a mugging or rape. What is the 'uneducated man' in any case to make of this when Genesis plainly and specifically says that the serpent was smart? Anyway, Luther is not sure whether the angels fell on the second or third day, but Satan apparently fell with them from the 'heavens' though 'whether the heavens at that time were finished or still crude and unfinished' we don't know. This is an amazing mixture of the esoteric deduction (ie it was Satan, not just a walking snake) and crass literalism (perhaps heaven still had the scaffolding up). Whatever would the 'uneducated man' make of it? Whatever would he make of Luther's novel assertion that the 'tree of knowledge of good and evil' was actually a whole *grove of trees*, as was the 'tree of life' with diverse medicinal properties to promote eternal youth?

Luther says that 'on the day' in 2:5 'is to be understood in the sense of indefinite time' – presumably to the confusion of the 'uneducated man'. So what reason does Luther give for savaging the views of his heroes Augustine and Hilary on the *six* days? Basically that the account contains the language of time – seemingly missing the point that if the main metaphor used *were* in terms of days, then one would expect the language of time to be used. Anyway, according to Luther, Eve was made near the end of the sixth day, whilst God gave Adam the command not to eat of the tree (or grove?) 'early on the seventh day'. Luther does not explain why the sequence in Genesis Ch. 2 (presumably written for the 'uneducated man') is entirely different, both from the creation order in Genesis 1 and from that in Luther's own reconstruction. Paradise in Genesis is (he says) literal, but that referred to by Christ on the cross 'is an allegorical paradise'. On the story of Eve made from Adam's side, he exclaims (several times): 'what could sound more like a fairy tale?' – but enjoins us to believe it literally anyway. This is the whole problem with his approach. If it suits him then reason is used (eg to deduce that Satan speaks and not the snake) – but if not then we have to believe the irrational anyway. To grasp some bits the holy fathers are essential for the uneducated man, on other bits the holy Fathers are proclaimed childish and stupid.

Luther's account is similarly muddled over the Sabbath. In chapter two he notes that it says God rested, but Jesus in John 5:17 says 'My Father works until now'. Luther argues that God no longer *creates*, but still *maintains*. He gives the 'uneducated man', however, no way to avoid seeing the seventh day as extending (as Jesus implies) until now, and no explanation of how thorns, thistles and bugs appeared only after the fall without constituting 'creation' rather than maintenance. He also notes Jesus' words that 'the Sabbath was made for man' – without reconciling the implication he sees in Genesis that God did it purely for himself.

Luther, then, produced perhaps the most literalistic commentary up to that time. Though the oft quoted remark of his that Copernicus was 'a fool' is actually based on hearsay[69], it is entirely in keeping with his approach, language, and the way he speaks of the sun and stars in his commentary. The Munich Professor of Systematic Theology, Wolfhart Pannenberg claims that as late as 1707 Lutheran theologians in Germany rejected Copernicanism on biblical grounds.[70] Overall, Luther's literalism was adamant if patchy.

The other best known Reformer, John Calvin, was rather more measured in his approach. On the one hand he clearly rejects

---

[69] See Russell (1985) p. 42, Goodwin & Russell (1991) p. 67.
[70] Pannenberg (1993) p. 53.

Augustine's idea of things created all at once, and attacks Origen.[71] On the other hand, he repeatedly asserts that Moses 'does not speak in a philosophical manner' (ie what we would mean by a scientific manner).[72] He is highly critical of those who 'embrace by faith' a view which suggests (contrary to science) that there are really 'waters above the heavens'.[73] Moses had no intention to teach us science, says Calvin sternly, and:

> He who would learn astronomy, and other recondite arts, let him go elsewhere.[74]

Moses is simply speaking in terms of common appearance not of science, he is just referring to ordinary clouds. In our terms, Calvin is saying that science should not be done from Scripture. Thus eg the moon is the 'lesser light' although we now know its light is reflected and it is smaller than saturn. Calvin applies his principle to astronomy, but on the other hand, seems not really to follow it regarding the 'days' (though he seems to make no great play of 24 hours). We are left on the whole with a mixture – with rather less depth than Augustine (whom actually Calvin usually followed in theology). The new age of science however, was now beginning to dawn.

Interpreting Genesis 1-3 in the Age of Geology

What was the effect on biblical interpretation of the various stages of development in geology that started in the last part of the seventeenth century? In a later section we will find that a lot of Christians were involved in the actual science at all stages, but what biblical interpretations were involved?

John Wesley, who died in 1791, could not really be blamed for still believing the world was 6,000 years old. It was really by about the start of the nineteenth century that geology had concluded that the great thickness of strata indicated an ancient earth. During the period (say) 1819-1833 there was still one school which believed that over long time periods there had

---

[71] Calvin Commentary on Genesis Tr King (1969) p. 78 & 114.

[72] King (1969) pp. 79, 84, 120.

[73] King (1969) p. 80.

[74] King (1969) p. 80.

been successive inundation's - the last could be identified with Noah's flood. By around 1833 mainstream geology had concluded that:

1. Strata were laid down by water (aqueous) and molten rock (igneous) over long time periods.
2. Periodically there were cataclysms marking off one major series from another.
3. Within and particularly between series particular fossil types were associated with particular periods.
4. There was a succession of fossil types – with major orders of animals appearing successively – but no evidence of evolution.

In the period 1833-1855 all the major strata series known today were established.[75] It should be noted that this was all *before* Darwin published the *Origin of Species* in 1859, and that virtually *all* the geologists involved rejected evolution – including Charles Lyell. There was *no* sense in which evolution was assumed by those who constructed the geological column, and, as we will show in a later section, some of the key geologists were evangelical Christians.

So how did Bible-believing Christian leaders react to geology and the geologists in their midst? Four basic alternatives were on offer:

1. **A Flood Geology:** Put forward an alternative geology with all or most strata ascribed to one flood, so that a young earth (c 6000 years) can be kept.
2. **The Age-day View:** The 'days' were taken to be long time periods.
3. **The Gap theory:** That between Gen 1:1 and Gen 1:2 there was actually a long gap (into which dinosaurs etc could fit), then 'the earth *became* without form and void'. The rest of Genesis 1 describes its reconstitution.
4. **The Framework View:** Basically following Augustine & co in a belief that the 'days' are purely schematic.

The first of these was taken up in books by the so-called U.K. 'Scriptural Geologists' listed in Table 1 below.

---

[75] The Ordovician was *named* later, but this was a nomenclature dispute.

Table 1: UK 'Scriptural Geologists'	
1822 1825	**Granville Penn (1761-1844):** *Comparative Estimate of Mineral and Mosaic Geologists (2 eds)*
1826	**George Bugg (1769-1851)** *Scriptural Geology (1826-7)*
1829	**Andrew Ure (1778-1857)** *A New System of Geology*
1833	**Frederick Nolan (1784-1864)** *Analogy of Revelation and Science Established*
1834	**Henry Cole (1792?-1858)** *Popular Geology Subversive of Divine Revelation*
1837	**Thomas Gisbourne (1758-1846)** *Considerations on Modern Theories of Geology*
1837	**Samuel Best (1802-1873)** *After Thoughts on Reading Dr Buckland's Bridgewater Treatise*
1833 1837	**George Fairholme (1789-1846)** *General View of the Geology of Scripture* *Mosaic Deluge*
1837	**William Rhind (1797-1874)** *Elements of Geology and Physical Geography*
1838	**James Mellor Brown (1796-1867)** *Reflection on Geology*
1838	**John Murray (1786?-1851)** *A Portrait of Geology*
1838	**George Young (1777-1848)** *Scriptural Geology*
1838 -44 1849	**William Cockburn (1774?-1858)** *Letters etc* *A New System of Geology*

When the *Geological Society* was founded in 1809, its emphasis was on empirical research rather than overall theory. As people realised in the 1820's and particularly in the 1830's that actually a geological consensus was now being reached, some reacted by rejecting it and looking for an alternative. Flood-geology was essentially a phenomenon of the 1830's, at a time when the full evidence for the new geological consensus could easily not be known by figures who were (as most of them were) slightly out of date with their mugged-up science.

But how did Evangelicals in the 1820's and 30's react? Support was given Scriptural Geology by the Calvinist editor of the weekly paper *The Record* - whose dour controversial tone was deeply distasteful to many Evangelicals.[76] Its attitude was abhorred by major evangelical leaders like Simeon, Sumner and Henry Venn.[77] Sumner himself, regarded by Toon as one of the few whose evangelical credentials were above reproach, castigated Ure without hesitation.[78] In any event, a modern study can state: 'the following of the Scriptural geologists, for all their vociferousness and the plenitude of their tracts, was small and consistently so.'[79] Mortensen, who is highly sympathetic to these 'Scriptural Geologists' in his recent PhD thesis, nevertheless shows how by 1850 (note: nearly a decade before Darwin published his book on evolution) *all* the major orthodox commentaries had abandoned any support for such schema.[80] Ronald Numbers' monumental book identifies only the *very* obscure Lord brothers as advocating flood geology in the U.S.A. after 1850 (Lord's magnum opus being in 1851).[81]

Actually, Paul Marston's own PhD thesis (Sec 6.2) shows that, in the crucial 1820's and 1830's, mainstream geology was accepted by both Anglican and non-Anglican Evangelicalism, as well as the High Church – ie all those in the church who regarded the whole Bible as inspired. This point is important, for it seems not always to have been well understood even in some modern historical works.[82] In this period, the mouthpiece of the moderate evangelical Anglicanism of Simeon, Wilberforce, Sumner, and the so called 'Clapham' group central to British Evangelicalism, was the *Christian Observer*. Though it would print letters from 'Scriptural Geologists' (and even from the more extreme Hutchinsonians who rejected Newton), its editorial line consistently supported mainstream geology and the position of clerics like Conybeare and Sedgwick who were geologists. On the other hand it equally clearly rejected any suggestion (such as that made by Powell at Oxford) that the

---

[76] See G R Balleine (1908), p 163.
[77] F K Brown(1961), p 129; A Ashwell (1880-2) p. 219; E Stock (1899-1916) 4, p. 60.
[78] See P Toon (1979) p. 4.
[79] J D Yule (1976), p 328.
[80] Mortenson (1996).
[81] Numbers (1992) p. 28.
[82] Eg Thackray & Morrell (1981) which exaggerates broad church influence and minimises the significant evangelical contribution in science.

Bible might contain historical or scientific mistakes. Amongst Church of Scotland Evangelicals, key leaders like Thomas Chalmers, and geologist Hugh Miller, were equally clearly committed to the value of geology. Amongst leading non-Anglican (or 'Dissenter') Evangelicals, John Pye Smith wrote his book *On The Relation Between the Holy Scriptures and Some Parts of Geological Science* in 1839. His acceptance of mainstream geology was continuous (his correspondence with geologist John Phillips is extant in Oxford and we have read it) and a final version was issued just after his death in 1854.

The most common views amongst leading Evangelicals between 1815 and 1859 (when Darwin published his book) were the age-day and gap theory. The exact origins of these two views are hard to discover. As we have seen, the idea of the 'days' as millennia was very early in Christian and Jewish thinking, but there would have been no possibility to associate them with *geological* ages until geology reached this point in the eighteenth century. The age-day theory can actually be traced back to Buffon in *Epoques de la Nature* (1778), but was influentially revived by the Evangelical G S Faber in his *Genius and Object* (1823), and had its most illustrious pre-1859 geological advocate in Hugh Miller in his *The Testimony of the Rocks* (1857). Miller actually portrays the days as visionary or prophetic - but argues that they are also indicative (with some caveats) of time periods in history.

The gap-theory is traced by Ramm to some figures in the seventeenth century,[83] and work in progress by Michael Roberts may in due course produce further evidence of its early occurrence.[84] In the nineteenth century it owed its popularity to Chalmers in T*he Evidence and Authority of the Christian Revelation* (1817), to John Pye Smith's *On the Relation between the Holy Scriptures and Certain Parts of Geological Science* (1839) (and in later works like G H Pember's *Earth's Earliest Ages* (1876)). Influential geological advocates were Buckland in *Geology and Mineralogy Considered With Reference to Natural Theology* (1836) - supported by high church scholar Pusey. Amongst the evangelical geologists, in America Hitchcock

---

[83] B Ramm, *Op Cit* p 172.
[84] A paper was presented to the CiS conference in Autumn 1997.

supported it, and in Britain Sedgwick also tended towards it though later was more wary of committal.[85]

Variants of the age-day and the gap-theory dominated Evangelicalism in the years before Darwin. Two other ideas, however, caused reaction without achieving popularity as systems. First, in J H Kurtz's *The Bible and Astronomy* (1842) a form of gap theory was combined with the idea that the six days were visions given to Moses rather than intended to have any real reference to time periods. Secondly, in 1857 the evangelical naturalist P H Gosse published his *Omphalos*. The word means 'navel', and Gosse drew attention to the obvious fact that if Adam was created directly then he did not need a navel as he had no mother - yet surely God would have created him *with* a navel. In other words, Adam, as an instantaneous mature creation, bore marks of a history which did not in fact occur. All of what we have called type-ii miracles actually involve creating an apparent history. Thus e.g. changing water into wine gives it an apparent history of fermentation etc. Gosse carried this to its logical (or some thought ludicrous) conclusion, and suggested that all the fossils etc had been placed there as part of an apparent age - the earth might really be only a few thousand years old. Philosophically this is, of course, unassailable, it is just that (to most people) going to quite that extreme seems rather far fetched. On the other hand Gosse's point about apparent age does have to be taken into account for any creative acts performed as type-ii miracles.

Interpretation in an Evolutionary Age

There was, of course, some following for Lamarckian evolution before Darwin published his *Origin of Species* in 1859. It was, however, in a minority of scientists, mostly anatomists, and mostly deists or atheists. Darwin's theory brought evolution, with his mechanism of 'natural selection' into the mainstream. We are not here concerned either with the scientific merits (or otherwise) of evolution, or whether Evangelicals were 'right' in

---

[85] See Paul Marston, (1984) p 529 etc. Davis Young summarises such attempts at concord in (1992) p 55 etc and in (1987).

how they reacted. We are concerned here just with how it affected understanding of Genesis 1-3.

Basically, the same four pre-1859 understandings of the timescale were still available, but now a couple of them were subdivided:

1. **A Flood Geology:** An alternative geology with all or most strata ascribed to one flood, so that a young earth (c 6000 years) can be kept. Creation is instantaneous.

2. **The Age-day View:** The 'days' were taken to be long time periods. And
   either: (i) God created species instantaneously at points throughout geological history
   or: (ii) God created species through slow evolution

3. **The Gap theory:** That between Gen 1:1 and Gen 1:2 there was actually a long gap (into which dinosaurs etc could fit), then 'the earth *became* without form and void'. The rest of Genesis 1 describes its reconstitution. The new species were created instantaneously.

4. **The Framework View:** Basically following Augustine & co in a belief that the 'days' are purely schematic. Then
   either: (i) God created species instantaneously at points throughout geological history
   or: (ii) God created species through slow evolution

In a nutshell, all the versions of (2) – (4) were held by different evangelical leaders. The young-earth creationism of view (1), in contrast, was virtually absent between 1859 and 1920, whilst from 1920-1950 had few advocates and those it had were almost all Lutheran pastors or Seventh Day Adventists in America. It rose to its present comparative popularity only after the publication of *The Genesis Flood* (1961) by Henry Morris and John C Whitcomb. None of this is an issue of opinion but of incontrovertible fact, and the twentieth century part of it can be verified largely from Henry Morris' own writings.

In the period 1860-1910 there were some conservative theologians who rejected evolution (eg T R Birks (1810-1883) a Cambridge Professor and founder of the Evangelical Alliance) and a number who were open to it – but none advocated a young-earth. One can, of course, find the occasional eccentric even in this period. In England there was a flat earth society which gave A R Wallace some grief. In America, a book by a New York engineer claimed that a true biblical Baconianism would not reconstruct any kind of organic past for fossils which could not be seen, but just analyse them as bits of stone.[86] We can, however, find *no* leading figure amongst Evangelicals who advocated a literal six day original creation or a young earth.[87]

In our next section we will consider evangelical scientists, but here we note in the context of theologians that Morris' reconstruction of events is a strange mixture of fact and myth. He writes:

> As long as the scientists believed in creation, Christian leaders were quite content to believe in the inerrancy of Scripture and the literal historicity of the Biblical accounts of Creation and the Flood... But as soon as the scientists turned to evolution, theologians and church leaders in almost every denomination scurried in a hasty retreat to the old compromising types of exegesis used by early theologians, such as Origen and Augustine, in order to accommodate evolution and the geological ages in Genesis ...[88]

But Christian leaders before 1859 certainly did *not* take Genesis 'literally' in Morris' sense, and evolutionary theory was in no sense a watershed in the development of Biblical intepretation. Lamenting their failure to stand on the Word of God, Morris bewails that:

> Certain very popular religious leaders of the day who were believed to be orthodox Bible-believers, such as Frederick Farrar, James Orr, Charles Kingsley, and Henry Drummond, were tremendously influential in persuading rank-and-file Christians to accept theistic evolution. The same was true in the United States, where even such stalwarts as B.B.Warfield and A.H.Strong - known as strong defenders of the faith - capitulated to evolution.[89]

The only notable 'exceptions' cited by Morris are Spurgeon, Moody and Charles Hodge of Princeton. Spurgeon (1834-92) was a leading South London Baptist, a renowned preacher rather

---

[86] See Hovencamp (1978) ch. 8.
[87] Numbers (1992) fully backs up and much extends our own research.
[88] Morris (1984) p. 37.
[89] Morris (1984) p. 38.

than a theologian or profound thinker. He remained against evolution, yet in one review wrote:

> We look upon evolution as a questionable hypothesis. It is not yet an ascertained or acknowledged truth of science, and assuredly the time has not come to incorporate it with our faith in revelation.

Colin Russell, who cites this review, gives a more balanced view of Spurgeon's undoubted anti-Darwinism.[90] Moody was a mighty preacher, much used by God in British universities and elsewhere, but was neither theologian nor philosopher - and made no claim to be. Moody was a close friend of evolutionary apologist-theologian Henry Drummond, and also of R A Torrey of whom more presently.

Only the third of Morris' supposed 'exceptions', Charles Hodge, carries any real theological weight - and he was very influential on Calvinism of the whole period. Unfortunately Morris either has not read or totally misunderstands him. Hodge actually accepted a form of age-day theory, *emphatically* denying that the 'days' of Genesis must be literal and fully accepting orthodox geology. What of evolution? In his 1874 book *What is Darwinism?* he concluded 'it is atheism' - but this is misleading. He defined 'Darwinism' to include the three elements (i) evolution, (ii) natural selection, and (iii) rejection of design. Obviously if this third point is included in a *definition* of 'Darwinism', then Darwinism *is* atheism. But Hodge was quite clear that someone could believe in evolution by natural selection (like Asa Gray whom Hodge quotes in criticising Darwin) and still be a Christian though not a 'Darwinist' in Hodge's sense of that word. In other words, Hodge saw no particular problem in reconciling the purely scientific theory of evolution by natural selection with Christian faith.[91] What he then went on to argue was that Darwin and Wallace had in fact added to this system the metaphysical concept of 'pure chance' as an alternative agent to God. Unfortunately Hodge's use of terms has left many confused about his real position. G M Marsden in his interesting work on fundamentalism, left the definite impression that Hodge saw all evolution as

---

[90] Russell (1985) pp. 170-174.
[91] Hodge (1874) p. 48 etc. Hodge is totally explicit on these things.

incompatible with the Bible.[92] In actual fact Hodge's book shows clear sympathy with what Marsden presents as the most general view at the 1873 Evangelical Alliance in which Hodge participated. Some, like the respected evangelical theologian James McCosh, accepted evolution. Others thought it difficult to accept - though even then there was no apparent support for 'literal' recent creation in six days. Finally M B Anderson, in a popular speech, pointed out the two ways of using 'evolution' - either as God's method of development or as pure chance. Evolution, however, was not a 'verified law, but only a 'working hypothesis'. Hodge's later book said just the same. Untenable and untrue comments on Hodge's position are, however, rife amongst modern historians.

Morris is, however, correct in his assessment that major theologians of the period such as B B Warfield and A H Strong mainly moved to accept evolution. Moore and Livingstone add numerous other leading Evangelicals including A A Hodge, S Van Dyke, James McCosh, Landey Patton, W T Shedd, and a number of others. Their attitudes varied from basic acceptance to acknowledging its compatibility with Evangelicalism but questioning its inductive base (with good reason as we have seen!). Many distinguished evolution as part of science from the philosophy figures like Huxley and Tyndall might build on it.[93]

The next period involves the birth, from 1910-1915 of 'Fundamentalism'. The word arose as a nickname (in the 1920's) for those who contributed to a series of twelve volumes (later reissued as a four volume set) called *The Fundamentals,* edited by R A Torrey and A C Dixon. The essential points of fundamentalism were:

- The inspiration and error-free nature of the Bible.
- The virgin birth of Jesus.
- The sacrificial death of Christ – taking our sins on him.
- The bodily resurrection and ascension of Christ.
- That Jesus performed supernatural miracles in his ministry.

They were concerned to defend classic evangelical Christianity against the liberal ravages of 'Higher Criticism' of the Bible, but

---

[92] Marsden (1980) pp. 19-20.
[93] Eg A A Hodge (1890) Ch. viii.

they were *not* literalists in any modern sense. We have followed up all of those we can who wrote for *The Fundamentals,* and have been unable to find a single one who either took the 'days' literally or believed in a young earth.

R A Torrey (see below) thought belief in literal 'days' would show 'hopeless ignorance'. Baptist leader A C Dixon wrote against 'evolution' – but what he was attacking was Spencer and the Social Gospel. One biographer writes:

> Dixon upheld the possibility that Darwinian evolution could find a place in the Bible, with God as Evolver and evolution as his method of creation.[94]

What did the contributors, the real original 'Fundamentalists' believe? Morris cites two: Torrey himself (cf below) was a gap theorist and W Griffith Thomas an age-day theorist. Contributor C I Schofield put the gap theory into his famous reference Bible. Another contributor was prominent Southern Baptist theologian E Y Mullins (1860-1928) who elsewhere wrote:

> There is also a difference between the purely scientific and the philosophical conception of evolution, As a purely scientific theory it refers only to the facts of nature ... When a man turns his doctrine of evolution into materialism, monism or theism, it thereby ceases to be science and becomes philosophy.[95]

Could Richard Dawkins and Philip Johnson both please note! Another contributor was prophetic writer and linguist A C Gaebelein (1861-1945). Though 'literal' in places, he specifically believed the world millions of years old and adhered to the gap theory.[96] Another contributor, Melvin Grove Kyle, followed the orthodox geology of Professors Wright and Salisbury.[97] Another contributor, gynaecologist Howard A Kelly, indicated that, whilst believing in special creation of humankind, he was open to the possibility of "continuous sequence in the history of the lower creation."[98] Another contributor, renowned Bible teacher Campbell Morgan (1863-1945), was open to literal days, the age-day or (his own view)

---

[94] Brena M Meeham (1967) p. 54.
[95] Mullins (1905) p. 61.
[96] Eg Gaebelein (1913) Introduction.
[97] Kyle (1912).
[98] Cf Numbers (1992) p. 72.

the gap theory![99] Like another contributor (James M Gray (1851-1935) – President of Moody Institute) he enthused over Pember's version of the gap theory (which incidentally included pre-Adamite mankind).[100] Contributor George L Robinson, a Professor of Old Testament Literature, remarked:

> In order to accommodate it to human capacity, the whole picture is set in a framework of 'seven days'... the author intended to teach *order* rather than geology.[101]

One contributor, lawyer Philip Mauro, elsewhere wrote articles attacking evolution (which he associated with materialism) as incompatible with Christianity.[102] Mauro knew very little (and said very little) about science, but adopted the 'gap' theory in his popular book *Man's Day*.

The Fundamentals themselves contained two short articles that were anti evolution – one anonymous and the other by a total unknown (Henry Beach). Their main focus is, again, human evolution, they do not argue for 'literality'. Dyson Hague also attacks evolution, particularly human, but cites orthodox geologists Dawson and Etheridge. Four renowned scholars and professors who wrote for *The Fundamentals* were explicitly open to the possibility that macro-evolution *was* the means God used to create: Princeton Professor B B Warfield (1851-1921), Glasgow Professor James Orr (1844-1913), Oberlin Professor G F Wright (1838-1921), and the Baptist Professor A H Strong (1836-1921). Both Orr and Wright expressed their openness to the possibility of some version of macro-evolution in long and learned articles published in *The Fundamentals*. What we have here are the leading theologically conservative Presbyterian, Free Church of Scotland, Congregational and Baptist scholars of their age – the flower of early Fundamentalist scholarship. All were open to organic macro-evolution; none saw any conflict with their faith. All this is simple fact, yet we find in young-earth 'Scientific Creationist' material statements like:

---

[99] Morgan (1947) pp. 14-16.
[100] Gray (1920) p. 15: Pember (1876).
[101] Robinson (1906) p. 1.
[102] Mauro (1922).

Fundamentalists supported a biblical creationism based on a literal reading of the Holy Bible.[103]

This is just demonstrably untrue. Sadly, it is typical of the demonstrably untrue statements (on this and other topics) that litter such literature, and are taken by unsuspecting readers as truth. If an author chooses to claim that all the major conservative Evangelicals and early Fundamentalists were 'really' theological liberals in disguise that is one thing, but to ascribe to them views they plainly never held is another.

Three further points can be made. One is that the view of evolution prevalent in the scientific community in this period was more Lamarckian than Darwinian[104] – and it was this they were open to.[105] The second is that generally they wanted to make some kind of exception for human development. The third is that they were conscious that *some* scientists were illegitimately using Darwinism to exclude design. Wright (like Hodge & co) is adamant against these:

> By no legitimate reasoning can Darwinism be made to exclude design. Indeed, if it should be proved that species have developed from others of a lower order, as varieties are supposed to have done, it would strengthen rather than weaken the standard argument from design.[106]

The Rise of Young-earthism

Many people today who adopt the American brand of young-earthism (ie that the world is about 6,000 years old and made in six literal days) do not realise what are its roots. They presume that they are acting in the general tradition of Evangelicals or of Fundamentalists. This is simply not so.

Around the turn of the century there was, however, one group that was highly critical of the Fundamentalists. A self educated Baptist farmer William Miller (1782-1849) had raised a big following with predictions that Christ would return in 1844. The Adventist church (formed in 1845) transmuted this into a belief that some kind of new investigation had started in heaven

---

[103] J N Moore in Selvidge (1984) p. 120.
[104] Cf Bowlby (1992) – also acknowledged in Numbers (1992) p. 33.
[105] See eg Orr *The Bible on Trial* (4th Edn) p. 219.
[106] *The Fundamentals*, iv, p. 77. Numbers (1992) treats Wright in detail.

around that time. Its main prophetess, Ellen Gould White (1827-1915) had little formal education, but was a lady with intelligence and fervour. A major part of this new post-1844 situation was to be the re-establishment of the Saturday rather than Sunday as the Christian Sabbath – a reform she believed prophesied by Isaiah. White accepts the heritage of eg Wycliff, Huss, Luther, the Pilgrim Fathers and Wesley – but is highly critical of evangelical leaders in her own day who have not accepted the prophesied Sabbath reform. Those, for example, who mix temperance work with Sunday observance 'disguise poison by mixing it with wholesome food'. In her book *The Great Controversy* (1888, 1907, 1911), scholars are suspect:

> The truths most plainly revealed in the Bible have been involved in doubt and darkness by learned men, who, with a pretence of great wisdom teach that the Scriptures have a mystical, a secret, spiritual meaning, not apparent in the language employed. These men are false teachers... The language of the Bible should be explained according to its obvious meaning unless a symbol or figure is employed.' (Ch. xxxvii)

Those so castigated cannot be liberals (who say no such thing) but Evangelicals. Learning is, indeed, unnecessary, perhaps even dangerous:

> Humble men, armed with the Word of truth alone, withstood the attacks of men of learning, who, with surprise and anger, found their eloquent sophistry powerless against the simple straightforward reasoning of men who were versed in the Scriptures rather than in the subtleties of the schools. (Ch. xxvi)

The reason theologians 'have no clearer understanding of God's Word' is 'they close their eyes to truths they do not wish to practice.' A grim future is predicted for American Protestants as they reject the Sabbath truth for satanic Spiritualism and suppression of freedom. As for science:

> To many, scientific research has become a curse... even the greatest minds, if not guided by the Word of God in their research, become bewildered in their attempts to investigate the relations of science and revelation. (Ch. xxxii)

Elsewhere she claims that:

I have been shown that without Bible history, geology can prove nothing.[107]

In saying 'shown' she refers to the 'vision' she had when she was:

Carried back to the creation and was shown that the first week, in which God performed the work of creation on six days and rested on the seventh, was just like every other week.[108]

The perspective of this vision determined her view of geology:

Geology has been thought to contradict the literal interpretation of the Mosaic record of the creation.[109]

The gap theory and the age-day theory both 'destroy the force of the Word of God' and 'do violence to His word'. So she adds:

Each of these periods Inspiration declares to have been a day consisting of evening and morning like every other day since that time.

She gives us an example of geology 'guided by the Word of God' in *Patriarchs and Prophets* (1890, 1913), saying that at the time of the Flood:

Immense forests were buried. These have since been changed to coal, forming the extensive coal beds that now exists and also yielding large quantities of oil. The coal and oil frequently ignite and burn beneath the surface of the earth. Thus rocks are heated, limestone is burned, and iron ore melted. The action of water upon the lime adds fury to the immense heat. As the fire and water come in contact with ledges of rock and ore, there are loud explosions, and volcanic eruptions follow.

This is the kind of stuff she put up in opposition to the learning of Evangelicals and early Fundamentalists who were seen by her as rejecting the post-1844 prophesied restoration of the Sabbath.

How her word, though, must have struck a young Seventh Day Adventist like George McCready Price (1870-1963). True he had little formal education and no training in either science or geology[110] – but the prophetess had said that all he needed was the Bible and enthusiasm. True the unanimous ranks of scholars

---

[107] Cited in White (1929) p. 227.
[108] White (1864) p. 91.
[109] White (1903) p. 128-9.
[110] Cf Numbers (1992) Ch. 5 or Clarke (1966) for a wealth of background.

and leaders amongst Bible-believing Evangelicals and Fundamentalists believed the earth old and the days non-literal – but the prophetess had in any case pronounced them apostate as they rejected the prophesied restoration of the truth of the Sabbath. At times, indeed, Price was almost seduced by evolutionary creationism – but each time was saved by prayer and re-reading the words of the prophetess.[111] He even speaks of:

> Our faith in the simple Bible narrative, supplemented by the writings of Mrs E G White.[112]

His geological views were arrived at before any study of the rocks, on the basis that orthodox geology was crucial to evolution and evolution was wicked. In 1902 Price published his first anti-evolution book, in 1906 (whilst working as a handyman) a book identifying geology as the weakest link in evolution, and in 1913 a new system of geology made comprehensive in his 1923 magnum opus *The New Geology*. Price was fundamentally an 'armchair geologist', but all the work of the previous century of geologists was reinterpreted as due to the one Flood. The seven days – crucial to the Sabbath for Seventh Day Adventists – were indeed literal. Price argued that if a person:

> does not believe that there ever was a real Creation at some definite time in the past, how can we expect him to observe the Sabbath as a memorial of that event, which in his view never occurred?[113]

In his books, however, Price generally tends to focus more on the supposed impossibility of orthodox geology, and does not much emphasise the implications of his literality. A lot of the myth about development of geology which still lurks in books today was created by Archibald Geikie and transmuted by Price. It is hard to say which is the least accurate of the two.

In the early years Price's system made little headway. It was predictably savaged by contemporary Fundamentalists.[114] Morris himself makes the extraordinary admission:

---

[111] See Lindberg and Numbers (1986) p. 400, Numbers (1992) p. 88.

[112] Cited in Numbers (1992) p. 88.

[113] Cited in Numbers (1992) p. 87.

[114] See Lindberg and Numbers (1986), Numbers (1992).

Almost the only writers to advocate literal recent creationism during this period, however, were to be found amongst the Lutherans and Seventh Day Adventists – no doubt partly because their respective founders, Martin Luther and Ellen G. White, had taught six-day creationism and a worldwide flood.[115]

Luther liked literalism so that the 'uneducated man' would not need the help of the church scholars (whom he thought apostate) to understand it; Ellen G White liked literalism so that 'Humble men, armed with the Word of truth alone' would not need the help of Evangelical or Fundamentalist scholars (whom she thought apostate) to understand it. In any event, Morris then lists Adventists (H W Clark, F L Marsh and E S Booth, etc) all of whom were taught by Price, and then cites Lutherans (Byron Nelson, Graebner, Rehwinkel, etc), none of them scientists, who based their views on their sixteenth-century founder and also on Price. One of the very few with scientific training who accepted Price's theories in the mid-1920's was D J Whitney (1884-1964). Morris judges that from his letters:

Whitney was irascible and highly impatient with anyone who disagreed with him about almost anything.[116]

Price's appeal, according to Morris, was to fellow Adventists under the sway of their prophetess, unscientifically trained Lutherans, and the occasional 'irascible' individual (perhaps a euphemism for 'bigot') with some science background.

On the famous 1925 'Tennessee Monkey Trial' we have consulted not only secondary sources but the memoirs of chief participants.[117] The trial was not actually even about evolution but about *human* evolution.[118] William Jennings Bryan, a liberal champion of the rights of woman and workers, was concerned at the 'dehumanising' potential of current versions of human evolution. His *Memoirs* show his focussing not on *The Origin of Species* but on Darwin's *The Descent of Man* with is aggressive naturalism about human descent. The issue was not whether

---

[115] Morris (1984) p. 60.
[116] Morris (1984) p. 105.
[117] Bryan's own *Memoirs* plus defence lawyers Darrow (1934) and Hays (1937), defendant Scopes & Presley (1967). We will put some materials on our website.
[118] Numbers (1992) p. 72.

Scopes should be free to hold such views, but whether as a paid state employee he should be state funded to peddle implicit atheism whilst Christians had to build and fund their own schools to teach theism. Actually, Bryan himself held an age-day theory and believed the earth was very old, and even had no general problem with evolution. Though he was, of course, less of a scholar, his position in objecting to purely naturalistic human evolution hardly differs from (say) McCosh[119] or Orr[120] and indeed most other Evangelical/Fundamentalist evolutionary creationists. Morris himself accepts that Bryan was an age-day theorist who rejected Price and accepted orthodox geological time scales.[121] The thinly disguised account in the play *Inherit the Wind*[122] is, of course, fairly cliched drama and totally inaccurate history.

Here is a list of all the various figures *identified by Morris himself* as key to fundamentalism and 'creationism' in this time, together with his own descriptions of them in italics:

1.R A Torrey (1856-1928)

'*A highly successful evangelist*' and '*one leading figure*' in the Fundamentalist movement, his book '*served as one of the key "textbooks" motivating the fundamentalist movement.*' Torrey once remarked that someone could 'believe thoroughly in the absolute infallibility of the Bible and still be an evolutionist of a certain type.'[123] He also actually stated that anyone who tries to insist that the 'days' of Genesis must be literal:

> displays a hopeless ignorance of the Bible. Anyone who is at all familiar with the Bible and the Bible usage of words knows that the word "day" is... frequently used of a period of time of an entirely undefined length.[124]

Ironically, in view of these strong words, Torrey reputedly took the infant Henry M Morris in his arms in 1919 and prayed that

---

[119] McCosh (1872) p. 45.
[120] See eg the 4th Edn of *The Bible Under Trial* p. 220.
[121] Morris (1984) p. 66.
[122] By J Lawrence and R E Lee – we have seen both the 1960 film with Spencer Tracey and a later version with Kirk Douglas.
[123] Cited in Numbers (1992) p. 39.
[124] Torrey (1907) ch, 4.

the Lord himself would use him in His service.[125] Torrey himself accepted the orthodox geology of Dana under whom he studied, and was a gap-theory creationist. He also followed earlier evangelical teaching on the existence of pre-Adamite mankind.

2. W B Riley (1861-1947):

He was *'one of the most outspoken fundamentalists and creationists of the period'* and *'a key personage in the fundamentalist revival.'* Riley was an age-day creationist who asserted that there was not:

> an intelligent fundamentalist who claims that the earth was made six thousand years ago, and the Bible never taught nay such thing.[126]

3. H Rimmer (1890-1952)

'The most widely known creationist of this period.' He was *'recognised by fundamentalists as the greatest Christian apologist of his generation.'* Rimmer was a gap-theory creationist, believing Noah's flood only regional, although he did also (inconsistently) refer favourably to Price.

4. W H Griffith Thomas (1861-1924)

He was *'another key leader of the fundamentalist movement... a scholarly writer and speaker, publishing many outstanding volumes of biblical and apologetics studies...'* Thomas was an age-day creationist, believing in a local flood, and he recommends Dawson and McCosh.[127]

5. I Brown

'Perhaps the most godly, gracious Christian gentleman I ever met, as well as one of the finest Bible teachers and creationist scientists.' Brown was a gap-theory creationist.

6. Carl Schwarze

'Obviously a fine scientist and also a fundamentalist...' Schwarze was a gap-theory creationist.

7. L Allen Highley

'Another fundamentalist... a very gracious Christian gentleman.' Highley was a gap-theory creationist.

---

[125] Morris (1984) p. 58.
[126] Cited in Numbers (1992) p. 45.
[127] Thomas (1946) pp. 25-35.

Obviously Morris is excluding from his list anyone who was Fundamentalist and believed in evolution, but even if we accept *his* selection *NOT ONE* of them gave credence to any young-earth literal-day scheme. This was not because it was unknown to them. Indeed, as Ramm asserted in his famous 1955 book, Price and Whitney sent a stream of articles to mainstream Christian magazines – though those Ramm cites as actually having swallowed the system are the Lutherans and Seventh Day Adventists cited by Morris. What one does find is reference to Price from those who actually accept the gap or age-day theory, and seem unaware that his system radically differs.

In Britain, the main forum for discussion of such issues between evangelical theologians and scientists was the *Victoria Institute*, and we have studied the minutes of its annual meetings. R L Numbers describes it during this period as a:

stronghold of liberal Evangelicalism and theistic evolution.'[128]

Now if here the word 'liberal' simply means 'open minded, not prejudiced' (*Concise Oxford Dictionary*) this is true. But if 'liberal' is meant *theologically* it is totally misleading. Those in the Victoria Institute at this time were doyens of British Conservative Evangelicalism, in the tradition of Wesley, Simeon, Sumner, Chalmers, Wilberforce, James Orr and the Fundamentalists. In the UK there was, of course, a tradition of evangelical scholarship, and no particular reason to believe or need the yokel with a translation, or the prophetess with a vision, to be as well able to construct a theology of Genesis as the Hebrew scholar. Nonconformity in the shape of the Open Brethren movement (which was strong at this time) valued scholarship no less than the Anglican establishment.

In 1914 E W Maunder summarised the then current views of Genesis 1 for the Victoria Institute – noting that recent creation was believed 'at one time' but no one now accepts it. In this period there was discussion for and against evolution – but no young-earthism. In 1924 (pp. 97-116) and 1925 (pp. 167-183) George McCready Price himself presented two papers.[129] He met with a mixture of polite British incredulity and hostility.

---

[128] Numbers (1992) p. 140.
[129] Numbers (1992) p. 142 says he went to every meeting he could in 1924-28.

Another flood-geology paper was presented in 1929, after which it sank into total oblivion – Price's own subscription lapsed in 1930. In 1927 engineer Sir John Ambrose Fleming became President and with ornithologist Douglas Dewar argued against evolution[130] whilst others argued for. No one advocated young-earth flood geology. In 1932 the *Evolution Protest Movement* began. Its founder/President was Fleming, called by Morris '*one of the century's foremost scientists, but also a strong creationist.*' Fleming accepted orthodox geology and the existence of pre-Adamite mankind. The EPM member called by Morris '*the most prolific creationist writer in England*' was ornithologist Douglas Dewar. Dewar was a gap-theorist, rejected flood geology, and also wrote:

> I see no harm in the theory of evolution in the fullest sense being adopted as an alternative hypothesis to that of creation, but I consider it suicidal to adopt evolution as a creed, to distort facts to cause them to conform to it... Dr W R Thompson well says:... "The fundamental difficulties about the theory of Evolution are, in fact, not theological, but rational and experimental."[131]

Dewar would have abhorred Morris-type creationism. Morris accepts that virtually the only 'Britisher' in the period to accept young-earth creationism was the obscure Major E C Wren whose style was '*marked by pungency and impatience... much like that of D J Whitney.*'[132]

This remained true into the 1950's. The Victoria Institute had members who were evolutionary creationists and also had in R E D Clarke a man who rejected evolution but thought Price's flood geology both absurd and less scientific than evolution. In the Victoria Institute, as in the Cambridge Conservative Evangelical circles where Roger Foster became a Christian in the early 1950's, young-earthism simply did not exist. This was true as the age of Rendle Short, R E D Clark and P J Wiseman led into that of Oliver Barclay, F F Bruce, Douglas Spanner and (an article in 1961) R J Berry. Some of these we have been (and are) privileged to count as friends. Growing up in British

---

[130] Eg Dewar (1938).

[131] Dewar (1938) p. 205.

[132] Numbers (1992) presents the same picture, though sometimes muddles up 'Conservative Evangelicalism' with anti-evolutionism.

Conservative Evangelicalism in this whole period, there was debate between pro and anti-evolution – but no one espoused a young earth.

We are less familiar with the American developments. Of key interest is Bernard Ramm's famous 1955 book in which he expresses incredulity and some nervousness about Price – but is secure in the overwhelming consensus of conservative scholarship which differs on the extent of evolution but accepts mainstream geology. For details of American developments, however, the reader may refer to Ron Numbers' book.

In any event, in 1961 came the publication of *The Genesis Flood* by the Baptist engineer Henry M Morris and the Lutheran pastor John C Whitcomb. It is virtually a straight copy of Price's 1923 *New Geology* – and Morris himself has, of course, acknowledged the debt. The only real addition was a rejection of the new radiometric dating methods. Through this book flood-geology entered the mainstream of evangelical thought. In Britain the faltering Evolution Protest Movement – its eccentric secretary A G Tilney hardly even noticing it – abandoned its previous position for this new one. 'Creationist' groups started in Britain, America, Australia etc. Books produced since by its advocates have varied in levels of understanding (scientific, linguistic and theological) and in tone, but all give the same basic message. Again, we do not wish here to repeat what Numbers chronicles in detail.[133]

The young-earth approach of Henry Morris has some bizarre implications. Having shown that virtually all those he accepts as spiritual Christian leaders between 1859 and 1940 were gap-theory, age-day or evolutionary creationists, he elsewhere proclaims all such ideas to be equivalent to evolution which he says is inherently atheistic and 'pictures God as a sadistic ogre'.[134] Having accepted that all these evangelical leaders saw no inconsistency in interpreting the Bible in harmony with their views, he nevertheless maintains that theories like the age-day theory are in 'flagrant contradiction' with Genesis, and that he has 'conclusive proof, that the 'days' were literal and speaks of

---

[133] Numbers (1992).
[134] Morris (1976) p. 54.

'pervasive theological apostasy amongst the major evangelical figures of the late nineteenth century.'[135] What Morris implies, therefore is that all the spiritual giants of the church over a period of a century or more followed a sadistic ogre, believed in theories in flagrant contradiction to the Bible and were theologically apostate. Only with the light of his own movement (mainly post 1961) has the self-evident biblical truth been re-established. Young-earther Bowden is similarly happy to apply a test for who is a 'Bible believer' which would exclude most of the major early church figures and Christian leaders throughout history – including virtually all nineteenth century evangelicals and all the early Fundamentalists.[136] The reader - Christian or non-Christian - will have to make his or her own assessment of the plausibility of such extreme claims.

Conclusion

The aim of this section was firstly to reduce the scepticism of those who regard biblical Christianity as 'really' teaching a flat earth with a hard sky, which can be rescued only with desperate 'reinterpretation'. But it was also aimed at those who may be attracted by the seeming plausibility of the young-earth creationist claim to represent historic Bible-believing Christianity. What have we shown?

1. The earliest Jewish and Christian understanding identified 'allegorical' and 'literal' meanings, but the literal meaning was also taken to have some symbolic and metaphorical language in it.

2. The later Christian Fathers, Celtic Church, Middle Ages, Scholastic period etc, contained a strong stream of non-literal understanding, with a view of the 'days' as non-literal a very strong element in this.

3. After the coming of geological science, evangelical Christian leaders from 1820-1920 reached a strong consensus on an ancient earth made in non-literal days. This extended in the period of Fundamentalism and up until at least the 1950's.

---

[135] Morris (1988) pp. 37-38.
[136] Bowden (1998) p. 41.

4. After 1859, a number of key Evangelicals and early Fundamentalist scholars were open to evolution as the means God used to create.

Some of these details were put in our *Reason and Faith*, giving rise to some very silly comments from some critics. One proclaimed that Basil, Augustine and Origen all took Genesis in a 'sensible literal sense' – a claim which is (in the critic's meaning of 'sensible') debatable for Basil and demonstrably untrue for the other two.[137] Another critic said that those open to evolution were 'just a glitch' in the general realisation amongst Bible-based Christians that evolution was a doctrine of Satan. Yet, as we have seen, *the* leading scholarly Fundamentalists from the Presbyterians, Baptists, Free Church of Scotland and Congregationalists *all* took this view. Hardly a 'glitch'.

Finally, the word 'creationist' is itself confusing. The creatorship of God is central to Christianity, and it is in our view impossible to be *any* sort of a Christian *without* being a 'creationist'. So to a Christian theist who believes that God can work through 'natural' processes, when does a so-called 'progressive creationist' become an 'evolutionary creationist'? Exactly how much micro-evolution is acceptable? R L Numbers, having called his book *The Creationists*, seems to want to limit it (for some reason) to *non-evolutionary* creationists – though at times is hard put to delineate them. Morris and other young-earthers seem to use the confusion of language to disguise their own origins. To them the word 'creationist' is a flexible word. Sometimes it means just those who believe in a literal six days and recent earth – at other times it includes the many figures in the last two centuries who have accepted mainstream geology but not macro evolution. By juggling the terms, the radical break marked by young-earth creationism with mainstream Evangelicalism is masked. Let us be clear on this one thing. Young-earthism *is* a clear and radical break differing in its whole approach to the issues – and its modern roots are in Seventh Day Adventism not in later nineteenth century Evangelicalism nor in early Fundamentalism.

---

[137] Note also our earlier comment on another critic Bowden (1998).

8

Interpreting Genesis Today

The Challenge of Literalism Today

How should we understand Genesis 1-3 today? We would wish to stand in the tradition we find amongst Bible-based Christians throughout history – not necessarily in adopting their particular conclusions but in taking their approach.

Our first commitment must therefore surely be to truth – to harmonising the truths in Genesis with the truths of nature because both reflect the same God. But we may also sympathise with one who said:

> Usually even a non-Christian knows something about the earth, the heavens, and the other elements of this world... and this is knowledge he holds to as being certain from reason and experience. Now, it is a disgraceful and dangerous thing for an unbeliever to hear a Christian, presumably giving the meaning of Holy Scripture, talking nonsense on these topics, and we should take all means to prevent such an embarrassing situation, in which people show up vast ignorance in a Christian and laugh it to scorn.[1]

Much ignorance is, alas, displayed in some books available today in which the 'science' cited is out of date, nth-hand or just plain wrong.

Another traditional principle is humility and forbearance in interpretation. This has several aspects. Firstly, throughout Christian history there has been an extraordinary tolerance of alternative views on such 'scientific' issues. Men not noted for tolerance like Augustine, as well as Aquinas, Grosseteste, and many others, gave their reasons for their own conclusions but did not denounce as heretics those who had reached different ones. Would that all those with divergent views today could be so tolerant. We say again, therefore, that to us the spirituality of men like Henry Morris is not in question – what we doubt is the rationality and hermeneutic of their young-earth system which

---

[1] Augustine: *The Literal Meaning of Genesis* i.19.

we believe to be factually incorrect both theologically and scientifically.

The other aspect of this humility is recognition that conclusions are themselves tentative – and may change as science itself advances. Both Augustine and Aquinas are clear on this very point. We are right to try to reconcile Genesis with current scientific ideas – but should do so as tentatively and discerningly as Aquinas linked it with his Aristotelian science.

Finally, we should recognise that decisions about what exactly is, and is not, figurative, are *not* straightforward. One young-earth critic of our *Reason and Faith* wrote:

> It is the general view of many Christians that where the passage is CLEARLY allegorical it is to be taken as such, but all other passages which CAN be interpreted as an accurate account, are to be accepted as a true record.

Apart from apparently identifying 'true record' and 'accurate account' with *literal* account, this has another major flaw. To Origen, Augustine, and many church figures throughout history (including virtually all leaders amongst Evangelicals and early Fundamentalists), the six days were *'CLEARLY'* figurative. R A Torrey (editor of *The Fundamentals*) joins Origen to specifically say it is *silly* or *ignorant* to take them literally. Yet the young-earthers *do* take them literally. On the other hand we suppose one *CAN* take the snake story to be just about snakes and not about Satan or some greater principle of evil which is not mentioned. But how many young-earth creationists do so? Their mentor herself, the prophetess Ellen White, even says that half of the speech in Gen 3:14-15 was addressed to the unmentioned Satan.[2] To suggest that anything which *can* possibly be taken literally *should* be is not only naïve but young-earth creationists don't even apply it consistently.

What Christians *should* be doing is to use linguistics, study of Hebrew culture, classic Christian understanding, and empirical science, to see what the most sensible way is to understand a particular verse – whether literally or figuratively. This, we believe, has been what most Christian leaders throughout history have tried to do.

---

[2] White *Patriarchs & Prophets* p. 47.

The 'Days'

Some readers may still be unconvinced, so let us first look at a kind of 'test case'. We have seen that from the very beginning there were strong streams of Christian teaching which took the 'days' non-literally. Yet there are avowed modern 'literalists' for whom the days *have to be* literal chronological twenty-four-hour periods. So what arguments do they put forward for this? We will assess these arguments without any mention of 'modern science', but simply in terms of the teaching and words of Jesus.

1. God should say what he means:

The 'days' of Genesis Ch. 1, it is asserted, MUST be literal 24 hour periods because this is the Word of God and:

'God is well able to say exactly what he means.'[3]

The problem with this is that Jesus was presumably 'well able to say what he meant' when he told Nicodemus to be 'born from above', promised someone 'living water' etc.[4] Neither Jesus nor the Genesis writer should be accused of not 'saying what they mean' if their hearers 'take them literally' when they expect spiritual discernment.

2. The 'Sabbath' law implies literality:

Exodus 20.8-11 reads:

Remember the Sabbath day to keep it holy...For in six days the LORD made the heavens and the earth and the sea, and all that is in them, but he rested on the seventh day...

Does this imply literal days? Is the writer saying that our Sabbath really is to commemorate God taking a twenty-four hour break after 144 hours of toil? We might, if this were true, ask what did God do on the eighth day, and did he rest again on the fourteenth? But does Jesus say anything which might reflect on such a 'literalistic' view? Well firstly, Jesus cryptically remarked on the Sabbath to over literalistic Pharisees: 'My father works until now and I work.' (John 5:17). The context, remember, is that Jesus has just done 'work' on the Sabbath. There would be no point in him saying 'my father works until now' unless this somehow implied that God works 'on his

---

[3] Morris (1976) p. 31.
[4] As noted above and in Jn Ch. 3 and Jn Ch. 4.

Sabbath'. It is very hard to see any meaning for this unless it is that *all* the time since the creation *is* the 'seventh day', and God is still in some sense active in it (therefore Jesus can be active in his literal Sabbath). We have seen no convincing 'literalist' interpretation which makes it mean anything else.

The second thing Jesus says is that the Sabbath was made *for man* and not man for the Sabbath (Mark 2.27). A 'literal' understanding of Exodus 20:11 would be that the Sabbath was simply to commemorate a rest day for God - but Jesus says that it is, rather, to benefit mankind. Jesus is neither legalistic nor literalistic on the Sabbath.

As a final point we might mention Hebrews Chs. 3-4. In Ch. 3 the Israelite entry to the promised land is spoken of as 'entering my (God's) rest'. Then we read:

> And God rested on the seventh day from all his works... again he sets a certain day, "Today" saying through David, so long afterward in the words already quoted, "Today when you hear his voice do not harden your hearts"... So then there remains a Sabbath rest for the people of God, for whoever enters God's rest also ceases from his labours as God did from his...

This whole passage is a highly allegorical understanding of the 'Sabbath rest' of the people of God.

3. The word 'day' is always literal elsewhere:

> the Hebrew word for 'days' ... which is used over 700 times in the Old Testament, never in any other place necessarily means anything but literal "days". Even when used in the singular, as it is several times in Genesis 1, it normally means literal day...[5]

There are a number of major faults in this argument. The first is that it misunderstands the whole basis of the use of metaphor. Suppose someone says: 'I am broken hearted because you broke your promise to mend my broken computer'. The figurative use of 'broken' conveys meaning only because it has a known literal meaning. It is the *context* which determines which kind of meaning applies - not the word itself. Suppose, moreover, someone argued like this:

> The Greek word 'body' is used in the Gospels 40 times. In 37 cases it is clearly literal. The other three are all in Jesus' phrase 'Take. eat,

---

[5] Morris (1977b) p. 24.

this is my body'. Therefore it must be literal here too. To deny this would lead to the danger that the resurrection accounts where they found not the body' might also be taken figuratively - casting doubt on the central doctrine of the resurrection.

No one actually argues like this - even the most ardent 'literalist', takes 'this is my body' in a spiritual sense and most of us take it as metaphorically as Jesus' words 'I am the vine'. Yet this is exactly the same argument as applied to 'day' above.

What makes the whole argument even more absurd is that both the plural and the singular word for 'day' are used many times in the Bible in contexts where there is *no* intention of 24 hour periods, and in some instances clearly refer to longer time spans. The plural is used elsewhere very commonly in phrases like 'full of days' (= old: in Gen 35:29, 1 Chron 21:3, 27:28, 2 Chron 24:15) and 'in those days' (Gen 6:4, Ex 2:11, Judg 17:6, 18:1, 2 Sam 28:1) variants of which are the most common use of the word. In none of these are 24-hour periods being emphasised. Even more marked is the use of the singular 'day'. Throughout Isaiah, for example, it is used countless times, in hardly any instance meaning a period of literally 24 hours after which it stops. In Jer 11:4 God says that he gave Israel a command 'In the day that I brought them forth out of the land of Egypt ...' - reference to Deut 11 shows that the event described actually happened well after their exit. Jer 34:11 similarly refers to a covenant made in that day - whereas Ex 19:1 shows it was made 'on the third new moon after' they went forth. Both these are very similar to Gen 2:4.

One modern writer has argued for literality because:

> Whenever the word "day" is used with a number in the OT ("first day" etc) it means a literal day.[6]

His commentary may be of spiritual value, but the writer's unfamiliarity with the sources is shown in that throughout Jewish and early Christian writing it is emphasised that the Hebrew reads 'one day' not 'first day'. More generally, the argument has no linguistic value. Of course, in general when numbers are used it will be in a context where literality is intended. To argue from this that no one could use the same

[6] MacDonald (1992) p. 34.

phrase figuratively in a prose-poem like Genesis 1 is absurd. Language just isn't like that, and to suggest that 'consistent interpretation' requires words to mean exactly the same in all contexts is untenable if not bizarre. Even sillier are arguments for literality based on the observation that elsewhere 'in approximately 95% of its occurrences' it is literal.[7]

It has also been suggested on similar lines that literality is indicated by specific use of the terms 'evening and morning'.[8] Yet not only do these have metaphorical meanings in some other contexts (Ps 65:8) but their use here would only heighten the drama of the metaphor. E J Young himself rightly remarks:

> If the word "day" is employed figuratively, i.e. to denote a period of time longer than twenty-four hours, so also may the terms "evening" and morning", inasmuch as they are component elements of the day, be employed figuratively.[9]

Actually, as Augustine long ago noticed, night is not mentioned at all, only twilight and morning.[10] Augustine (noting the difficulty anyway of having night and day before the sun was made) suggests either a physical meaning beyond our senses, or else a highly figurative one which emphasises the dependence of Creation. Others might, however, from the same starting point, almost paraphrase: 'there was a twilight and a dawning of a new creative unfolding in God's work...'

To be fair, Henry Morris' approach to language probably works well enough in engineering. But he simply cannot seem to grasp the fact that if a picture is being used metaphorically, then details in it are just part of the metaphor. It is as though one argued that Jesus must have meant that he was literally a 'vine' because he goes on to speak of fruit and pruning.

4. The 'slippery slope' argument.
The 'slippery slope' argument is that if we let some uses be figurative where will it all stop? If, argues Henry Morris, parts of the creation accounts are seen as myth or allegory:

---

[7] Morris (1985) p. 223.
[8] Morris (1985) p. 224.
[9] E J Young (1964) p. 104.
[10] Augustine: *City of God* xi, 7 (*Nic & Post Nic Fath* 1, I, 209).

what is to prevent our interpreting any other part of Scripture in the same way ? Thus the Virgin Birth may, after all, be only an allegory, the Resurrection could be only a myth or suprahistory, the Ten Commandments only a liturgy, the crucifixion only a dream.[11]

In a sense we answered this in our previous paragraph. A metaphorical or spiritual understanding of 'this is my body' does not negate a literal disappearance of the body from the tomb - it is context which decides which meaning applies.

All these arguments, then, against the classic Christian understanding of the 'days' as non-literal, go against both sense and the use of language in Scripture itself.

Is Complete Literality an Option?

Is it actually meaningful to talk about a completely 'literal interpretation' of Genesis 1-3? We believe not, for such an interpretation would be impossible to any sane person. Anyone, avowed literalist or not, is led by context to take *some* terms figuratively – even when strictly speaking it *could* be taken literally. The simplest way to illustrate this is from the works of the three leading avowed 'literalists' already mentioned: Morris, Young and Andrews. We shall see how they are all forced to take key points figuratively. Some readers may think that this is obvious, and wish to skip these paragraphs, but to others it may be a question of some importance.

Henry Morris, effectively a founder of modern young-earth creationism, as we have seen, makes the bold claim that he takes nothing allegorically in Genesis. When, however, he actually comes to consider the text, we find the following:

(a) Waters above the skies

God's creation of these is noted in 1:7, but what are they? Aquinas, for example, gives a whole list of possibilities – and is careful to come to no dogmatic conclusion.[12] Most of us today may take them as a poetic reference to clouds. In Psalm 148 the Psalmist calls upon various created things to praise the Lord in his day, including in verse 4: 'Praise him, you highest heavens, and you waters above the skies. Let them praise the name of the

---

[11] Morris (1984) p. 116.
[12] See eg Lindberg & Numbers (1986) p. 64.

LORD, for he commanded and they were created. He set them in place for ever and ever.' The plain Hebrew text (testified by all translations from LXX onwards) indicates a past creative act (as in Gen 1:7). and a present calling for the waters to join in the praise of God. Morris, however, wishes to interpret Gen 1:7 as a 'water vapour canopy'[13] which disappeared in the Noachic flood. Without the slightest linguistic basis he then interprets Ps 148.4 as a future event describing waters which 'will be established 'for ever and ever'.'[14] This is not only non-literal, but seems a distortion of the obvious meaning.

(b) Dominion

God's instructions to subdue and have dominion are, says Morris:

military terms - first conquer, and then rule. In context, however, there is no actual conflict suggested.[15]

In what context ? Morris has painted a picture of a pre-fall world without physical death and where the fundamental laws of physics are radically different from today - all of which   is highly speculative and not accepted by all his sympathisers. It is on this basis that he, effectively, denies the meaning of the word 'dominion' - though he does not explain why God used it if it was 'not what he meant'.

(c) The Rib

Morris emphasises that the 'rib' is really a 'side',[16] but presumably Adam was not literally one-side-missing after Eve's creation, and Morris emphasises its immediate and   ultimate spiritual interpretations.

(d) Death

God warned Adam concerning the forbidden fruit that in the day you eat of it, dying you shall die.'   The latter phrase is a common Hebrew construction emphasising the certainty of the event, thus the NIV 'you shall surely die'. Clearly Adam did NOT die physically in the day he took the fruit but lived on to reach a great old age. Those of us who take Genesis 2.17

---

[13] Morris and Whitcomb (1961) p. 255 and elsewhere.
[14] Morris (1976) p. 61.
[15] Morris (1976) p. 76.
[16] Morris (1976) p. 100.

straightforwardly (bearing in mind both early Jewish ideas eg of Philo and even more the clear inference of Rom 7:9) take it to mean spiritual death, and that Adam did spiritually die in the moment he sinned. John Wesley, interestingly, argued exactly this against those who denied any spiritual death and therefore any need for regeneration![17] Morris, however, has as a mainplank of his system the idea that human and animal physical death began with the fall. He therefore takes Gen 2:17 to mean that Adam:

> died both spiritually and (in principle) physically the very day he ...disobeyed.[18]

This 'in principle' is not a literal interpretation.

(e) The Snake

The curse of the snake Morris takes as

> more than a reference to the physical enmity between men and snakes'.[19]

The 'real thrust' of the curse was not, he says, on the literal snake but on 'that old serpent called the Devil'. Indeed, Morris (like Ellen G White) imports into Genesis an elaborate picture of Satan or Lucifer as a 'fallen angel' based on verses from Isaiah, Ezekiel and the New Testament, which were written centuries after Genesis. Genesis itself mentions neither Satan nor 'the Devil' by name, and a 'literal' reading would take it that there was only one character involved and that was an intelligent physical snake. Morris introduces two - the physical snake and the spiritual fallen angel, in a complex reinterpretation of the text.

(f) Dust

On the snake's gastronomic preferences Morris remarks:

> It 'would not "eat dust" in a literal sense, of course ... the expression is mainly a graphic figure of speech.[20]

But how could the 'plain man' know this except through science and reason? Some, indeed, have tried to argue that there must be *some* species of snake which now eats dust, just as it originally

---

[17] Wesley (1756).
[18] Morris (1976) p. 94.
[19] Morris (1977b) p. 76.
[20] Morris (1976) p. 119.

had legs which dropped off. We agree with Morris that this is not sensible, we *interpret* it as he does. But it is as obvious to us (and to many Christians throughout history) that the 'days' are not about early cosmology as it is that the 'snake' is not about biology.

(g) Seed

In reference to the seed of the serpent' and 'seed of the woman' Morris says:

> The term "seed" of course has a biological connotations, but this is not strictly possible here. Neither Satan, who is a spirit, nor the woman would be able to produce actual seed.[21]

We note first that male snakes do, of course, have 'seed' - it is only Morris' interpretation of the 'snake' as 'Satan' which raises any problem for 'literalism'. Likewise, Gen 4:25 seems to refer to Eve's literal seed. A literal reading of 3:15 would therefore see a prediction of enmity between snakes and humans. Morris, however, takes the seed of the woman as: 'those in the human family who are brought into right relationship with God through faith...' The seed of the serpent is those who 'knowingly and willingly set themselves at enmity' with these faithful people. This is a HIGHLY metaphorical interpretation.

(h) The Blood

Morris appears not to interpret literally Gen 4.10: 'the voice of his brother's blood cries unto me from the ground.'[22] Elsewhere he adds:

> 'The blood of animals could only figuratively cover sins, of course.'[23]

(i) Places

Morris does not interpret literally the biblical use of the place names before the flood, but thinks them 'carried over' and reapplied to entirely different post flood locations.[24]

(j) The 'Days'

Morris allows the word 'day' in Gen 2:4 to mean 'the whole period of creation' i.e. six days,[25] even though elsewhere he says

---

[21] Morris (1976) p. 121.
[22] Morris (1976) p. 139.
[23] Morris (1976) p. 119..
[24] Morris (1976) p. 90; (1977b) p. 38.

that the word 'never' means a 'definite period of time with a specific beginning and ending'.[26]

We may now turn to theologian E J Young, who is also highly regarded by many who claim to 'take the Bible literally', and who himself claims that Genesis is 'straightforward, trustworthy history'.[27] When we look, however at his two books *Studies in Genesis One* and *Genesis 3*, and at the book *In The Beginning* which transcribes his lectures, we find the following:

1. 'we say: 'God said'. That does not mean that he spoke in Hebrew. It does not mean that he even uttered sounds. I cannot positively say what it does mean...''God did not speak with physical organs of speech, nor did he utter words...'[28]

2. 'The Hebrew word Yom is much like our English word day, and it is capable of a great number of connotations ... The first three days are not solar days such as we now know... the work of the third day seems to suggest that there was some process, and that what took place occurred in a period much longer than twenty four hours...' 'The length of the days is not stated... The first three days were not solar days such as we now have...' 'It is almost universally taught nowadays that man is millions of years old... if it could be proved that some of the figures that are being used are correct, it would not affect what is stated in the first chapter of Genesis.'[29]

3. 'We do not know how God breathed. That is certainly an anthropomorphic expression.'[30]

4. 'Genesis two... a chronological order is not intended here.'[31]

5. 'I do not think we have to maintain that Adam died physically on that particular day.' 'He did die, although not in a physical sense, the moment he disobeyed God.'[32]

6. 'What is meant by the 'seed of Satan'? I am inclined to think that it refers to evil men...the serpent seed is found in evil spirits.'[33]

---

[25] Morris (1976) p. 84; (1984b) p. 127.

[26] Morris (1977b) p. 24;' (1977) p. 60; (1984b) p. 127.

[27] E J Young (1964) p. 105.

[28] E J Young (1976) p. 56.

[29] E J Young (1976) p. 43; (1964) p. 104; (1976) p. 44.

[30] E J Young (1976) p. 69.

[31] E J Young (1964) p. 74.

[32] E J Young (1976) p. 109: (1966) pp. 64.

[33] E J Young (1976) p. 106: (1966) p. 116.

7.   'the eating of dust is not necessarily to be understood as referring to the serpents' food.. To declare... that serpents do not eat dust ... is to miss the point of the language.'[34]

Interestingly, E J Young's son Davis A Young is also an Evangelical but is a professional geologist. His own commitment to a 'non-literal' account of the days etc is even clearer - in spite of his evident respect for his father's theology.[35]

The leading British scientific sympathiser with Morris' ideas is probably Professor E H Andrews. Actually, in his later works, Andrews seems to be moving away from Morris on some points. Although now he still retains a number of philosophical inconsistencies largely copied from Morris or Whitcomb, we can find much to agree with in what he says. Though he sometimes forgets it (referring to the 'plain meaning' where it is far from plain), he does recognise the importance of metaphor in human speech, and his commitment to non-literality is explicit:

if we try to interpret the Bible literally at all points we find ourselves in all kinds of trouble...[36]

When, for example, it says 'God spoke' Andrews takes this as an 'anthropomorphism', and in fact: the word 'spoke' implies something far more significant in its metaphorical than in its literal meaning, and this is clearly the import of God's speaking in Ch. 1.[37]

Another important example concerns the apparent differences in sequence between Ch. 1 and Ch. 2:

If we turn to the second chapter we find that man was apparently created before animals for that is the order in which their respective creations are presented. If we interpret these chapters wholly literally we have a difficult contradiction on our hands ...

Once again, however, we recognise that a literary, rather than a literal, interpretation is in order. That is, a dramatic device is being employed in Genesis 2...[38]

---

[34] E J Young (1966) p. 98-99.
[35] D A Young (1977) and (1982).
[36] Andrews (1986) p. 80.
[37] Andrews (1986) p. 81.
[38] Andrews (1986) p. 81.

In one place Andrews writes that 'to deny that the days of Genesis 1 were normal days' would be to deny the context.[39] Elsewhere, however, he finds acceptable the suggestion that the first day was millions of years long (even though Exodus 20:11 'plainly' says that everything including the heavens and earth was made in six days), and that the other days may not have been solar days either.[40] On the fourth day the sun and moon were not 'made, as a plain reading of Gen 1.16 would imply, but simply 'became visible'. There is no way the Hebrew of the text can mean this. Referring to the words in 2:17, Andrews takes the death as physical but that Adam 'died in the sense that he became mortal' - which is another very oblique interpretation.[41]

Finally we might mention Francis Schaeffer, founder of L'Abri, whose *Genesis in Space and Time* strongly defends the objectivity and historicity of the creation accounts. Yet he retains a deliberate openness, for example, on whether 'day' in Ch. 1 means an 'era' or some other 'non-literal' interpretation.[42]

In spite of Morris' words about nothing in Genesis being allegorical it is plain that he and those like him interpret many points metaphorically. Also, we note that those who claim that the meaning is very clear and does not need 'interpreting', themselves disagree over the interpretation on some important points. To Morris the six days are all literal, to Andrews only five of them are, whilst to Young just three have to be literal. To both Morris and A E Wilder-Smith, it is vital to believe that before the fall of Adam neither death nor the second law of thermodynamics (which implies 'decay') existed.[43] Andrews, in contrast, believes that there were no carnivores, but there WAS death and the second law of thermodynamics did operate.[44]

Why have we wandered through the inconsistencies, allegory and confusion of these avowed literalists? Neither to deny their zeal nor to suggest that it is 'all myth and fable'. The point is:

---

[39] Andrews (1985) p. 101.
[40] Andrews (1978) pp. 111-112.
[41] Andrews 1986) p. 87.
[42] Schaeffer (1972) p. 57.
[43] Morris (1976) p. 127; (1985) p. 212; Wilder Smith (1974) p. 282.
[44] Andrews (1985) pp. 82, 87.

1. No sane person could possible take all Genesis 1-3 literally and no one does.

2. *All* modern avowed literalists actually interpret *some* parts figuratively which could (with the kinds of ingenuity they exhibit in imagining eg Adam kept in suspended animation whilst God plants a garden, or the earth spinning in 24 hours through a sunless universe) be taken literally.

3. Once it is recognised that it is really a question not of 'should we take it literally?' but of '*how* literally should we take it?' we can get back to the humility of Augustine, Aquinas, Grosseteste etc and away from any approach which proclaims alternative views as decadent and heretical.

Having said that, we would wish, calmly and prayerfully, to look more at what exactly is 'on offer' as part of the young earth package. Some readers may wish to skip the following sub-section, but any involved in or tempted by it should at least be aware of the novelties in theology which are involved.

The Young-Earth Theology

We have consistently defended what we believe to be the traditional Jewish/early church approach to understanding Genesis. In Western countries today, however, the young-earth 'creationist' movement has achieved an unprecedented influence, and it will be useful to some to consider the particular system put forward by the effective founder of the modern young-earth system Henry Morris. We want here to assess this not from a *scientific* but from a *biblical* viewpoint. Morris' system can be summarised:

- The earth is only a few thousand years old, and was completed in 144 hours.

- Physical death of both man and animals started only after the sin of the first man and woman, which occurred at least 24 hours after the creation of birds and sea creatures.

- There were, therefore, no animal predators in the original creation, and all of them were vegetarian throughout the first day or so of their existence.

- At the first human sin (or the 'fall'), substantial changes occurred both in biology and in physics. Though some young- earthers deny it, Morris also emphasises that the second law of thermodynamics began only at that time.

- Just after the fall of man, God somehow withdrew his hand, allowing an undirected process of evolution by natural selection to occur, leading to animals developing structures specialised for predatory habits.

- During the period between Adam and Noah (c 1000 years?), all the structures for predatory habits found in fossils developed. This universal flood laid down all the strata and engulfed the now fossilised animals.

Many young-earth creationists simply do not realise the total package they are 'buying into'. Because Henry Morris is a sincere Christian man, he has tried to think through in detail the implications of his system. Not only has this led him (as we have seen) in practice to admit that major parts of Genesis 1-3 are figurative/allegorical, but it has also led to the anomaly that he actually has a greater belief in the efficacy of evolution by natural selection to change animal structures than anyone else we know. Though he may call it 'degeneration', it actually means that highly complex new structures evolved over a period of just a few thousand years! He states his views thus:

> It seems unlikely that God actually either created or 'made' thorns or thistles at this time. He did not 'create' death in the direct sense, but rather withdrew that extension of his power which maintained a 'steady state' of life and order, thus allowing all things gradually to disintegrate toward disorder and death... God merely "allowed" certain plant structures which previously were beneficent to deteriorate into malevolent characteristics... In terms of modern genetic knowledge, such changes probably were in the form of mutations, or random changes in the molecular structure of the genetic systems of the different kinds of organisms... If deteriorative mutational changes occurred in plants, it seems reasonable and even probable that they would also occur in animals. As smoothly rounded structures deteriorated to thorns in plants, so perhaps teeth and nails designed for a herbivorous diet mutated to fangs and claws which, in combination with a progressively increasing dietary deficiency of proteins and other essentials, gradually created carnivorous appetites in certain animals... Parasites and viral systems may also have developed in some such way.[45]

---

[45] Morris (1976) p. 125.

He later calls mutations 'random disruptions in their highly ordered genetic structures.'[46] Let us be clear here how novel is this suggestion. He is saying that as originally created all animals were vegetarian, and there was no animal death. Then at the moment of that first sin of Adam, God 'withdrew' his power in some way, leaving the physical world to a new system of physics which operated in some sense independently of God. Animal life evolved very rapidly (within a few thousand years between Adam and Noah) to transform the originally vegetarian structures of the Genesis 'kinds' into carnivores with claws and teeth for tearing, into parasites etc. The mode by which these changes occurred was random mutations - not God-directed in any way, but (Morris seems to imply) by natural selection. When, therefore, we look today e.g. at a member of the feline 'kind' (i.e. a cat), we see a structure which is unrecognisable as the original vegetarian creature God made, but has 'degenerated' into the lissom, efficient hunter with claws and teeth we know so well.

It is a supreme irony that Morris seems to have a greater belief than any other writer we know in the efficacy of a purely godless system of mutation and natural selection to produce intricate and amazing new structures within a very short time-span. There may be considerable scientific problems in believing in such rapid evolution by completely 'natural' processes, but here we need to think about its theological novelty and how far it may be reconciled with the Bible.

Relevant Genesis passages are as follows:

- Gen 1:12; 1:31 God pronounces creation 'good'.
- Gen 1.28 God tells mankind to 'subdue' the earth.
- Gen 1.29-30 God gives humankind plants and trees for food, and animals vegetation for food.
- Gen 2:17 God tells Adam that in the day he eats of the tree of knowledge of good and evil 'dying you shall die'.
- Gen 3:17 God says the ground is cursed and in the fields 'thistles will grow for you', so the Man will need to toil to 'eat bread'.

---

[46] See also Morris (1974) p. 238.

- Gen 4:4 Abel brought the 'fat portions' of firstlings as a sacrifice - Cain brought vegetables.

Do these and other Bible passages point to Morris' system?

Firstly, the word 'good' does not imply pain-free. God's promise in Deut 8:7 to bring the Israelites into a 'good land' does not suppose it to be without struggles. The word may mean 'fitting' or 'beautiful' amongst a wide range of meanings. That most unfanciful of early commentators, Ambrose of Milan, took God's pronouncement that the sea was 'good' to imply its beauty (seen as the same for us to appreciate today) and added:

> Notwithstanding all this, I am of the opinion that the beauty of such a creation is not to be estimated by the standard of our own eyes, but is to be gauged in the design of the work as a whole by its conformity and agreement with the intention of its Creator.[47]

Chrysostom, likewise, took God's pronouncement of 'good' to apply to the created world as we now see it.[48] No one seemed to take it that it implied a world free from predatory habits and pain which was inconceivably different from the present.

Secondly, the command to 'subdue the earth' seems to imply some degree of strife - even if some kind of strife-free garden were envisaged in Genesis 2.

Thirdly, the promise of death:

1. Seems (as both Paul and eg Philo take it) to refer to spiritual not physical death.
2. Is specifically directed at Man - not at animals (hardly surprising as it is spiritual death).

There is no indication here or anywhere else in the Bible that it introduced death for animals. Indeed, if physical death had not been familiar to Adam, then it is hard to see what meaning at all God's warning could have had to him. We understand the concept of the second or spiritual death only by analogy to the physical one with which we are familiar.

Fourthly, the curse of thistles is again specifically directed at humankind. It is not that thistles are newly created, but that Man stands in different relationship to his environment - it says

---

[47] Ambrose, *Hexameron* tr Savage (1961) p. 238.
[48] Chrysostom *Homilies on Genesis.*

nothing about changes in *animal* structures or general ecology outside the garden. It certainly says nothing about a slow degeneration through evolution from that point.

The strongest positive evidence for anything remotely like Morris' system comes from Gen 1.29-30. Does it imply that all animals (though not, we note, all fish) were initially vegetarian? There would be two major problems for the Christian in taking it thus. The first is that elsewhere in the Old Testament it seems to imply that eg the lions seek their prey from God (Psalm 104:21). It seems to be God who provides prey for the lion and ravens and eagles (Job 38:39-41; 49:27-30). The second is that Jesus did not advocate vegetarianism before or after his resurrection (cf eg Mk 6:41; John 21:6&13; Lk 24:42-3). Paul sees the vegetarian (in his cultural context) as the 'weaker' in faith (Rom 14:2), the Kingdom of God is about deeper things, which food at most symbolises. Neither read Genesis as implying literal vegetarianism was part of some higher estate - whether now or in the coming kingdom. Isaiah 11:6-9 and 65:25 speak, indeed, of the coming kingdom of the Messiah where:

> The wolf and the lamb shall graze together, and the lion shall eat straw like the ox; and dust shall be the serpent's food.

Is this really about animals? Does he mean this 'literally'? Well in Isaiah 35:9 he says that there will not be any lions there at all, so presumably the lion part isn't literal. Surely, also, the reference to the serpent and dust refers back to Genesis 3:14? It is not snakes' diets in view, but it means that in the Messiah's kingdom Satan is defeated. It ties in with Revelation, where, as we shall further explore, Satan is portrayed as a defeated serpent. It is interesting for us as traditionalists to turn, eg, to Matthew Henry's famous 1710 commentary on this:

> God's people, though they are sheep in the midst of wolves, shall be unhurt; for God will not so much break the power of their enemies as formerly, but he will turn their hearts, will alter their dispositions by his grace... Satan shall be chained, the dragon bound, for dust shall be the serpent's meat again...

Matthew Henry sees the whole thing in terms of a picture about the people of God, not about animals at all. His comment on Genesis 1:30 is also interesting:

> Yes, certainly he provides food convenient for them, and not for oxen only but even the young lions and the young ravens are the care of his providence. He is a great housekeeper and a bountiful one, that satisfies the desire of every living thing. He that feeds his birds will not starve his babes.

The reference to lions and ravens reflects Psalm 104 - which surely does not hold with a literal vegetarian view of their diet?

Amongst modern conservative commentators, Oswalt rejects a literalistic view that Isaiah 11 is about physical lions, and again takes a figurative view that it is about felt security during the Messiah's reign.[49]

Gen 1:29-30 is fundamentally about the bounty of God - in contrast to views of other nations at that time which thought the gods created mankind to supply their own needs. It may be that the writer expressed this in contemporary terms,[50] or just that the food chain does, of course, ultimately come back to vegetation.

Were we to wish, however, to 'take it literally', there is no indication in the actual Genesis text that vegetarianism was abrogated until Gen 9:3. Yet Abel apparently brought the 'fat portions' to sacrifice in a way in which Lev 7 indicates the rest of such sacrifices was eaten. Nothing anywhere, of course, is said about God giving animals permission to eat each other. It is hard to avoid the feeling that trying to take Gen 1:30 in some literal sense risks missing the point and tries to make it speak to issues it never envisaged.

Does the New Testament give any support to Morris' ideas? Rom 8:19-22 says:

> The creation waits in eager expectation for the sons of God to be revealed. For the creation was subjected to frustration, not by its own choice, but by the will of the one who subjected it, in hope that the creation itself will he liberated from its bondage to decay and brought into the glorious freedom of the children of God. We know that the whole creation has been groaning as in the pains of childbirth right up to the present time. Not only so, but we ourselves, who have the firstfruits of the Spirit, groan inwardly as

---

[49] John N Oswalt (1986) p. 283.
[50] Westermann (1984) notes a widespread ancient view that early animals were vegetarian.

we wait eagerly for our adoption as sons, the redemption of our bodies.

The word 'frustration' means powerless, ineffectual or aimless.[51] The word 'decay' means destruction or corruption.[52] In Paul's writings (Rom 8:21; 1 Cor 15:42,50; Gal 6:8; Col 2:22) it seems to take the meaning of mortality. Paul does not say in Romans 8:21 at what time God subjected the creation to a servitude to mortality which he pictures as a state of ineffectuality. It is far from clear that it was the fall and involves moral evil. This could be one possible interpretation, but it is also possible that it was at creation, and that mankind's task was to transform and give it purpose by the introduction of altruism and eternity.

The coming Kingdom is pictured in Revelation 21:4 as a place with 'no more death or mourning or crying or pain.' The context, however, is clearly one of human experience, and we have seen that this is also true similar passages in Isaiah 11 and 65. Whether there will, in fact, be a new order of animal-kind is hard to tell from the hints we are given about the new heaven and new earth. It is not even possible to say whether we are intended to be 'vegetarian' (if, indeed, such categories have any meaning for those who are to be 'like the angels' (Mt 22:30)). As we noted, Jesus, in his resurrected state, ate a piece of fish (Lk 24:43) so to say the least this must be in question. If we consider the world of nature, the Bible, surely takes it that *this* world is God's created world. Psalm 104, for example. pictures God in verses 5-9 as making the earth. It then passes smoothly into God's continuing activity in making springs bring waters to present animals (104:10-12), in growing grass (104:14), etc. There is not the slightest hint here to support the novel young-earther idea that God somehow withdrew and let the second law of thermodynamics take over. The lions (104:21) seek their food from God - not from the effects of altered physiology (claws, teeth etc) in a struggle for survival introduced by God's withdrawal from nature after the first human sin (as Morris seems to suggest). Psalm 104:25 speaks of the sea teaming with living things implying that these are the ones mentioned in the

---

[51] *Mataiotes* see Brown (1971) vol i pp. 549-51.
[52] *Phthoras* see Brown (1971) vol I pp.467-71.

previous verse 'in wisdom you made them all, the earth is full of your creatures.' Then verse 26 mentions the frolicking leviathan (also found in Job 41) which you formed', going on to speak of all those sea creatures also looking to God to feed them.

When today we go for a walk and admire 'the beauty of God's creation' we are looking at a nature that is quite definitely based on predatory habits and the laws of thermodynamics. One without this would be inconceivably different. Classically the church has always taken it that it is *this* world which is God's created world - not one which effectively perished at the instant of humankind's first sin. Only early Gnosticism (as we have already noted) took it that the actual present world was *not* the work of the one true God but of some kind of inferior deity. Ironically, it was exactly this view that the present physical world was 'evil' that was attacked strongly by all early christian leaders. Consider, for example, our own wonderfully made bodies, with all the mechanisms of white blood corpuscles, immune systems etc. None of this should have been necessary before the fall introduced the possibility of disease - so presumably Morris believes it all to be the product of a couple of thousand years of blind chance mutations and natural selection in a nature from which God had 'withdrawn'. Is such a view really compatible with the Bible where David sings praise to God in Ps 139:13-14 for forming him in the womb, and because he is fearfully and wonderfully made'? Is it compatible with a situation where the divine 'Word became flesh and dwelt amongst us'? Was the body of Jesus not subject to the second law of thermodynamics? Morris' conclusions are surely absurd, yet in a sense they are the 'logical' ones from his starting point.

Surely the Christian view is that the wisdom and power of God is seen in *this* world, not in a world where physics, biology and ecology were totally different and which degenerated into ours when God supposedly 'withdrew' in some way from nature at the time of the first human sin. The hints of Gnosticism, semi-deism, and various other historical heresies implied in consistent young-earth theology should give much cause for concern as its advocates clearly think of themselves as orthodox.

Some of these concerns were raised in our previous *Reason and Faith*, but, although various young-earth reviewers 'nit picked', *no one* has even made any attempt to answer them. Well-meaning Christians take up some of the young-earth ideas thinking they are being 'true to Scripture'. Few seem to try to actually think through the implications. All credit to Henry Morris for attempting it - but the results are far from orthodox and are in conflict with the traditional approach taken by people like ourselves.

Approaching Genesis 1-3

Before we come to any real conclusions about Genesis 1-3 we need to understand what *kind* of literature it is. As a document it falls into two distinct parts 1:1-2.3 and 2:4-3.24, which in turn form part of a wider pattern of sections of Genesis each beginning with the words: 'These are the generations of...' (Gen 2:4; 5:1; 6:9; 10:1).[53] At one time critics tried to argue that these were two rival accounts from different sources, but we see no reason to doubt the traditional view (accepted by many modern scholars)[54] that the two passages were from the beginning seen as complementary. Gen 1:1-2:3 serves as a kind of prologue, whilst Gen 2:4-3.24 speaks of what was engendered in a human sense from the creation of earth and heavens. Some scholars have emphasised a supposed role of the passages as a prologue to a covenant document made by God with Israel.[55] There may be some truth in this, though it seems clear that both accounts are intended to deal with far more fundamental issues of God's relationship with the physical world and with mankind.

A second point about both accounts concerns their mode of inspiration. However strong one's belief in Biblical inspiration, clearly there are historical books like Luke's Gospel which in the words of Morris himself who strongly defends 'plenary verbal inspiration':

> ...were very definitely written by the human authors, using their own observations and researches and expressing their own feelings and convictions.[56]

---

[53] See eg Blocher (1984) p. 30; E J Young (1964) p. 59; Kidner (1967) p. 23 etc.
[54] See Blocher (1984) p. 30 etc.
[55] M G Kline (1975) and H Van Till (1986).
[56] Morris (1974) p. 168.

Gen 1:1-23 and 2:4-3:24 are not like this. They are divinely inspired accounts intended by God to explain his relationship with his world and mankind. As such we find a problem in that they are (with the possible exception of some poetic passages e.g. in Job) unique kinds of document. This should make us wary of too hasty or dogmatic a classification of them with other kinds of literature in the Bible - whether historical, poetical, philosophical or prophetic.

Both creation accounts are in carefully constructed patterns. The early distinction of the work of 'separation' (days 1-3) and 'adornment' (days 4-6) led to recognition from the time of the Fathers of the symmetry of the two triads of days. Sometimes these are called 'form' and 'fullness', reflecting the changes in the creation of a world 'without form' and 'void' in Gen 1:2.

SEPARATION (FORM)	ADORNMENT (FULNESS)
DAY 1: Light and Dark	DAY 4: Lights (Sun, Moon & Stars) of Day/Night
DAY 2: Sea and Sky	DAY 5: Creatures of Water and Air
DAY 3: Fertile Earth	DAY 6: Creatures of the Land

Modern commentators identify a complex pattern of tens, threes and sevens in Ch. 1[57] and some discern a literary pattern in Ch. 2 as well.[58] Both, and especially the second, contain Hebrew plays on words.

Henry Blocher asks: 'Is it prose or poetry? The choice is a gross oversimplification.' Clearly any[59] who insist that it is not 'poetry' in the sense, say, of Job 38, are right. But does it contain elements of the poetic? Hebraists who have denied this usually seem to believe that it represents a very primitive worldview and adhere without question to the Wellhausen multiple-author late-composition view of Genesis. Von Rad, for example, said there was 'no trace of the hymnic element'[60] –

---

[57] See eg Kidner (1967); Blocher (1984); Wenham (1987); Hamilton (1990) – Filby (1964) gives much detail.
[58] Blocher (1984) pp. 54-55.
[59] Eg Sailhamer (1996).
[60] Von Rad (1961) p. 47.

though also asserted eg that the writer thought the firmament was a hard roof and that the snake story is just about snakes. The Hebrew expert most often cited by young-earth creationists is James Barr – who certainly says that the passages are meant literally.[61] To Barr, however, the picture implied is a flat earth with a tin roof and 'fundamentalists' (amongst whom he includes all Conservative Evangelicals) are silly in trying to see it figuratively to save biblical inspiration. The young-earth writer Bowden suggests that we have 'missed the point' that Barr is not an Evangelical and yet thinks the accounts were meant literally.[62] If Barr had no axe to grind and yet held this view then this might be significant – but he clearly does have an axe to grind and that axe is to discredit Evangelicalism. Bowden *still* cites *not one* single other Hebrew scholar, and relies on a 1984 letter from Barr which vaguely claims that many other Hebraists support him *again without citing a single other name*.

As for Barr's views, as Hamilton remarks:

> It never occurs to Barr that there may be other reasons why a nonliteral interpretation may be advanced than to keep biblical inerrancy from being refuted.[63]

Other scholars have not supported Barr. Classically, Professor James Orr, writing in the original work from which we got the name 'fundamentalism', called it a 'sublime proëm'.[64] Likewise, the major modern commentaries – including theologically conservative ones – seem to identify poetic elements. Claus Westermann, sees the passage definitely as a 'prose poem'.[65] The renowned Jewish Professor Cassuto (an emphatic defender of the unity of composition of Genesis) states that:

> Verses with poetic rhythm like i 27... and a number of other poetic features... also point to a poetic tradition among Israelites anterior to the book of Genesis...[66]

Walter Brueggemann states that:

---

[61] Barr (1978) p. 40.
[62] Bowden (1998) p. 41.
[63] V P Hamilton (1990) p. 54.
[64] Orr in *The Fundamentals* vol 1 Ch. xi.
[65] C Westermann (1971) p. 38 and (1974) p. 126.
[66] U Cassuto (1961) p. 11.

The text is a poetic narrative that likely was formed for liturgical usage... At the outset we must see that this text is not a scientific description but a theological affirmation.[67]

Gordon Wenham writes:

Gen 1 is unique in the Old Testament... It is indeed a great hymn, setting out majestically the omnipotence of the creator, but it surpasses these other passages in the scope and comprehensiveness of vision. In that it is elevated prose, not pure poetry, it seems unlikely that it was used as a song of praise as the psalms were.[68]

David Atkinson writes:

The poem of beauty and grandeur which for the opening chapter of our Bibles is a hymn of praise to the majesty of God the Creator... Through its structured harmonies our hearts are tuned to the music of the heavens.[69]

Even Young who wishes to see in Genesis 1 only 'straightforward history', recognises without any sense of inconsistency that this chapter

is written in exalted semi-poetical language.[70]

Ernest Lucas asserts:

It is often said that Genesis 1 is not Hebrew poetry. This is true in the strict sense. However, neither is it simple prose. It has some of the features of Hebrew poetry, such as repetition of phrases, parallelism, and carefully balanced phraseology.[71]

Blocher likewise states that we do not find 'the rhythms of Hebrew poetry' nor its 'parallelism' - but concurs with the common view of scholars that it can be seen as a kind of 'hymn' which is a unique blend of prose and poetry. This does not mean, of course, that it is fictional. Many hymns contain a great deal of factual and historical reference, but they often couch this in metaphorical forms.

---

[67] Brueggermann (1982) pp. 22-5.
[68] Wenham (1987) p. 10; to Youngblood (1980) it is 'almost liturgical' (p. 21) and he also espouses eg Augustine's view of the non literality of the days.
[69] Atkinson (1990) p. 15.
[70] E J Young (1964) p. 82.
[71] Lucas (1989) p. 91.

Literality and the Relationship of Chapters 1& 2

Whether we call them two 'accounts', or 'chapters' (as Young and Morris), or 'tablets' (as Blocher), it is obvious that Gen 1:1-2,3 and 2:4-2.25 overlap in what they describe. Two immediate points arise. The first is that the order of events in the two chapters appears different, and the second is that chapter 1 speaks of six days whilst in 2:4 we read:

> These are the generations of the heavens and of the earth when they were created, in THE DAY that the Lord God made earth and heaven..
> And no plant of the field... And the Lord God formed man... etc

The obvious implication of non-literality in the contrast of six days and one was seen by those in the second century who defended Christian orthodoxy against critics.[72] A plain 'literal' reading of Gen 2.4 would imply that all the succeeding events (described with no break) took place on the 'day' mentioned, and in the order described. There are, then, three possibilities:

i.   the two are contradictory.
ii. one account is intended as literal in chronology and time span and the other one not.
iii. neither are intended to give strict chronology and literal time spans.

Unbelieving critics have sometimes suggested the first, but it is frankly incredible. Even atheists must accept that whoever compiled Genesis was intelligent, and it would have been careless to leave together two obviously contradictory accounts. Clearly the Hebrews did not understand their own language in any sense which would imply this.

So was just one, or were both intended non-literally? We have already described the widespread early Hebrew-Christian view, which took neither as literal. Is this kind of traditional non-literal view the most obvious one? We have argued that it is the context, which determines whether a word is to be taken literally or metaphorically, and this we should apply.

---

[72] See Origen *Against Celsus* vi 1 (*Ant Nic Fath* iv 596).

Modern supposed 'literalists' such as Young and Andrews accept that the 'day' in 2:4 is non-literal. With some apparent reluctance Morris also concedes that the:

> Hebrew word *yom* can, if the context justifies, be translated 'time' in the general sense., and that the context of 2:4 'perhaps does justify such a meaning.[73]

What of the 'days' in Genesis Ch. 1? It may be added that the reasoning in Gen 2:5 also seems to indicate non-literality. It would hardly be logical to argue that the lack of crops or vegetation at the time of man's creation was due to a lack of rain or cultivation if it had only to have existed since its creation for less than two and a bit literal days.[74]

Now what of the chronology or order of events ? The two chapters seem very similar in structure. Both chapters describe a sets events, all couched in the same simple past tense, and linked by the word 'and' (Hebrew *waw*, Greek *kai* in the Septuagint version). Now Young, Morris and Andrews are all insistent that Ch. 1 is chronological and Ch. 2 is not. But what justification can they give? Young argues:

> I have been very insistent that the first chapter is to be understood chronologically. This is seen by the order of development, the progression of thought. It is also seen by the chronological emphasis - day one, day two, and so on. You do not find that in the second chapter of Genesis ...[75]

This is a piece of special pleading. A traditional early Jewish-Christian understanding did *not* see the 'days' as especially implying a time sequence, and the language used in the two chapters is otherwise very similar. To back up the claim that Ch. 2 is non-sequential, Young sarcastically asks what God would have done with the man if he really made him before the garden.[76] Actually this would be quite a minor problem compared with creating night and day two days before the sun and moon! To get around the latter problem for Ch. 1, Young suggests that on the fourth day 'God constituted the universe as we now know it.' This is unwarranted from the text, as is the

---

[73] Morris (1976) p. 84.
[74] See Dawson (1890) p. 142; also M Kline (1958) p. 15; Blocher (1984).
[75] E J Young (1976) p. 70.
[76] E J Young (1976) p. 70; (19640 p.74.

similar idea that the sun and moon were just 'made to appear' on the fourth day. The Hebrew language was perfectly well able to express this idea had the writer wished – but he did not. It is, then, simpler to assume that the Ch. 1 like Ch. 2 was not intended to be chronological.

Morris has no problem with God keeping Adam somewhere west of Eden whilst God planted directly the garden. He has, however, to suggest interpreting 'and' (*waw*) as 'also' and 'formed' (*yatsar*) as the pluperfect 'had formed' in 2:19. The NIV is the only version we can find which renders it thus, and, as the Hebrew is a simple past tense, its motivation is plainly theological not linguistic. It is hardly a 'straightforward' reading, and the Septuagint rendering ('God further formed') shows that the Jews never took it thus. Having thus artificially rearranged the time sequence in Ch. 2, Morris preserves the sequence in Ch. 1 by suggesting that God created the light from the sun and moon three days before he created the actual objects. Though this last interpretation was taken by some early Christian writers, for someone who (unlike them) has claimed that there is no need to 'interpret' Genesis at all, it seems extraordinary lengths to maintain a preconceived interpretation. Let us be blunt. Taken 'literally' Gen 2:5 'clearly' states that there were no shrubs and no plants of the field' before the creation of man – whereas Gen 1:11-12 'clearly' puts them three days earlier.

Andrews explicitly accepts (as quoted above) that the apparent order in Ch. 2 indicates a 'literary rather than literal' interpretation, for it is a 'dramatic device'. Yet when some of us, trying to interpret Scripture consistently and following the approach of leading early Jewish and Christian teachers, suggest the same about Ch. 1, he bizarrely sees this as 'attacking the Bible'. Andrews, as we saw, accepts a first day millions of years long, and reinterprets the creation of the sun and moon in day three as making them appear'. There is no linguistic basis at all for this in either the Hebrew or Greek versions, and it is not what the text says. Andrews gives no clear reason for rejecting the view that Ch. 1 is to be taken (as he takes Ch. 2) as a dramatic device not intended chronologically. The only reason he seems to give is that his interpretation does not 'diminish in any way the miraculous act'. This does not seem to us to be a proper motive for Christian theism which - as Andrews himself clearly elsewhere says - sees God active in all natural processes.

All this confusion and divergence amongst supposed literalists only underlines for us that those early Jewish and Christian teachers - following up indications in the actual text and the 'non-literal' interpretations of Jesus himself on the Sabbath - were right in taking both Ch. 1 and Ch. 2 as dramatic devices rather than literal in chronology. Andrews himself says:

> their contents are presented plainly as historical fact. Those facts may be expressed using a variety of dramatic and literary devices, but the author nevertheless claims to be relating events, which actually took place. The narratives are accounts, not of myth but of reality.[77]

We would agree that the contents are historical fact in the sense that God really did create the heavens and earth *ex nihilo* and the subsequent appearance on the planet of vegetable, animal and human life was according to the unfolding of a divine plan. But both chapters do contain dramatic and literary devices; neither was intended to give scientific detail or strict time sequence, and neither should be pressed to do so.

Conclusions on the Form and Nature of Genesis 1-3.

So what is on offer today? Leaving aside pure 'Gossism' (which no one takes seriously) we have:

The 'Literal' Interpretation

1. *Roots:* Basil (partially) - really in Luther – E G White
2. *Recent Support:* 'young-earthers' following G M Price.
3. *Hebrew:* Support mainly from those who see Genesis as primitive myth (Von Rad, Barr) – parts on 'making' sun etc not permissible renderings in their own terms.
4. *Consistency:* Never applied consistently (eg on the snake), Gen 2 contradicts Gen 1 if both interpreted consistently.
5. *Physical Coherence:* Sun made on 4th day.

Concordist Interpretations: Age-Day and Gap

1. *Roots:* Age = millennium in 2nd C; mostly post geology.

---

[77] Andrews (1986) p. 82.

2. *Recent Support:* key nineteenth century Evangelicals and nearly all early Fundamentalists.
3. *Hebrew:* Both are not obvious ways to render the Hebrew, few modern scholars seem to support either (though Kidner cautiously accepts age-day)
4. *Consistency:* Fair – though no obvious reason to take Gen 1 chronologically and Gen 2 not.
5. *Physical Coherence:* Still does not explain sun made on 4th day.

Literary or 'Framework' Understanding

1. *Roots:* 1stC (Philo); 2ndC (Origen); 4thC (Augustine); 7thC Celtic Church; 13thC Aquinas etc.
2. *Recent Support:* eg Henri Blocher (France), M G Kline (America), Victor P Hamilton (America), the Dominican scholar M J Lagrange, Ernest Lucas (Britain), A Noordtzij (Holland), D F Payne (Britain), Bernard Ramm (America), N H Ridderbos (Holland), J A Thompson (Australia), Gordon Wenham (Britain), and R Youngblood (USA) [Wiseman's 'days of revelation' seems to us a variation on this].
3. *Hebrew:* All those cited in 2 are Hebrew scholars.
4. *Consistency:* Consistent in looking to all 3 chapters for theology, not details of biology or cosmology.
5. *Physical Coherence:* Advocates *throughout history* had no need to discuss days without a sun, or celestial water tanks.

Two other points to mention. First, in personal conversation with other Hebraists (eg William Lane (America) and Hugh Williamson (Britain – Barr's successor!) and Robert Fylde (Britain)) we have found no support for literalism. Some other unmentioned Hebraists might go as far as Jewish Professor Nahum Sarna:

> The literalistic approach… tends to obscure the elements, which are meaningful, and enduring, thus distorting the biblical message and destroying its relevancy.[78]

The second point is that we see no particular advantage in the schema of P J Wiseman[79] or Alan Hayward[80] that the 'days'

---

[78] Sarna (1966) p. 3.
[79] Wiseman (1949).
[80] Hayward (1985).

were days of 'vision' or 'divine fiat'. It is, of course, possible, because the material had to be revealed in some way (even Adam missed the first five days!) but there is no linguistic basis in the text to take it thus, so why deviate from the traditional view?

Our own position, then, is along lines of the traditional one, ie it is the third of those listed. Genesis 1-3 is to answer theological questions, not scientific ones. Some of those theological issues are, of course, 'historical' – ie that God *really did* create the present universe. The 'days' however, should be seen primarily as a logical or literary device intended to confirm the readers (particular the Hebrew readers) in their majestic monothestic faith and in contrast to prevailing polytheistic myth. Indeed, we follow the tradition since Philo in asserting that there is no myth in Genesis 1-3. It is divinely inspired narrative saga, true in every sense it intends. Like the language of Jesus, it conveys truth in a way which needs spiritual discernment and understanding – sometimes (alas) not found in modern equivalents of that 'teacher of Israel' Nicodemus. There is no intention to teach a geocentric system with the sun as an afterthought, the biology of snakes, or human rib anatomy. There is every intention to teach that the sun is a creation and neither a divinity nor the ultimate source of light and life, that evil is not co-eternal with God but is in conflict with his purposes, and that man and woman are intended in marriage to be a union of allies and partners. Finally, though we see nothing threatening in the idea that the final redactor of Genesis (like the author of Luke) used different sources, we sympathise with the most recent swing back towards seeing a unitary and early authorship for Genesis.

An approach grounded in the culture of the text recognises that just as Genesis 2 does not imply a literal timescale and order of events, neither does Genesis 1. The chapter is a polemic work, designed to reassert the truth of God's supremacy and creatorship against the claims of worshippers of chaos, sun, stars or other created things. The sun, then, is just a 'lamp' (the normal ancient word for the sun which implied divinity is not even used) created by God on the fourth day and so not responsible for light or for life. But this is theology, not cosmology. The events described do follow a logical order (the most casual observer would surely put creation of plants before creation of animals to eat them), which in some instances happens to follow the geological order. This is, in many ways, coincidental, and was not part either of the writer's purpose nor (necessarily) of the guiding Holy Spirit's purpose. The chapter was not intended to be a framework for science but for theology.

This does not, of course, mean that the account of the creation is 'not historical'. As we have seen, some of Jesus' own words described historical events in metaphorical ways. We also have to recognise that early Hebrews had an approach to chronology different from American engineers. The Gospels are historical but from the very beginning the Christians recognised e.g. that Mark 'the interpreter of Peter, wrote down accurately, though not indeed in order, whatsoever he remembered of the things said or done by Christ'.[81] They were historical but not wholly chronological. Mark did not consider that the chronological order of the events was of any significance, and arranged them for continuity of theme rather than chronology.

Likewise in Genesis 1-3 the events did occur, but from before the time of Jesus, leading Jewish and Christian commentators explicitly recognised that its writer never intended them to be taken as chronological. In the two accounts of Ch. 1 and Chs. 2-3 incidents are arranged to bring out particular theological points. Chapter 1 deals with God-'s pre-eminence and relationship to all creation. In it Chaos is denied divinity and shown as a stage in creation from which God was never absent. The celestial bodies arrive in day three, given not a divine role but a subordinate one in the affairs of mankind. In Ch. 2 the same events are arranged in a different order to bring out the relationships of man, woman and God. We have already looked at Paul's reference in 1 Tim 2,13 to Genesis 2. Paul refers to the order of events, but if, of course, he were really arguing on a literal chronological basis, then he would have to accept that the animals (formed even before Adam) stood to Adam as Adam to Eve - and Paul's whole argument would fail. Paul's argument holds only if we take the Genesis writer to be rearranging events

---

[81] Eusebuis quoting Papias: *Church History*, iii, 39, 15.

to bring out a theological point in dealing specifically with mankind's human relationships.

To try to use Genesis 1-3 to derive either a chronological order of events or technical scientific detail, would be to misuse the passage to derive information from it which it was not intended to give.

What we would emphasise is that we are *not* saying that Genesis 1 is 'only', a literary framework. The passage describes real events in amazingly powerful way, magisterial in its vision of God, and the word 'only' is wholly inappropriate. This whole understanding may come as a disappointment to those brought up on the kind of statement: 'Isn't it amazing that God put into his Word all the correct orders revealed by modem science...' But this kind of statement was trying to make it do something it was never intended to do. God's word does not need that kind of support. Its majesty stands on its own merits, and we consider it totally fitting that it was actually read on man's first trip to the moon. Its teaching is timeless, and no less relevant today than to those in the ancient world who first heard it. God is the Creator, he creates and acts in space-time, but his design is in eternity.

Finally, though we do not believe that Genesis 1-3 somehow contains foreknowledge of later scientific discoveries, we do not believe either that it implies a 'flat earth with a tin roof' view of nature. This is sometimes implied by Evangelicals[82] but we think it mistaken. Suppose that the ancient Hebrew people were to be given a divinely inspired message about God's creation of the universe. One of two things could happen. They could, of course, first be given a divinely inspired physics textbook – perhaps containing Maxwell's equations and quantum mechanics – after which the creation account can be couched in suitable scientific terms. Alternatively, God could use the terms which are commonly available: eg the land and the sky or 'firmament'. They are being used as 'observer language' – the creation of the sky and the land is something, which is comprehensible to anyone in any era. If those words, to some ancient cultures, went with a picture of a flat earth etc, then this does not imply that it was a part of the meaning carried by the

---

[82] Eg Allan Day in (1998) in an article which otherwise has much useful material and in no way means to denigrate Scripture.

message. It was just that no other terms were available in which to describe it. Each culture can, however, quite properly understand the words in terms of its own level of scientific understanding. The whole point of the words is their theology, not any particular implied 'scientific' picture. The imagery intended is neutral: it is neither primitive nor modern.

Mechanisms of Creation

We have repeatedly insisted that any Christian theism has to recognise that God can work both within and outside 'natural processes'. It is God who 'creates the winds' (Amos 4:13) - but nothing 'supernatural' in involved in the sense of a type-ii miracle. So is God also involved in the processes of organic descent? Suppose, for example, that we accept that all Darwin's finches descend from one original 'finch kind'. Is it really right to deny that God *created* the species of finch? We really cannot see any *philosophical* objection from a consistent Christian theist to the idea of God 'creating' species through a natural process of organic evolution, any more than 'creating' winds though a natural process of meteorology.

What, however, about the *specific language* of Genesis 1-3? If there is no *philosophical* objection, could there not be something in the actual *text and language* of Genesis, which indicates (say) a type-ii miracle type of creation?

The simple answer to this is 'No'. The strong word for create[83] used in Genesis 1 is, indeed, always used with God as its subject. Though it does not necessarily mean 'out of nothing' (indeed humankind was not created out of nothing but out of dust) it does imply a freedom of expression to God. The same word (*bara*), however is also used for the creation of the winds as mentioned. There is no implication carried by the Hebrew language that such 'creation' is either instantaneous or a type-ii miracle. It *could be*, of course, but the context and other evidence and not the language has to determine this.

It is, of course, highly unlikely that the human writer of Genesis 1 had in mind an evolutionary process for 'creation'. He probably, however, did not have had in mind any particular

[83] See eg Wenham (1987) p.14.

process at all - natural or type-ii instantaneous fiat. Hebrew writers generally just did not ask such questions - any more than the Israelites stopped to wonder if the plagues in Egypt were 'natural processes' or 'type-ii' miracles.

Some have felt that the words 'let the earth bring forth...' (1 Gen 1:24) rather than just 'let there be...' implies some kind of spontaneous generation. Certainly some early writers took it that the earth was given a kind of fecundity principle for spontaneous generation. We doubt, however, that this kind of meaning should be assigned. The writer was simply not addressing such issues.

The Jewish-Christian doctrine of 'Creation' is a statement about person and purpose. In this context 'evolution' describes a natural physical process, whilst 'creation' speaks of the purpose behind it. The geneticist can 'create' a new strain of wheat - ie bring into being a strain which (s)he has first had in mind. The fact that (s)he uses natural processes in that creation does not negate the purpose behind it. The analogy is not, of course, perfect, for in the instance of God the natural processes only have any continuing reality through his continuing will - they have no existence outside of him.

We are well aware that there are atheists like Richard Dawkins (and, alas, Christians like Phillip Johnson) who portray 'evolution' as incompatible with 'creation'. Obviously there are some versions of evolution which *are,* because they include within them a denial of intention or design. But this is not inherent in the idea of organic descent of one species from another - or indeed one genera from another. The language of Genesis 1 tells us nothing about the mechanism or mode of 'creation'. This was, as we have seen, the view of many key late nineteenth century Evangelicals and early Fundamentalists – and we believe that they were right.

Details of the Accounts - Mainly Chapter One

Genesis Ch. 1 begins with the simplest and most majestic statement of the Creationist doctrine which is central to all Christian Theism: 'In the beginning God created the heavens and the earth...' The physical universe as we now see it is not eternal, it had a beginning. This is by no means self-evident.

Chaos is not a divinity but is itself a stage in purposeful design. The world is not, moreover, some kind of by-product of warring gods, but the result of planned creation by the only true God. The sun and stars are not divinities, but created products - and the dramatic effect of not even introducing them until the fourth day must have been shattering to the star-worshipping, neighbours of the Hebrews! There are many ways in which the chapter can be seen not as having affinities with other accounts (like the Babylonian) but as a devastating attack on their presuppositions.[84]

What is the essence of 'Creation'? The Bible clearly presents it as the activity of a personal God: 'And God said "Let there be light", and there was light.' God first formed the idea of light in imagination, then decided to make that thought actual, and then it appeared in physical reality. As already explored, we, like God, are personal beings and (though our own experiences of volition are unlike his, in being tied to the physical bodies and brains he has given us) we may experience 'from the inside' something of 'choice, in creative activity. Our mental picture precedes the thing which we later make.

But this leaves some basic questions about God's creative activity. The word 'created' *(bara)* is used only three times: to refer to the heavens and earth (1:1), the animal life (1:21) and mankind. (1:27) Does the word itself always imply 'created out of nothing' (or as some prefer to word it 'created not out of anything'). Are, as Andrews for example takes it, all the creative acts of Genesis 1 type-ii miracles as we previously defined them? To make such assumptions, however well meaning, if the Bible language itself implies otherwise, is neither intellectually acceptable nor honouring to God. We may note again Jesus' clear theistic teaching that God is at work in natural processes like feeding the birds. Thus when Scripture says that 'God creates the winds...' (Amos 4:13) we can take it that he does this through the natural processes in which he operates.

If the language itself, then, does not tell us, are there other indications of whether type-ii miracles are involved ? In the case of the very first event, elsewhere the Bible states: 'By faith we

---

[84] See Heidel (1951) or Van Till (1986) Ch. 2.

understand that the universe was formed at God's command, so that what is seen was not made out of what was visible (Heb 11:3). Possibly this creation out of what is not visible could be stretched to mean what physicists call a 'singularity', which is not visible in any usual sense, or to mean 'quantum space, which is not quite the same as literally nothing. Personally, however, we favour the traditional interpretation of *ex nihilo*, as literally created out of nothing (or not out of anything) - implying that quantum space itself is a creation.

The nature of the creation of animal life (1:21) is less easy to determine. Obviously if we took the 'days' literally then the creation would have to be type-ii miracle, but we have already seen that consistent interpretation of Scripture would be against this. This being so, there is no obvious necessary reason to take creation of animal life as a type-ii miracle - though of course it may well have been. Some of the earlier language 'Let the earth bring forth....' fits at least as well any idea of vegetation emerging through natural processes of spontaneous generation. Some early support may be found for spontaneous generation' in both Basil and Augustine, eg:

> as mothers are pregnant with young, so the world itself is pregnant with the causes of things that are born.[85]

Neither Jewish thinking nor early church teaching rules out the idea of a natural fecundity in the earth.

If we consider human creation there is a clear Biblical sense in which all mankind is created and (unless we take such Biblical statements in a highly oblique and allegorical sense) they are 'created' through the natural processes of human procreation (Ps 89:47). God, indeed, is specifically said to have formed man out of pre-existing material (Gen 2.7) just as he 'formed' (Heb: *yatsar*) Jeremiah in the womb (Jer 1:5) and his servant in Isaiah (49:5). If there is no reason to suppose that Jeremiah's prenatal growth involved any type-ii miracle we should have to accept that the Scripture language concerning the forming of Adam's body may have needed none either.

What of the breathing into man's nostrils of the 'breath of life' (Gen 1:7)? We have seen that even Young takes this as an

---

[85] Augustine *On The Trinity* iii 9 (*Nic & Post Nic Fath* 1, iii, 62).

'anthropomorphic expression', and it is hard to determine how far the metaphor goes. Mankind shares with animals the breath of life (Gen 1:30), and other poetic references to the 'breath of the Lord' (Job 37:10) seem to indicate that it may also imply working through natural processes.

Where does all this leave us ? What it emphasises is that it is not good enough - whether we are devout Christians or sceptical enquirers - simply to 'read into' Genesis a weight of presupposition on what it 'must mean'. To be faithful to the text we should look to the Bible language itself to set the limits of interpretation. Genesis certainly does not 'teach' organic evolution, nor does it 'teach' a series of type-ii miracles. Both these ideas involve modern categories of understanding neither relevant nor present to the ideas of the human writer. God could, of course, have used type-ii miracles in all his creating and forming, but the language used does not necessarily have to carry this meaning. If anything, in fact, phrases like 'Let the earth bring forth...' and the deliberate reference to the pre-existent materials of man's body, could give a hint of the use of natural processes. Certainly if this is what is meant, then it gives an even greater contrast to some of the pagan early accounts where there is a nature independent of the gods who create in acts of magic. On balance, however, we would conclude that the Genesis accounts are neutral as far as deciding whether God used natural processes or type-ii miracles after the first initiating act. If we do feel that it is important to decide this question, then we will have to look to other sources of information, rather than force the Genesis accounts to give information they were evidently not intended to give.

Of Trees, Snakes and Gardens

We have seen how even ardent 'literalists' take parts of Gen 2-3 figuratively. Surely, as we consider *how much* of the trees, garden, snake etc is meant to be literal and how much allegory, we should look to the Bible itself (and in particular the New Testament) for guidance?

God planted a garden in Eden, where the trees included the 'tree of life' (2:9). The other four Old Testament occurrences of this phrase 'tree of life' are all figurative (Prov 3:18, 11:30,

13:12, 15:4) – as are apocryphal references in 1 Enoch 24:4, 2 Enoch 8:3-9 and 2 Esdras 8:52). It is also mentioned in Revelation 2:7 as being (present tense) 'in the paradise of God'. The word 'paradise' (from the Persian for 'park' or 'garden'[86]) is exactly the same word as used in the LXX of Gen 2:8 for 'garden' of Eden. Is it literal? The whole of Revelation is full of picture imagery, and to 'take it literally' would be absurd. Thus when the tasting of the 'tree of life' is linked with blessings for 'washing one's robes' (22:14) it is not really about laundering - and the exclusion of 'dogs' (22:15) need not concern literalist members of the canine defence league. The trees of life and the knowledge of good and evil *could*, of course, have been literal in Genesis, but as we look to the New Testament to guide our interpretation we tend to take the account of them as metaphorical history. Man faced a real, historical choice between life and the knowledge of good and evil - but the language used to describe this choice (like so much of Jesus' language) is metaphorical. The 'paradise of Eden' was taken by pre-Reformation commentators partly as literal and partly metaphorical. One commentator claims it was Luther who:

> broke fundamentally with earlier views of paradise. He distinguished between the paradise of Genesis 2 and that of the New Testament, and he rejected the allegorical interpretation of paradise.[87]

We would wish to reassert the more traditional (ie pre-Luther) view of this, and accept that the New Testament writer's very deliberate use of identical terms is no coincidence.

It is actually worth looking in detail at the deliberate parallels between the 'first things' in Genesis 2-3 and the 'last things' in the book of Revelation:

1. The heavens and earth were completed (Gen 2.1).
   I saw a new heaven and a new earth (Revn 21.1).
2. The Lord God brought the woman to the man (Gen 2:22).
   The bride/wife (which is the city) comes down from God for her husband who is the second Man (Revn 19:7, 21:2 & 10).
3. The gold is good and the bdellium and onyx stone (Gen 2.12).
   The city is gold, jasper and precious stones (Revn 21:18-19).

---

[86] Morris (1987) p. 62.
[87] Sailhamer (1996) p. 217.

4. There is a river flowing which divides into four rivers (Gen 2:10). There is a river of the water of life (Revn 22:1).
5. There is a tree of life in the midst of the 'garden of Eden' (Gen 2:9; 3:22).
   There is a tree of life in the 'garden (paradise) of God'(Revn 2:7) on both sides of the river (?) with twelve fruits, and leaves for the healing of the nations (Revn 22:2).
6. Cursed are you more than all cattle - cursed is the ground (Gen 2:14; 2:17).
   Every curse will be no longer (Revn 22:3).
7. The serpent (Gen 3, cf 2 Cor 11:3).
   The serpent is Satan (Revn 12:9), is bound (20:2), and thrown into the lake of fire (20:10).
8. The serpent said 'You shall not surely die' (Gen 3:4 cf Jn 8:44).
   Nothing unclean shall enter it, or one practising abomination or a lie. (Revn 21:27).

Revelation is a book absolutely full of allegorical/figurative imagery: Churches have central lampstands, cities are also women, Christ is a lamb and has a sword coming out of his mouth, a dragon is also a serpent, and angels pour out bowls of woe. So how should we take the narrative in Revelation:

- See it as a primitive fairy story?
- Take it all literally?
- Say 'well I see a figurative/allegorical meaning but I *also* think the church "really will" be a great gold cube which is also a woman'?
- Take it as meant purely figuratively, and discern the real issues and events God wishes to speak to us about through it?

The first two of these are not options for any serious commentator. The third seems to us absurd - it would not be a sign of spirituality but stupidity on the level of saying 'Well I understand Jesus' words in John 15 had an figurative meaning but I also think he really is a vine.' Why, then, do people so often try to say something fairly similar about (say) the 'tree of life' in Genesis? John's deliberate use in Revelation of the same imagery and language shows clearly how first century Jews understood Genesis - and as we believe him to have been writing by God's direction there is especial reason for us as Christians to take our lead from it. We have little doubt, then, that the 'tree of life', the 'serpent' and the other imagery in these passages is intended as pure symbolism (and not literally as well) both in Revelation 20-22 and in Genesis 2-3. It deals with real events and issues, but describes them in figurative terms.

Perhaps we should just look at the 'snake' of Gen 3 in more detail. Taken 'strictly literally', the story would imply:

1. Before man's fall there was only one serpent and he walked upright, had great wisdom, and talked.

2. After man's fall that particular serpent was cursed and made to crawl (note that no ban on walking was put on his descendants if we 'take it literally').

3. Also, the serpents would be particularly enemies to man, would bruise their heels, and eat dust as part of their diet.

To take it thus would not only be absurd, but would miss its point. New Testament writers make explicit the contemporary Jewish interpretation which sees the serpent as Satan - though Satan is not 'literally' a serpent since in the same breath he can be spoke of as a 'dragon'. (Rev 20:2). The 'seed' of Satan are his followers - a 'brood of vipers, as the gospels say (Mt 12:34; Lk 3:7). Just as the serpent denied that God had really spoken to mankind, so his 'seed' denied that God had really spoken or acted through Jesus (Gen 3:4; Mt 12:24). The serpent Satan lied because the truth was not in him (Jn 8:44), his offspring spoke falsely because of what was in them (Mt 12:34). The word 'seed' can, of course, be taken either as singular or plural, but the 'seed' of the woman is referred to in Gen 3:15 as 'he' and is a clear reference to the coming Messiah. There was, then, enmity between the 'brood of vipers, and 'seed of the woman' - the bruising of whose heel may speak of the crucifixion during which a nail was driven into it. The church, as Christ's non-literal body, also enters into the conflict (Rom 16:20). If, then, we take the New Testament as our guide, we see the snake as the embodiment of Satan.[88] It *could*, of course, have been a literal embodiment - but whether it was is irrelevant. It is, however, more difficult to accept an approach like that of eg Ellen Gould White or the more recent E J Young to read into the account two separate characters (a physical snake and Satan).

---

[88] We dealt in *Reason and Faith* with questions about the reality of spiritual forces, and will put some comment on our web site.

Not only is it a highly artificial interpretation, but Young is inconsistent - slipping inadvertently into speaking as though the snake *is* Satan and at times taking a highly figurative view. Our own view is that the serpent, tree of life, forbidden fruit etc are all most consistently seen as intended figuratively.

Of Adam and Eve

We have insisted that much of the setting in the 'Paradise of Eden' is allegorical. So were 'Adam and Eve actual people or is the *whole story* an allegory? We must firstly insist that to those who (like ourselves) take a high view of biblical inspiration, the account of the creation of Adam and Eve is one of the most important in the Bible. Jesus cites this passage (eg in Matt 19:4-6) to teach that God intended marriage to be a heterosexual, monogamous and lifelong commitment. Our own clear commitment to interpreting it as the basis for marriage and family life is shown elsewhere.[89]   Like Jesus (and Philo, and Origen and Augustine etc) we believe the account to be inspired and to be intended to convey important truths to us.

But does this mean it is all meant to be 'literal'? Does 2:19-20, for example, imply that God 'literally' trooped all the world's land and air creatures (including over 2 million species of insects) before a bachelor named Adam as he sat on the veranda during the afternoon of the sixth day? Or is it rather to tell us two basic truths:

(a) Mankind alone was created with an in-built urge to create conceptual language in 'naming' animals.

(b) No animal can have a truly personal relationship with a human person in the way epitomised by marriage.

God *could*, of course, have literally put Adam to sleep and used a rib to 'build' Eve - but we do not believe the story was intended to imply this. For one thing the order of events would then contradict Ch. 1, and for another the actual word means 'side' not 'rib'.[90] As the first century Jew Philo asked:

---

[89] Cf Paul Marston's own books *The Biblical Family* (1982) and *God and the Family* (1983).

[90] See eg Victor P Hamilton (1990) p. 178.

> If he filled up with flesh (the place of) the one which he took, are we to suppose that the one which he left was not made of flesh? Truly our sides are twin in all their parts and are made of flesh.[91]

Surely this is not about a lopsided Adam or human anatomy, but a deeper truth. As Wenham says:

> The whole account of woman's creation has a poetic flavour: it is certainly mistaken to read it as an account of a clinical operation.[92]

Blocher describes some of the richness of Hebrew word-play involved, and also the spiritual meaning taken throughout Christian history by Augustine, Aquinas, Matthew Henry etc.[93] Woman was not created from Man's head to rule, nor his feet to serve, but from his side as a companion and equal - reflecting the phrase 'a powerful ally suitable for him' in 2:20. Were we actually to 'take it literally', two questions might be asked. Why should God put Adam into a deep sleep to do it? Since it was (presumably) miraculous anyway, he could surely have done it painlessly with Adam awake – on a local rather than a general anaesthetic principle? Secondly, if Adam had been asleep, how did he know that Eve was 'bone of his bone, as soon as he saw her? God might, of course, have told him - though one then wonders why the text does not mention it. Douglas Spanner suggests[94] that the 'deep sleep' was so that God could speak to Man in a dream about the building of Woman from his 'side'. In any event, all these kinds of question illustrate the futility of trying to make this a lesson in surgery and anatomy rather than about theology and marriage.

Granted that *elements* of the account were clearly meant figuratively, were 'Adam and Eve' actual individuals? Before looking in more detail at New Testament references to Genesis 1-3 we must note one key linguistic point. The Hebrew word *'adam'* simply means 'Man', and is used in this sense throughout the Old Testament. It *can* also be a proper name, but it is not clear where it is first used in this sense in Genesis. Hebrew expert Gordon Wenham remarks:

---

[91] Philo *Allegorical Interpretation* II 20.

[92] Wenham (1987) p. 69.

[93] Blocher (1984) p. 98-100.

[94] Spanner (1987) p. 65. Douglas is not, of course, a literalist.

(adam) "man" in Gen 1-4 is usually preceded by the definite article "the man" except when preceded by an inseparable proposition such as *(l)* "to" (2:20; 3:17,21). In omitting the article with the preposition *(l)*, *(adam)* behaves like *(elohim)* "God." In chap. 5 *(adam)* is used without the article as a personal name "Adam", but from 4:1 and 4:25 it is evidence that even with the article "Adam" may be the better translation, just as *(ha elohim)* may well be translated "God," e.g. 22:1 (cf Cassuto, 1:166-67). This fluidity between the definite and indefinite article forms makes it difficult to know when the personal name "Adam" is first mentioned (LXX 2:16; AV 2:19; RV and RSV 3:17; TEV 3:20; NEB 3:21). The very indefiniteness of reference may be deliberate. *(adam)* is "mankind-humanity" as opposed to God or the animals (*(ish)* is man as opposed to woman). Adam, the first man created and named, is representative of humanity...

Nowhere in chaps 1-3 does God give mankind a name, although "man," literally "the man" , is often mentioned. But from 4.25 to 5.6 the anarthrous form "Adam," the proper name, is used. However such a translation here is jarring in English and most commentators adopt the generic term here.[95]

The ambiguity of *adam* not only makes dogmatic interpretation of Genesis itself impossible, but is also reflected in New Testament references to which we now turn.

Paul and Adam

Paul, even more than Jesus, seems to use Rabbinic forms of argument. We know that he often 'disputed in the synagogues' throughout Acts, and many of his letters have a kind of 'debating' air, as though he is trying to convince a Jewish critic. In some instances his arguments actually make sense only if some of the Genesis account is *intended* as a kind of allegory. If it is purely literal reporting of historical events, then why should it imply anything about how we should live now? In 1 Tim 2:11-15, for example, Paul[96] wrote:

> For Adam first was formed, then Eve. And Adam was not deceived but the woman being deceived became a transgressor. But she will

---

[95] Wenham (1987) p. 32 & 126; we have transliterated the Hebrew in his text (shown italicised) to make it easier for non-Hebrew readers.

[96] We are aware of the controversy over the authorship of the Pastoral epistles, but it is not relevant to our present theme.

be saved through the childbearing if they continue in faith and love...

We should note first about this that it is not given in a kind of history lesson context, but is advanced by Paul as a basis for how men and women should behave in the church. As such it actually has *more* force not less if we see the Genesis account as a divinely inspired allegory intended to teach us truth about humanity. Bearing in mind the clear prophecy in Gen 3.15 about the 'seed of the woman' (whom we take to be Jesus the Messiah), surely 'the childbearing' must refer to the Messiah? The unaccountable switch in the Greek text from 'she' to 'they' seems best understood in terms precisely of a concept of 'Eve' as representative woman. In 1 Cor 11 he is arguing on a point of symbolism between men and women, and states: 'For man was not out of woman, but woman out of man' (11:8). His argument carries weight only if Genesis is about a meaning deeper than anatomy. Paul's words also might leave some doubt about the literality of Adam as an individual.

In 1 Cor 11 Paul refers simply to 'Man' and 'Woman' - ie seeing the Genesis story as personifying the species and gender as a whole. He could, of course, have said 'the man' was not out of the woman', or even more explicitly implied names 'Adam was not out of Eve'.

Rom 5:12-19 parallels the 'one man' Adam and the 'one man' Christ, seemingly seeing both as individuals. But great care needs to be taken in considering such passages in Paul. Firstly, he is reacting to existing ideas in Judaism. One of Paul's basic points is that the 'second Man' was not (as some rabbis held) the nation of Israel[97] but was focused in on *one man*, the Messiah. His argument actually carries *more* force if the Adam (or Man) in the Genesis account is intended *primarily* as a 'type' (5:14) rather than as a simple account of events. We really need also to remember that to Paul 'Christ' was not a name, and wherever it appears in his letters it could actually be translated 'Messiah'. His theology reorientates Jewish thinking to be 'Messiah centred'. It is interesting to compare some of his language with his contemporary Philo:

---

[97] Cf N T Wright (1997b) p. 262 etc.

1. In Philo the 'earthly man' is the 'earthly and perishable mind' whilst the 'heavenly man' is the pure mind 'after the image' and set in God. In Paul the 'earthly man' is the one in Genesis 2, the 'heavenly man' is the Messiah (1 Cor 15:47-8).

2. In Philo the 'pure mind' is set on heavenly things with reason controlling passion, whilst to Paul the 'pure mind' is also set on heavenly or spiritual things but in the Messiah, the heavenly man (Rom 8:1-5).

3. In Philo immortality is a property of the soul; in Paul it is a resurrection gift to those who have identified with the Messiah (Rom 6:5-6, 1 Cor 15:54 etc).

We may note not only the Jewish background, but that in his whole imagery of the old and new Adam, old and new Man, Paul plays on the plural/singular nature of the words. Compare:

- Our old man has been crucified with him (Christ) that the body of sin might be done away with. (Rom 6:6).
- You have put off the old man with his practices and have put on the new (Col 3:9-10).
- For he (the Messiah) is our peace, the one having made us both one...that he might create in himself one new man in the place of the two...that you put off, concerning your former conduct, the old man which grows corrupt according to the deceitful lusts, and be renewed in the spirit of your mind, and that you put on the new man which was created according to God in true righteousness and holiness (Eph 2:15, 4:22-4).

Paul *nowhere* speaks in the plural of 'new made *men*' or of 'your former *selves*'. There is *one* old man (Adam), and *one* new man (the Messiah). Our old Man/Humanity has been crucified *with* the Messiah, and Christians accept God's judgement in this by burial in baptism and rising again to share in the resurrection life of the new Man/Humanity (Rom 6:4-6). As well as this once-for-all acceptance of God's provision, we also have to make a continual 'putting off' of the old Man/Humanity, and a 'putting on' of the new one. 1 Corinthians raises the same theme:

- For as through man (or 'a man') came death also by man (or 'a man') has come resurrection from the dead. For as in Adam all die, so in the Messiah shall all be made alive. (1 Cor 15:21-22).

- And so it is written, the first man Adam became a living being, the last Adam became a life giving spirit... The first man was of the earth, made of dust, so also are those who are made of dust: and as is the heavenly man so also are those who are heavenly. And as we have borne the image of the man of dust, so also shall we bear the image of the man of heaven. (1 Cor 15:45-9).

- Therefore just as through one man sin entered the world and death through sin, and thus death spread to all men because all sinned... therefore, as through one man's offence judgement came to all men, resulting in condemnation, even so through one Man's righteous act the free gift came to all men resulting in justification of life...(Rom 5:12-18).

As we noted, to Paul the 'heavenly man' was the Messiah, bringing a new dimension of *spiritual* life. Adam is the 'old man' and Christ is 'the new man' - and in both cases there is a collective as well as an individual identity. Though through individual acts came both transgression and salvation, it seems that we have to 'opt in' in both cases. Paul describes his own 'fall' in a passage, which comes, soon after his reference to the fall of 'Adam' (5:12):

I was alive once without the law, but when the commandment came sin revived and I died. (Rom 7:9)

Sin is in our world and environment, but it was at the point where Paul 'opted in' that he died. The reference is, of course, to spiritual not physical death. This reflects his contemporary Philo who suggested that since after sinning Adam lived and had children, the phrase in Gen 2:17 'you shall die the death' refers to the 'death of the soul' which is 'the decay of virtue and the bringing in of wickedness'.

Other near contemporary Hebrew/Christian writings reflect similar ideas. The book of 2 Baruch, which dates from around 100 AD, was probably translated (into Syriac) from Hebrew. It contains the following interesting passage:

For although Adam sinned first and has brought death upon all who were not in his own time, yet each of them who has been born from him has prepared for himself the coming torment. And further, each of them has chosen for himself the coming glory. For truly the one who believes will receive reward. But now, turn yourselves to destruction, you unrighteous ones who are living now, for you will be visited suddenly, since you have rejected the understanding of the Most High. For his works have not taught you, nor has the artful work of his creation which has always existed persuaded you. Adam is, therefore, not the cause, except only for himself, but each of us has become his own Adam.[98]

A recent paper comments on this:

> The parallels with the Pauline Romans here are startling. In Romans God may be known by what he has made (1:20), destruction is in store for those who have rejected God from their understanding (1:28), whilst reward is for those who believe (3:22). To Paul, we note, Adam has 'brought death on' those who followed (5:12). Surely the Pauline 'because all sinned' (5:12 and cf 7:9) is also reflected in the phrase 'each of us has become his own Adam'? What is, of course, missing, is the Pauline insistence that to believe is efficacious only because of the faithfulness of Jesus the Messiah (3:22 correctly translated). Much else, though, shows the parallels with Paul who was reinterpreting not abrogating Jewish approaches.[99]

We already noted that Paul speaks ambiguously, sometimes speaking as though 'Adam' is 'Man'. In 1 Cor 15:21-22 he says:

> For since through man (or 'a man') came death, so also through man (or 'a man') came the resurrection of the dead. For as in (the) Adam all die, so also in (the) Christ all shall be made alive.

The word 'man' (15:21) has no definite article and there is no indefinite article in Greek, so it could mean 'man' or 'a man' (reflecting Romans 'one man'). But in verse 22 the tense is present (all *die*), so surely a historical individual cannot be meant? A few paragraphs earlier he has said:

> For just as the body is one and has many members...so also is (the) Christ. (1 Cor 12:12).

This refers to the church as the 'body' of Christ. In sense it seems as though the 'old humanity' is both plural and singular, just as 'the Christ' is both plural and singular.[100]

In Romans 5 Paul speaks of the coming of sin. He tells us that unless a moral law is recognised (either explicitly or in one's conscience) there is no sin (Rom 5:13). In Eden Man recognised that law, broke it, and so fell into sin. In doing so he had grasped

---

[98] 2 Baruch 54:15-19 tr A Kiljn (1983)

[99] Justin Marston (1998).

[100] Compare Dan 7:13-14's messianic receipt of the kingdom with the receipt by the saints in Dan 7:18.

an experiential 'knowledge of good and evil', but at a cost predicted by God. This cost was spiritual 'death' (Gen 2:17) which thus entered through one man (Rom 5:12). This is logical enough, as there must have been a first explicit recognition of the authority of a divinely revealed moral law. In this sense there surely must have been *an* 'Adam' - an individual whose experience initiated and epitomised the experience of Man with sin and spiritual death. Paul goes on (5:12) to picture death as spreading to all men because all men sinned. Neither the spreading of the sin, nor the parallel spreading of salvation through Jesus is automatic - both involve choices of the individuals. Paul later reflects in his own experience this spreading of sin and death. In 7:9 he relates how before he felt the authority of moral law he was alive, but on recognising it and committing sin for the first time 'sin revived and I died'. But as Adam's sin released a sin principle which came to all men in this way, so the righteous act of the Messiah has brought the 'free gift resulting in justification of life to all men' (Rom 5:18). Those (and it is everyone) who have submitted to and accepted the sin principle died, but those who submitted to and accepted the free gift of God in the Messiah have a life more abundant than that lost.

There was, of course, not the slightest doubt in the mind of Paul that Jesus the Messiah was a historical figure. So was it essential to Paul's understanding to believe that Adam was also a historical individual?   This is hard to say. He does use collective language, though he also uses individual language. James Dunn, in his scholarly *Word* commentary, is doubtful as to how far Paul expected his readers to understand the plural ambiguity of '*adam*'; yet Dunn also asserts of Romans 5:12 etc:

It would not be true to say that Paul's theological point here depends on Adam being a "historical" individual or on his disobedience being a historical event as such. Such an implication does not necessarily follow from the fact that a parallel is drawn with Christ's single act: an act in mythic history can be paralleled to an act in living history without the point of comparison being lost. So long as the story of Adam as the initiator of the sad tale of human failure was well known, which we may assume (the brevity of Paul's presentation presupposes such a knowledge) such a comparison is meaningful. Nor should modern interpretation encourage patronising generalisations about the primitive mind naturally understanding the Adam stories as literally historical... such tales told about the dawn of human history could be and were treated with a considerable degree of sophistication, with the literal meaning often discounted. Indeed, if anything, we should say that the effect of the comparison between the two epochal figures, Adam and Christ, is not so much to historicise the individual Adam as to bring out the more than individual significance of the historic Christ.[101]

If the main point of Paul's teaching about the earthly *adam* was that he was a 'type' of the one man the Messiah, then his argument certainly depends upon accepting the divine inspiration of the Genesis account of 'the man', but it is less clear that his argument requires this to be a literal individual – although on other grounds we may conclude that it was.

The Early Church and Augustinianism

How did the early church interpret these things? They seem fairly generally to have taken the story of the creation of Eve from Adam's side figuratively. The second century anti-Christian Celsus ridiculed the passage on a literal basis - but even he had to admit that:

> the more modest among Jews and Christians are ashamed of these things and endeavour to give them somehow an allegorical interpretation.[102]

We previously noted Origen's pre-eminence amongst the early teachers who wrote in the Greek (the language of the New Testament). Origen also learned his Hebrew from living sources, and so his comments are of special interest when he notes that:

> in the Hebrew language Adam signifies man, and that in those parts of the narrative which appear to refer to Adam as an individual, Moses is discoursing upon the nature of man in general. For "in Adam' (as the Scripture says) 'all die;' and were condemned in the likeness of Adam's transgression, the word of God asserting this not so much of one particular individual as of the whole human race.[103]

---

[101] Dunn (1988) pp. 289-90.

[102] Quoted by Origen in *Against Celsus* iv, 38 (*Ant Nic Fath* iv 516).

[103] Origen *Against Celsus* iv 40 (*Ant Nic Fath* iv, 516).

Augustine, coming some two centuries later, can hardly be called 'early church', though we have seen that he was no more a crude literalist than Origen. We have also noted, however, some of his novelty in theology, perhaps due to Manichaean influences. One of these was an idea that all babies are born inheriting the guilt of Adam (which he thought washed away in physical baptism). This idea of hereditary guilt is found in *no* Jewish source[104] and in no early church figure. It would, though, obviously necessitate a literal single man from whom all present people descended. Augustine's supposed biblical basis for this was a mistranslation in his Latin version of Romans 5:12: 'death passed on all men for in him all sinned'.[105] This translation is simply not possible, but it led him to the novel idea (found in no previous Jewish or Christian commentator) that we inherit the guilt of Adam. Theologically conservative scholarly commentaries (eg that of Sanday and Headlam) have long ruled out any such rendering of Romans 5:12, and Cranfield's more recent work, even though written from a fairly Augustinian position, states that it 'should surely be rejected'.[106] John Murray, another Augustine sympathiser, actually admits:

> The clause should not be rendered 'in whom all sinned'.... If Paul meant that death passed upon all because all men were guilty of actual transgression this is the way he would have said it. At least, no more suitable way could be considered.[107]

Murray's subsequent suggestion that one has to be a 'Pelagian'[108] to believe Paul meant what he said (ie that spiritual death came because of their own sin) is unconvincing. Augustine bolstered his novel idea of inherited guilt with various other verses taken out of context. The most common is Psalm 51:5 which says nothing about inherited guilt and in any case is a cry of anguish no more intended literally by David than the preceding words of Psalm 51:4. Though inherited guilt found its way from Augustine into Reformed theology, it has no

---

[104] Cf Edersheim (1900) i p. 52 who is quite explicit.

[105] Augustine: *On the Forgiveness of Sins and Baptism* i 10 (*Nic & Post Nic Fath* 1 v 26 etc).

[106] C E B Cranfield (1980) vol 1 p. 276.

[107] Murray (1965) p. 183.

[108] 'Pelaglians' are usually taken to believe we can save ourselves by good works.

biblical foundation whatsoever. Our own reasons for firmly rejecting such ideas are purely biblical,[109] and in no way depend on the question of whether we all descend from one human pair.

We have made this point at length to show that the Augustinian/Calvinist tradition may have particular reason to insist on a single progenitor, but that this reason is not biblical. This is not, however, to prejudge the actual issue of the literality of Adam to which we shall return shortly.

Back to Beginnings

We have noted that in the early chapters of Genesis the more modern versions are right to translate 'Adam' simply as '*the* man' - it usually contains the definite article. It is really only from chapter 4 or perhaps even 5 onwards that it can *definitely* be seen as a name. Were Adam and Eve the sole humans on earth in Genesis 4:1? If so then Cain's fears in Gen 4:14 would seem a bit bizarre: 'Whoever finds me will kill me'. If, at this point, his mum and dad were the only other humans on the planet and he was already full-grown, he must have been of a very nervous disposition to be worrying about such distant future eventualities. Then, in verse 17, Cain 'had sex with his wife' - where did *she* come from? Adam's next son Seth and other offspring are mentioned in 5:3-4. But before these are even mentioned, Cain had a son, and built a city named after him. Who lived in it? Wouldn't it have seemed a bit pretentious for just the three of them? Now, again, sceptics have sometimes suggested that the writer of Genesis was a complete simpleton to whom such questions never occurred. This is implausible. Surely either the writer intended us to understand that at the time of a historical Cain there were many other human beings around who were not in his immediate family, or else he intended the whole story of Cain and Abel to be seen allegorically, and the real history of the individual unambiguously *named* Adam for the first time in Gen 5:1, to begin from that point.

---

[109] See the appendix of our (1973, 1989). We would, of course, emphatically assert the biblical doctrine that all people sin and are in need of a Saviour.

So how *is* it all to be put together? Firstly, we would want to assert that the import of the passages for us (which was the concern of Jesus and Paul) is pretty clear. In particular:

- Humankind are in the image of God in that they have cognitive language, morality, and self-conscious social interaction.

- In the 'deep-knowing' unity of heterosexual lifelong marriage commitment, we reflect the interacting plurality of persons in a personal God.

- Humankind are in a fallen moral state, looking to a representative 'seed of woman' to crush the forces of evil.

On how it ties *historically*, rather than on its implication for us, it would be foolish to be dogmatic. It seems clear to us that the 'trees' and 'snake' were intended figuratively. It also seems likely that the story of 'the Man' and 'the Woman' in Genesis 2-3 (where the terms carry the definite article) is a picture of Everyman - certainly each of us (like Paul) have our own personal fall as we 'opt in' to the sin principle in the world. In that sense an individual 'Adam' may be seen as our 'Federal Head', and it may be that we should picture it that all humans 'opt in' to his sin. With the 'second Man' or 'last Adam' (ie Jesus the Messiah) the 'faithfulness of the Messiah'[110] in his atoning act of self sacrifice is 'opted into' through faith - and this opting in is done by believers both before his death (eg David and Abraham) and after it. If we want to take Paul's parallel seriously, then perhaps we might suggest that the sin of 'The Man', so graphically recorded in Genesis 2-3, has been 'opted into' by humans living both before and after the event happened in space-time.

Can Genesis be used to date the 'Adam' whose generations begin in Gen 5:1? Genesis 5 contains a list of genealogies, but again the New Testament can guide us as to how to interpret these, When Mt 1:6-11 repeats the genealogies of 1 Chron 3:10-19, it omits several of the names. This was neither a mistake nor a deception, but a deliberate use of an accepted literary convention of the times. Matthew's readers recognised that Hebrew genealogies did not have to be strict father-son

---

[110] See Wright (1997) p. 106.

relationships, so no misunderstandings could arise. This, then, applies to the genealogies of Adam's descendants. When it gives the age at which 'X begat Y', the word 'begat' could mean (as evidently in Matthew) that X begat the forebear of Y at that point. The early church did tend to believe that the time since Adam was in thousands of years. Most actually gave it as earlier than Ussher's famous 4004 BC in the seventeenth century. Thus e.g. Theophilus placed it at 5529 BC,[111] Clement of Alexandria c 5590 BC,[112] Julius Africanus at 5531 BC,[113] etc, But the difficulties of any certainty bearing in mind the difficulties of interpreting the genealogies were often noted. What does seem clear is that the time since the time of the Adam referred to in Genesis 5 onwards, is to be seen in terms of thousands rather than hundreds of thousands of years.

One final point to note, which we will pick up on later. The humankind in Genesis 1 seem to be 'hunter-gatherers'- cultivation is not mentioned. In Genesis 2:15 'the man' is to cultivate and keep the garden, although hard labour does not seem to be envisaged (see also 2:6). In Gen 4:2 we find a contrast between Abel, a keeper of flocks (with a nomadic lifestyle?), and Cain, an agriculturist who begins human violence and then goes off to build a city. If this were really a kind of allegory instead of or as well as a literal history, it would be very apt. With cultivation comes settlement and building and territory - and with territory comes violence and war. New Testament references to Cain and Abel (Matt 23, Heb 11, 1 John) seem to speak as though they were actual individuals, but at the very least they are representative of wider issues.

The Flood

We have seen that, taking guidance from the New Testament, the Genesis accounts of creation and Eden are historical but couched in fgurative language, and Adam himself can be taken as 'Man'. What, then, of Noah and the account of the flood?

Unlike Adam, the Bible seems always to regard Noah as an individual within a particular historical context. The flood

---

[111] Theophilus *to Autolucus* iii, 24-8 (*Ant Nic Fath*, ii, 118-120).
[112] Clement *Stromata*, i. 21 (*Ant Nic Fath*, ii, 332-3).
[113] Julius Africanus *Fragments of Chronography*, iii (*Ant Nic Fath*, vi, 130).

passages of Genesis describe historical events in a style more like that of normal observer style than in one of symbolic language. An acceptance of the authority of the Old Testament seems, therefore, to imply that there was an individual called Noah and some kind of physical flood. This understanding is reflected eg in the first century Jewish thinker Philo. Not only does Philo insist that Noah is no myth, but, in contrast to his treatment of Adam and Eve, his 'literal' interpretation of the account is really fairly literal.[114] Like the New Testament, of course, he is *also* interested in the allegorical meaning – but that is another story. All the early Jewish and Christian sources seem to have held to Noah as an actual figure.[115]

To be faithful to Scripture, however, we still need to ask two important questions:

1. What did the actual words mean to the writer; ie to what concepts in his mind did they relate?
2. In what way is the language being used eg as literal, sarcasm, hyperbole, etc?

On (1), the point of departure for interpreting any biblical passage must be to try to understand what the writer intended by the language (s)he used. To do this, one needs first to understand the concepts in the mind of the writer. Some have suggested that the Genesis writer tied the ideas to some kind of primitive cosmology, but we are unconvinced of this. On the other hand, there is no indication that the writer had a concept of a spherical planet earth. The Hebrew word *eretz*, which is translated 'earth' in Gen 1:1 and various verses in Gen 6, did not (to the writer) mean planet earth as we now think of it. Though we may choose to read this *into* Gen 1:1, this is a modern reinterpretation. The writer simply meant 'earth' as distinct from the heavens or as distinct from the sea (Gen 1:10). No particular cosmology, either primitive or modern, was implied.

Whatever they believed about cosmology, it is very unlikely that any early Old Testament writer had in mind a globe when (s)he used the word *eretz*. Elsewhere the word is actually more commonly translated 'land' (1476 times) or 'country' (140

---

[114] See Lewis (1968) Sec III and Colson F H & G H Whitaker (1991).

[115] See Lewis (1968), D A Young (1995).

times) or 'ground' (96 times).[116] Thus to translate 'the whole *eretz*' as 'the whole earth' is really misleading to the modern reader, for we think of 'earth' in terms of a 'globe'. To translate it 'the whole land', would much better convey the kind of concept in the mind of the writer – and often it does not even imply the whole of the then known world.

This can amply be illustrated from some of the other places in which similar phrases are used. In virtually every case to render it 'globe' in any literally implied sense would make it nonsense. Thus in Gen 41:57 when 'all the *eretz* came to Egypt... because the famine was severe in all the *eretz*.' We are surely not to take this as literally global or even as the whole of the inhabited world. In Ex 10:5 the locusts are said to have covered 'the face of the whole *eretz*' but meaning the whole land in question. In Num 22:5, 11 Israel was said to 'cover the *eretz*'. In 2 Sam 15:23 (kjv) 'all the *eretz* wept with a loud voice', whilst in 2 Sam 18:8 (kjv) the battle was 'scattered over the face of all the *eretz*'. In 1 Kings 4:34 and 10:24 'all the *eretz* sought to hear Solomon's wisdom.' King Cyrus, in claiming 'all the kingdoms of the *eretz*' in 2 Chron 36:23 was quite aware of other kingdoms beyond his boundaries. Jer 12:11-12 (kjv) reads: 'the whole *eretz* is made desolate because no man layeth it to heart... for the sword of the Lord shall devour from one end of the *eretz* even to the other end of the *eretz;* no flesh shall have peace.'

The meaning of phrases like 'the whole *eretz'* (as 'for any flesh') must be taken from the context. Generally, the use of the phrase elsewhere would not allow any modern reinterpretation of it to mean 'all the globe'.

The use here of the word 'reinterpretation' may seem strange to some, who have always thought that this was what the Noah account literally said. But this is precisely what it is - a reinterpretation. It involves reading *into* the word *eretz* a concept which it never contained in its Old Testament usage.

There may possibly be some justification for such a reinterpretation of the word *eretz* in Gen 1:1 and we would not rule it out for Gen 6:1, 6:5, etc, though it may not be the most natural reinterpretation to make. What we have to recognise,

---

[116] These numbers are given in Filby (1970) p. 83.

however, is that if we ask whether the flood was global or non-global we are asking a question which the language of Genesis was not intended to answer – and either conclusion is a *reinterpretation* into modern terms of the original concepts.

On the point 2, to fail, for example to recognise the hyperbole in Jesus' teaching in Matthew 23:24 or Luke 14:26 could lead to some strange ideas! Of the way in which language is used in the Old Testament, G B Caird writes:

> Overstatement is... characteristic of the Hebrew style, and the Old Testament abounds in examples of it.[117]

Thus when, for example, there is a reference to the 'nations that are under the whole heaven' in Deut 2:25 (KJV), this is exaggeration or hyperbole. This may also apply to very similar expressions in Genesis, as when it says that 'all the high hills... under the whole heaven were covered' (7:19 KJV).

So what did the writer on the Flood mean? Clearly, (s)he was referring to a cataclysmic event, for Noah and his contemporaries. Their known world was evidently destroyed. But need it have been the whole planet as we now know it? Christians have asked this question almost since the global nature of the planet was known. We may wonder if any light is thrown on this question by the reference to the flood in 2 Pet 3:5-7 (KJV) which reads:

> By the word of God the heavens were of old and the earth (Gk *ge*) standing out of the water and in the water; whereby the world (*cosmos*) that then was, being overflowed with water, perished, but the heavens and the earth (*ge*) which are now, by the same word kept in store, reserved unto fire against the Day of Judgement.

The New Testament uses *ge* 248 times, mainly to mean the soil or land.[118] What does the word *cosmos* mean? In classical Greek it could mean 'world order' or 'created universe'. In the Greek Old Testament (LXX) it can be translated as 'world' (in *any* sense) only in the late apocryphal books of Maccabees and Wisdom. Apart from the created universe, it can mean the human order[119] or take the sense as in 'honoured throughout the world' (Mk 14:19; Rom 1:8). It *never* seems to imply a *globe*.

---

[117] Caird (1980) p. 133.
[118] Brown (1978) i, p. 517.
[119] Brown (1978) i, pp. 521-6.

In the New Testament, Paul uses the word to the sophisticated Greeks to say, 'the God who made the world (*cosmos*) and everything in it is the Lord of heaven (*ouranos*) and earth (*ge*)' (Acts 17:24). Although the idea was rejected by more philosophical Greeks, the old myths had held *Uranus* and *Ge* to be the primal sky and earth gods – and Uranus long survived in popular cults along with other deities. Paul asserts that *everything* (ie the universe or cosmos) was created by God – and heaven and earth are created things under his rulership. In this context Paul's background would have made him well aware that his hearers believed the earth to be a globe, though whether it was or not is irrelevant to his point about God's lordship. By the word *cosmos*, however, Paul here surely means 'the sum total of everything linked to space and time', as in say, Aristotle.[120] He does not mean 'the globe'.

The word *cosmos* can be used to mean the inhabited area of possession, as in 'gain the whole world', but most commonly in the New Testament it means the system of human affairs.[121] Interestingly, even then Luke in Lk 4:5 replaces the word *cosmos* (used by Matthew and Mark) with the word *oikoumene* (inhabited earth), which elsewhere he uses in a more restricted sense to mean the 'civilised world' of the Roman Empire (eg in the census of Lk 2:1).[122]

Where does this leave us? When 2 Pet 2:5 says that God destroyed 'the ancient *cosmos*' or '*cosmos* of the ungodly' in a flood, the reference is most likely to mean the evil system of human affairs (as Peter also uses the word in 2 Pet 1:4 and 2:20). When in 2 Pet 3:5-8 he says that the *ge* which is formed out of water was destroyed with water, he means the 'land'. To make either verse refer to a globe is to reinterpret his words in a way the language simply does not imply. To insist that he must mean total planetary coverage is to force his words way outside their real meaning.

If Peter's language does not necessarily imply literal universality, what of his context? He was arguing against 'scoffers' who 'followed their own evil desires' ie who rejected

---

[120] Brown (1978) i, p. 521.

[121] Brown (1978) i, p. 524.

[122] Brown (1978) i, pp. 518-9.

God. The point at issue was not whether or not the flood was global, but whether or not God was active in his own world. Our God is a God of morality and judgement, who acts in history – this is central to Christianity. But whether the judgement was applied to the 'land' or literally across the planet is relevant neither to Peter's point nor to the Christian faith.

One interesting point is that the New Testament writers are actually more interested in the allegorical or typological meaning than the literal one.[123] The references of Jesus to the flood are to illustrate his point about the coming judgement (Mt 24 and Lk 17) and Peter uses it first as a type of baptism (1 Pet 3:20) and then (as it is used eg in 1 Enoch) to parallel to the coming 'flood of fire'(2 Pet 2:5 etc). Origen emphasised that this 'flood of fire' was allegorical – based on 1 Cor 3:10-15. Indeed, in that passage Paul seems to picture the fire of final judgement as testing the work each one has put into building the church. The 'you' in '*you* are God's temple' in verse 16 is, of course, plural – the church *collectively* is the 'temple' of God. The building with 'gold, silver and precious stones' seems to reflect the building of the church in Rev 21:18-19 where the city is gold, jasper and precious stones as we have seen relating in turn to Gen 2.12. Paul, surely, does not intend a 'literal' building and fire here?   We have, then, to be careful with Hebrew apocalyptic writing, but this is not to deny that the flood was seen as some kind of literal event. The typology, however, is not really dependent on a literally global flood.

It could, perhaps, be objected that if it were only a local flood then the ark would have been unnecessary because Noah and the animals could have been saved through migration. Whilst this is, of course, true, the ark would have been just as purely symbolical if the flood were literally universal, for God could quite easily have saved Noah and all the animals by putting them into suspended animation. He could, indeed, have vaporised the wicked (or used a virus) without sending a flood at all. Perhaps God chose this method in order to emphasise mankind's stewardship over the animal creation. As for Noah, his motivation for building the ark and collecting animals, was

---

[123] For early Christian equivalents see Cohn (1996) (though his later treatment of 'fundamentalism' is less helpful.).

not some kind of modern ecological enthusiasm. He did it in obedience to God. Whatever point God intended by working this way remains unchanged whether literally all species or just species in the region concerned were thus preserved.

When, therefore, we ask today whether or not the flood was global, we are asking which of two ways to reinterpret the language of Genesis. Since the time when scientific knowledge raised the question, people have taken it to mean:

(a) a global and all-covering flood

(b) a global but not all covering flood

(c) a local to 'the land' flood

Its language could plausibly be reinterpreted to fit any of these.

That the earth was a globe was, of course, well known to Philo, probably known to Paul though maybe not to Peter, and well known to the early fathers. So how did they understand the flood? Early rabbinical sources were not interested in the 'scientific' issues at all, though some thought on biblical grounds that either Israel or Eden might have been spared the flood.[124] Philo seems in one place to suggest that it might have just been the Mediterranean basin, though is inconsistent.[125] The leading church fathers give no indication of thinking it localised – though they were dealing with a Greek culture which had its own flood tradition. Augustine, in line with his general approach, discusses the 'scientific' problems of covering all the high mountains with water, gives a tentative suggestion, but advises against dogmatism.[126] All of them thought that secular or 'scientific' information should not be ignored in exegesis, and Augustine especially warned against putting people off Christianity by talking scientific nonsense. Young cites one 5thC Christian source which indicates that 'many now say' the flood covered only the inhabited earth.[127] We may pick out just a few more stages in thinking – though Young deals with it in much more detail. Leonardo de Vinci (1452-1519) seems to have suggested a local flood.[128] Luther (1483-1546) referred to

---

[124] See Lewis (1968) p. 143.

[125] Marcus (1929,1953) Supp 1; Young (1995) p. 11.

[126] Young (1995) pp. 17-18.

[127] Young (1995) p. 27.

[128] Young (1995) p. 39.

no recent science (ignoring issues raised by the rediscovery of America) and thought the flood global and landscape-changing. As the seventeenth century progressed, however, increasing numbers of Christian scholars questioned the universality of the flood. Young mentions the Jewish convert Isaac La Peyrere who in 1655 suggested both pre-Adamites and a local flood.[129] Isaac Voss in 1559 suggested that the flood covered only the inhabited earth. In 1662 a local flood was suggested by the learned and orthodox bishop Edward Stillingfleet[130] followed by Rev Matthew Poole, an Anglican of Presbyterian sympathies, in 1670.[131] All this, we note, is before any development of geology – either flood-geology or any other kind.

Because the Genesis language is open to the different interpretations, later Christians continued the early church tradition in taking scientific knowledge into account in deciding how it should be taken. In the late 18thC, for example, there was a common belief in a world-wide (though not necessarily all-covering) flood. Andre Deluc, a careful scientist working consciously in the Baconian tradition, was one sincere Christian who constructed one of the best known theories. He believed that Noah's flood was world-wide, but that some animals were left on uncovered mountain tops. Thus he asserted of Gen 6:13:

> The more literal translation of the latter part of the verses is: 'I will *destroy* them and the *earth with them.*' We see that the term 'earth' does not here signify the 'terrestrial globe' but 'land' inhabited by man. Conformably to this we read in chapter 1, verse 10: 'And God called the dry land *earth.*'[132]

Almost identical arguments were used by some of the leading evangelical British and American geologists and theologians in the last half of the 19thC. evangelical geologist and theologian Hugh Miller wrote *The Testimony of the Rocks* in 1849 with clear arguments for interpreting the Bible to mean a local flood. The Congregationalist John Pye Smith wrote his influential book *Relation Between the Holy Scriptures and Some Parts of Geological Science* in 1839, which included detailed arguments

---

[129] Young (1995) p. 51; Voss (1559).
[130] Young (1995) p. 53; Stillingfleet (1662) bk 3 Ch. 4.
[131] Young (1995) p. 53; Poole (1670).
[132] De Luc (1809) pp. 389-90.

for a local flood.[133] Later, American geologists J W Dawson[134] and G F Wright[135] wrote similar strong lines of argument, linguistic and theological. As a valid reinterpretation, this received further support from scholars such as the great Hebrew commentator Delitzch. There were, of course, some who continued to interpret the flood as global, but its interpretation as local was widespread among Evangelicals during this period.

So what about today? Some modern writers have argued strongly that Genesis must mean a universal flood.[136] Yet most of their supposed biblical arguments are merely emotional, eg:

> So frequent is the use of universal terms, and so tremendous are the points of comparison... that is it impossible to imagine what more could have been said than actually was said to express the concept of a universal deluge.[137]

The problem with this is that it is an insistence on pressing a narrative (in a manner both Morris and Whitcomb do constantly elsewhere) to answer modern questions it was never intended to answer, at the cost of an almost cavalier disregard of the actual language and intent of the writer. Morris and Whitcomb then back this up not with clear biblical exposition, but by appeals to points of their supposed modern science (eg the depth necessary to cover mountains in the Sumerian region).

Actually, any theory like that of Luther, Woodward, or modern young-earth creationists, holding that the whole face of the earth changed by the flood, does face a major biblical problem. This is that the details of rivers etc mentioned before the flood in Gen 2.14, match those after the flood. For those who, like us, are less adverse to broader interpretation this might not be a problem. But it is a problem for avowed literalists. Why would the names be used in evident expectation that they would be recognised if absolutely nothing of the region remained? There seem also to be biblical problems with Morris' idea of a

---

[133] Smith's letters on this to geology Professor John Phillips (in the Oxford Geology Museum) show his care to check scientific facts.
[134] J W Dawson, eg in (1880).
[135] G F Wright eg in (1896).
[136] F Delitzsch (1899).
[137] Morris & Whitcomb (1961) p. 57.

304 REASON, SCIENCE AND FAITH

water vapour canopy which disappeared with the flood and so caused a more extreme climate. The idea of a perpetual warm climate before the flood is not, of course, explicitly denied in Scripture (though ironically it is explicitly denied by Lactantius so cannot be early orthodoxy![138]). It would, however, seem rather strange for God to go to the trouble (as Morris seems to suppose) of saving two of each kind of dinosaur etc on the ark, knowing full well that the change in climate would kill them off immediately afterwards. This is in addition to the rather forced view of Ps 148:4 if the water vapour canopy really disappeared with the flood.

We believe, therefore, that the Bible implies there was an individual Noah and a physical flood 'throughout all the land'. It leaves it open to modern reinterpretation whether or not 'land' implies the whole globe, though the actual language would tend on the whole to imply not. There is, then (if the expression may be pardoned) no question here of watering down the flood account. It is a question of understanding what it actually meant as written, and to which modern concept this relates.

The question of whether it was universal as far as mankind was concerned is a different issue. The language of Gen 6:6 would seem to offer the strongest indication that it was, ie that all the existing human population was involved. The problem is that, again, we wonder how far this is pressing the language to answer questions it was not intended to answer. This too, therefore, we would still wish to leave open.

Summary

What we have tried to do in this chapter is to explore the meaning of Genesis 1-11, and particularly 1-3, simply from the Bible itself and early Jewish and Christian insights. Our conclusions could have been reached a millennium ago (many of them were!) and are in no way dependent on 'modern science'. The task of seeing how they relate to what we know from modern science will be left to a later chapter.

---

[138] Lactantius *The Divine Institutes* ii 13 (*Ant Nic Fath*, vii, 60).

9
Belief & the Rise of Science

The Issues

In Section 7 we looked at ways in which Christian teachers approached the understanding of early chapters in Genesis throughout history. We were more interested in the theology than in looking at the nature and methods of the developing scientific ideas. The present section is connected, therefore, with Section 7, but takes a slightly different perspective. It aims to ask the following three questions:

1. Have great scientists on the whole been religious or irreligious?
2. How much have theologians through history opposed empirical findings of science and persecuted scientists?
3. Has the Bible been (or should it be) a starting point for science, or has science (or should it have) begun by looking for order in nature?
4. Did mainstream geology develop on unempirical and/or atheistic grounds?

The first two of these issues is one which may concern both Christians and the uncommitted. The third will mostly concern claims of young-earth creationism and some design theorists (particularly Moreland). The fourth will mainly concern the claims of young-earth creationists.

Scientific and Religious Minds?

In the late nineteenth century Francis Galton, a cousin of Darwin and scientist in his own right, put forward a new thesis that 'the pursuit of science is uncongenial to the priestly character.'[1] Rejecting the Christian views of the Christian home (happy by his own admission) in which he had been brought up, he advocated the 'improvement' of the human race by scientifically controlled selective breeding, ie eugenics. Ironically, as he was

---

[1] Galton (1874)

using his scientific mind to explore his main interest of genetics, the real breakthrough in that area of science was being made by an Austrian priest, Abbot Gregor Mendel.[2]

So how general is this? Have great scientists in general been more or less religious than their contemporaries? One must, of course, recognise various problems or dangers in analysing this. Firstly, there are sometimes difficulties in identifying religious convictions of scientists - the potted biographies in encyclopaedia may fail to mention even the most profound evangelical commitment. Thus eg the latest Encyclopaedia Britannica (CD ROM) says of physicist James Clerk Maxwell (1831-1879) that he is:

> regarded by most modern physicists as the scientist of the 19th century who had the greatest influence on 20th-century physics; he is ranked with Sir Isaac Newton and Albert Einstein for the fundamental nature of his contributions.

The article fails, however, to mention his conversion and deep Christian beliefs.

Secondly, there may be a problem in assessing exactly where in the theological spectrum a person's convictions should be placed, and how deep those feelings run. A person who is nominally 'orthodox' may actually be less profoundly 'Christian' than someone with a deeply felt and thought through personal faith which includes elements of unorthodoxy.

Thirdly, there may be problems of 'selectivity' – who are to be regarded as the 'great' scientists?

Even with these provisos, however, it is obvious that the general public greatly underestimates the religion of scientists. Justin Marston, founder-chair of *Christian Students in Science* did a 1997 survey of some 850 British students across ten universities. One of the questions was to obtain student's impressions of whether particular scientists were more religious, about the same, or less religious, than their contemporaries. Table 2 shows some of the results of students' views on the religion of some major founders in areas of science:

---

[2] Cf Mendel's 1865 and 1869 papers in Stern & Sherwood (1978); see also S Finn (1996).

Table 2: Students' Views on Religion of Scientists				
Name	Main Area(s)	More religious	About the same	Less religious
Kepler	Solar System	10.9	63.1	26.0
Galileo	Dynamics	16.2	54.1	29.7
Descartes	Methodology	19.6	50.6	29.8
Newton	Physics	20.1	60.8	19.1
Boyle	Chemistry	6.0	77.5	16.5
Mendel	Genetics	32.0	42.5	25.5
Faraday	Electricity/Physics	10.4	74.5	15.1
Kelvin	Physics	4.5	77.7	17.8
Planck	Quantum Physics	5.0	64.1	30.9
Einstein	Relativity	15.5	48.2	36.3

Galileo was at least as devoted a Catholic as most contemporaries, Descartes probably more so. Kepler, Boyle, Newton, the Abbot Mendel, and Faraday were all *markedly* devout in their faith. Kelvin was a committed Christian. Comments on these are given on the CSIS and our own websites,[3] but we will give here some comment on the religion of the two key 20th century figures in the table.

Max Planck (1858-1947) revolutionised our understanding of the physical world with his quantum physics. In his 1937 lecture "Religion and Naturwissenschat" he said that God was everywhere present and that 'the holiness of the unintelligible Godhead is conveyed by the holiness of symbols.' Atheists, he thought, attach too much importance to what are merely symbols. Planck was a churchwarden from 1920 until his death, and believed in an almighty all-knowing beneficent God (though not necessarily a personal one). Both science and religion wage a 'tireless battle against scepticism and dogmatics, against unbelief and superstition' with the goal 'toward God.'[4]

Albert Einstein (1879-1955) is associated with major revolutions in our thinking about time, gravity, and the conversion of matter to energy ($E=mc^2$). He was not a Christian, but the Britannica CD Rom states:

> Firmly denying atheism, Einstein expressed a belief in "Spinoza's God who reveals himself in the harmony of what exists".

---

[3] www.csis.org.uk and www.reason-science-and-faith.com
[4] See also Heilron (1986).

This actually motivated his interest in science, as he once remarked to a young physicist:

> I want to know how God created this world. I am not interested in this or that phenomenon, in the spectrum of this or that element. I want to know his thoughts, the rest are details.

His famous epithet on uncertainty "God does not play dice" was a real statement about a God in whom he believed. His religion was a mystical pantheism, whose famous saying was 'Science without religion is lame, religion without science is blind.'[5]

What the key scientific discoveries of the 20th century and who made them? There is quantum theory in which Planck's constant plays a central role. There is relativity, discovered by Einstein. There is the big bang in cosmology discovered by the Belgian Priest: Georges LeMaitre (1894-1966). There is the neo-Darwinisn synthesis, central to which was Cambridge geneticist/statistician R A Fisher (1890-1962), a regular chapelgoer and a preacher. The key biological concept, DNA, was found by two atheists Watson and Crick – though it is interesting that Watson's successor as head of the human genome project is Francis Collins, a committed born-again Christian.[6]

The predominance of Christian faith amongst earlier famous scientists is even more remarkable, and Dan Graves *Scientists of Faith* (1996) outlines 48 mini-biographies. Historians like Hooykaas (1972) and Jaki (1986) argued that the rise of science was fostered by a Christian framework expecting a rational universe from a rational creator-God. We will consider later how far a 'scientific' approach contrasts with religious faith.

The Conflict Thesis

Suppose we accept, however, that leading scientists were often religious, surely 'the church' (or at least theologians in it) were in constant conflict with science? T H Huxley, nicknamed 'Darwin's bulldog', thought so:

---

[5] For details on Einstein see Paul (1986), Highfield & Larter (1993) and Goldernstein (1995).

[6] Collins' testimony is on the CSIS video *Encounter* (1999).

'Extinguished theologians, lie about the cradle of every new science as the strangled snakes beside that of Hercules...'[7]

This graphic picture was given by Huxley in the late nineteenth century, and it is often the picture which the media and person in the street still has. Theology and science are seen as somehow naturally in conflict with each other, and 'the church' thought to have persecuted scientists for their beliefs.

As we shall see, Huxley's picture has little or no justification, and it is useful to see why he put it forward. To Huxley, free scientific inquiry was an end in itself to be pursued with the vigour of a military campaign - regardless of socio-religious consequences, In 1864 Huxley and eight fellow scientists formed a dining club - the 'X-Club' united in what one member called: 'devotion to science, pure and free, untrammeled by religious dogmas.'[8] Colin Russell has shown how the X-Club fitted into a context in which it sought independence for science, and to establish scientists (rather than any other group) as leaders in society to whom people looked for answers.[9] Though Huxley also had (as we shall later see) Christian associates who shared some of these aims, the agnostic members of this club would naturally want to portray organised religion in a bad light in any science-religion issues. Yet they did not represent the greatest scientists of the period (which included eg the illustrious Faraday and Maxwell), and it seems unlikely that they reflected the views of the majority of 'ordinary' scientists. A contemporary survey by Galton is cited by Moore who asserts: 'most scientists were religious men'.[10] Huxley was, however a brilliant publicist, active in science education at all levels, and for a time the X-Club dominated the Royal Society and British Association for the Advancement of Science.

Two books in particular added to the 'conflict thesis'. J W Draper, a Lancashire man who became a New York science professor, published *History of the Conflict Between Religion and Science* in 1875. He set out to portray history as a 'narrative of the conflict of two contending powers', adding 'no one has

---

[7] Huxley (1894) Vol II p 52.

[8] See J V Jenson (1970).

[9] See C A Russell (1983) p. 239 etc, and (1985). p. 192.

[10] Moore (1979) p 84.

hitherto treated the subject from this point of view'. Everthing in Draper is seen through his novel distorting medium of a conflict thesis. He therefore supposes that with the breakdown of the old religion of the Roman Empire, religious affairs: 'fell into the hands of ignorant and infuriated ecclesiastics, parasites, eunuchs and slaves'. Early church figures (eg, Lactantius) he portrayed as rejecting as 'heretical' what actually they rejected on quite good common sense grounds. Medieval Christians (e.g. Bede) who speculated on cosmology he dismissed as 'preposterous, and ignorant with no real attempt to understand the observational base of what they thought'. Draper's book was effective propaganda, but not history.[11]

The second book was the 1895 *A History of the Warfare of Science with Theology in Christendom* by A D White, first President of Cornell University. Ecclesiastical opposition to his liberal policies seemed to lead him to see science and 'Dogmatic Theology' as locked in a struggle. Admitting his debt to Draper, White's own work is more temperate but still fails to come to terms with the thinking of earlier ages, It fails (in terms of the great idealist historians like Collingwood) to understand the thinking of those studied, and it suffers from a triumphalist tendency to assess all ideas with the hindsight presumption that they are 'good' only if they correspond with present ideas.[12]

As a tool to achieve particular ends the 'conflict thesis' was effective, but as history it is unacceptable and has come under increasing criticism from modern historians. Claude Welch's chapter in a recent book begins with 'The Warfare Myth' and is heavily critical of Draper and White.[13] Professional historians of science today simply do not think in these terms.

There have, of course, been clashes. When a new scientific idea is put forward, it may conflict both with previous scientific ideas and with current ideas of how to harmonise in areas of overlap between theology and science. Important new scientific ideas do not simply add facts, like bricks to an existing wall. Often they involve quite new perspectives. Sometimes (eg the motion of the earth) when first suggested, they face apparently

---

[11] See also Welch in Richardson & Wildman (1996).

[12] See *The Conflict Thesis and Cosmology* (OU Unit), p 30.

[13] In Richardson and Wildman (1996) see also Brooke (1991) Introduction,

overwhelming physical objections, and lack any conclusive evidence. Scientists themselves can (at least with hindsight) sometimes be unduly conservative. An example of this is cited by atheist Richard Dawkins, speaking of the indignant disbelief of Zoologists in 1940 when Galambos first reported that bats use sonar. No religious issue was involved here - just a quite natural reluctance to believe what seemed preposterous. But no one would use this to proclaim that there is a conflict between zoologists and science![14] Theologians, like anyone else, can be unduly reluctant to accept new scientific ideas. But the notion that theology-science conflict has been rife is simply not true.

As so often, however, popular opinion and the cliches of the media have lagged behind informed opinion. This has not been helped by the prominence given in the media to scientist atheists like Peter Atkins, Richard Dawkins and Lewis Wolpert, whose lack of expertise both on history and philosophy is generally unknown to the public.

Science and Theologians: Suggestions and Beginnings

If, then, we reject as unhistorical the 'conflict thesis', how should we characterize the historical interaction of theology and science? We are going to suggest a number of generalisations:

i.   Where new scientific theories met opposition, there have usually been strong physical reasons for doing so.

ii. In any scientific controversy there have usually been Christians of equal sincerity on both sides.

iii. The use of biblical verses to settle 'scientific' questions has been common only where no observational evidence existed, as a part of a synthesis of 'known facts'. Its use to reject observational science has been rare amongst acknowledged Christian leaders.

iv. Scientific speculation itself has not been outlawed, but there may have been objections to presenting speculation as 'fact' to those whose faith might thereby be damaged.

v.   Objections have sometimes been made to scientific theories which in fact contain their own religious metaphysics.

---

[14] Dawkins (1986) p. 35.

vi. Whatever the disagreement, scientists have very rarely, even in times of shocking, unchristian, religious intolerance, had life or liberty threatened for purely scientific speculation.

It may be useful to make a few general comments on these. Obviously Christian leaders have sometimes been mistaken over physical details of the world - but then so have most scientists as well so this is of no great surprise or significance. Clearly, too, there have been exceptions to (iii), i.e. where individuals have tried to fit science and observation into preconceived schemes they think they find in Scripture. We are arguing only that the mainstream of Christian thought has not believed that the language of Scripture was specific enough to dictate points of physical science. On (vi), we are not denying that there has sometimes been deplorable religious intolerance. But it was possible for Koestler as a non-Christian observer to write:

> Giordano Bruno and Michael Servetus (burned in 1553 by the Calvinists in Geneva) seem to be the only scholars of repute who became victims of religious intolerance in the sixteenth and seventeenth centuries - not, of course, because of their scientific but because of their religious opinions.[15]

Koestler saw scientists as a kind of species of 'sacred cow', ambling unmolested through the bazaar of religious persecution. Ironically there are instances of persecution by irreligious authorities. During the avowedly anti-Christian French Revolution, one of history's greatest chemists (Antoine Lavoisier) was guillotined on a trumped up charge reputedly with the words 'France does not need men of science'.[16] In Soviet Russia there was a more overt clash of science and irreligion, as eminent adherents of the scientific Mendelian geneticists were mercilessly persecuted because the theories were thought to contradict Marxist ideas. Atheistic systems do not regard scientists as sacred cows.

We could not hope here to demonstrate the above suggestions comprehensively, but we can illustrate them in some key areas.

Early Christian leaders frequently made two points of criticism of Greek Philosophers. The first was that there much disagreement amongst them over basics, and many of their ideas

---

[15] A Koestler (1959) p. 451.
[16] D Mckie (1962), p 306.

were speculative and offered no means to determine whether or not they were true. Today this is hard for us to understand, for we are brought up to recognise a huge body of scientific 'facts' based on observation. Secondly, 'natural philosophy' (ie science) had no moral use, little practical use, and questions of faith and ultimate destiny were far more important. Again, today we automatically link science with technology and with improving the physical welfare of mankind - and often fail to understand how recent is this link. At the time they were made, such criticisms were both reasonable and valid. However, the early Greek 'Fathers' Justin Martyr (c100-165), Clement of Alexandria (c150-215) and Origen (c185-254)) were very positive towards secular learning about nature, though aware of its deficiencies.[17]

In second century North Africa began the tradition of Latin Fathers. The lawyer Tertullian (c160-c225) was influential in developing Latin style, though his theological influence was more limited. He did, however, begin an unfortunate tradition of lawyers writing slightingly of science they fail to really understand. Tertullian, though, stands virtually alone. His contemporary, for example, the more orthodox Minucius Felix, portrayed Greek natural philosophy from Thales onwards as pointing to the one true God. Augustine, though himself tinged with neoplatonism, was fairly critical of Greek philosophy. He does not, however, appear to wish to construct what we would call science from the Bible, nor reject empiricism. Thus in, for example, his commentary on Psalm 104, Augustine shows no inclination to build a cosmology, but takes a highly figurative approach. When he tentatively advances biblical reasons for believing the antipodes uninhabited, he specifically prefaces this by pointing out that it is a question on which 'scientific conjecture' can offer no evidence. We have already noted his repeated warnings against being dogmatic on science issues.

We have seen that Basil claims to 'take all in the literal sense'. Yet he keeps an open mind on key scientific questions:

> Let us admit that the earth rests upon itself or let us say that it rides upon the waters; we must still remain faithful to the thought of true religion and recognise that all is sustained by the Creator's power...

---

[17] Some more details are on our website.

Grand phenomena do not strike us the less when we have discovered something of their wonderful mechanism.

In general, church leaders in the early centuries accepted empirical findings of 'science' of their age, and did not 'do science from the Bible'.

Cosmology and the Rise of Science

Some of the older 'conflict theory' books make incorrect statements that eg Lactantius opposed the sphericity of the earth on religious grounds. Actually, his opposition was based purely on reason not theology – and can be seen as a plea for empirical science rather than speculation![18] Such issues were just not seen as being settled from the Bible – thus whilst Augustine thought the antipodes probably uninhabited his contemporary Jerome thought they were![19] The scholastics adopted the science of Aristotle – a science based firmly on observation and common sense. They believed, of course, that the earth was small and spherical (only television companies think that people in the days of Columbus thought it flat!).

As we briefly consider the development of cosmology, in particular of the solar system, we will make two firm assertions:

1. Fear of religious persecution was rare and if it did happen was due to more complex situations than simple 'science versus theology'.
2. Scientists, even when devout, did not derive their science from the Bible.

Actually, one of the *first* works arguing in detail for a possibility of a moving earth was written in 1377 by Oresme, Bishop of Liseaux, by order of the King of France. In *Le Livre du Ciel*, Oresme counters physical objections, and says of Bible verses which appear to imply a stationary earth:

> One can say that [the Bible] conforms in this part to the manner of common human speech, just as it does in several places as where it is written that God repented and that he became angry and calm

---

[18] Lactantius, *The Divine Institutes*, III, 3 & 24 & 39 (Ant.Nic,Fath., vii, 71I & 94 & 237); for further details of this and other such points see our website.
[19] Augustine, *The City of God*, XVI, 9 (Nic. & Post Nic Fath, 1, ii 315), Jerome in his commentary on Ezekiel 1:6.

again and things of the same kind, which are not in fact at all as the letter puts it.

On issues such as that of 'long day' of Joshua 11:12, or the sun going back in the time of Hezekiah, he suggests it more in line with God's general working to 'disturb the common course of nature' in a small local way (i.e. in the earth) than in the whole universe.

Copernicus (1473-1543) was actually a conservatively minded devotee of Greek science, yet it was he who created the first mathematical system based on a moving earth (*Revolutions of the Heavenly Spheres*, 1543). A canon of the Catholic church, he received nothing but clerical encouragement during his lifetime. The first resumé of his system was given in 1532 by the Pope's private secretary in the Vatican gardens.[20] In 1535 Cardinal Schoenberg (a confidant of the Pope's) urged Copernicus to publish. Copernicus' most immediate disciple, Rheticus, stood high in the Lutheran camp when he published *Narratio Prima* (1540) summarising his mentor's views: the rejection of Copernicanism by Melancthon and German Lutherans[21] did not imply any suppression of its adherents. Copernicus' reluctance seems to have been from fear of common ridicule rather than religious persecution - coupled with the knowledge that he had no evidence for the truth of his system which was at least as mathematically cumbersome as the old one.

White's conflict thesis, predictably, asserts: 'All branches of the Protestant church... vied with each other in denouncing the Copernican doctrine as contrary to Scripture.'[22]

Actually Luther appears not to have referred to the question in any published work - the story often related of his supposed opposition comes from someone else's recollection 27 years later of an after dinner remark.[23] Calvin seems to mention it in only one sermon - and then his rejection is on 'common sense' rather than biblical grounds.[24] His commentary on Genesis (as

---

[20] Koestler (1959, 1972) amazingly remains the most readable book for these details, and they are accepted in essentials by all historians of science.

[21] Panneberg (1993) p. 53.

[22] White (1896) vol 1, p 126.

[23] See C Russell (1985) p 42,

[24] See R Hooykaas (1959) p 154 n27.

we noted) clearly says that if one is interested in studying such things one should study astronomy – not try to get them from Genesis. Melanchthon rejected Copernicanism - but numbered admirers of Copernicus amongst his friends. The absence of scientific intolerance here is all the more remarkable if we remember that these 'Reformers' were steeped in an Augustinian view of God which encouraged persecution of dissenting Christians (such as the Mennonites or Anabaptists) and led to them being killed, imprisoned, or exiled.

A generation later the pious Lutheran Johannes Kepler published in 1609 the true elliptical orbits of planets (including the earth) about the sun. Koestler suggests, as we noted, that the reason why Kepler (like Rheticus in the generation before) could move so freely in Catholic Europe was that scientists were 'sacred cows'. Kepler's great reputation led to his appointment as imperial mathematician to the Catholic Emperor Rudolph III.

Perhaps the most famous 'persecution' is that of Kepler's contemporary Galileo. There are good modern books on this so here we will just give a bare outline.[25]

Galileo was a man who reveled in debate, and ridiculed opponents in it. This was a good way to win debates but also to make enemies. Though he claimed to have long been a Copernican, his public interest came only after his improvement of the telescope (around 1609), and the telescopic discoveries which he tried to portray as relevant to the issue. In 1615, following some after dinner conversation, he launched himself into the controversy with a Letter to the Grand Duchess Christina. The leading Cardinal Bellarmine in a letter to Galileo's disciple Foscarini set out the Catholic church's view. If a physical proof of the earth's motion could be produced then the church would be prepared to rethink its biblical interpretation (ie rethink the current synthesis of theology and science).[26] Until that time Galileo was, he said, prudent to speak only hypothetically about earth motions.[27]

In 1632 Galileo published a *Dialogue on the Two World Systems*. This was supposed to present 'both sides', but was a

---

[25] Original documents are found in Finocchiaro (1989) and Drake (1957)

[26] See Fantoli (1994) p. 173, Sharratt (1994) p. 114, etc.

[27] Cf also Sharratt (1994) p. 188 etc.

thinly disguised argument for the earth's movement. In its final section the favourite argument of the Pope on the issue (that we should avoid dogmatism since God could use many different means to an effect) was put into the mouth of the dunce in the Dialogue; the Pope (who had previously been an admirer of Galileo) was furious.[28] Scientifically Galileo's book would have been out of date even if published 15 years earlier. He ignored Kepler's elliptical orbits (published 24 years earlier), and gave the impression of circular ones which would have been absurdly inaccurate. Tycho's system of a static earth but with the planets going around the sun had been accepted by leading Jesuits because it fitted best the data and lack of observed stellar parallax.[29] Galileo ignored it and pretended the choice was between his own and Aristotle's. All the physical proofs presented in his book were either wrong (as his key theory of the tides) or would apply equally to Tycho's system. It was a popular book rather than a real academic contribution written in pithy Italian rather than academic Latin.

So what was the fuss? In today's terms the real issue might be seen as one of the social responsibility of a scientist rather than one of academic freedom. Do scientists have a duty to publish any and all discoveries or ideas they have - irrespective of the social effects of such publication? Should Galileo have popularised a system for which he had no proof and premature publication of which might have had an destabilising effect on ordinary people? Bellarmine, rightly or wrongly, had thought not, and in Galileo's later trial the only real issue was whether or not Galileo had received and disobeyed a specific personal order' from Bellarmine in 1615.[30]

Throughout all this period Galileo had many supporters in all branches of Catholicism, but also made personal enemies. When, however, a young firebrand denounced Galileo from a pulpit somewhere, more than one leading member of the order might express to Galileo their regret that such ignorance existed.[31] In his 1633 trial, the evidence is that a 'plea bargain'

---

[28] See eg Sharratt (1994) p. 169, 175.

[29] See eg Fantoli (1994) p. 31 etc.

[30] See Drake (1978), p 348, or (1980). p 78, Sharratt (1994) p. 130.

[31] Drake (1980) p. 239; Fantoli (1994) p. 167.

was scotched by the pope - either under political pressure or from pique at believing Galileo had mocked him in the *Dialogue* - and the issue was therefore forced.[32]

Galileo was never thrown in the dungeons but placed under comfortable house arrest. He was not pronounced heretical (the verdict was 'suspicion of heresy') but was made to recant and his book placed in the prohibited Index. (Copernicus' book had been on the Index from 1616-1620 pending very minor corrections.) Three of the ten Cardinals refused to sign the sentence anyway.[33] The various recent books on the affair contain all the documents and details - though on any reading of them a simple 'science versus religion' view is hopelessly naive. Ironically, it was after the Inquisition turned him away from his rather sterile astronomical speculation, that Galileo did some of his really useful work on dynamics in the last years of his life - feted and honoured by all.

We have no axe to grind in 'defending' the Catholic Church over the Galileo affair, and note the Church's own recent heart searchings over it.[34] But to see it as a simplistic 'faith versus science' or as epitomising science-faith relationships is simply not tenable. Isaac Newton was born in the year (1642) that Galileo died, and wrote the *Principia* in 1687. Any 'religious' opposition after this (eg from the 'Hutchinsonians' who derived their science from the Bible) was regarded as cranky.

Science: Biblical or Empirical?

Did scientists who were Christians begin their science from the Bible or from observation? As we have seen, both Kepler (1609) and Galileo (1633) put forward theories that required a physically moving earth adrift in space. Kepler was a devout Lutheran, whose astronomical works actually contained much Christian symbolism. Kepler, however, argued that when 'the sacred writings' speak concerning ordinary matters in which:

> it is not their normal function to instruct men, they do this in a human manner so that they may be understood by men.

---

[32] See eg M A Finnochiaro (1989) p. 37.
[33] Drake (1980) p 351.
[34] Cf Sharratt (1994) Ch. 10.

Some, he says, are mistaken in thinking:

> Psalm 104 to be wholly concerned with physics, since it is wholly concerned with physical matters... the psalmist is a very long way from speculation about physical causes. Rather he is unfolding a hymn 'in Psalm 104 to be wholly concerned with physics, since it is wholly concerned with physical matters... the psalmist is a very long way from speculation about physical causes.

Rather he is unfolding a hymn 'in which he runs through the whole world as it appears to our eyes.'[35] Kepler's astronomy is full of reference to the Trinity and other parts of Christian theology – but he was clear that science began from observation and reason not from the Bible.

Galileo, a confirmed Catholic, cited Augustine and Peter Lombard in support of his basic tenet that:

> The Holy Bible can never speak untruth - whenever its true meaning is understood. But... it is often very abstruse, and may say things which are quite different from what its bare words signify ... This being granted, I think that in discussions of physical problems we ought to begin not from the authority of scriptural passages but with sense experiences and necessary demonstrations; for the Holy Bible and the phenomena of nature proceed alike from the Godhead.[36]

This is very clear. The Bible is totally inspired and true, but it is not the starting point for science. Actually, Galileo's early opponent on the moving earth, the scholarly Cardinal Bellarmine, believed something not much different. Noting that the Council of Trent forbade any teaching contrary to the early Fathers, he wrote to Galileo's disciple Foscarini:

> If there were a real proof that the sun is in the centre of the universe ... that the sun does not go round the earth but the earth round the sun, then we should have to proceed with great circumspection in explaining passages of Scripture which appear to teach the contrary, and rather admit that we did not understand them... But as for myself, I shall not believe that there are such proofs until they are shown to me.[37]

Bellarmine was clearly *not* saying here that he could prove the earth stationary from Scripture. He was open to the possibility

---

[35] From Kepler (1609).
[36] *From the Letter to the Grand Duchess Christina* (1615).
[37] Cited eg in Fantoli pp. 174-176.

that it might one day be proved that it was not, and *took it for granted* that scientific observation would be the means of that proof.

Coppleston's famous *History of Philosophy* spoke for many modern scholars in stating:

> Modern philosophy is generally said to have begun with Descartes (1596-1650) or with Francis Bacon (1561-1626) in England and with Descartes in France.[38]

Francis Bacon's *Novum Organum* (1620) was a radical book which had a profound effect on the thinking of scientists. Today (like Descartes) he is often misrepresented and caricatured. He wrote in flowery picture language, but actually made some astute observations. He emphasised that science should be built on a good observational base – it was a mistake to jump very quickly to conclusions and then defend these with ingenuity against future observation. For example, there might turn out to be atoms, but the Greeks jumped to the idea with too little observational base, and then thought up clever ways to defend their ideas. A slow process of induction was the path forward – with a particular emphasis on controlled experimentation to *interrogate* nature. Bacon particularly identified four 'idols' which prevent us getting at the truth in science:

1. *The Idols of the Tribe:* Are perspectives which we have because we are human.
2. *The Idols of the Cave:*   Perspectives and ideas due to our individual upbringing.
3. *The Idols of the Theatre:* The effects of language on our perceptions.
4. *The Idols of the Market Place* The effects of philosophical systems – eg scholasticism.

Of course, by modern standards Bacon failed to perceive some of the problems of induction. He failed to recognise that we definitely need prior concepts, and that observation is inevitably theory-laden. But there is still much astute thought there, and Bacon was indubitably influential on scientific thinking.

He was also influential on science-faith issues. The following passage sets out key ideas of Bacon on theology and science

---

[38] Coppleston (1960) Vol 4, p. 13.

(though note that in his day 'science' was referred to as 'natural philosophy', and the word 'scientist' had not been invented):

> The school of Paracelsus, and some others ... have pretended to find the truth of all natural philosophy [ie of science] in the Scriptures; scandalising and traducing all other philosophy as heathenish and profane. But there is no such enmity between God's word and his works. Neither do they give honour to the Scriptures as they suppose but embase them. For to seek heaven and earth in the word of God, whereof it is said 'Heaven and earth shall pass away but my word shall not pass away' is to seek temporary things amongst eternal; and as to seek divinity in philosophy is to seek the living among the dead, so to seek philosophy in divinity is to seek the dead amongst the living... the scope or purpose of the Spirit of God is not to express matters of nature in the Scriptures, otherwise than in passage, and for application to man's capacity and to matters moral or divine. And it is a true rule: 'What a man says incidentally about matters not in question has little authority; for it were a strange conclusion, if a man should use a similitude for ornament or illustration sake, borrowed from nature or history according to vulgar conceit, as of a basilisk, an unicorn, a centaur, a Brierus and Hydra, or the like, that he must needs be thought to affirm the matter thereof positively to be true... In this vanity some of the moderns have with extreme levity indulged so far as to attempt to found a system of natural philosophy on the first chapter of Genesis, on the book of Job, and other parts of sacred writings; and repression of it is the more important, because from this unwholesome mixture of things human and divine there arises not only a fantastic philosophy but also an heretical religion.[39]

Bacon says that God has laid before us:

> two books or volumes to study if we will be secured from error; first the Scriptures revealing the will of God, and then the creatures expressing his power.[40]

Descartes' Discourse on Method was published in 1637. Though he emphasised reason where Bacon emphasised observation, the differences between them are fewer than often supposed.[41] Though God was central to his whole system, knowledge of the physical world was to be based on observation and reason.

---

[39] Bacon: *Advancement of Learning* (1605) bk 11, see also *Novum Organum* (1620) vol lxv.
[40] Bacon *Valerius Terminus* (1734) – though similar in other works.
[41] See R M Blake (1960) chs 3-4.

One could hardly exaggerate the standing and influence of Bacon, both on Western science and on the thinking of Bible-believing Christians in their attitude to it. Newton, for example, whilst by no means uncritical of Bacon, himself wrote of 'two books' which should be read separately, though he believed them to have similarities since God was author of both.[42] Other early members of the Royal Society tended to see themselves as Baconians, and his approach was standard to scientist-Christians in the seventeenth and eighteenth centuries. In fact, mainstream scientist-Christians in Western Europe for well into the nineteenth century (if not later) saw themselves as following the traditions of Bacon, Descartes or both. George Marsden presents Bacon as 'the pre-eminently revered philosopher' in dominant evangelical colleges in America for much of the nineteenth century, and indicates that a version of Baconianism (albeit sometimes rather simplified) was influential into early twentieth century.[43] Interestingly, Henry Morris cites Bacon as a 'great creationist scientist' and the 'originator of the scientific method'.[44]

Put briefly, the two books idea is this:

Two Divine 'Books':	BIBLE	NATURE
	|	|
Human Interpretations:	THEOLOGY	SCIENCE

Both the 'book of God's word' (the Bible) and the 'book of God's works' (nature) are true and infallible, but human interpretations of them are not.

It might be useful to make clear what this is *not* saying. Firstly, Bacon was not saying that the Bible speaks only spiritual truth and never refers to historical or physical facts. The fact of the Resurrection, for example, is not incidental to the truth of the account, but basic to it. The Bible relates God's dealings with men in actual history and in the physical world, it would make no sense to try to 'spiritualise' away all space-time references.

Secondly, to say that the Bible is not a textbook of science does not mean that it contains wrong science. Neither Bacon nor

---

[42] See F E Manuel (1974).

[43] Marsden (1980) pp 55-62, 111-12, 169, 214-5 etc.

[44] Morris (1984) p. 26.

his followers implied this. To say, moreover, that the language of the Bible is often 'observer language' rather than 'technical language's (eg on the Flood) is not to say that what it described was mistaken.

Again let us spell out the implications of all this.

- Kepler was a devout Lutheran.
- Galileo was an Italian Catholic with an absolute belief in the inspiration and truth of Scripture.
- Descartes was a French Catholic for whom God was central to his system.
- Bacon was a devout English Protestant.
- Newton was devout (though Arian in theology) with a very high view of biblical inspiration.

They represent the very heart of the scientific revolution – and their views are reflected throughout the Royal Society and the subsequent rise of science. They all operated in an uncompromisingly supernaturalist and theistic framework – but they were all as adamant that science should begin from observation and not from the Bible, as they were sure that ultimately (when both were interpreted correctly) nature and the Bible would be in harmony.

The Origins of Geology

Our first task will be to outline the history of the development of geology, and assess Christian reactions to it. After this we will return to consider alternative models suggested today to fit what happened.

Earth science based on observation basically dates from the mid seventeenth century.[45] We might distinguish three main important areas of actual field-work:

i.   Structure (i.e. recognition that strata had a structure).
ii. Composition (i.e. mineralogy, what the rocks were made of).
iii. Fossils (in the modern sense of living remains turned to stone).

---

[45] Porter (1977) p. 10.

On structure, Steno (1631-1686), who later entered holy orders, was one of the first to suggest study of strata on the obvious presupposition that they indicated an order of deposition.

In the systematic study of the structure of mineralogy and rock composition John Woodward (1665-1728) founded a system which, though not profound, makes Porter describe him as 'remarkable' and 'prophetic' in pointing the way forward.[46]

Fossils had long puzzled observers. Some looked like living creatures, others didn't, and opinions on their origins varied. Woodward began a useful collection of fossils and minerals, still intact in Cambridge. At that time there was no obvious reason why living creatures should 'turn to stone', and no obvious reason why fossils should not (like minerals and crystals) be chemical products of the rocks themselves.[47] Nevertheless, the consensus view by the early eighteenth century was that fossils were the remains of once living creatures.[48]

Naturalists at that time also faced the wider problem of constructing a theory to explain how strata formed, why fossils were found on tops of mountains and how (since they were all Christians of varying orthodoxy and piety) this fitted Genesis. It should, however, be noted that they all generally took a Baconian approach, not tailoring nature to the Scriptures, nor feeling any great theological pressure to do so, but simply developing their theology and science together in seeking an ultimate unity of knowledge.[49] Though, of course, individuals sometimes failed in the application of this approach to which they were committed, science 'confirmed' Scripture but did not begin from it.[50]

One suggestion was that most of the earth's surface structure was laid down during the one Noarchic flood. Two Cambridge scholars on what Porter describes as 'on the liberal and rationalistic wing' of the church put forward such theories.[51] Both Burnet's (1681) and Whiston's (1696) theories proposed

---

[46] Porter (1977) p. 56.
[47] Davis A Young (1982). P. 28.
[48] Porter (1977) p. 166.
[49] Porter (1977) p. 64.
[50] Porter (1977) p. 70.
[51] Porter (1977) p. 70.

non-supernatural mechanisms, though neither were practical naturalists. Theologically, Whiston was unorthodox, whilst Burnet took Genesis very allegorically. They found few followers scientific or theological.

A third 'flood-geology, was that of Woodward, *An Essay Towards a Natural Theory of the Earth* (1693). Woodward suggested that in the flood the stone, minerals, chalk etc 'lost their solidity' and were 'sustained in the water', eventually resettling in the order of different specific gravity'. Contemporary Christian naturalists like the pious Ray, Lhwyd, Nicholson, Baker, etc, found this to make neither scientific nor theological sense. They pointed out that neither the strata nor fossils are in order of specific gravity, it would have required far more water than the Bible implied, the shells would also have dissolved (leaving no fossils) etc.[52] Woodward was forced to introduce type-ii miracles supposing that normal gravity was suspended etc. This (though modern 'flood geologists' usually resort to similar stratagems) all rather defeats the original object of constructing a scientific theory of the flood - given enough miracle *any* theory can be made compatible with observation.

More biblically minded critics also pointed out that the Bible referred to the same rivers before and after the flood, that the curse dated from the fall of Adam and not the flood, and that the Bible implied a longer period than the 14 days in May suggested by Woodward to account for fossil leaves.[53] Woodward was a pioneer in observational geology, but his actual system was scientifically impossible and biblically unsound.

There was also another important model which gained some support, due to Robert Hooke (1635-1703). Though Hooke believed in the Bible and the widespread effects of Noah's flood, he believed that marine fossils were found on mountains because the earth's surface was in a constant cycle of uplift and fall - a series of catastrophic earthquakes over a long period of earth history. His system prefigured the later one of Hutton

---

[52] Baker to Woodward on 15th April 1700 (Camb MS no 35); John Edwards to Woodward on 4th February 1697; Ray to Lhwyd on 8th June 1696.
[53] *Ibid* p. 23.

(whom some have suggested knew of it) and also some ideas of William Smith.[54]

It should actually be noted that in general (and Woodward was an exception) 'most theorists were not field-workers, and most field-workers did not write theories'.[55] Field workers - like Ray and Lhwyd, were all too aware of the shortcomings of theories. Davis Young rightly portrays how Ray puzzled about how to construct one.[56] Earthquakes might raise sea floors - but not to the extent needed for mountains. A single flood of short duration could not account for distributions of rocks and fossils without great ad hoc introductions of miracle. Thus, though most naturalists suspected that a worldwide flood might have something to do with fossils on mountains, ideas (like Woodward's) that all the Strata were laid down in one universal flood were never part either of scientific or of Christian orthodoxy. Men like Hooke, Ray and Lhwyd believed no less in the flood than Woodward, but could not believe it the sole agent for laying down the strata.

In the eighteenth century, the most important figure in biology was probably Carl Linne or Linnaeus, the man who adapted Ray's system of organic classification into the one which is still used today. Linnaeus like Ray, specifically rejected the possibility that all the fossils could have been laid down in the Genesis Flood.[57] Such, in fact, was the effect of accumulating evidence that one modern study states that by 1750 Woodward's theories: 'were so undermined that they could no longer be accepted, even by those geologists who emphasised the flood's role.[58] One of the few prominent 18th century 'flood geology' naturalists was Alexander Catcott, who held a tense mixture of Woodwardian and Hutchinsonian ideas.[59] Hutchinson rejected Woodward as insufficiently 'literalist', and Hutchinsonians continued as a minority (much as modern Young-earth

---

[54] See Yushi Ito (1988). Like later writers, Hooke's belief in an ancient earth was based on strata thickness. Ellen T Drake (1981) suggests Hutton was aware of Hooke's writings

[55] Porter (1977) p. 24.

[56] Young (1982) p. 30.

[57] J Ray *Reflections on the Study of Nature* Tr Smith 1786.

[58] R Rhappaport (1978).

[59] M Neve and R Porter (1977).

Creationists). They were never, however, regarded as mainstream or orthodox. John Wesley, for example, was himself interested in 'scientific' literature and encouraged his preachers to be. He read (with them) various books on Hutchinson's system, and his growing criticism culminated by 1758 in saying: 'I am more and more convinced that they have no foundation in Scripture or sound reason.'[60]

By the late eighteenth century *all* schools of geology had concluded that the world was much older than previously thought. There were, however, two major areas of controversy:

1. *Aqueous vs Igneous:* 'Neptunism' held that virtually all rocks had been laid down by the agency of water, except relatively recent volcanic rock. 'Vulcanism', held that a number of rocks (e.g. basalt, granite) were formed from molten lava - ie were igneous in origin.

2. *Progressivism vs Steady State:* This concerned whether the process showed a beginning ('primitive' rocks which contained no fossils), or was simply endlessly cycling with no trace of any beginning.

Neptunism was generally progressivist, vulcanism could be either. In these movements the figureheads (though not the founders) came to be Werner and Hutton. Hutton argued that even granite was igneous, and was a strong advocate of a 'steady state' theory. He did not necessarily reject catastrophes as part of geological history, but saw them as part of a steady-state system.

Hutton himself was deistical, but there was no lack of Christians (eg Rev Playfair) amongst his most prominent supporters. His steady state system merely says there is no apparent trace of a beginning; God could, of course, have created the whole thing instantaneously as an ongoing system. It was never a simple issue of theological differences, and (though many were also interested in theology) the arguments were, with few exceptions, based on observational evidence.

In the early 19th century there were two further developments. The first was the recognition by English engineer

---

[60] John Wesley, *Works,* 3rd Edition 1872 (1986 printing), II, p 454; see also p 388, 389, and 441.

William Smith, that particular strata could be systematically identified by their fossils. It should be noted that Smith's ideas began from the practical experience of work in mines, cuttings, and road surfaces (which were just bare rock and not covered). The flat strata around Bath where he lived showed fairly clearly how different fossils appeared at different layers. Smith was not a theoretician, and his approach was structural rather than thinking in terms of 'dating'.[61] No particular 'theory' was assumed, and certainly no concept of evolution.

The written dissemination of Smith's idea owed much to the writings of Brongniart and Cuvier. Cuvier was a renowned French Protestant who experienced religious renewal. He also opposed and rejected the contemporary theories of evolution (due to Laplace) as unempirical. Cuvier also developed an influential idea (based mainly on data from around the Paris Basin) that there had been successive widespread floods. In England, William Buckland (a Dean who wrote about the design of God in creation and whose wife attended an evangelical church[62]) developed this into a notion of successive worldwide floods, of which the flood of Noah might be the last.[63] This form of 'catastrophism' (i.e. successive 'catastrophes') became popular. A leading advocate for it was the Cambridge Professor of Geology, Adam Sedgwick. Its leading opponent was probably the Scottish naturalist John Fleming, who rejected it (in favour of a tranquil flood) on both geological and biblical grounds.[64] Both were highly competent scientists. Theologically, Sedgwick identified his views with those of Charles Simeon - acknowledged as one of the foremost evangelical leaders of his generation[65] - whilst Fleming was part of the evangelical revival which split the Church of Scotland. On *both* sides of the debate, then, leading protagonists were firm Evangelicals.

The standard 1820's geology textbook was co-authored by W D Conybeare (whose 1839 book on the Christian Fathers shows

---

[61] See also, Hugh Torrens (1988) pp. 83-93.

[62] E 0 Gordon (Ed) (1894), p. 111.

[63] W Buckland (1823).

[64] See Paul Marston (1984) p. 396.

[65] Marston (1984) section 2.3; the letter quoted by Evangelical Carus in *The Churchman* of February 1889 contains Sedgwick's reference to Simeon.

a highly orthodox theology) and Phillips (who held to the orthodox 'gap theory' of Genesis).

Of the first three decades, then, of the nineteenth century, we can make the following clear generalisations:

1. No serious geologist believed the world 6000 or so years old, or that the strata were laid down in one big flood.

2. No school of geology or leading geologist assumed or even believed in organic evolution - although the idea had been put forward both in Britain and in France.

3. Christians (including Evangelicals) were prominent in the development and dissemination of the ideas of geology.

4. Their ideas developed not because of some anti-Christian agenda, but simply because of what they saw in the rocks.

By around 1830 various controversies had become settled amongst serious geologists:

A. Neptunism had been right in believing the rocks to show a one-way history rather than an endless cycle (as Hutton had thought)..

B. Neptunism had been wrong in supposing that mineral type indicated age of rock - granite, for example, was fossil-free not because it was 'primitive, (ie before organic creation), but because it was igneous (ie solidified from molten rock, which could be of any period).

C. Neptunism had been wrong, and Vulcanism right, in the igneous origin of basalt, granite etc, and igneous rocks played a major part in earth history.

D. The association of fossil type with age was accepted.

E. The successive worldwide flood theories were abandoned, and Fleming's slow processes were accepted.

Sedgwick's own field work, for example, led him to a public admission in a Presidential Address to the Geological Society in 1831 that his former views on (B) and (C) had been wrong. Dean Buckland, Reader in Geology at Oxford, made the same admission in footnotes in a work of natural theology of 1836.[66] These ideas were the basis of the work from 1830-1855 which

---

[66] W Buckland (1836).

saw the development of the geological column still accepted by geologists today.

We need at this point to assess the work and influence of Charles Lyell, a lawyer turned geologist about which more baloney has probably been written (by Christians and non-Christians) than any other figure in geological history. Lyell put forward two distinctive theories:

i.   'Rate-uniformity': he assumed that rates of all processes had been constant, and actually tried to work out time spans based on it.[67]

ii. 'Steady-state': Lyell assumed that all the genera of animals had always existed in a steady cycle of species change - there was no 'progression' of animal forms.

On (i), his sympathisers never numbered more than a small minority of geologists - the general view (well expressed by Sedgwick) was that it was a gratuitous assumption. Lyell's attempts at actual time spans were never accepted, and by the 1860's even he admitted it was hopeless.

Lyell's steady state theory fared even worse, he won no notable converts, and this has led Michael Bartholomew in his detailed studies to call Lyell a 'singular figure'.[68] Lyell's famous *Principles of Geology* (1830-33) was a best selling introduction, but neither of his distinctive ideas convinced the geological world. What was more influential was its version of geological history - a version which was really propaganda. Porter calls it 'mythic history'.[69] His praise of Hutton and criticism of Werner as heads of two supposedly warring factions in the earlier period is misleading, as are his exaggeration of the importance of Hutton and of himself in geological development. Unfortunately his version of history passed into folklore, copied in the historical works of Whewell and Geikie and down to modern ones like D H Hall in his 1976 *History of Earth Sciences* and even to a recent book by John David Weaver who studied his geology in the 1960's-1970's.[70]

---

[67] See M Rudwick (1977).

[68] M Bartholomew (1980), M Rudwick (1972), A Hallam (1983). p 54, Peter J Bowler, (1976), p 5.

[69] R Porter (1976).

[70] Weaver (1994) repeats the Lyell myth but in general his book is good.

What of Lyell's more general beliefs? Lyell (unlike, say, Sedgwick) does not seem to have been a naturally pious man. But his inaugural lecture as a professor in the orthodox Kings College in 1832 included the classic argument from design and consistency of geology with Scripture.[71] On evolution, Lyell was still (as his notebooks show) clearly thinking throughout the 1850's in terms of a supernatural origin of new species.[72] In fact, he was a vehement anti-evolutionist and the second volume of his *Principles* is an anti-evolution polemic clearly rejecting the evolutionary ideas of Lamarck. Lamarckian evolution, he thought, would undermine the specialness of human nature. One modern expert on Lyell even states: 'Lyell feared evolutionary ideas in part because they contradicted... Christian theology'.[73] His anti-evolution was so extreme that he rejected even the idea of any overall progression in organic forms - on which point he differed from all the other geologists.

So how crucial *was* Lyell to geology? Note first that the Evangelical Fleming had been leading an assault on Bucklandian catastrophism in 1825-6 when Lyell was still a catastrophist,[74] and Fleming was justifiably angry when Lyell later tried to claim the credit for its demise.[75] Fleming, Scrope and Prevost, were probably at least as influential as Lyell on professional geologists like Sedgwick. Sedgwick's own field observation was the *real* reason for his change of mind which occurred between 1827 and 1830 ie *before* Lyell's book was published.[76] In any event, what was distinctive in Lyell's system remained an oddity, and some modern evangelical geologists have doubted if even Lyell himself fully accepted it.[77] Certainly many key geologists retained either the neo-catastrophist ideas of Elie De Beaumont on mountain building (as did Sedgwick), or the neo-catastrophist glacial theories of Agassiz (as did

---

[71] See M Rudwick (1974).

[72] See e,g, P Bowler (1976) p. 76.

[73] Bartholomew (1973). Browne (1995) p. 362 also connects Lyell's anti-evolutionism and religion.

[74] See Hallam (1983) p. 46.

[75] Flemings letter to Sedgwick of 15th November 1831 is in the Cambridge Sedgwick collection.

[76] See Paul Marston (1984) section 7.3, especially p 415.

[77] R Van De Fliert (1978).

Buckland). Lyell's excessive belief in constancy of rates was not accepted by the majority of those who established the geological column.

The geological column, then, was essentially completed by 1855 (later changes were merely verbal) - four years before Darwin published his *Origin of Species,* and three key points need to be made about this:

1. It did *not* assume evolution, and key geologists were vehemently anti-evolution.
2. It did *not* assume uniformity of process rates and most geologists were catastrophists.
3. It did *not* depend on a circular 'dating the rocks from the fossils and the fossils from the rocks'.

Let us take each one of these in turn. We have already noted the anti-evolutionism of Lyell. Most orthodox geologists rejected Lyell's idiosyncratic 'no change at all' system, and held that different orders of creature came into being at different stages; but this did not even imply 'progression' at any more detailed level, let alone organic evolution. Lyell himself was a contributor mainly to the study of later strata. The Evangelical Sedgwick made major contributions to the older Cambrian, Ordovician (by another name), Silurian, and Devonian. Later, the Evangelical Hugh Miller made great contributions on the Carboniferous, and unitarian Agassiz (lauded as a creationist by Morris) on glacial theory. Sedgwick, Miller and Agassiz all vigorously opposed evolution in written critiques of works by Chambers and/or Darwin. All three (unlike Lyell but like most geologists) were catastrophists.

What about the 'circularity' of geological method? We already noted that William Smith discovered the fossil-strata association empirically - particularly from undisturbed strata. A mine dug in one spot revealed the same sequence of fossils as one dug elsewhere in the vicinity. But what about the older rocks where the strata were less simply 'layered' and much more folded? Adam Sedgwick, the major pioneer of the stratification of older rocks, wrote in 1846 of his method:

> In every country which is not made out by a pre-existing type, our first labour is that of determining the physical groups, and establishing their relations by natural sections. The labour next in

order is the determination of the fossils found in successive physical groups; and, as a matter of fact, the natural groups of fossils are generally found nearly co-ordinate with the physical groups ...[78]

Sedgwick claimed that his method (which he saw as the classical method of William Smith) began by finding the rock succession in a particular locality using three dimensional mathematics and the tracing of rock types up from a base line. The initial identification of fossil types must be made on the basis of their position in some local succession. Only then do they become a useful tool to correlate rocks in far apart localities. There is no more circularity involved here than in any other area of science.

To illustrate the kind of totally false statements about this which one is unfortunate enough to find in too many Christian books, consider the following quotation from a 1998 book:

> How do geologists arrive at the geologic timetable when the record of the earth does not show it? By the means we have so often seen – assuming that evolution is true and applying circular reasoning.
>
> We noted earlier that one of the primary "evidences" for evolution is the fossil record. Here the simpler or earlier fossils are believed to exist in the "older" rocks. The circular reasoning can be seen as follows: the *age* of the rocks is determined by the index fossils they contain. The ages assigned to the index fossils is determined by their stage of evolution. So the stage of evolution of the fossils determines the geological age of the rocks; the geological age of the rocks in turn determines the sequences of the fossils; the sequence of fossils in the rocks in turn demonstrates evolution... Again, strata are *dated* by the fossils they contain. For example trilobites found in the Cambrian strata date the Cambrian strata based on the evolutionary assumption that trilobites fit in a particular order of evolution from the less complex to the more complex. The fossil age is then determined by the rock stratum in which the trilobite was found, again based on evolutionists' assumptions...[79]

Adam Sedgwick is universally accepted as the geologist who first mapped the Cambrian (along with most of the rest of the Palaeozoics). There is absolutely *no doubt whatsoever* that:

---

[78] Cf Paul Marston (1984) p. 449 which analyses this.
[79] Ankerberg & Weldon (1998) pp. 297-8; *The Genesis Flood* itself contained similar claims.

1. Sedgwick *never* accepted evolution, but always regarded it as unempirical.
2. Sedgwick specifically denied that later species were 'more complex' – the development was only in terms of appearance of new major orders.
3. Sedgwick mapped out the Cambrian strata using a base line, careful measurement of dip, strike etc, three dimensional strata mathematics – and fossils as an interactive backup.

So how is the average reader to know that the assertions made by the learned authors – sporting umpteen doctorates between them – are sheer fictional moonshine (perhaps along with various other assertions they make)? How is it that respectable Christian authors, whose expertise is in some other field of study, feel able to make up demonstrably false statements on subjects about which (it seems) they know nothing, and publish them in books carried in Christian bookshops world-wide? Their motives are not in question, but 'young-earth' literature contains a great deal of such material.[80] We find it puzzling.

We have looked at the assumptions and methods of mainstream geology in this period. In Section 7 we looked at the various 'Flood geologists' in *theological* terms. In *geological* terms we may note:

1. Most were quite respectful to geologists, seeing themselves as 'reinterpreting', what the geologists were finding.[81]
2. They vary in the extent of their actual fieldwork experience, with perhaps a couple of them having a reasonable level of local expertise. Only one, Ure, was in the Geological Society - though he was really a chemist and had joined in early days of a more lax membership.

The reaction of an 'orthodox' geologist like Sedgwick to these 'Mosaic geologists' is instructive. Sedgwick, of course, believed in both the Christian gospel and the Bible. But he strongly held to the Baconian ideal (advocated by Galileo and others too) that science should not be derived from the Bible - even though the same God was author both of nature and Scripture. He knew that current geology had been built up over decades by careful

---

[80] Ian Taylor (1991) is another tome full of historical error.
[81] The exception was the vituperative Henry Cole, a scientific ignoramus.

empirical work - he himself had recognised his earlier errors through empirical observation. Flood geology simply could not explain either the huge volumes of rock (especially in his specialism, the Palaeozoics) or the orderliness of fossils. His criticism of the chemist Ure, the ignoramus Cole, and the unscientific Dean Cockburn were equally strong.[82]

Geology and the Lyell Myths

We have already noted how classical conflict theory started with agnostic propaganda, and there are similarly agnostically motivated popular modern 'conflict theory' productions which are critical of Christianity. Sadly, however, there are also modern works by young-earth creationists which, in the words of one informed article on the history of creationism, are 'the warfare model with the role of cowboys and indians reversed.'[83] Though we do not doubt the sincerity of the writers (whose theology of salvation may often be little different from our own), these are again full of demonstrable historical mistakes, total inconsistencies, and highly improbable speculation, and they leave an impression at least as misleading as the atheist versions of the conflict theory.

The comment made above was actually referring to Malcolm Bowden's book, *The Rise of the Evolution Fraud* (1982). Bowden is not a trained or accredited historian of science, and relied heavily on early books by Irvine (1956) and Himmelfarb (1959).[84] These particular secondary sources were interesting in their day but would not be taken as reliable by serious historians of science today. His other main source was L Wilson's biography of Lyell (1972), which made some untenable assumptions about geology in the period.[85] As we shall see, much of Bowden's historical account is demonstrably mistaken or is highly improbable speculation. Henry Morris, however, copied many of Bowden's ideas in his own *A History of Modern Creationism* (1984). Apart from the specific historical errors, Morris (and to some extent Bowden) tended to take a 'big man'

---

[82] See Clark & Hughes (1890) i, 362, i 403 and ii, 76.
[83] M B Roberts (1986).
[84] W Irvine (1956), G Himmelfarb (1959).
[85] See eg R Porter (1977) p 129.

approach to the history of science. An individual is identified as 'Father of X-ology', obscuring the essential continuity of the development of science, and creating the myth that an individual 'superhero' (or villain) can change the course of science. Young-earth writers since Morris and Bowden tend to copy their model for the history of geology, without knowledge either of the original sources or of the volumes of work being done by real historians of science. Most of the model is demonstrable nonsense, but it is a feature of young-earth literature that long exploded myths continue to be repeated and passed around (with or without a 'Chinese whisper' effect) - so we may as well consider the originals rather than derivatives.

To begin with, Morris' use of the most basic terms shows a central self-contradiction. In one of his books Morris asserts:

> ... the evolutionary model of origins and development is itself fundamentally atheistic ...
>
> ... a popular semantic variation of theistic evolution is a system called progressive creationism... it is almost impossible, either scientifically or Biblically to distinguish progressive creation and theistic evolution the progressive creationist... visualises a bumbling sort of god.[86]

Both progressive creationism, and gap-theory creationism are, according to Morris, just semantic variations of what he calls theistic evolution - and belief in evolution is itself inherently atheistic. One might, therefore, expect him to argue that progressive and gap-theory creationists were really crypto-atheists. Actually (as we saw in our previous section) virtually all those he cites as great 'creationist scientists' and all those he acknowledges as spiritual giants of the century 1850-1950 were progressive, gap-theory, or evolutionary creationists - there were virtually no important advocates of young-earth creationism. By using the term 'creationist' in a woolly way, he disguises the fact that at times he writes as though young-earth creationists were the only real ones, and at others implies the opposite.

A second point about terminology concerns the term 'uniformitarian'. It is unfortunate that the literature (secular and religious) contains such divergences of use of this term that it is inadvisable to use it as a term on its own. As a physical theory

---

[86] Morris (1984b) p 107, 114.

(and so aside from any religious meanings e.g. a scepticism of the supernatural) it has two basic meanings:

i. To mean a belief that present fundamental natural laws of physics and chemistry are similar to those of the past.

ii. To mean that *rates* of geological *processes* (which are produced by particular combinations of the laws of physics and chemistry have always remained the same.

This distinction was made in the 1830's by Professor of Geology Adam Sedgwick[87] and it has been repeated in different form since by Hooykaas[88] by Stephen Jay Gould,[89] and others. Unfortunately there is no consistency about which of the two meanings the term 'uniformitarian' properly has. The often cited phrase 'the present is the key to the past' could, of course, equally be cited of either of these two meanings - and only muddles the issue further. For this reason we will call (i) 'actualism', and (ii) 'rate-uniformitarianism'.

Put simply, young-earth creationists (repeating a mantra started by Price based on Geikie) often state that modern geology is based on uniformitarian principles, - and find no shortage of secular geologists (most of them poorly informed on the history of geology) to cite to 'prove' it. If they mean 'actualism', then the claim is true, and it is true for all branches of science. Science itself is possible only if it may be assumed that nature behaves in a law-like way. This is not to say that scientists rule out type-ii miracle, but just that science as such can deal only in regularity. If, on the other hand, it is asserted that modern geology was built on rate-uniformity, then the claim is demonstrably false - as we have seen. Lyell was unable to convince his contemporaries of this, and most major contributors to the geological column were catastrophists.

Let us look at those Morris praises for their piety and creationism. Apart from Woodward, Morris cites two key 'Bible-believing' naturalists from the earliest period: the 'founder of natural history' and 'strong Christian' Ray (1627-

---

[87] Clark & Hughes (1890) vol i p 369.

[88] R Hooykaas (1963) p 32.

[89] Morris (1984b) p 305 says Gould 'was one of the first to distinguish' between these two meanings of uniformitarianism - but actually Sedgwick made a similar distinction in the 1830's.

1707) and the 'founder of systematic biology' Linnaeus (1707-78). Linnaeus is also cited as a 'creationist' by Bowden and as a 'man of great piety and respect for the Scriptures' by Morris.[90] Linnaeus, like Ray, specifically rejected the possibility that all the fossils could have been laid down in the Genesis Flood.[91] By the end of his life he had even concluded that most species had evolved. Pearcey and Thaxton, billing Linnaeus as a 'devout Lutheran' whose 'scientific work was something of a religious enterprise', note that in later years Linnaeus actually thought that only the *orders* had been created by God, and species had evolved.[92] Ironically, this is not far removed from 'arch villain' Darwin's famous statement in the *Origin of Species* about God originally breathing into a few primal forms![93]   Moving on, Hutton is cited as a founder of 'uniformitarianism' by Morris,[94] by Bowden,[95] and others, he merely shared the universal 'actualism, of geologists and was not particularly a rate-uniformitarian in the later sense of Lyell.

In the early nineteenth century, Cuvier is a key figure in establishing the fossil-strata link associated with geology (and progressive creationism). Yet both Bowden and Morris cite Cuvier as a 'famous creationist scientist' who 'discovered' comparative anatomy and vertebrate palaeontology.[96]

Bowden and Morris assume:

i.   That geology in the 1830's was a bit of amateur dabbling by gentlemen, without much empirical base or history.

ii. That Lyell was a kind of 'Hercules' figure, taking the feeble geological establishment by storm to establish 'uniformitarian principles'.

iii. That Lyell himself was a secret evolutionist, dedicated to overthrowing Genesis.

---

[90] Bowden, (1984) p 10; Morris (1982) p 40, 49.

[91] Ray (1786); Davis Young (1995) pp. 89, 96, etc.

[92] Percey & Thaxton (1994) p. 102.

[93] Quoted, interestingly, at the end of a (1996) book on evolution by three Cambridge scientists Majerus, Amos and Hurst!

[94] Morris & Whitcomb (1961) p 95.

[95] Bowden (1984) p 19.

[96] Bowden (1984) p 219; Morris (1984b) p 463-4.

iv. That the geological column was then developed on Lyellian principles, preparing the way for evolution.

All these points are demonstrably historically mistaken. On (i), Morris states:

> Throughout the eighteenth century and well into the nineteenth, most theologians and scientists of the western world believed that the Deluge was responsible for the major fossiliferous strata of the earth.[97]

As we have to say so often, this is demonstrably untrue, but Morris extends this mistaken idea even to the nineteenth century, and so makes a quotation (actually taken from a secondary source dated 1946) to Buckland's 1820 work, to show that Buckland 'abandoned' flood geology for Cuvier's multiple floods.[98]. The quotation is made out of context, and a scientist of Buckland's generation would have been little more likely to have ever believed in flood geology than to have believed that the world was flat.

Points (ii) and (iii) are clear in Bowden's portrayal of a supposed group of amateur gentlemen, and his citation of Himmelfarb's early (long since discredited) assertion that geology was 'in so feeble a state that it could not resist the determined assault' of Lyell's theory.[99] A similar but more detailed perception due to Rachel Laudan is considered at some length in Paul Marston's PhD Thesis. Laudan's suggestions are misleading because there is in fact a breadth of continuity in observational work, a point not very clear in her later work.[100] Morris, however, follows Bowden's misunderstanding on this, listing a supposed circle of 'untrained' geologists (inexplicably including Chambers, whom *no-one* regarded as a competent geologist and who contributed nothing).[101] Neither explains what kind of training they would have expected geologists to have. In the 1830's, of course, there were no 'professional' scientists in the modern sense, and the modern route into science

---

[97] Morris & Whitcomb (1961) p 113 (see also p 91).

[98] Morris & Whitcomb (1961) p. 93.

[99] Bowden (1984) p 23.

[100] Paul Marston (1984), p. 356 etc. R Laudan (1987).

[101] Morris (1984b) p. 302.

of specialist degree, PhD research etc, did not exist.[102] Nevertheless there were ways for researchers to be recognised as 'competent' and as genuine contributors to the ongoing advance in observational science.[103] Geologists 'trained' by studying the literature on the observational results which had been accumulating since about 1700, and by working with experienced geologists.

Morris too claims that the views of Cuvier and Buckland were 'eclipsed by the Lyellian school of uniformitarian geology'.[104] Ascribing to Lyell's influence both widespread use of fossils for dating, and 'uniformitarianism', Morris asserts: 'Lyell is then a figure of key importance in the sudden conversion of the world from creationism to evolutionism...'[105] We have already seen that Lyell's effect was not crucial to geology in this respect - all this is simply (as Porter inferred) myth (even allowing for the wrong equating of geology=evolutionism).

Bowden seems to misunderstand not only Lyell's effect on geology, but also his religious motivation. He cites a letter of Lyell's referring to 'freeing the science from Moses' and to the harm of 'Mosaic systems', and applauding Bishop Sumner's castigation of Ure.[106] Bowden takes 'mosaic systems' as 'a typically oblique reference to the accounts of Creation and the Flood, as given in Genesis'. Not so. Lyell did not mean to attack Genesis, obliquely or otherwise, and in his inaugural lecture in the orthodox Kings College in 1832 he included the classic argument from design and consistency of geology with Scripture. By 'Mosaic Systems' he was referring to those who tried to found systems of geology on Genesis rather than observation. Bishop Sumner is regarded as one of the most incontrovertible Evangelicals of the period, and for Lyell to applaud him against Ure (whose religious orthodoxy and personal life both had some question marks amongst his contemporaries) can hardly be presented as due to hatred of Scripture. The Evangelical Professor Sedgwick wrote a stinging

---

[102] See eg C A Russell (1983)

[103] M Rudwick has analysed this in (1982) p. 190.

[104] Morris & Whitcomb (1961) p. 95.

[105] Morris (1961) p. 95.

[106] Bowden (1984) p. 94.

review of Ure's geology. Lyell's attitude to Ure, then, was unexceptional. Bowden's suggestion, moreover, that 'Lyell's sole purpose in rapidly befriending Darwin and promoting his interests was in order to use him as a means of propagating the theory of evolution' is sheer fantasy. Darwin's main mentors during his famous 1830's Galapagos trip were Adam Sedgwick and John Stevas Henslow - an emphatically orthodox Anglican rightly described by Bowden as 'deeply religious'. Darwin was a pleasant and promising naturalist and Lyell's interest in him was no more remarkable than theirs. We have seen how Lyell was in this whole period firmly anti-evolutionary, and we find him even in the late 1860's struggling to come to terms with a thoroughgoing Darwinianism. It would be ludicrous to see him as secret evolutionist in the 1830's. Bowden's more recent book actually reasserts:

> As I have pointed out (Bowden82), Lyell admitted that he wrote this work (Principles of Geology) specifically to undermine a literal belief in Genesis. It provided the huge time spans needed by evolution.[107]

The absurdity of suggesting that Lyell wrote his geological (and anti-evolution) text for negative religious reasons and to facilitate evolution beggars belief. It is followed by a suggestion that the doyen of Scottish Evangelicalism, Thomas Chambers, wrote his 'gap theory' of Genesis in 1814 to 'combat the long ages proposed by Hutton and later Lyell'. How Chalmers could write a book to combat a work written 17 years later is not explained. Bowden further believes that when Lyell visited Darwin in 1836 he 'suggested to Darwin that he should write about evolution which would make him famous.'[108] Words fail us. Everything we know about both of them makes this totally impossible.

What of the geological column? Morris asserts in his *The Genesis Flood* (1961) that fossil dating of rocks was based on 'the two assumptions of uniformity and evolution' (p 132). Both these suggestions are demonstrably untrue. Rate-uniformity was

---

[107] Bowden (1998) p. 33 and 104. What is even more puzzling is that Bowden is supposed to have read our *Reason and Faith* in which evidence against this kind of nonsense on Lyell is presented.

[108] Bowden (1998) p. 140.

assumed by almost no one who contributed to the geological column - Lyell being a singular figure - and most were catastrophists. The nonsense about depending on evolution has been endlessly copied by his followers and the geological column often labelled 'the evolutionary geological column'[109] even though we know of not one single evolutionist who made any serious contribution to it – and several (eg Sedgwick, Miller and Agassiz) were key and lifelong anti-evolutionists. British young-earth professor, E H Andews, in the 1997 version of *From Nothing to Nature*, still writes:

> ...geologists have used (and still use) the idea of evolution to help them work out the age of the earth... they are trying to agree with the theory of evolution that needs enormous lengths of time to explain all the forms of life we know today. Evolution and geology are both setting their own clocks by the others.[110]

This is a slightly different 'circularity' claim than that looked at earlier, for this concerns timescales. Historically, however, it has no credibility. It was anti-evolution geologists who concluded that rates of sediment deposition were very slow and very long periods of time were involved. They did so because of clear indications in the rocks themselves, instances of weathered and then overlaid rocks, and other lithological indications. Most guessed at no specific figures, but by 1855 none doubted that the earth was very ancient. To suggest the ancient-earth belief was due to evolutionary supposition is simply untrue. Even the actual dating today, the 'millions' superimposed on the 1855 column, is based on radiometric dating, a technique which does not depend on evolution. The actual figures now held are substantially below those Darwin thought.

What we get, then, from young-earth writers is a mass of self contradiction (viz the number lauded as 'creationists' who were progressive old-earth creationists and therefore crypto-evolutionary traitors in Morrisian terms) and demonstrable historical mistakes. So why do they go on repeating it all?

One reason is Archibald Geikie (1835-1924). Geikie wrote *Founders of Geology* (1897, 1905), which was a kind of resumé-sequel to the mythical history in Lyell's *Principles*. To Geikie,

---

[109] Again in Bowden (1998) p. 351 for example.
[110] Andrews (1977) p. 57-63.

'uniformitarianism' was the principle of 'modern' geology, and Lyell was its founder and prophet. Though Lyell had not convinced his contemporaries that his distinctive ideas were anything but gratuitous hypotheses, though the geological column had been built by geologists who were preponderantly catastrophists, the myths were still propagated. George McCready Price's books on flood geology took Geikie's myths as though they were history. The same ideas have been copied fairly uncritically by Morris and Whitcomb in their 1961 *The Genesis Flood,* and repeated endlessly by their followers.

Let us be clear on this. Lyell made only two distinctive claims:
1. All the major groups of organisms have always existed.
2. Processes in geology have always proceeded at the same rate and intensity.

Both of these are now totally rejected by present geology. The first is long gone – Lyell himself had abandoned it explicitly by the 1860's. On the second, it is now fairly well recognised that there is great evidence for sudden cataclysmic changes ('catastrophes') eg at the end of the Permian and the end of Cretaceous. This is exactly what Sedgwick would have claimed and Lyell denied in the 19th century! So strong, however, is the Lyell myth, that in an 'Evolution Weekend' on British TV in 1998 a programme which hailed Lyell as the 'founder of modern geology' was followed by one which demolished in detail his distinctive uniformitarianism by describing the catastrophes now accepted by virtually all geologists! Apparently no one noticed the inconsistency!

Darwin's Theory - Introduction and History

Darwin's evolutionary theory can be summarised briefly:
i.   There are variations (for reasons not then known) amongst the offspring of any living creature.
ii. These variations will mean that some of these offspring are better able than others (in the given conditions) to survive and reproduce.
iii. There will, in turn, be differences amongst the offspring of these successful reproducers - the most successful in turn reproducing.

iv. This process will imply what may be called a process of 'natural selection', in which competition to survive in successive generations organism produces a cumulative evolutionary trend.

This theory began to emerge in Darwin's unpublished sketches in the 1840's. In 1858 A R Wallace independently arrived at it and sent Darwin a paper (not knowing that Darwin had already reached this conclusion). This forced Darwin's hand, and led to the publication the following year of *The Origin of Species.*

Darwin's main arguments for the theory were:

- An analogy with breeder selection (eg in dogs or pigeons) and the presumption that there was no limit to the changes which could occur by this selection.

- A kind of 'what would we expect if I am right' argument. Darwin did this very well - though critics suspected that given sufficient ingenuity he could have explained almost anything.

These two kinds of argument made evolution plausible, but did not show it was true. Darwin had little or no positive evidence that it had actually happened. He had to explicitly admit ignorance of the laws governing inheritance, of the cause of particular variations, of the reasons for hybrid sterility, of the reasons for rarity or extinction, of the conditions favourable for new species, of the means of transport, and of reasons for embryo variation. The fossil record, except in very broad outline, was an embarrassment to be explained away (in Ch. 9) rather than a proof. It showed little or no evidence of gradation from one species into another, and Darwin had to argue that it was very incomplete - failing to convince his old mentor Sedgwick amongst others. Positive evidence against the theory was produced by physicists like Kelvin and Jenkin.[111] This was that the cooling rates of the sun and earth did not (on known laws of physics) allow enough time for evolution. The physicists were open to suggestions for possible sources of energy, but found none plausible - and could not at that time have known that a nuclear source of energy would later be identified.

---

[111] Cf eg Burchfield (1975) and Hull (1973) for details.

On a scientific level, then, the debate was not one between unprejudiced Darwinians and obscurantist conservatives. On a basis of observation alone, any rational person would have had to reject Darwin's theory as the observable evidence was against it.[112] Science, however, is a search beyond immediate observation for a coherent overall view - and it was a belief that they had found this (in spite of contrary evidence) which motivated the evolutionists.

Darwin presented the debate in The Origin of Species as though it was between simple 'flash bang' creationists on the one hand, and his own theory on the other. This was misleading. Those (eg Sedgwick and Agassiz) who rejected evolution often veered towards a complex concept of 'archetypes' - a kind of 'variations on a theme' approach, which might also be held by non-Darwinian evolutionists (which probably included the leading anatomist Richard Owen).

On the actual laws of inheritance Darwin had speculated unconvincingly, but formed no viable theory. Around the turn of the century Mendel's ideas were 'rediscovered' (though put in a slightly different form), producing some further problems for Darwinian theory. Gradually, however, over several decades a reconciliation between the ideas of Darwin and those of Mendel was affected, largely through the mathematical work of Haldane, R A Fisher, and Sewall Wright. This resulted in what has become known as Neo-Darwinism. By the 1930's this was generally accepted outside a few religious circles. Developments since are the arguments of Gould and Eldridge that evolution happens in punctuated equilibrium (which explains the lack of transitional forms), and an ongoing (often acrimonious) debate between Gould and Dawkins as to how far the 'gene' and how far the organism is the unit of selection.

It must be emphasised that all these developments are movements within neo-Darwinism - not attacks on it. The neo-Darwinian assumption remains overwhelmingly predominant amongst biological scientists - and no one should be misled on this by the careful selections of quotations (often out of context) which appear in some anti-evolutionary literature. Books

---

[112] See also Gale (1982).

heralding the imminent demise of evolution have been published virtually continually over the last century - with less credibility today than ever. How good the *evidence* is for evolution is another question, but modern anti-evolutionists should not delude themselves about its   overwhelming predominance amongst professional biologists.

'The Church' and Darwin

In the light of modern historical scholarship, a number of points may be made about the religious aspects of the evolution debate in the century after Darwin:

i.   Virtually all main evangelical scientists and spiritual leaders during the period accepted an ancient earth – it was never about 'literalism'.

ii. At times Darwin's own work read in a 'reductionist' way, going beyond scientific theory to imply a lack of design.

iii. Religious objections were usually not to evolution as such but to this implicit reductionism.

iv. Evangelicals were to be found in Darwin's closest circle of scientific supporters on both sides of the Atlantic.

The supposed rantings against Darwin of ignorant contemporary clerics is a classic part of the 'conflict theory' folklore. Often portrayed as a supreme example of this is the June 1860 British Association debate at Oxford, where the 'ignorant jibes' of Bishop 'Soapy Sam' Wilberforce were supposedly silenced by the cool scientific precision of T H Huxley in what is taken to be a 'turning point' of the evolution debate. Actually Wilberforce (the high churchman son of the famous evangelical anti-slavery campaigner) was a competent amateur naturalist, had been primed by Owen the greatest comparative anatomist of the age, and (by Darwin's own admission) made all the most telling points against Darwin in an article in the *Quarterly Review* of July 1860. It seems highly unlikely that this was any kind of 'turning point', or indeed that many people thought Huxley to have 'won' the debate. The gleeful undergraduate uproar was probably more to do with the fact that Huxley had been publicly rude to a bishop. No modern historian of science would see it as Huxley liked to think, or as, say, his grandson presented it.[113]

Christians Doing Science in the Nineteenth Century

Many leading nineteenth century scientists were strong theists, some were also Christians with a high view of the Bible. What was their attitude to science and its relationship with theology?

Sedgwick professed (in the Geological Society tradition) to be following Francis Bacon.[114] John Herschel wrote his *Preliminary Discourse on Natural Philosophy* in 1831, again eulogising Bacon[115] though he also recognised that the sources of inspiration for scientific ideas were independent of the process of their testing and justification.[116] *Whewell's Philosophy of the Inductive Sciences* (1840) was altogether more sophisticated, recognising the theory-laden aspect of observation.[117] Whewell was influenced by Kant – Sedgwick and Herschel hardly at all. Though Whewell and Sedgwick saw empiricism as basic to the study of natural phenomena both refused to extend this empiricism to morality. Morality and metaphysics were not reducible to natural phenomena.

How did such scientist-Christians see the relationship of their science and theology? On this there was pretty well agreement amongst all the leading nineteenth century figures including the three just cited, and it was along the lines of the comments above by Francis Bacon (who was often referred to).

1. 'Natural causes' have no existence independent of the will of God.

---

[113] Julian Huxley and H Ketterwell (1965) p. 78. White and Gribbin (1995) give a highly biased account which is high in triumphalism but short on evidence - in general their book is poor compared with eg Desmond and Moore (1989).

[114] See eg Sedgwick's *Discourse* of 1833, 1834 and 1835. A lot of detail on Sedgwick's methodology and its relationship with theology is in Marston (1984).

[115] Eg Herschel (1831) p. 104, 114.

[116] See eg Losee (1993) Ch. 9, Marston (1984) Sec 7.5.

[117] See Whewell (1840) also Losee Ch. 9, Marston (1984) , and our next section.

2. Uniformity in nature (essential to the success of science) can be assumed because God is 'unchanging in his operations'.[118]

3. Science is the study of 'natural causes', and is to be begun from the study of nature, *not* from the Bible.

4. Structure in nature evidences intelligent design, and divine design is essential to this – this implies a certain degree of 'idealism' ie the primacy of mind which is not 'reducible' to matter.

5. Materialistic evolution, which denies design, is equivalent to atheism.

6. Ultimately the findings of science and the true meaning of the Bible will be found to be in harmony.

These kinds of view were common to Cuvier, Fleming, Sedgwick, Herschel, Buckland, Whewell, Brewster, Lyell, Miller, Phillips, Hitchcock, Owen, Mivart, Gray, Dana, Dawson, Pasteur, Mendel etc – and indeed to chemists like Dalton, physicists like Maxwell, Faraday, Tait, Kelvin, and most scientists who called themselves 'Christians'. Some theists (like the unitarian Agassiz and liberal Baden Powell) would have probably accepted all but the last one, but we will restrict our comments here to those who were more theologically orthodox.

Science and theology were not totally 'separate' to Christians who were scientists. Points (1), (2), (4), (5) and probably (6) all imply some kind of connection – but the connection is Baconian and traditional in form. Number (1) was held firmly – no one was suggesting that God was only in the 'gaps' of natural explanation. Geologists (eg Buckland and Sedgwick) who concluded from empirical observation that species had originated preternaturally, noted that this formed a more powerful design argument than Paley's. Paley himself, in the classic (1802), had based his design argument purely on structure – for in his day there was no empirical proof that the universe and all its species had not always been there. Christian geologists in the 1830's argued that the sudden appearance of new species now showed that God was not a Deistic absentee landlord but still actively involved in creation. But they were explicitly adamant that natural processes were not independent

---

[118] Sedgwick reported in the *Athenaeum* October 5th 1844.

of God – he was not restricted to 'gaps' in them (we already quoted Buckland in Section 5).

On (3), that science was not properly begun from Scripture they were all adamant. Some of the 'Scriptural Geologists' (or 'Mosaic Geologists' as Lyell and Sedgwick called them) in the first half of the century *did* begin their 'science' from the Bible, but those who did were generally not scientists and did not contribute to science. Neither leading scientist-Christians nor leading conservative theologians (even going back to the days of Bellamine!) accepted such an approach. Sometimes Christians (eg Kepler or Maxwell) may have got *inspiration* from their theology on specific science issues, but they did not claim to derive them as known truths from Scripture.

What of (5) and (6)? Purely physicalist systems from Hobbes onwards seemed inevitably to be reductionist, to leave no room for freewill or morality, and (in strict form) to deny both God and consciousness. Hardly surprisingly, scientist-Christians rejected this adamantly – not just for 'biblical' reasons but because it was unempirical, irrational, and negated all theism. In the early nineteenth century, materialistic reductionism was rife in the Edinburgh school (including people like anatomist Robert Grant, and Robert Knox) and associated with a form of Lamarckian evolution. Where scientist-Christians like Sedgwick and Owen made theological objections it was to a perceived materialism in eg Chambers *Vestiges* or Darwin's *Origin*, not to the evolutionary idea as such.[119]

As Baconians, the scientist-Christians listed above would have held to (6). The biblical flood, for example, was presumed to be a real event. This did not mean that they started geology from the Bible, but it did mean that (as true Baconians) they looked for the truths of science and truths of theology about the flood to harmonise. This is so not just for the Evangelical Sedgwick, but for Charles Lyell who writes at the end of his *Principles:*

> For our own part, we have always considered the flood, if we are required to admit its universality in the strictest sense of the term, as a preternatural event far beyond the reach of philosophical enquiry, whether as to the secondary causes employed to produce it or the effects most likely to result from it.

---

[119] See Marston (1984) section 7.6, Desmond (1982) pp. 60-1 for details.

There is no indication here that Lyell thought the Bible might simply be mistaken, he assumes both that the Noachic flood is a real event (possibly though not necessarily universal), and that it is supernatural (or preternatural).

Where scientist-Christians believed in the likelihood of some kind of 'creation' of species departing from natural processes, we can say that in general:

1. They arrived at the conclusion empirically, not *a priori* from Scripture.
2. They did not regard 'creation' as part of science itself but as something science might point to.

Whewell, for example, deals in detail with the issue of creation and science in his *History of the Inductive Sciences* (1837, 1857). Geology was, he held, a 'historical' science. It should have the three phases of:

i. **Descriptive Geology:** what is there.
ii. **Geological Dynamics:** by what mechanisms can such things be produced.
iii. **Physical Geology:** hence what were the causes of existing things.

He was convinced that there was at that time no natural process explanation for the appearance of species but added:

> Although it may not be possible to arrive at a right conviction respecting the origin of the world, without recourse to other than physical considerations, and to other than geological evidence; yet extraneous considerations and extraneous evidence respecting the beginning of things, must never be allowed to influence our physics or our geology. Our geological dynamics, like our astronomical dynamics, may be inadequate to carry us back to an origin of the state of things, of which it explains the progress; but this deficiency must be supplied, not by adding the supernatural to natural geological dynamics, but by accepting, in their proper place, the views supplied by a portion of knowledge of a different character and order. If we include in our Theology the speculations to which we have recourse for this purpose, we must exclude them from our Geology. The two sciences may conspire, not by having any part in common; but because, though widely diverse in their lines, both point to a mysterious and invisible origin of the world...It may be urged that all truths must be consistent with all other truths, and that therefore the results of true geology or astronomy cannot be

irreconcilable with the statements of true theology... but it by no means follows that we must be able to gain a full insight into the nature and manner of such a consistency... the impossibility of accounting by any natural means of all the successive tribes of plants and animals... when we enquire whence they came into this our world, geology is silent. The mystery of creation is not within the range of her legitimate territory; she says nothing, but she points upward.[120]

Whewell's sermons show him to be fairly orthodox in his theology – he was certainly not a theological 'liberal' in any modern sense of the term. Moreover, he in no way believed theology 'inferior' to geology – his demarcation of science and theology was Baconian not positivist. He certainly did not believe in some kind of total 'separation' of theology and science, for he is clear both that ultimately they are truths which must reconcile, and that the absence of any 'natural' explanation 'points upwards'. On the other hand he did believe that within geology itself only natural causal patterns were permitted, and (in common with all the renowned scientist-Christians of his times) that all science should start from observation not from Scripture. We could go on to illustrate the same basic approach from Herschel, Sedgwick and probably virtually all the others named above. It was standard throughout the century.

Scientist-Christians and Evolution

In the late 1850's and early 1860's Darwin's 'inner circle' actually included a number of highly religious men. Adrian Desmond rightly remarks that even the crusade of the X-club was never simply a matter of Church-baiting rationalists triumphing over religious obscurantism, but a more subtle attempt, jointly undertaken by 'agnostics', deists and some Christians, to professionalise science and put it at the disposal of the mercantile middle classes.[121]

The key evolutionists in the 1860's were from almost every conceivable religious viewpoint. A R Wallace, who independently formulated and consistently supported the theory of evolution by natural selection, became a lifelong spiritualist.

---

[120] Whewell (1837, 1857) iii pp. 486-8.
[121] Desmond (1982) p. 17.

In England the circle of close supporting naturalist friends around Darwin and Huxley included the Unitarian W B Carpenter (1813-85) who proposed Huxley for his FRS, and the Broad Churchman W H Flower (1831-99), There was the Methodist W K Parker (1823-90), whose 'lifelong almost rustic piety was reminiscent of Faraday's' with an 'exuberant belief in Old Testament miracles' and an 'abiding sense of the Divine presence.'[122] There was J W Hulke, a 'deeply religious Calvinist' who was Huxley's formidable ally'.[123] Then, in those early years, there was Professor of Zoology St George Mivart, an Evangelical who became a Roman Catholic in 1844 during the revival of Anglo-Catholicism. A keen evolutionist he was almost one of Darwin's inner circle, and a close friend of Huxley; his later move to belittling natural selection was a bitter blow to the group.[124] In America, the foremost supporter of Darwin was indubitably the Harvard botanist Asa Gray (1810-1888), who was the first one outside the English circle to whom Darwin revealed his theory. The Encyclopaedia Britannica says of Gray:

> Gray was one of the few persons whom Darwin kept fully informed concerning the publication of his Origin of Species (1859). Gray was a devout Christian, however ...

Livingstone states of Gray:

> his convictions were thoroughly evangelical. He stated that the Nicene Creed encapsulated the heart of his faith., Moore states: a moderate Calvinist and an adherent of the fundamental doctrines of evangelical Christianity.[125]

Darwin's leading American proponent, then, was an Evangelical. On the other hand the leading scientific anti-Darwinian in America was probably Agassiz. Agassiz was a theist but no Evangelical, and Livingstone suggests that he found Unitarianism congenial to his views.[126] Agassiz believed so strongly in special creation that he opposed racial intermarriage because he thought the different races had been

---

[122] Desmond (1982) pp. 51-53.
[123] Desmond (1982) p. 134.
[124] Desmond (1982) p. 137 and see Moore (1979) p. 117.
[125] Livingstone (1987) p. 61.
[126] Lovingstone (1987) p. 58.

made separately. This is ironical since Morris, Bowden and others all laud Agassiz as a 'creationist' and 'Bible-believing' champion of orthodoxy, and Morris (following Price's lead) decries evolution for its supposed connection with racism and imperialism.[127] But let us note that in America the foremost scientific figures on both sides believed in a God and accepted orthodox geology, but Darwinian-evolution was defended by the Evangelical (Gray) and attacked by the theologically-liberal racist (Agassiz).

An associate of Gray was the evangelical Congregationalist minister G F Wright (1838-1921). A linguist and philosopher as well as a theologian. Wright also became an expert on glacial geology in the region.[128] Both his orthodoxy and intellectual stature were generally recognised, and he allied himself with those who became Fundamentalists in the twentieth century.[129]

A second geologist was J D Dana (1813-1895), Morris says that Dana was one:

> of the most prominent American geologists... at first opposed Darwinism, but eventually accepted evolution. Nevertheless, he continued to be a firm believer in Biblical Christianity.

This is true (even though on Morris' premises it should be impossible!), and is confirmed both by Livingstone and by the Encyclopaedia Britannica.

The Rev George Macloskie, a Presbyterian and Princeton Professor of Biology, held to inerrancy but came to an evolutionary view of creation - being troubled that some churchmen had sanctified the position of Agassiz who was 'not a theologian and scarcely a Christian'.[130]

Alexander Winchell 'played a major role in organising geology as a science in the United States',[131] and though Winchell tended to the neo-Lamarckian end of evolution, his commitment was clear.

---

[127] Morris (1984b) p. 463, (1984) p. 45, etc.
[128] Moore (1979) p. 280-282, 295-296, Livingstone (19870 p. 65-70.
[129] Moore (1979) p. 42.
[130] Cited in Livingstone (1987) p. 93.
[131] Livingston (1987) p. 87.

Morris cites three 'Creationist geologists' who fought 'evolutionism'.[132] The first was Benjamin Silliman (1779-1864). who reconciled the creation statements in Genesis with orthodox geology. The second was the evangelical Congregationalist Edward Hitchcock (1893-1864). an advocate of orthodox geology who favoured age-day, or gap-theory, In 1859 Silliman was 80 and Hitchcock 66 - neither lived long to reflect on the new theory and both would have thought ludicrous Morris' brand of young-earth creationism. The third of Morris' anti-evolutionary geologists was J W Dawson (1820-1899). Dawson was actually a good friend of Lyell, he adopted the age-day theory and firmly accepted orthodox geology.[133] In his later work he accepted that:

> there may be a theistic form of evolution... It necessarily admits design and final cause.[134]

In the last section we saw that no leading Evangelical/ Fundamentalist theologian of the period (unless you count Ellen G White!) would have countenanced Morris' young-earth creationism. We have now seen that none of the 'creationist' scientists he cites (and there were, indeed, many Evangelicals amongst leading scientists) would have countenanced it either. None of them would have accepted the views of Morris or J P Moreland that it would be legitimate to begin science from the Bible rather than observation. Some did reject evolution, usually on empirical grounds, but many (and Moore even argues that they were the more orthodox!) accepted some kind of evolution whilst, of course, rejecting pure physicalism.

What exactly was the objection to Darwinism of scientists like Sedgwick, Owen, and Guyon? There could be four possible bases:

1. **Biblical literalism:** objections from the wording of Genesis.
2. **Philosophical theology:** evolution was inherently atheistic.
3. **Materialistic linkage:** evolution was linked to materialism in Darwin.

---

[132] Morris (1984) p. 39.
[133] Livingstone (1987) p. 82.
[134] Quoted from Livingstone (1987) p. 84, from J D Dawson: *Modern Ideas of Evolution.*

4. **Empirical evidence:** actual geological evidence was against organic evolution.

Amongst scientists and theologians (1) seems rare. None of them, of course, believed the accounts 'literal', and there seemed no reason to suppose that the Hebrew word 'make' should not imply a process. Likewise for (2). Since they were *theists* they believed that God worked as much through natural processes as in the supernatural. This is why writers like Ronald Numbers and Neal Gillespie have so many problems in deciding whether some of them (eg Herschel, Owen and Wright) were 'really' creationists or evolutionists. There was simply no sharp dividing line. Wright, for example is often lauded as a 'creationist' but actually was 'evasive' (says Numbers) about whether he still believed in evolution, and:

> Wright, especially in his later years, refused to regard creation and evolution as mutually exclusive explanations.[135]

Of course he did! Terms like 'creation' and 'design' spoke of divine intention, whereas evolution spoke only of mechanism. Whether the mechanism God used for 'creating' was an instantaneous miracle or a process was largely an empirical issue – and it admitted of degrees. Even Linnaeus, as we have noted, had come to accept evolution of all the species within the main orders. Hugh Miller likewise says of evolution:

> Nor, be it remarked. Is there positive atheism in the belief. God might as certainly have originated the species by a law of development as he maintains it by a law of development...[136]

Miller (who notes that Sedgwick and Brewster agree with him) was concerned for some kind of special creative involvement in mankind – a common view amongst Christians. But he had no inherent theological objection to evolution – he thought it unempirical. Sedgwick argued (4) – there was no empirical evidence for evolution and the fossil evidence was against it. But, again, the objection was not to evolution on philosophical/theological grounds. What Sedgwick (who was both a geologist and a Church Canon) objected to was the implicit *materialism* in Chambers' earlier evolutionary work

---

[135] Numbers (1992) p. 35.
[136] Miller (1849) p. 12. The entry on Miller in the recent *Dictionary of Evangelical Biography* is by Paul Marston.

(1844) which 'annulled all distinction between the physical and moral.' He also suspected the *Origin of Species* of being a 'dish of rank materialism'. It was the reduction of spiritual to physical which Sedgwick believed both philosophically foolish and theologically unacceptable. Materialism did need and assume evolution, but 'a doctrine may be true and yet may be turned to evil purposes'.[137] Owen is similar. Like Sedgwick he also rankled at the triumphalism in Darwin's *Origin*, he thought Darwin had given no real evidence for his suggested mechanism, and he objected to materialism.[138] It would be tedious to go through all the other 'anti-evolutionist' scientists, but the pattern seems common.

Darwin and Religion

About Darwin there are more myths than about Galileo and Lyell put together. As a scientist he was well trained. At Edinburgh (1825-7) he attended courses by Robert Jameson (including field trips[139]) and Thomas Hope - representing the two then main schools of empirical geology.[140] He read other books, eg by the (evangelical) botanist John Fleming, and worked together on marine invertebrates with the (atheist) anatomist Robert Grant.[141] In Cambridge (1827-31) he worked intensively with the botany Professor John Stevas Henslow[142], and completed his science education with a brief geological tour of Wales with leading geologist Professor Sedgwick in 1831.[143] Suggestions made by critics that he was some kind of 'amateur' are nonsense – he had one of the best scientific trainings of the age. Robert Grant was a Lamarckian evolutionist, and Darwin had also read his grandfather's evolutionary work, but his own

---

[137] Cf Marston (1984) sections 5.6.2 and 7.6, the latter is on our web site.

[138] Cf Desmond (1982) pp. 43, 61: there is also a manuscript letter to Sedgwick in the Sedgwick collection in Cambridge.

[139] Cf Secord (1991) He later claimed he stopped going – but his notebook shows otherwise! See also Desmond & Moore (1991) p. 42.

[140] Cf eg Browne (1994) pp. 69 etc, Desmond & Moore (1991) p. 42.

[141] Browne (1995) Ch. 3., Desmond & Moore (1991) ch 3.

[142] Second (1991) notes Henslow's own excellent previous work in geology.

[143] Cf Desmond & Moore (1991), and Browne (1995) – who unfortunately repeats the old myths fostered by Thackeray and Morrell (1981) of a 'broad church' Cambridge Network.

evolutionary speculations seem to have begun after his Galapagos trip in 1831-2.

On the religious front, he met with a rampant materialism at Edinburgh, and toyed with it in private notebooks – but seems not to have gone far into it. As he went to Cambridge he was thinking of entering the Anglican Ministry, and read and appreciated the Evangelical John Bird Sumner's *Evidences of Christianity*.[144] He was delighted with the logic of Paley's *Evidences* when he read it as part of his Cambridge degree.[145] He was greatly influenced by the devoutly Christian Henslow - also by Sedgwick, Whewell and other Anglican Dons. Early in 1831, when he graduated, he had to assent to the 39 Articles of the Anglican church. Over time, his reasonably orthodox Anglican beliefs slowly changed to a general theism, and Desmond and Moore suggest that the death of his daughter Annie in 1851 brought a final demise to the idea of a *benevolent* creator. He was still, however, a theist when he wrote *The Origin of Species* in 1859, though this in turn degenerated. In 1887 he denied ever being an atheist though accepted the term 'agnostic'; John Hedley Brooke, however, argues that Darwin meant this in a sense rather different from Huxley - in actual fact Darwin wavered, was undecided, and could speak differently on different occasions not from deception but from uncertainty.[146]

Sometimes stories are circulated that Darwin had a 'death-bed conversion', and renounced the wicked theory of evolution.[147] The stories are usually based on a probably true incident when he was visited by the temperance campaigner and evangelist Lady Elizabeth Hope. If we read her own account rather than a newspaper report (such reports usually tend to garble things!) we can gather what probably happened.[148] Knowing that a young (39), personable, devout Christian lady, campaigning for a temperance cause he supported, was coming to visit him, the fragile 72 year old Charles 'just happened' to be reading the

---

[144] Desmond & Moore (1991) p. 48.

[145] Desmond & Moore (1991) p. 78.

[146] See eg Brooke's 'Darwin's Science and His Religion' in J Durant (Ed) (1985). Our present treatment is also based on personal discussion with the author.

[147] A British 'daily reading' booklet carried the story yet again in late 1998.

[148] James Moore (1989) contains both.

book of Hebrews (rather than, say, *Das Kapital*) at the time he knew she would arrive. He commented that it was a 'Royal book', said he liked to hear some of the modern hymns, and regretted the use some had made of his theory. He did *not* profess 'conversion' and did *not* renounce evolution; in any case it would not have occurred to him that a theory of evolution was incompatible with Christian belief[149] (especially as he knew a number like Asa Gray who combined both). That any supposed death-bed return to Christianity would have been kept from, or kept quiet by, his pious wife and daughter and revealed only to a passing stranger (however personable) is so silly a notion that it cannot be taken seriously. Lady Hope made no such claim – and those who do make it should read her account more carefully.

Darwin struggled over the question of design. On the one hand natural selection seemed to open the door to the possibility that creatures could have evolved purely accidentally, and he felt a moral revulsion against the idea that suffering and death could form a part of a design plan. On the other hand he found it hard to escape a conviction that the universe as a whole must be more that a product of undesigned chance. His friend Gray (and, according to Darwin, Lyell) thought that perhaps God worked through designing the variations worked on by natural selection. In 1861 Darwin wrote to him:

If anything is designed, certainly man must be: one's "inner consciousness" (though a false guide) tells one so; yet I cannot admit that man's rudimentary mammae, bladder drained as if he went on all four legs, and pug-nose was designed.[150]

By the *Descent of Man* (1872) he could write:

The birth of the species and of the individual are equally part of that grand sequence of events, which our minds refuse to accept as blind chance. The understanding revolts at such a conclusions, whether or not we are able to believe that every slight variation of structure... have all been ordained for some special purpose.

When the Duke of Argyll (a disciple of Owen) suggested that it was impossible not to see design in nature, the ageing Darwin famously responded:

---

[149] He wrote this to an enquirer in 1879 cf F Darwin (1887) vol 1 p. 307.

[150] F Darwin (1887) vol 2 p. 382.

'Well that often comes to me with overwhelming force, but at other times,' and he shook his head vaguely, adding 'it seems to go away.'[151]

Even in 1881 he wrote to Graham of an inward conviction that 'the Universe is not the result of chance' – repeating, however, earlier doubts about the capacity of the human brain, if it were really a product of natural selection purely for survival, to arrive at truth in such matters.[152] Finally, he was a determinist who denied libertarian freewill but wanted to maintain morality. Darwin, as he repeatedly wrote to Gray in the early 1860's, was 'in a muddle'. It was as big a muddle as Dennett, the Churchlands, Dawkins, and those like them are in today – trying to maintain meaning and morality in a purposeless, deterministic, and reductionist reality. The heart of his problem was not evolution, but materialism: but unlike them Darwin realised it.

Neal Gillespie and The Problem of Creation

Neal Gillespie's book *Charles Darwin and the Problem of Creation* was published in 1979. It is a book deeply flawed by contradiction and a failure to understand the mainstream of scientist-Christians of the period. Unfortunately, it has been taken as a sensible analysis by modern 'design theorists' like J P Moreland (who admits he is 'not a historian of science'), and others who want to portray evolution as inherently evil.

Gillespie suggests two basic *'epistemes'*, or basic approaches to the nature of truth in science, for the nineteenth century:

> The positivist limited scientific knowledge, which he saw as the only valid form of knowledge, to the laws of nature and to processes involving "secondary," or natural causes exclusively. The creationist, on the other hand, saw the world and everything in it as being the result of direct or indirect divine activity. His science was inseparable from his theology.[153]

The first two sentences seem clear enough. The 'positivist' is a physicalist for whom *only* the physical is real and *only* science is knowledge. The 'creationist' includes *all* theists of any

---

[151] F Darwin (1887) vol 1 p. 316.
[152] F Darwin (1887) vol 1 p. 303. 316.
[153] Gillespie (1977) p. 3.

description (eg Sedgwick, Miller, Agassiz, Lyell, Whewell, Buckland, Herschel, Owen, Phillips, Gray, Dana, Guyon, Parker, Maxwell, Kelvin, Mivart, Wright, and possibly even Darwin at the time of writing the *Origin*). One would have, of course, to be circumspect about the 'inseparability' of science and theology. Theological concepts were not used in science, though they underpinned it and related to it. But, on these definitions, 'creationist' and 'evolutionist' were not alternatives because they related to different questions. One dealt with context and meaning and the other with mechanism. Virtually all those cited would have agreed with this.

Had Gillespie stuck with this schema it might have had some use. As we have seen, theological objections of eg Sedgwick, Owen and Hodge to Darwin were to a perceived materialism, not to evolution as such. A book could certainly have been written about Darwin's struggle to maintain meaning as he slid to materialism and determinism.

Gillespie, however, gets thoroughly confused about his terms, and makes all kinds of puzzling assertions. One base of his problem seems to be that he sees positivism as modern and creationism/theism as obscurantist, and really cannot empathise with consistent Baconian theists. His only nod to the latter is:

> Many creationists followed the accommodating Baconian tradition of insisting on a pragmatic ad hoc divorce of science and religion as a way of warding off conflict, they were, nonetheless, incapable of receiving a scientific teaching that appeared to conflict with theological truth.[154]

Rather than a carefully considered *episteme* which formed the basis of the scientific revolution Baconianism is presented as a kind of '*ad hoc*' pragmatic shambles, a cheap trick to avoid clashes between science and religion. And what 'scientific teaching' were they supposed to have been incapable of 'receiving'? Was it evolution? If so his statement is untrue. Was it materialistic physicalism? In which case they were quite right to refuse to 'receive' it as it is an incoherent metaphysic not a scientific theory.

Let us just recap on what consistent Baconians did believe:

---

[154] Gillespie (1979) p. 13.

1. Theology underpins science and the consistency of God makes nature law-like.[155]
2. Science itself involves looking for natural causes – though absence of them may indicate some miraculous or preternatural agency.
3. Empirically (c1859) the evidence was against evolution.
4. If natural causality were found this would not negate 'creation' ie divine design.
5. Materialistic reductionism would negate design, and is both untrue and inconsistent with faith.

All the many Christian naturalists Gillespie cites would have accepted (1), (2), (4) and (5) – their disagreement was over (3) and (perhaps) over how far particular evolutionary schema had slipped into (5). Gillespie seems to thoroughly confuse the issues, as we may illustrate:

(a) Compatibility of Theism and Positivism

Gillespie has defined positivism as a belief that the 'only valid form of knowledge' is a science which deals exclusively with physical causes. Thus there is no metaphysics, religion or theology that is 'knowledge'. Now we personally believe that such a view is internally incoherent (on what basis can science be done except on metaphysical assumptions?), but its definition is clear. Yet Gillespie goes on to assert on p. 153 that 'Theists could also be positivists.' In his sense of 'positivist' this is nonsense. It is like saying 'Of course, there are some circles which can in fact be square.' How could a theist see science as the 'only valid' form of knowledge? But if by now Gillespie has dropped this definition, what, really, *is* positivism? Is it just a belief that nature is law-like? On p. 44 we learn that 'Whether "being scientific" meant being like Herschel or being like Lyell it meant being positivistic.' But both Herschel and Lyell were theists – how were they positivistic? No one could do *any* science if nature were not law-like, and no consistent theist would deny it. It is all very confused. Does 'positivism' perhaps mean an *a priori* ruling out of type-ii miracles? This seems to be implied on p. 152. Yet according to Gillespie (p. 26) all his arch-

---

[155] Gillespie cites Gray on p. 38 defining a law as 'the human conception of divine and orderly Divine action.'

Creationists 'did not believe in miraculous creation in 1859'. Actually no consistent theist rules out type-ii miracles *a priori*, and Gillespie may in any case be exaggerating their empirical rejection. Men like Sedgwick were open to whatever degree of lawlikeness 'creation' of new species turned out to have.

(b) Empirical vs Theological Groundings

Gillespie aserts:

> In its pure form creationism predicted that no purely physical explanation of speciation would be found.[156]

There is a lot of difference between saying that no explanation *has been* found or looks empirically likely, and saying that it is ruled out by theology. Now geology, we are told, was the 'practical exemplar of the new orientation'. Gillespie cites Hitchcock and others as claiming that "No other science presents us with such repeated examples of miraculous intervention in nature."[157] British geologists would have agreed. Gillespie, having narrowly decided on the basis of 'recent work' not to class Sedgwick as a 'mere biblicist', pronounces him as 'one of the foremost British geologists of the century'.[158] But he just does not understand how Sedgwick can be thoroughly and instinctively theist, seeing God in every part of nature, yet believe in a Baconian separation of theology from empirical science. He cannot understand that Sedgwick, whilst objecting to materialism, has no particular theological problem in evolution although he thinks the empirical evidence is against it. Thus Gillespie states:

> British geologist Adam Sedgwick shared Hitchcock's suspicion that attempts to account for new species by means of "secondary laws" were inherently materialistic and atheistic.'[159]

This is, to say the least, misleading. Nowhere in any of Sedgwick's published or extant manuscript works is there any statement that evolution as such is inherently atheistic. Sedgwick's comments were on the specific schemes of Chambers and Darwin which he believed tended to be. Thus

---

[156] Gillespie (1979) p. 6.
[157] Gillespie (1979) p. 23.
[158] Gillespie (1979) p. 30, p. 15.
[159] Gillespie (1979) p. 22.

Darwin had said that if natural selection had produced eg the beehive structure, then it was 'not very wonderful'. Sedgwick responded that even if it could be shown to be due to secondary causes ('which no mortal can prove'), it would not negate 'final cause' – to Sedgwick nature was all very wonderful and saturated with God.[160] Secondary causes were not a problem – though Sedgwick thought that empirically the evidence was that present understandings of them could not account for the origin of species. Gillespie actually admits this for Cuvier, Owen, Sedgwick and others on page 26 – and also states that they 'did not believe in miraculous creation in 1859' – which forces him to invent all kinds of new terms 'nomothetic creationist', 'nescience' etc. On page 29 Owen is clearly shown to have rejected evolution on empirical grounds, whilst asserting that were laws to one day be discovered governing the origins of life:

> We should still retain as strongly the idea... we call 'creation;, viz that the process was ordained by and had originated from an all-wise and all powerful First Cause

There have been, of course, atheists who pronounce that evolution 'must be' true – and on their creed this is so. But Christians saw no *a priori* reason either way to decide whether 'creation' of new species involved a type-ii or a type-i miracle. God could have used either.

(c) Baconian Empiricism

Gillespie says:

> To interpret nature according to "a regular system of secondary causes" alone was the heart of the positive view of science. Whilst these are Charles Lyell's words, he could not have accepted the idea that "secondary causes" alone could explain nature.[161]

To interpret nature according to a regular system of secondary causes was also at the heart of the Baconian view of science – which well predates positivism. But Gillespie simply cannot grasp a Baconian belief in orderly natural processes as the concern of science. Thus he speaks of:

---

[160] Darwin: 6th Edn *Origin* p. 246; Clarke & Hughes (1890) 2, p. 358, F Darwin (1887), 2, pp. 247-50.
[161] Gillespie (1979) p. 41.

The naturalists of the old episteme, while developing in their practice a protopositivism as manifested in their preference for nomothetic creation and in their purely naturalistic work in geology...[162]

No Christian could be 'purely naturalistic' if this implies a denial of all underlying divine intention or design. However, if the 'old episteme' was actually a Christian Baconian creationism, then it would quite properly refer *only* to natural processes in its scientific practice. If this is what Gillespie means by 'purely naturalistic work' then it is no sign of 'proto' or any other kind of positivism. But we could multiply examples of this basic confusion in Gillespie.

Gillespie's whole understanding seems to reflect a fairly naïve positivism tinged with a triumphalism, which the total annihilation of twentieth century logical positivism should at least have made him question. He simply cannot understand the approach to science of Kepler, Galileo, Bacon and, indeed, the great majority of those who formed and developed the scientific revolution. He presents his 'twin epistemes' and adds 'I hasten to point out the artificial nature of these epistemes'.[163] It is not so much 'artificial nature' as total confusion as to their meaning which is the problem. We will return to the multiplied confusion this has caused in leading 'design theorists' in our next Section.

Conclusion

The 'conflict model' of science and theology – whether presented by agnostics or well meaning 'creationists' – is unhistorical. Theologians seldom opposed scientific ideas purely on theological grounds, and mainstream practising Christians were usually involved centrally in major scientific development. The almost universal approach on the science-faith relationship amongst leading scientist-Christians has been that of Kepler, Galileo and Bacon: theology underpins science but scientific study begins from and is based on empirical observation not on Scripture. We will come back to consider whether this approach is still useful today after looking at some developments in the philosophy of science.

---

[162] Gillespie (1979) p. 52.
[163] Gillespie (1979) p.3.

10
Nature of Science & Belief

The Issues

This section begins with consideration of the general nature of science, and continues to explore its relationship with religious belief. Is the kind of thinking needed in science sharply different from that in faith, can we find a criterion for making demarcation between science and non-science, and can 'God' legitimately form part of a scientific explanation? These are the questions we shall address, greatly expanding on earlier brief comments in Section 1.

Christians (like anyone else) often simply assume that it is 'obvious' what is the nature of science and scientific truth. Alternatively, they choose the latest fashion in the philosophy of science (empiricism, Popper, Polanyi, Kuhn or whatever) and show that Christianity has always said almost the same thing.

The problem is that the nature of science is far from obvious, and the nature of knowledge and of science have been and still are topics of intense debate among scientists and philosophers. As it happens Paul Marston has a special interest in the philosophy of science (on which he currently teaches a university course) and he began his study of it under the tutelage of Karl Popper, Imre Lakatos and Paul Feycrabend in the LSE in the late 1960s. The next few paragraphs attempt to portray something of recent thinking, though those who find it heavy going might want to skip to the 'Conclusions on the Nature of Science' paragraph!

Logical Empiricism

To begin with, an unreflective view of scientific methodology might be something like this:
1. A scientist first observes objectively, making sure he or she has no presuppositions or prejudice.

2. His or her observations accurately represent what really is 'out there', and general patterns of cause and effect which necessarily operate.

3. These patterns are formulated into scientific laws, which, once verified, are certain truth.

In actual fact the logical positivism (or more moderate logical empiricism) which dominated secular Western philosophy in the 1940s-1950s was not much removed from this. The circle included Moritz Schlick, A J Ayer, Gustav Bergmann, Rudolf Carnap, Herbert Feigl, Philipp Frank, Kurt Gödel, Otto Neurath, and Friedrich Waismann. W V Quine studied under Carnap, though departed in key ways from the group.

The movement's basic tenets might be summarised thus:

1. Any statement (other than a definition) had meaning *only* if it were capable, at least in principle, of complete verification.

2. Verification implied specifying an observation which demonstrated its truth.

3. Neutrality of observation and the language used to describe it was a desirable aim.

4. Knowledge was actually about human sensations. A table was real in the sense that it expressed a continual possibility of a sensory experience. Non-directly observable concepts, like atoms, were real only in the sense that they were words useful as a shorthand way of speaking of possible sensations (eg of seeing chemical reactions).

A J Ayer (who cited Carnap as the one to whom he owed most) was fairly clear on all these points in 1936.[1] There is argument as to how far others in the group held all of them – particularly (4), though some think it essentially true of all logical empiricism.[2] Positivism had a track record of redefining terms so that apparently 'traditional' views could be maintained, and Schlick accepted that knowledge was ultimately about sensation but argued that this was the meaning of 'real'.[3] This is some evidence that Carnap modified his views on this under the

---

[1] See Ayer (1946).
[2] Se eg Boyd (1991) p. 7.
[3] In 1932/3 as printed in Boyd (1991) ch 1.

later influence of Neurath.[4] Even on basic issues of their philosophy there continues to be controversy.[5]

In any event, logical positivism was something of a crusade. Statements made in religion, metaphysics etc, were not simply wrong, but, as one could not state any specific sensory observation which would 'verify' any of them, were all literally meaningless and to be abandoned forthwith.

The whole system, however, simply did not hold water. There were obvious immediate problems. No empirical observation could be specified which would 'verify' the principle itself – which was therefore meaningless. Historical statements, statements about what others were thinking, etc, could not be 'verified' by any present observation. One of its chief critics, Sir Karl Popper, also raised problems concerning science. Scientific laws are generalisations (eg 'Electric current always produces a magnetic field'); but we never *observe* generalised laws as such, we observe only specific instances of them (eg 'In 1,000 observations, in each case an electric current produced a magnetic field'). How, then, can we make the logical jump from specific instances - however numerous - to the universal statement that it always happens? To do so we need to make two assumptions. The first is that nature always behaves uniformly or consistently. The Christian, of course, has good reason to assume this, as (s)he believes in a consistent Creator-God behind nature. But why should the atheist believe it? Early attempts such as that of J S Mill to defend it rationally look very much like circular arguments.[6] Science, of course, cannot be done at all unless nature does behave consistently, but for the atheist the belief that it does so must be an act of faith. In a logical sense, a universal law is falsifiable (as we have only to observe one counter instance) but never verifiable.

The second problem is that we can never be sure that there is not some qualifying condition which we have missed. Inevitably, in making observations we are selective: we could not note the total state of everything in the universe at the

[4] See eg Gillies (1993) p. 119 etc. also Preston (1997) sec 3.2.
[5] Eg Oberdan (1998).
[6] Mill (1843).

moment of observation. Thus, for example, electricity might behave differently under conditions of super-cooling.

The experience of the leading English positivist, A J Ayer is noteworthy. In 1936 Ayer wrote his *Language, Truth and Logic,* setting out in great clarity this wonderful new system. Problems like the above led Ayer in the second edition of his book in 1946 to a long preface, full of special pleading and tortuous logic, in which he tried to argue that single observations' might be totally objective, neutral and verifiable with certainty, whilst universal scientific laws were 'weakly verifiable' rather than strongly so. It was unconvincing. By 1956 (in *The Problem of Knowledge*) Ayer was fighting to preserve any sense for knowledge, and by 1978 he said of positivism: 'I suppose that most of the defects were that nearly all of it was false.'[7]

Logical empiricism's demise had also been caused by a further problem. This was, in essence, that all seeing also involves interpreting - there is no such thing as pure objective observation. Books by Hanson (1958), Polanyi (1958) and Kuhn (1962) emphasised this and heralded a new phase in the philosophy of science, but it had been explored in some depth over a century earlier by William Whewell. Whewell was a Cambridge Don whose sermons show a real depth of Christian commitment, but who had a high reputation in scientific circles and actually invented the word 'scientist' in 1834. Whewell was critical of the naive empiricism derived from Locke and Hume, which viewed the mind as a kind of blank sheet passively receiving objective reflections of reality. 'There is,' wrote Whewell, 'no sensation without an act of the mind.'[8] The mind is active. In observing we interpret, though we may not be aware that we are doing so. A modern illustration might be to imagine Aristotle, Newton and Einstein all watching an apple fall. Aristotle sees a piece of solid matter (=earth, one of the four elements) returning to its natural place. Newton sees the acceleration effects of mutual force of gravity between the earth and the apple. Einstein sees the stable behaviour of an apple in the warp in the time-space continuum introduced by the presence of the earth. In 'seeing' the event each also 'interprets'

[7] Interview in *The Listener* 2nd March 1978.
[8] Whewell (1840, 1847) p. 28

it, not as a separate act but as part of the perception. An implication of this recognition that observation is not purely passive is that scientific discovery is creative. It actually involves a mixture of painstaking methodical work together with creative intuition and imagination.[9] Seeing, then, always also involves interpreting. This does not mean, however, that literally *any* interpretation is a good one. If Aristotle, Newton and Einstein were joined in looking at a falling apple by someone who 'saw' a pink elephant floating in custard we would call this a hallucination not a 'perception' at all. To accept that seeing involves interpreting does not imply that it is arbitrary.

Major figures in the development of ideas of 'perceiving is interpreting' were pragmatist C S Peirce, and in the early twentieth century the Catholic physicist and philosopher of science Pierre Duhem.[10] Logical positivism (or logical empiricism) was in many ways an anachronism. Its proponents' naivety on questions discussed so profoundly by the Christian Whewell nearly a century earlier is hard to explain, except on the grounds that their anti-religious fervour blinded their eyes. The criticisms of Hanson and Kuhn restated these old insights, and contributed to the demise of logical empiricism.

Post Empiricism: Popper, Kuhn. Lakatos and Feyerabend

By the end of the 1960's logical empiricism was dead, but what was to replace it? Karl Popper offered 'falsificationism'. Laws of science could not, he said, be *verified*, but they could be *tested.* A theory was scientific if, and only if, it made predictions specific enough to test. It must, therefore, be possible to specify a set of conceivable observations which would be deemed to have refuted the theory. For example, a general law that 'all electricity produces a magnetic field' would be refuted if we ever found an instance where it didn't happen.

It was, of course, pointed out by Duhem in (1906) that no theory can be tested in isolation because other theories are assumed in testing it.[11] Quine (1951) and Braithwaite (1953) made similar points. Popper argued for a convention to regard

---

[9] See eg Beveridge (1968) or Medawar (1969).
[10] Duhem (1906).
[11] See also Gillies (1993) ch 5.

particular observations (and therefore background assumptions) as 'not in question.'[12] To many this seemed somewhat arbitrary and unrealistic - in practice scientists do not in any case regard a single counter-instance as a refutation. Others took Popper's ideas just to mean that one was testing a set of theories for consistency – much as Duhem had emphasised.

T S Kuhn began from quite a different standpoint. Instead of beginning, as had the positivists and Popper, from a logical construct, he began from a consideration of the way in which science had actually advanced in history, it was 'historical philosophy of science'. A key Kuhnian term was 'paradigm'. Initially he used this word 'paradigm' very vaguely, but later took two main meanings:

1. **Exemplars:** results and ideas known and explicitly recognised in that scientific discipline.
2. **Disciplinary matrices:** a more subtle idea meaning a 'conceptual framework' within which phenomena are perceived.

Kuhn portrayed 'normal science' as development of ideas routinely within a scientific specialist area or discipline. Periodically, however, he suggested that anomalies built up to such a degree that the whole disciplinary matrix had to be changed in a revolutionary way, and phenomena viewed from a new perspective. An example of this might be the change from thinking of the earth as stationary to thinking of the sun as stationary - the whole way of perceiving the world changed. Similarly, in the twentieth century the change from Newtonian mechanics to those of Einstein involved a major change in the way of looking at things. Those with such radically different paradigms may use the same words, but they view them so differently that a simple test cannot decide between them: the two paradigms are 'incommensurable'.

Many criticised Kuhn because scientific development does not fall neatly into 'normal' and 'revolutionary' science, but there was a more fundamental question. He had portrayed science as being unlike a building programme, where each new brick is added on to those already built up. Rather he had seen it as a

---

[12] Eg Popper (1968) p. 106 where they are called 'basic statements'.

process of building (normal science), but with a periodic demolition and entire reconstruction from a different perspective (revolutionary science). But in what sense, then, could one speak of 'scientific progress', and in what sense could any scientific concepts refer to 'real' things which were 'out there', since they might always be changed by a new perspective? The implication of Kuhn seemed to be that science must ultimately be subjective. Later Kuhnian emphasis was on development of ever more specialised areas of scientific knowledge, which Kuhn compares with the process of evolving ever more specialised organisms in biological evolution.[13] As well as emphasising evolution over revolution, Kuhn in his later works continues to emphasise 'incommensurability'[14] ie that earlier theories may 'see' phenomena entirely differently from later ones, and not be strictly comparable. In this context also specialisation may mean that there is no common language to link theories in different areas. The later Kuhn portrays a 'candidate for true/false' as a statement in which language rules forbid asserting both the statement and its contrary, and accepts that 'the rules of the true/false game are... universals for all human communities' ie that in all communities have such statements. But which *particular* statements are candidates for the true/false category depends on the particular community's set of word meanings or 'lexicon', and:

A statement can be a candidate for truth/falsity in one lexicon without having that status in the others.[15]

This means that he rejects what Suppe called 'metaphysical realism' ie the idea that theories increasingly 'correspond' to some kind of external reality. Rather, each community has an evolving language, which implies a particular way of perceiving reality. For those into Kant (cf also below), Kuhn compares these to an evolution of different species of Kantian 'categories' seen as 'preconditions of possible experience.'

Reactions to Kuhn varied. Feyerabend and his school thought Kuhn not radical enough. Feyerabend moved from positivism in the 1940's, to his own brand of Popperian anti-positivist

---

[13] Kuhn (1990).
[14] See Kuhn (1962), also Hacking (1983) ch 5.
[15] Kuhn (1990) in Tauber (1997) p. 240.

realism.[16] By 1968[17] he had moved significantly again. Science, he said, did not develop 'logically' and no ideal methodology was possible. Whilst Feyerabend believed in basing science on observation, he did not believe this would lead, even ultimately, to a single 'One True Theory'.[18] Later this view became more extreme. Science was, some said, simply an 'ideology' like any other, with no special claim to truth. In this school of thought 'objectivity' is simply institutionalised belief.[19] This kind of view has cut little ice with real scientists, and other philosophers of science have heavily criticised it. One of its basic problems is that it leads logically to pure relativism: the assertion that any set of beliefs is as true as any other. The internal inconsistency of this approach is seen precisely in the fact that it makes an apparently absolute assertion concerning the relativity of truth - yet it denies that assertions can be absolute! The apparent inability of its proponents to live with the logical implications of their approach (ie that no objective statements at all would be possible) is not surprising. In practice it is unlivable. We have touched on such ideas in our comments on 'postmodernism' in our early sections.

A view, which stood somewhere between Popper and Kuhn, was that of Lakatos.[20] Lakatos asserted that:

> For Kuhn scientific change – from one 'paradigm' to another – is a mystical conversion.[21]

He saw 'sophisticated falsificationism' (the later view of Popper) as accepting both that theories could not be tested in isolation, and that they were not considered 'refuted' until a 'better' was available. But how could one tell if a new set of theories were 'better'? even sophisticated falsificationism, he thought, had to come back to some kind of Duhemian reliance of 'good sense'. In Lakatos' own view this was better conceived in terms of a succession of research programmes. In each

---

[16] See Preston (1996) and (1997).

[17] The year Paul Marston attended a seminar series Feyerabend gave at L.S.E.

[18] Feyerabend (1975), also Chalmers (1982) Ch 12, Lossee (1993) Ch 13 and Preston (1997) chs 9-10.

[19] See Bloor (1976) and Stanesby (1985) ch. 3.

[20] Lakatos & Musgrave (1970) also Chalmers (1982) Ch 7, Lossee (1993) Ch 14. Mayo (1996) more recently revisited the Kuhn-Popper debate.

[21] Lakatos & Musgrave (1970) p. 93.

programme there would be a 'hard core' of assumptions accepted as basic to that programme. But there would also be:

> A partially articulated set of suggestions or hints on how to change, develop the 'refutable variants' of the research-programme.[22]

Lakatos thinks Kuhn envisages just one dominant paradigm, whereas he himself wants to see competing paradigms - where the movement to 'better' ones over time is based on their capacity to generate 'factual novelty' ie to predict new things. Though Lakatos sees himself as basing his scientific rationality on Popper's, his 'research programmes' do not seem to be as different from Kuhn's 'paradigms' as he imagines. Popper based his ideas of 'truth' on Tarski, a view that is essentially 'realist'.[23] Lakatos' view is not; as Hacking puts it from his own 'realist' perspective:

> Lakatos tries to make the growth of knowledge a surrogate for a representational theory of truth.[24]

Lakatos reacts strongly against what he sees as Kuhn's relativism, but actually his own system seems fairly parallel to it. In neither is 'truth' regarded as correspondence to some kind of reality.

Nothing, of course, is straightforward in philosophy! Most clearly stated views have to be modified in the small print, and this brings unexpected similarities. However, in general distinction from both Kuhn and Lakatos have stood various critical realist schools of thought, reasserting (though usually redefining) objectivity and the view that science follows a reality external to ourselves.

Critical Realism and Instrumentalism

In 1977 Frederick Suppe edited the second edition of *The Structure of Scientific Theories,* a book originally based on a 1969 symposium. In the introduction he stated:

> Much has happened to the philosophy of science in the eight years since the symposium: (1) Positivistic philosophy of science has

---

[22] Lakatos & Musgrave (1970) p. 135.
[23] Popper (1963) p. 223 etc. His (1956) is dedicated to Tarski who argued for objective truth.
[24] Hacking (1981) p. 141.

gone into near total eclipse; (2) the more extreme Weltanschauungen views of Feyerabend, Hanson and Kuhn no longer are serious contenders for becoming a replacement analysis and (3) philosophy of science is coalescing around a new movement or approach which espouses a hard-nosed metaphysical and epistemological realism that focuses much of its attention on "rationality in the growth of scientific knowledge"...

Suppe is heralding 'critical realism'. In general terms this may be characterised thus:

1. Scientific theories (at least in the 'mature' sciences) are typically approximately true, and more recent theories are closer to the truth than older ones in the same domain.

2. The observational and theoretical terms within the theories of a mature science genuinely refer (roughly), there are substances in the world that correspond to the ontologies presumed by our best theories.

3. Successive theories in any mature science will be such that they preserve the theoretical relations and the apparent referents of earlier theories, that is, earlier theories will be limiting cases of later theories.

4. Acceptable new theories do and should explain why their predecessors were successful insofar as they were successful.[25]

Suppe thought Lakatos not 'realist' enough. He also thought Toulmin's instrumentalist approach to theories 'is incapable of accounting for the epistemic success of science.'[26] He followed Shapere[27] in believing that the accepted 'theory-ladenness' of observation 'does not compromise the objectivity of scientific knowledge.'[28] Pluralism was restricted to recognition of Shapere's 1969 concept of different 'domains' in knowledge, introduced as 'fundamental conceptual tools for illuminating the nature of science'.[29] They seem, however, even more vague than Kuhn's paradigms, and we are given little clue about how to recognise a domain which is truly scientific.[30] Suppe's

---

[25] The four points are taken from Laudan (1981).

[26] Suppe (1977) p. 681.

[27] Writing in Suppe (1977) p. 518 etc.

[28] Suppe (1977) p. 692.

[29] Suppe (1977) section vii, also Shapere (1984) Ch. 13.

[30] Even in Shapere (1984) (ch. 14) there is little elucidation on domains.

disarming admission that Shapere: 'has not yet supplied an analysis of what it is to be a scientific hypothesis' is also a bit worrying. Though he claims there are:

> patterns of good reasoning which do enable one to rationally assess whether or not a particular knowledge claim is *likely* to be true.[31]

The details of these patterns fall short of conviction.

Suppe was right about the well-deserved demise of positivism[32] but his triumphalism concerning critical realism was unfounded. It continued to run into questions and problems. It is, in any event, *not* straightforward, and there is some debate as to who counts as a real 'realist'! What is known as 'naïve realism' is the view that our ideas or concepts reproduce exactly the true properties of externally existing objects. Allied to this is 'representative realism' which holds that our ideas *represent* externally existing 'real' things though may recognise that some properties (eg the 'tickliness' of a feather) are 'secondary' in the sense that the properties cause particular effects in us. In the history of philosophy[33], the comparative realism in Locke (at least about particular objects - he was a nominalist about universals) led Berkeley to doubt that matter existed at all, and Hume not only to suggest that 'perceptions' were the only reality but effectively that 'cause' was nothing but mental expectancy. The reaction of Kant was to suggest that as humans we *cannot* perceive except in terms of particular categories eg space, time and cause. We do not know what 'things in themselves' are like, because we can never step outside our human perceptual framework.[34] Thus to Kant space and time are 'empirically real' – they are not illusions and they are given to any human experience. However they are 'transcendentally ideal' in the sense that they apply only to human experience and not necessarily to the nature of 'things in themselves'. After Kant, no thinker could take naïve realism seriously. Not only, as we noted, do non-realists like Kuhn have a debt to Kant, but

---

[31] Suppe (1977) p. 702.

[32] It exists today only in the imaginations of the authors of seemingly interminable books entitled 'Qualitative Methodology for Xologists'!

[33] We are not going to give umpteen references to Locke, Berkeley etc, though any general work [eg Copleston (1964)] will contain them.

[34] This also relates to T Nagel (1974) 'What's it like to be a bat?' mentioned in our Section 3.

naïve realism has to give way to '*critical* realism'. *Critical* realism asserts that 'behind' it all there is a unique 'reality' but also recognises that perception always involves interpretation, and aspects of this are inevitable to being human.

Suppe, as we saw, had a kind of triumphalist optimism about critical realism, combined with a recognition that much needed to be done. So how have critical realists sought to overcome the problems of Kantian perspective, theory-ladenness of observation, incommensurabilty of paradigms, etc? Newton-Smith's *The Rationality of Science* (1982) finishes with the slogan: 'realism is the truth and temperate rationalism the way.' In this sense 'rationalism' means having a rational model for science which, he says, implies:

> a goal for the scientific enterprise and an account of the principles of comparison (a methodology) to be used to give guidance on making choices between two rival theories.[35]

Early in the book (p. 13) he suggests that 'rationalists' in this sense 'tend to be realists'. In the end, however, (after describing the systems of Popper, Lakatos, Kuhn and Feyerabend in detail), he lumps together Popper (a Tarskian realist) Lakatos (a pluralistic Kantian) and Laudan (an instrumentalist anti-realist) all as 'rationalists' in science. To Newton-Smith, rationalism in science seems to naturally imply realism, and:

> The answer to those who, like Feyerabend, deny the existence of scientific method is quite simply that the special fruits of science... indicate that there is something special about (it)[36]

Scientific *success* is, in fact, most commonly given as *the* proof of rationalism and realism in science.

Hacking (who is some species of critical realist) gives a useful breakdown of types and aspects of realism, as does the Christian writer Del Ratzsch.[37] Hacking himself believes that 'Experimental work provides the strongest evidence for scientific realism' and adds:

---

[35] Newton-Smith (1982) p. 266.
[36] Newton-Smith (1982) p. 269.
[37] Hacking (1983) ch. 1, Del Ratzsch (1986) ch. 5.

The vast majority of experimental physicists are realists about some theoretical entities, namely the ones they *use*. I claim they cannot help being so.[38]

To Hacking 'the lesson is to think about practice not theory'. It is pointless arguing on a *metaphysical* level for 'realism' – in *practice* what matters is whether eg scientists can *manipulate* electrons (or presumably quarks), not their metaphysics. A F Chalmers (1982) outlines his own 'unrepresentative realism' too briefly for us to make much of it, though it seems similarly pragmatic. Brown, writing as an ex-positivist in 1987, argues a Shapere-type domain-based realism.[39] Brown also says some interesting things about observation. He points out that aliens, whose perceptual apparatus might be entirely different from our, would have very different everyday 'perceptions'. Their *scientists,* however, might well arrive at (say) concepts of unobservables like electrons, which were very similar to ours. In this sense, paradoxically, unobservables could be more 'real' than everyday perceptions which are a function of our senses. Arthur Fine (1984)[40] begins 'Realism is dead' – killed off by neo-positivism and the quantum theory. Musgrave (1989)[41] argues that Fine's own views are a type of realism! Boyd in 1991 reaffirms his earlier (1983) realism, adding:

> Most realists now hold that methodological incommensurability is not a phenomenon sufficiently common in the relevant parts of the history of science to undermine the realistic picture of the growth of theoretical knowledge.[42]

Again, *success* is the main argument for scientific realism, and Tarski's ideas on objective truth are 'the most important piece of philosophical analysis of the first half of this century.' More typical, however, is the pilgrimage of Hilary Putnam. Coming from an empiricist heritage of Carnap and Quine, he began to develop a new realism in the late 1960's, and was a contributor in Suppe's book. To Hacking, Putnam was 'once the most realist of philosophers' but has finished up with an 'internal realism'

---

[38] Hacking (1982) p. 16, see also in Boyd et al (1991) ch. 13.
[39] Brown (1987) was reviewed by Paul Marston in *Nature* Vol 333 (April 1988).
[40] In Leplin (1984) reprinted Papineau (1996).
[41] Reprinted in Papineau (1996).
[42] Boyd (1991) p. 16.

which is really anti-realism![43] Putnam himself, claims that his internal realism is *Realism with a Human Face* – the title of his 1990 compendium. In this Putnam is *critical* of Tarski on truth:

> The paradoxical aspect of Tarski's theory, indeed of any hierarchical theory, is that one has to stand outside the whole hierarchy even to formulate the statement that the hierarchy exists.[44]

On the one hand Putnam rejects:

> the fashionable panacea of relativism – even if it is given a new name such as "deconstruction" or even "pragmatism" (by Richard Rorty).

On the other hand, of 'metaphysical realism' (a term accepted by Suppe) he says:

> I feel justified in having taken the "metaphysical realist" to be a philosopher who accepts what Harry Field calls "metaphysical realism$_1$" (the world consists of a fixed totality of mind-independent objects), *and* accepts "metaphysical realism$_2$" (there is exactly one true and complete description of the way the world is), *and* also accepts "metaphysical realism$_3$" (truth involves some sort of correspondence).[45]

It is, of course, by no means clear that these are connected. Personally, for example, we would accept a theological version of "metaphysical realism$_1$" but not the other two. However, given that he links them and given that he has just asserted:

> Elements of what we call "language" or "mind" penetrate so deeply into what we call "reality" that the very project of representing ourselves as being "mappers" of something "language-independent" is fatally compromised from the very start.

it is little wonder that he rejects metaphysical realism. One might, however, ask with Hacking 'Was any serious thinker a metaphysical realist?'[46] However, Putnam renounces:

> the dream of a picture of the universe, which is so complete that it, actually includes the theorist-observer in the act of picturing the universe.[47]

---

[43] Hacking (1983) p. 130 etc.
[44] Putnam (1990) p. 14.
[45] Putnam (1990) p. 30.
[46] Hacking (1983) p. 94.
[47] Putnam (1990) p. 5.

As for so many modern philosophers, the uncertainty principle and other elements of modern physics rule out such a view and make *Mind* much more central to the understanding of reality. Putnam's own approach to steering a course between relativism and metaphysical realism is based on Kant:

> Although Kant never quite says that this is what he is doing, Kant is best read as proposing for the first time what I have called the "internalist" or "internal realist" view of truth.[48]

This 'internal realism' (which he first advanced in the mid 1970's) focuses on the internal consistency and coherence of a set of beliefs within a rational community, rather than on any kind of correspondence to external realities. It *is* fairly Kantian, but quite how it differs from (say) Lakatos (or for that matter Pierce or even Kuhn) is not clear to us. It is also not clear what he meant when he said that (at least some) 'terms in a mature science typically refer'[49] and how far this fades in his later work.

In a very helpful summary of scientific realism, David Papineau suggests (1996) that it consists of:

1. An *independence* thesis (there is a world which exists independently of our awareness or perception of it).
2. A *knowledge* thesis (by and large, we can know which of our beliefs about that world are true)

Papineau points out that one can doubt:

Either (1) taking an *idealist* or *phenomenalist* view that knowledge is just about sensation, and a notion of a world 'behind' sensation is incoherent.

or (2) taking a *sceptical* view that we cannot know the truth about the world.

No one, of course, outside philosophy seminars, doubts that normal elephants or mail-boxes are 'real' in the sense that pink elephants 'seen' by inebriates are not. In this context, 'phenomenalists' are just questioning what 'real' means, and sceptics refer to other levels of 'knowledge'. 'Realism' more commonly refers to concepts found in physics (electrons, muons etc) – though these are, of course, foundational to any physical reality. Anyway, with the welcome demise of the

---

[48] Putnam (1982) p. 60, see also (1990) chs 1-2.
[49] Putnam (1978) p. 20.

phenomenalism in early logical positivism, Papineau rightly points out: 'In contemporary epistemology of science, scepticism is the main alternative to realism.'[50]

Two major figurest have been consistent in criticism of scientific realism. Larry Laudan points out first that the new realists (he particularly attacks Putnam, Newton-Smith and Boyd) are vague about the sense in which theories are 'successful'.[51] Could not theoretical concepts which we no longer accept as 'real' also be successful? He is also critical of the argument that unobservables in theories must be 'real' to have true consequences for observation. In logic, false premises can easily lead to true conclusions. The title of Laudan's (1996) book *Beyond Positivism and Relativism* indicates his own path. He is highly critical of Feyerabend. He is critical of Kuhn for supposing that there would only be one dominant paradigm rather than a plurality, and also calls 'unadulterated hogwash' the notion he attributes to Kuhn that there is never a point at which resistance to a new theory 'becomes illogical or unscientific'.[52] However, in this he picks 'obvious' examples (eg 'the four element theory of chemistry' and 'classical creationist biology'). As for any kind of general criteria for what is 'progressive', he repeats verbatim in 1996 his 1977 comment:

> What is required, if we are to rescue the notion of scientific progress, is a breaking of the link between cumulative retention and progress, so as to allow for the possibility of progress even when there are explanatory losses as well as gains.[53]

No progress, then, on this for over two decades. So if he can't do it who will? One other point repeated across the two decades is that there is no clear demarcation between 'scientific' theories and other forms of 'sound knowledge'. He does not, however, give us any idea how to recognise such 'sound' forms in different domains.

A more obvious contrast to 'realism' is 'instrumentalism' – the view that theories are *nothing but* good or poor instruments for prediction. The other most consistent critic of scientific

---

[50] Papineau (1996) p. 3.
[51] Laudan (1981) p. 26.
[52] Laudan (1996) ch 1 n29.
[53] In Hacking (1977) p. 149, and Laudan (1996) p. 81.

realism is Bas van Fraassen, whose 'constructive empiricism' is a form of instrumentalism:

> Science aims to give us theories which are empirically adequate and acceptance of a theory involves a belief only that it is empirically adequate.[54]

Van Fraassen holds that a 'good' theory is one which contains truth about observables – we need make no assumption about the 'reality' of unobservables in it. He then, of course, has problems in saying exactly what *is* 'observable'. The moons of Jupiter are 'observable' even though we in practice use a telescope because we know that the telescope just enables us to see what we could if we got closer. A microbe is not 'observable' because we rely on the theory of the microscope in interpreting what we see. Ideas about microbes may be 'empirically adequate' but we do not know if the entities are 'real'. He believes that it is reasonable for us to form expectations of future events, but that there is no specific form of inference used in such instances, and that no potential mode of induction has the potential to properly be such a form of inference. In simpler terms, no methodology guarantees scientific success.[55] We may, in any event, only be choosing between poor alternatives of theories.[56] Couvalis makes a spirited attack on van Fraassen from a realist position[57] – but the arguments will continue, and one writer suggests that what scientists actually *do* is compatible with either van Fraassen or Putnam.[58] The realism vs anti-realism arguments also continue in more general philosophy than that of philosophy of science.[59]

Probability and Bayesianism

One other approach has so far not been mentioned – that which involves 'probability' of theories. What *is* probability? Suppose that we ask the 'probability' of getting a head if a coin is tossed. This has actually been defined in three distinct ways. The first

---

[54] Van Fraassen (1980) p. 12 etc.

[55] Van Fraassen (1985) p. 277-280.

[56] Van Fraasen (1989) p. 143.

[57] See eg Couvalis (1997) Ch. 7.

[58] Kukla (1994)

[59] Eg Stirton (1997).

is the 'range definition', classically presented by Laplace.[60] It says that since the event sought (a head) is one out of two 'equally likely' events, then the probability is ½. The problem, of course, is that 'equally likely' means 'equally probable' which is what we are trying to define in the first place, so the definition is circular. The second is the 'limiting relative frequency' view. This says that in a very long run of tosses the proportion of heads would converge to ½. There are actually two versions of this. This first, represented by Richard von Mises and Reichenbach[61], sees it as an actual property of empirical events. The problem with this, of course, is that one could never *prove* it. In *theory* and *final* proportion is consistent with any *finite* empirical sequence – we might just have been 'unlucky' and got all heads for example. The other version is that eg of Popper[62] who speaks in terms of a theory of sets which are 'conjectured' to be applicable to actual sequences. The problem is, again, that any finite sequence is theoretically compatible with any hypothesised set features – we have to make a methodological decision to exclude the 'unlikely'. The final[63] version of probability developed eg by de Finetti[64] sees it as concerning subjective 'degrees of belief' or 'betting odds'. The laws of probability are then just laws which show how a rational person would combine betting odds on different events. None of these three approaches are watertight – which does not stop probability being useful in both science and insurance.

One other aspect of probability was stated in the Rev Thomas Bayes work in 1763. We can illustrate it like this:

- Suppose that 5% of a particular population are left-handed.
- If, then, we receive an essay from a randomly selected person there will be a 5% chance that the writer was left handed [this is called the prior probability P(LH) = 0.05]
- But suppose that we know that of left handed people 90% slope their writing backwards, whereas for right handed people only 8% do [this means Pr(Slopes if LH) = 0.9 etc]

[60] Laplace (1812).

[61] von Mises (1939), Reichenbach (1949).

[62] Popper (1959) Ch. 8.

[63] We discount 'logical probability' which has even less meaning.

[64] De Finetti (1939) in Kybug & Smolker (1964).

- Obviously, if the particular essay we receive slopes backwards, then it seems more likely that it came from a left handed person (because a lot more of them slope it backwards)

The Bayesian formula says:

$$Pr(LH \text{ if Slopes}) = \frac{Pr(\text{Slopes if } LH) \times Pr(LH)}{Pr(\text{Slopes if } LH) \times Pr(LH) + Pr(\text{Slopes if } RH) \times Pr(RH)}$$

This works out to :
$$\frac{Pr(0.90) \times Pr(0.05)}{Pro(0.90) \times Pr(0.05) + Pr(0.08) \times (0.95)}$$

which is about 0.37 or a 37% chance − much bigger than the 5% 'prior probability' as we would expect. Issues of 'probability' of theories have been raised by philosophers throughout history. Locke, for example, raised it both in regard to issues not open to empirical investigation (eg the existence of angels), and to the propositions of natural science which are only ever known with a high degree of probability. Poincare raised it in his 1905 book *Science and Hypothesis*. The subtitle of Braithwaite's famous 1953 book is 'A Study of the Function of Theory, Probability and Law in Science' − though he managed apparently without mentioning Bayes theory at all! When Paul Marston was studying both philosophy of science and probability theory at L.S.E. in the late 1960's, one of the professors (Durbin) was sympathetic to Bayesian and subjective views of probability, one (Stuart) wasn't, and Karl Popper, when asked, predictably renounced subjectivism in probability as in science!

The current relevance, however, is in a school exploring a mixture of subjective probabilities and Bayesianism as a guide to 'rational' belief in theories as continually amended by evidence. Boyd, in his (1990) 800 page book on the philosophy of science, suddenly remembers he has left it out and whacks it into a footnote (n15 on page 21). It has been explored in science context in the 1970's eg by Mary Hesse and R D Rosenkrantz[65], van Fraassen develops it in his own way[66] and it has, more recently been floated/mentioned by British philosophers of science Barry Gower and Anthony O'Hear.[67] Colin Howson has

---

[65] Hesse (1974), Rosenkrantz (1977) − Glymour (1981) is sceptical!
[66] van Fraassen (1980) chs 5-6.
[67] Gower (1997) and O'Hear (1989).

explored 'theories of probability'[68] (including Bayes and betting), and other American articles have appeared.[69] The present authors (slightly tongue in cheek!) applied Bayesian analysis to 'prove' the overwhelming likelihood of God in our *Reason and Faith* (1989)[70], and the ordained astrophysicist Rodney Holder brilliantly applies it to Hume's problem of miracles in a recent article.[71] Wesley Salmon argues for Bayesianism as a bridge between Kuhn and logical empiricism – though speaks of 'many unresolved issues'.[72]

There are two major problems with it. The first is that it typically involves using the Bayesian formula to multiply together the unlike 'degrees of subjective belief' and 'relative frequencies'. Indeed, relative frequencies are usually invoked to show that some degrees of belief are 'more rational' than others. The second problem is that it is usually impossible to see any 'rational' way to *decide* on a set of *prior* degrees of belief in a scientific theory. How, for example, could one have established 'prior' probabilities of Einstein or Newton being 'right' before the famous 1919 test observation by Eddington during a total eclipse? One is not reassured when Gower makes remarks like:

> As Carnap and his co-workers have shown, there are an indefinite number of different ways of measuring ranges and thus degrees of confirmation.[73]

The Bayesian approach to general science inference is good fun but generally unworkable except in very specialised situations.

Finally, before we think about conclusions, it is interesting to note that some of the so called 'science popularisers' seem to have wandered into the area of philosophy of science without much understanding. In the mid 1980's Paul Marston was at an Oxford conference where fellow speakers included Peter Atkins, Mary Midgely, John Durant, Arthur Peacocke, Don Cupitt and others. Peter Atkins, an eminent Oxford physical chemist,

---

[68] See Howson (1995), also Howson & Urbach (1993).

[69] Mayo (1997), Hellman (1997).

[70] And above in Section 4.

[71] Holder (1998).

[72] Salmon in a 1990 article reprinted in Papineau (1996).

[73] Gower (1997) p. 218.

'evangelical'[74] atheist, and author of a book on 'creation', astounded the various agnostics and brands of believer present by presenting an effectively naïve-realist view of science. Yet he continues in the media to be presented as a scientific guru. In an incredible diatribe against any religious content to Christmas, Atkins recently portrayed himself as standing:

> on the good side of the fence that divides innate-truth (that is, science) from wishful-thinking falsity (that is religion).[75]

If he has read any philosophy since the 1980's he hasn't understood it. Professional philosophers of science are also highly critical of Richard Dawkins (another militant or 'evangelical' atheist we looked at earlier) for his lack of understanding of the subject – although he is a Professor of the Public Understanding of Science. Lewis Wolpert, another biology Professor and chair of a committee for the public understanding of science, is a rather less 'evangelical' atheist. As, however, we mentioned in Section 5, he startled a conference in 1996 by proclaiming himself a follower of Hume. Now Hume held that all ideas were linked to perceptions – a notion that was silly in the eighteenth century and ludicrous in the twentieth century world of mysterious physics (irrespective of whether one is a realist or instrumentalist). Wolpert had even recognised the 'unnatural nature of science' which was the title of his 1992 book. Perhaps what he meant was that to Hume faith was only and always 'fideism' – belief without reason and evidence.[76] 'Show me the evidence for God' demanded Wolpert, as though one could look down a test tube and if it turned blue there was a God. As we have already pointed out, either the evidence is all around you or not there at all – it depends if you see it. But there is no 'evidence' in this sense for rationality itself, the possibility of science, the existence of any external objects etc – he applies a crude unphilosophical understanding of what constitutes 'evidence' It was silly even for Hume, and it simply doesn't work at all today. In an interview in which one of us was involved in the summer of 1998, Sir Anthony Hewish

---

[74] Ie in the sense of an someone wanting to spread the 'good news' of atheism – though why they bother is beyond us!

[75] *The Times Higher Education Supplement*, December 25, 1998.

[76] Wolpert (1992) p. 148.

(Christian, FRS and Nobel Prize Winner for the discovery of quasars) remarked that perhaps some chemists and biologists were a hundred years behind physicists – they had not yet recognised that there was mystery at the heart of science. Perhaps he was right.

Belief and Knowledge

At this point we make a brief detour to consider some issues of Christians and more basic current debate about what kinds of belief can be warranted or justified. Philosophers ask questions like 'what is the difference between true belief and knowledge?' or 'what does it mean for a belief to be warranted?'. Consider the following examples:

- Mary believes that there are some white elephants in India because she once dreamt that elephants come in all colours.
- Mabel believes there are some white elephants in India because she read it in an encyclopaedia
- Mildred believes there are some white elephants in India because she has been there and seen two.
- Mavis believes there are no white elephants in India because her encyclopaedia says they are 'grayish brown in colour'.
- Martha was zapped by cosmic rays, which changed her understanding of 'elephant' to mean 'plate', so she believes there are some white elephants in India.

Mary has the 'right' belief for the wrong reasons – so is this 'knowledge'? Is it really 'knowledge' for Mabel as it is on human testimony alone? Mavis is mistaken, but if she has very good reasons for her belief then does she have 'warrant' to believe it? Is she actually more 'rational' than Mary who has no 'warrant' for her beliefs? Does Martha have 'warrant' for her beliefs?

Christian philosophers today, like Richard Swinburne and Alvin Plantinga, take up such issues and we are broadly sympathetic to both of them but lack enthusiasm for quite such questions. Some of it resembles scholastic logic chopping beyond the bounds of sense, though some deals with real issues.

Plantinga usefully considers 'foundationalism' – the view that there are some certainly known 'foundational' facts on which we can build knowledge. His conclusion seems to be that if there are such then they are very limited, perhaps just:

- My knowledge that at the present instant I am having various qualia experiences (though not whether they are of 'real' objects).
- My recognition that certain functions of logic could not be otherwise (perhaps including eg 2+3=5).[77]

Descartes, of course, then went on to 'perceive very clearly' the validity of a rational argument that God must exist, and hence that sensory perception was reliable. Non-theistic foundationalists have no such luxury, and we agree with Plantinga that the two 'foundations' above are woefully insufficient for either a philosophy or a lifestyle. The prospect of somehow 'deducing' or 'building' a wider set of certain knowledge from these foundations seems bleak.

Plantinga couches his own analysis in terms of whether beliefs have 'warrant' (which in rough terms means a good rational basis). His conclusion is:

> Belief has warrant for me only if (1) it has been produced in me by cognitive functions that are working properly... in a cognitive environment that is appropriate for my kinds of cognitive faculties, (2) the segment of the design plan governing the production of that belief is aimed at the production of true beliefs and (3) there is a high statistical probability that a belief produced under those conditions will be true.[78]

The obvious problem is that 'working properly' and 'design plan' have clear meaning in a designed artefact, but none at all for organisms in a Dawkinsian world of unplanned natural selection. Plantinga recognises this, and counter-argues that:

> Surely it is common for an atheist to say that a kidney or other organ has a function...[79]

It is not clear that mere 'common use' is a sufficient warrant, nor that to Dawkins it is more than a manner of speaking. Dawkins' idea of 'function' is (or at least should be) nothing but an unconscious mechanism which has been more or less effective through natural selection to enable the genes

---

[77] Plantinga (1993) p. 182 etc.
[78] Plantinga (1993) p. 46.
[79] Plantinga (1993) p. 198.

programming it to survive and reproduce. Conscious design is absent. However, we do agree with Plantinga[80] that since Dawkins believes only that our brains were designed to enhance *survival* he can have no reason to believe they will perceive *truth*. The theist, Plantinga claims, has nothing 'impelling him in the direction of such scepticism' about his capacity to discern truth. It is not that the theist can use reason to rationally deduce a God who could underwrite reason (as did Descartes) – for this would be circular. Rather, *if* a belief in God is taken as 'basic' (ie as a belief 'not accepted on the basis of any other beliefs'[81]), then acceptance of reason is rational. If one believes there is no God (ie adopts 'naturalistic metaphysics') then because evolution would teach us that our minds are nothing but survival mechanisms, we would have no reason to believe that our minds could arrive through naturalistic reasoning at truth. Plantinga therefore argues that 'naturalistic epistemology [ie seeking truth through reason and observation] flourishes best in the garden of supernaturalist metaphysics [ie a belief in God]'[82] We are sorry that this involves a different definition of 'naturalistic' to that we have used earlier in this book. We have used the term in the *Concise Oxford Dictionary* sense of 'a theory of the world that excludes the supernatural or spiritual', whereas here Plantinga means no more than seeking truth through natural reason and observation. However, we have no desire to quarrel with Plantinga over word meanings – we agree with the philosophical point he is making.

Others who share Plantinga's Reformed approach to truth explore other aspects of seeing a belief in God as 'basic'. William Alston argues that we can perceive and experience God as directly as we can perceive and experience the physical world.[83] He is speaking not of deep mystical experiences, but the religious experiences of the ordinary Christian. In philosophical terms, there is no more reason to doubt that there is anything 'behind' the ones set of experiences than of the other. Wolterstorff shares Plantinga's enthusiasm for Thomas Reid,

---

[80] Plantinga (1993) p. 218.
[81] Plantinga & Wolterstorff (1983) p. 72.
[82] Plantinga (1993) p. 218.
[83] Alston in Plantinga & Wolterstorff (1983) Ch. 3.

and also emphasises that people arrive at a belief in God from many routes, and are entitled to believe it unless they have adequate reason not to.[84] Marsden explores Abraham Kuyper's more strongly Reformed ideas that belief in God depends upon 'God's inspiring communication of special grace'.[85] A belief in God can then be 'basic', ie not derived from any other belief, because it depends just on God's sovereign choice to make that person believe. We do not share in this theology, and we also concur with Roger Trigg that:

> Reformed epistemology appears to succumb to the temptation of retreating to a faith that is groundless.[86]

Plantinga, however, is critical of Kuyper[87] and insists that belief in God is basic but not *groundless*; there is no conflict between faith and reason. Moreover, even though a belief may be 'basic', it may be modified if it turns out to conflict with some other more basic belief when we think about it. In the end, then, *consistency* of basic beliefs is important.

Plantinga's work is presently strewn with phrases like 'roughly speaking' and 'I make no claim to completeness' – and we are not sure quite how much further some of the analysis takes us. We are sceptical of his development of ideas of probability, though reserve comment on this for our website. His connection of [theism] [design] [proper-function] [basic-belief] is certainly circular – but it has to be said that *all* justifications of reason at the most basic level are circular. All, at some point, require some kind of faith – a point we made in our opening section. We would prefer to speak in terms of rationality based on 'coherence' but would certainly include coherence of *experience* and presumption of *sanity* – so we do not mean by it the view Plantinga criticises as 'Coherence'.[88] In our view theistic belief makes the most sense of our human experience, and scientific study of natural processes makes the most sense when accompanied by a theistic metaphysics. This is in line both

---

[84] Plantinga & Wolterstorff (1983) Ch. 4.
[85] Plantinga & Wolterstorff (1983) p. 249.
[86] Trigg (1998) p. 151.
[87] Plantinga & Wollterstorff (1983) p. 88.
[88] Plantinga (1993) Ch. 10.

with Plantinga and his mentor Thomas Reid, though perhaps we may express things differently.

As far as concerns the argument from design, it is surely true that many people come to faith without ever thinking about it. For most, however, a perception of the idea of design is inseparable from the concept of God. The argument from design simply makes this connection more explicit – just as the 'argument for other minds based on analogy' makes explicit our natural feeling that other minds exist. The argument from design can have a role both in challenging the uncommitted, and in confirming the faith of the believer. Few thinking Christians *never* have doubts, and the rational perception that one's faith 'makes sense' helps the maintenance through such times of the 'commitment to believe' of which Plantinga speaks.

Swinburne actually uses terms like 'coherence'[89] and is the nearest to a modern day Descartes in terms of developing a belief system on rationalistic grounds. We have already expressed sympathy with his work, and do not wish to enlarge on this here.

Christians do need to ask basic questions about knowledge and belief, and in our view a belief in God 'makes the most sense' of our total experience.

Conclusions on the Nature of Science

Returning specifically to science, how can we put all this together? Can we draw out any commonly agreed features of science? This is not easy, but the following more or less have to be accepted within *any* credible modern philosophy of science:

1. Background Assumptions and Uniformity

Various basic background assumptions have to be made both about rationality and about the uniform behaviour of nature. Some such uniformity is necessary for science and has to be accepted as an act of faith which 'seems to work'.

2. Observation

All observation is 'theory-laden' ie perception *always* involves interpreting according to prior concepts. It is then expressed in

---

[89] Eg in his book the *Coherence of Theism* (1993).

particular human language which is never 'purely objective' or 'neutral' in terms of concepts. Some 'observation' uses instruments (eg microscope, telescope) which imply a lot more implicit and explicit theory. Absolute relativism (the idea that any notion is as good as any other) is absurd, but there may be a range of possible ways of 'perceiving' particular phenomena.

3. External Reality

All we ever experience is experiences, and the conclusion that there is anything 'out there' causing these involves a whole set of inferences. This applies even more to 'unobservables' like neutrinos, muons and quarks than to elephants and currant buns.

4. The Status of Scientific Laws

The fundamental choice is between seeing scientific laws as:
(a) purely instruments for prediction (instrumentalism)
(b) hypotheses about 'real' entities (critical realism)
Neither is convincing in its 'pure' form, and each in practice seems to adopt elements of the other.

5. Scientific Methodology

Emphasis can be put on prediction-testing, on 'research programmes' which are not altogether commensurate, or on evolution by Bayesian probabilistic inference. None works well for *all* past 'discoveries, and none is watertight philosophically.

6. Discovery

Scientific discovery comes not by pure observation, but by a combination of creative intuition, imagination, and logical thinking. Competing paradigms, or theories within a domain if you prefer this terminology, may involve different and on some points irreconcilable perspectives. In some cases apparently conflicting models may be applied to the same phenomena. But this does not mean that any theory is as good as any other.

7. Convergence

Simply stated systems (eg Atkinsian naïve realism, pure relativism or the 1936 Logical Positivism of A J Ayer) are always (to use Laudan's phrase) 'unadulterated hogwash'. When the six points made above are recognised, apparently opposite systems begin to converge. Thus it has been suggested that such apparently contrasting views as Carnap and Kuhn can be seen as 'allies'.[90]   Kuhn, Lakatos, Putnam, Laudan etc in some ways may reach the same island from different directions.

8. Restriction

Few modern philosophers of science would now claim that *scientific* knowledge is the *only* form of well founded knowledge. Putnam, for example, insists that '"scientific" is not co-extensive with "rational"'[91] Laudan that 'there is no fundamental difference in kind between scientific and other forms of intellectual enquiry.'[92]

Science and Theology as Disciplines

At the beginning of section 9 we mentioned the irony of Francis Galton proclaiming the unsuitability of the 'priestly mind' for science at the time when the monk Mendel was making the breakthrough in Galton's area of science. But, ironical as the particular circumstances may be, Galton's contention is one which many today may intuitively feel. Is it plausible? Are the attitudes of mind needed for faith and science so different that conflict is inevitable? Is (as eg Wolpert suggests) 'religion' just about feelings whilst science is about facts?

Clearly, there *are* great differences between the thinking relevant to the spiritual and that to the material world of science. Nevertheless, we might list some points which are broadly parallel to those involved in science:

1. Reality:

There is no ultimate 'proof' that there *is* an external physical world, ie that matter 'exists'. There is no ultimate 'proof' that there is an external spiritual world, ie that God and angels 'exist'. Realism, in either field, is an act of faith. Yet to many it makes sense to believe that our experiences are 'caused' by external realities (physical and/or spiritual) – even if our knowledge of them cannot be certain. Actually, If anything, it seems logical to be *most* certain that *consciousness* exists because we experience it – though Dennett tries to persuade us that even this is an illusion!

---

[90] Irzik & Grunberg (1995).
[91] Putnam (1990) p. 143.
[92] Laudan (1977) p. 153 and (1996) p. 85.

2. Observation:

Evangelicals are *realists* in believing that their theology refers to 'really existing' entities. There *really is* a God, he is external to us and the word 'God' is not just a shorthand way of describing certain religious experiences. They will, though, be *critical realists* in the sense that all observation involves perspective. Recognising perspective is not, however, the same thing as postmodernist relativism. If there is one unique reality, then there are limits on what are 'perspectives' of that reality and what are hallucinations.

3. Constructions:

We noted above Brown's suggestion that unobservable concepts might be less perception-dependent than observables. Could the same apply to concepts of the unobservable God?

4. Language:

Language is never neutral. Firstly, it affects the way we 'perceive', and secondly it often contains model and metaphor. At the start of section 4 we noted that science, like religion, uses language metaphorically. Ian Barbour and Mary Hesse, from their different Christian traditions, have both pointed out the parallels in this respect.[93] When we say God is a 'Father' the term is metaphorical – but this implies neither that it has no meaning nor that we can make it mean anything we like. Metaphor is also a way of conveying *truth*.

5. Imperfect Knowledge:

The notion that science is 'verifiable' is dead. Scientific knowledge is always partial, and even a scientific 'theory of everything' never will be total knowledge. Similarly, in religion present knowledge is 'partial' (1 Cor 13:12) and may later prove to be a limiting case of a wider reality.

6. Mental Processes:

From different Christian traditions, Robert E D Clark and Russell Stannard have compared the reaching of conclusions in their science with those involved in Christian faith.[94]

---

[93] See Hesse (1966) and in Watts (1998), Barbour (1974), (1998).
[94] Clarke (1961) Stannard (1982).

In the heyday of behaviourism and positivism there were philosophers who thought that the only 'real' knowledge was scientific. Even Popperian falsificationism sought a sharp demarcation between the nature of scientific and of other knowledge. Whilst today it is possible to find throwbacks to the behaviourist/positivist views (like Dennett) or philosophical amateurs who confusedly argue that metaphysical knowledge has no reference to anything (like Dawkins), these are not generally received views. Putnam, for example, argues that:

> "scientific" is not coextensive with "rational". There are many perfectly rational beliefs that cannot be tested rationally.[95]

Putnam moved away from his earlier Logical Empiricism, just as even A J Ayer in later life recognised its falsehood and took a more mystical approach to reality. We are not convinced that Taylor (in a generally good article) is helping to describe a rejection of a naïve positivism as 'partial post-modernism'.[96] The term 'critical realism' seems to use to serve better.

More recent thinking in epistemology (ie the question of obtaining and testing knowledge) emphasises, in the words of D L Wolfe, 'the production of a system of assertions which makes sense out of final experience'.[97] Wolfe recognises that an interpretative belief system 'constitutes the spectacles through which one experiences' but that in any such interpretative schema we search for:

1. **consistency:** freedom from self-contradiction.
2. **coherence:** internal relatedness of statements in the interpretive schema.
3. **comprehensiveness:** applicability to all experience.
4. **congruity:** appropriateness to the experiences covered.

This covers both scientific and religious schema and, indeed, the mixture of the two, which virtually all of us hold. Scientific thinking can never be independent of all meta-physical and religious beliefs, though does not imply that the subject mater of science contains religious concepts.

---

[95] Putnam (1990) p. 143.
[96] John Taylor (1998).
[97] Wolfe (1983).

Both scientific research and religious (more specifically, Christian) thinking involve a mixture of subjective and creative thinking and objective realities. Both work from the seen to the unseen in human experience, and regard, in some sense, the unseen as more real. Both involve the confession that our knowledge is partial.

Mixing Theology and Science

We began this book with clear assertions that there are metaphysical assumptions behind both rationality and science. Putnam, for example, points out that even a search for *coherence* and *simplicity* involves values in the sense of deciding that these are 'desirable'.[98] The decision to *do* science, or follow its conclusions, is a value decision.

Approaches to Science-Theology

Various conceptual schemes have been given for this relationship. Barbour[99], for example, presents:

1. **Conflict** (eg Dawkins, Johnson)
2. **Independence** (eg Gilkey)
3. **Dialogue** (eg Pannenberg, McMullin)
4. **Integration** (eg Montefiore, Peacocke)

From a different standpoint, J P Moreland[100] gives a not dissimilar breakdown. These categories are useful, but not necessarily mutually exclusive in practice. What we would like to present, however, are a different four benchmark viewpoints which are found amongst those identifying themselves as Christian theists today. Two initial points about this. Firstly, perception, to us, is never neutral, and in putting these forward we are inviting the reader to perceive things in this way because we believe it 'makes the most sense'. Secondly, these are *bench stops*. Their boundaries are fuzzy, and individuals may be cited between them. Brief descriptions of our four categories are as follows:

---

[98] Putnam (1990) p. 138.
[99] Barbour (1998) ch 4 (repeating his earlier ideas).
[100] Moreland (1994) *Introduction.*

1. Young-earth 'literalism' (eg Morris, Whitcomb)

- All biblical descriptions of natural phenomena take their plain 'literal meaning'.
- Science begins from biblical exegesis, and observation is used to fill in the details.
- In science there are incontrovertible facts (like the second law of thermodynamics), and 'models' (which are all that we can form for past processes).
- 'Creation' must mean a type-ii miracle – if it were possible to show that animals evolved by a series of natural processes then creation would be refuted.

2. Design Theory (eg Moreland, Dembski)

- There is no clear demarcation between science and religion/metaphysics.
- 'Design' in a concept proper to be included in scientific theory.
- 'Theistic science' means science itself includes theism.
- [It is legitimate to derive scientific truth from biblical exegesis] {Moreland only?}.
- ['Creation' must mean type-ii miracles – if it were possible to show that animals evolved by a series of natural processes then creation would be refuted] {?}

3. Post-Kantian Baconian Critical Realism (Us!)

- Decisions about whether to *do* science, whether it is rational, and what can be included in it are metaphysical and not part of science itself.
- Science is neither coextensive with rational belief, nor is it sufficient in itself to form a world view.
- Science *as science* properly adopts methodological naturalism, trying to construct systems of 'laws' which use physical concepts to enable prediction of events.
- Science can identify ' ' in natural law explanations which a wider world-view can either:
  - ◆ leave unexplained or 'mysterious'.
  - ◆ have the faith to believe will one day be filled.
  - ◆ ascribe to (personal) 'agent causation'.

- God works both *within* natural laws and (when he chooses) in a type-ii supernatural miracle pattern which differs from them. Particular events (whether eg described in Scripture, found by modern medicine, or surmised in geological history) could be ascribed to God whether or not in line with normal 'natural law'.
- Decision as to whether a particular event is a type-i or type-ii event can be made only on empirical grounds.

4. Theistic Physicalism (Peacocke)

- Decisions about whether to *do* science, whether it is rational, and what can be included in it are metaphysical and not part of science itself.
- Science is neither coextensive with rational belief, nor is it sufficient in itself to form a world view.
- Natural law (although dependent on God) is in general never altered. Regular natural processes are complete in themselves and not altered by agent causation (whether human or divine). As far as concerns type-ii miracles:
  - *Arthur Peacocke:* holds that no amount of evidence should convince us that a type-ii miracle has occurred and the New Testament reports are not of observable events.
  - *Donald MacKay:* held that some NT events were type-ii miracles.
- Science is the exploration of inviolable regular sequences of natural processes.

Some general points:

i. The Spiritual Dimension: All these accept the reality of God and the spiritual. We omit eg logical empiricism/ scientism which claims that scientific explanations are either the *only* or at least greatly *superior* forms of explanation.

ii. Realism/Instrumentalism: All these four (and, indeed, positivism) are compatible with either a realist or an instrumentalist view of physical phenomena.

iii. The Views and Evangelicals: None of the first three are inconsistent in any way with evangelical belief – and clearly aligned evangelicals are found in each. The Peacocke version of (4) is not consistent with Evangelicalism, and (as we have argued) is also difficult to reconcile with *any* God who *acts*. MacKay preserved his Evangelicalism by adopting a theological determinism parallel to physical determinism, as well as by allowing exceptions on special occasions. Where the 'Fuller School' of 'non-reductive physicalism' currently stands we are unsure. Nancy Murphy has already moved from a quantum-related form of dualism to her current position, and she now thinks that type-ii miracles 'have been made problematic by modern science'[101] and hints at adopting a Peacocke view of divine action (or lack of it).

Young-Earth Creationism

We have already noted that a supposed 'plain literal meaning':

1. Is spectacularly undelivered – even by Henry Morris.
2. Is out of line with Jesus' use of language.
3. It against much of traditional mainstream Christian teaching.

What, though, about its view of scientific methodology?

Sadly, it really misunderstands the traditional 'two books' Baconian approach. J C Whitcomb attacks what he calls the 'double-revelation theory', which he describes thus:

> The theologian is the God-appointed interpreter of Scripture and the scientist is the God-appointed interpreter of nature, each having specialised lenses for reading the true message of the particular 'book of revelation' which he has been called upon to study.[102]

The only reason Whitcomb seems to give for his rejection of the principle scientist-Christians have accepted for at least 300 if not (implicitly) nearly 2,000 years, is that he feels science has limitations in exploring past events, and that there are particular problems with some modern theories of origins. He does not mention the problems or limitations of theology and biblical interpretation.

Theologian E J Young quotes Whitcomb and adds that the double-revelation theory entails a low estimate of the Bible because:

---

[101] Brown (1998) p. 147.
[102] Whitcomb & deYoung (1978) p. 54.

Whenever "science" and the Bible are in conflict, it is always the Bible that, in one manner or another, must give way.'[103]

This is, of course, factually incorrect. It is not 'the Bible' but the fallible human interpretations of it made in theology which must 'give way'.

Morris also says that the double-revelation theory must be 'unequivocally rejected by Bible-believing Christians'. He argues that whilst nature needs interpreting:

the Scriptures, in fact, do not need to be "interpreted" at all, for God is well able to say exactly what he means.[104]

In view of the various theological controversies throughout history among Bible-believing Christians, not to mention disagreements amongst young-earth creationists themselves, this is breathtakingly unrealistic. Its inconsistency is amply confirmed when, as we have seen, Morris' own writings contain numerous allegorical interpretations of aspects of Genesis 1-3.

In Britain, young-earth creationist E H Andrews has attacked the historic Christian and Baconian position, under the term 'complementarity'. Andrews actually attacks the modern versions of it by Christians such as Ramm, Mixter and MacKay, seemingly unaware that what he is rejecting is not some modern aberration, but the thinking of Bible-believing mainstream Christianity for centuries. He says they are 'at a loss to know what to do with the doctrine of creation, and dare not mention miracles'.[105] This is most strange, since the great majority if not all those listed by Henry Morris as 'Bible-believing creationists' held this Baconian view, and so have the vast majority of Christians who have analysed and defended the miraculous. More fundamentally, however, he seems not to understand the logical relationships of nature, Scripture, science and theology. Thus he says:

The error of complementarity is that it places Scripture alongside science.[106]

---

[103] E J Young (1964) p. 53.

[104] Morris (1984b) p. 47.

[105] E H Andrews (1986) p. 71.

[106] E H Andrews et at (Eds) (1986) p. 10 and see Andrews (1986) p. 71.

and he emphasises the 'fallibility's and 'shortcomings' of 'human wisdom'. Neither Kepler, Galileo, Bacon, Sedgwick, Ramm, Mixter, MacKay, nor anyone we know places the Bible and *science* on the same level. It is the Bible and *nature* which are on the same logical level as self-revelations of God, and theology and science which are human interpretations of them. It is not the Bible but theology which needs adjusting as science progresses. Of course, human wisdom is fallible, but this is no more true in science than in theology or in writing young-earth-creationist literature. Andrews's own work differs on key points in interpreting Genesis from Morris or Young, so why should we accept his interpretation as infallible and free from 'human wisdom'?

Finally, a 1998 young-earth book tells us that the 'two books' approach 'irrelevant and dangerous' because:

> Science cannot even properly comment upon creation... It is undeniably true that the Bible teaches a supernatural divine creation in six days.   Even naturalistic critics and liberal theologians agree...[107]

Strange how leading Christian teachers throughout history and so many conservative modern Bible scholars failed to spot what was 'undeniably true'. Their use of the word 'even' seems to fail to spot that naturalistic critics and liberal theologians (presumably Barr – no one ever mentions anyone else!) want to argue this to ridicule Bible-believing faith.

We would, then, defend the classical Baconian approach to science-faith issues, which was rooted in earlier Christian ideas and has shaped the whole of Christian and scientific thinking on relationships of science and theology. Many of the greatest scientific minds in history have accepted it, and it is unrealistic for sceptics to view it as naive or obscurantist. On the other hand, two kinds of new theology should also be resisted. The Bible is neither to be 'spiritualised' out of all reference to the world of space-time, nor to be used as a source-book for scientific theory. Neither liberalism nor young-earth creationism have any claim to represent the historic mainstream of Bible-based Christianity.

---

[107] Ankeberg & Weldon (1998) p. 250.

As we have seen, neither objectivity nor knowledge in science can ever be absolute. On the other hand, there is a given or a 'reality' which means that scientists are not free to make up whatever laws they like. There are experiences of our world which are real, and though they may later be reinterpreted or seen as part of a larger truth, they remain undeniable experiences. Disagreements or uncertainties in present science do not imply it to be unreal or lacking any objectivity.

As science is the systematic human interpretation of God's 'book of nature', so theology is the systematic human interpretation of God's 'book of his word' the Bible. Theology too is about realities, and theologians cannot make up whatever theories they like. There are experiences of God which are real, and though they may later be reinterpreted or seen as a part of a larger truth, they remain undeniable experiences. Disagreements or uncertainties in present (or past) theology do not imply that it is unreal or lacking any objectivity.

To say all of this is to deny neither the God-givenness of nature nor the God-givenness of the Bible - but it is to affirm human fallibility in interpreting both.

In general, science and theology are concerned with different issues: the respective realms of the physical and the spiritual. They are not, however, totally independent realms, because God has acted in space-time. Thus on some things, such as specific events in the past, both nature and the Bible have something to say. The main point of a biblical account may be clear, but on details incidental to its main purpose it may not be. At any given state of human knowledge we have to study the two accounts (nature and Scripture) together, reaching whatever tentative harmony currently fits best. Thus, for example, in the Renaissance it may have been a harmony of Aristotelian science and theology. There should be nothing embarrassing for Christians in this when later science changed and a new synthesis of science- theology emerged - providing that we clearly recognise (as did Aquinas) the tentative nature of the synthesis in any given period.

The young-earth critique of Baconianism (by whatever name) is riddled with misunderstandings.

We may just briefly mention Morris' insistence that any part of science which concerns a reconstruction of the past is a 'model' rather than part of hard science. There is, of course, a difference between experimental and historical science which was recognised as early as Whewell. But the two are connected. Take forensic science. The first task may be to establish what is there (eg the physical state of a murder victim). Then one looks for possible physical laws which might account for this. Finally one puts the two together to achieve an 'explanation' of how this particular victim came to die. So is this less 'science' than (say) studying electron spin resonance which involves entities one cannot even see? Surely not. But this kind of threefold process was (as we saw in the last section) exactly how Whewell saw geology in the mid nineteenth century. Of course we use our 'laws of nature' to project back and explain present phenomena. If we (for example) observe a modern lava flow and it leaves a particular rock structure, then it seems reasonable to explain an older looking similar structure as the result of an ancient lava flow. Why is this a 'model'?

Young earth creationists, truth to tell, do not have much of an alternative to offer us for scientific methodology.

'Design Theory' and J P Moreland

Over the last decade or so a movement which we might loosely call 'design theory' has developed. Key figures include eg the biochemist Michael Behe, the philosopher J P Moreland, the mathematician/ philosopher William Dembski, and the lawyer Philip Johnson. Some or all of the following are held by members of the group:

1. Science is not independent of metaphysics, because in doing science we make metaphysical assumptions.
2. Theistic belief is the most secure basis for a belief in the coherence of the world and of our own rationality.
3. Nature has a structure and set of 'finely tuned' basic laws which evidence intelligent conscious design.
4. In nature there are 'irreducibly complex systems' for which natural process explanations of origins cannot presently be found, and for which some kind of miracle (either 'unlikely' type-I or a type-ii) is the best explanation.

5. Macro-evolution is incompatible with the language of Genesis 1-3.

6. Science should or may start from the Bible, which provides a basic structure within which observation fills in details.

Perhaps the seminal book was J P Moreland's *Christianity and the Nature of Science* (1989). Moreland has a knowledge of philosophy and the philosophy of science, and his book contains some useful summaries of various positions. We like the spirit of his writing, and can find a number of basic points to agree with, in particular:

1. **Philosophy Undergirds and Justifies Science:** 'Philosophy operates underneath science in a foundation way…providing its presuppositions…focussing on what constitutes good theories. Philosophy operates outside the domain of science…operates within and interfaces with science… helps to clarify internal conceptual problems.' (p. 44)

2. **Rejection of 'Scientism':** 'According to this view science is the very paradigm of truth and rationality…scientism… is self defeating.' (pp. 104-7)

3. **The Insufficiency of Pure Complementarity:** 'According to this view, science and theology are complementary, noninteracting, noncompeting descriptions of the world… Applied to the question of the origin and development of life, the complementarity view takes theistic evolution as the proper way to integrate theology and science… I respect this approach… However, the complementarity view fails as a total model of integration.. is too clean, too neat, too easy…'[108]

4. **Body-Mind Dualism – Rejection of Physicalism:** 'Certain varieties of physicalism regarding the mind-body problem that deny the existence of mind are self refuting…I have defended the irreducibility of the mind to matter elsewhere… some form of mind/body dualism is true…'[109]

5. **Seeking an Integrated Worldview:** 'From the beginning to the present., Christians have felt it necessary to integrate

---

[108] Moreland (1989) p. 12.
[109] Moreland (1989) pp. 54, 207.

their theological doctrines with rational beliefs from scientific, philosophical and other sources.'[110]

There are, however, some basic problems elsewhere in the book. The U.S.A. (unlike the U.K.) has a ban on teaching 'religion' in state run schools, and concern with this seems to us to distort the whole approach of Moreland's book. The American followers of George McCready Price and Henry Morris have developed what they call 'Scientific Creationism' and insist that this is pure 'science' so that it can and should be taught in American schools. In a 1981 hearing in Little Rock, Arkansas, Judge William Overton gave a decision that it was *not* science but religion. He defined science as follows:

1. It is guided by natural law.
2. It has to be explanatory by reference to natural law.
3. It is testable against the empirical world.
4. Its conclusions are tentative ie are not necessarily the final word.
5. It is falsifiable.

Apart from the first of these (which is meaningless) this would be unremarkable in the U.K., if fairly naïve. But Moreland begins his whole treatment in evident outrage at this, and with a determination to demolish it at all costs. Moreland begins with citing the judicial grounds on p. 23 which he proceeds to demolish, returns to it on p. 56, and focuses his conclusions around it with the argument that:

> God... is not necessarily a religious concept...the term *God* may be a mere philosophical concept or theoretical term denoting an explanatory theoretical entity needed in some sort of explanation, much like the terms *quark* and *continental plate*.[111]

For the American scene is it not enough that our synthesis of knowledge in a worldview may include theism; we will have to accept both that it is proper for the term *God* to be part of the *science* and that it is *not* a *religious* term so that *God* can be mentioned in schools. This is Moreland's motivation and argument. In our view, however, it leads to some very basic confusions, which were new need to consider.

---

[110] Moreland (1989) p.17.
[111] Moreland (1989) p. 221.

1. Definition of Science

Moreland's problem is that he wants to do two contradictory things. On the one hand he needs to break down the distinction between science and non-science so that the "Judge Overtons" cannot properly exclude *God* from American classrooms. On the other hand he wants to be able to speak of scientists like Mayr who 'overstep their bounds' (p. 51) and so speak of the 'limits to science'. Frankly, he can't have it both ways. If 'God' and 'person' and 'consciousness' are (as he claims) all scientific terms, we can hardly complain if atheists like Mayr, Dawkins, Dennett and E O Wilson make pronouncements about such things supposedly from their science.

We have clearly stated our view that there are metaphysical and philosophical assumptions *behind* science, and that science cannot be the only or even a 'superior' kind of knowledge. But this is not to say that it does not have, broadly at least, a particular subject area. So what does Moreland object to in (say) Judge Overton's view as above?

To the Overton point (1) he rightly notes that scientists actually have all kinds of motives. However, even as early as Herschel[112] in the 1830's it was recognised that how one arrives at a theory is distinct from its justification/testing.

On (2) he claims that mathematicians do not refer to 'natural law' whilst moralists may do: so reference to natural law is neither necessary nor sufficient for science. This is spurious. Mathematics is an aid to science, but surely is not in itself 'science' since pure maths is axiomatic. The fact that moralists or phenomenologists use the word 'natural' certainly does not imply that it has the same meaning as in 'natural law' – to drag it in is special pleading. Moreland goes on to point out that:

> Scientists sometimes explain something by appealing to a brute given that is not itself a scientific law and is not capable of being subsumed under more general laws.

This is not a sensible objection for two reasons. Firstly, unless ultimately there are *some* brute facts (even if it is only why there is anything rather than nothing) we would either have pure rationalism or an infinite regress. The point of science is not that

---

[112] Herschel (1831) see also Losee Ch. 9.

everything is explicable by natural law, but that natural law helps us explain one physical thing in terms of others – even though at base we have to accept some basic principles/laws as 'given'. Secondly, it is part of the legitimate aim of science to break down apparently brute facts into higher levels of theory and generalisation. The seventeenth century 'brute fact' of the general gas law was explained after 1845 by means of molecular movement in gases. Molecular movement was later explained by means of atomic structure – etc. The objection of Laudan cited by Moreland is that:

> Galileo and Newton took themselves to have established the existence of gravitational phenomena long before anyone was able to give a causal or explanatory account of gravitation.[113]

This is confused. Cavemen knew about 'gravitational phenomena' – what Galileo and Newton did was to formulate a mathematical law which most certainly *did* 'explain' why *particular* objects behaved in certain ways. The word 'explain' does not here mean answering an ultimate 'why' question, but giving more details of 'how' and subsuming particular behaviour under law and prediction. Like the general gas law, its formulation is explanatory on a certain level – even though it may be open to later more general levels of explanation.

Moreland also has some fun demolishing the idea of 'natural'. He seems to assume that it includes such ideas as Cartesian souls, moral values, and the Freudian use of the unconscious. There are two different issues here. One is that he seems to confuse 'physical' with 'immediately observable'. Thus 'ecosystems'[114] are non-physical, and statements about 'properties and relations of unseen theoretical entities' are 'metaphysical'. We do not find this convincing, any more than his confusion of 'causal' with 'deterministic'.[115] The other point is that we do not believe that 'moral values' or Cartesian souls or the 'unconscious' (at least as Freud defined it) are 'scientific' concepts. Indeed the insistence that 'consciousness' is a scientific term, subject therefore to scientific study, seems one

---

[113] Cited in Moreland (1989) p. 25.
[114] Moreland (1989) p. 27.
[115] Moreland (1989) p. 79.

of the worst errors in the work of those like Dennett and the Churchlands.

Much of the rest of the critique is special pleading or based on scientists' fallibility. What is a real surprise is that, at the end of it all, Moreland declares:

> In a general way science is a discipline that *in some sense* and *usually* appeals to natural explanation, empirical tests, and so forth. Nevertheless the italicised words must be kept in mind. There are borderline cases that are hard to classify.[116]

He also says that 'disciplines outside science, like theology, can be shown to use various aspects of scientific methodology.'[117] We are happy to agree with both these statements. But the point is surely that there *is* in general a discipline of 'science' which concerns natural law and empirical tests, and a discipline of 'theology' which is distinct and concerns God?

We may add that we believe that science and metaphysics are distinct, but of course there is *interaction*. Forensic science can establish 'facts' which (in the dimension of morality which is not part of science) establish 'guilt'. Archaeology can check the veracity of the Gospels. Medicine can establish evidence that a type-i miracle has occurred – which may have metaphysical implications. The latter, however (as we explored in Section 4) is precisely because in these circumstances *there is no scientific explanation* for the event.

The pure 'complementarity' (which we joined Moreland in criticising above) logically implies physicalism and an *a priori* necessity for theistic evolution – which to us is both incoherent and incompatible with faith. But theistic evolution (or as we prefer to call it 'evolutionary creationism') can *also* be adopted as an empirical conclusion within a non-physicalist worldview which is fully supernaturalist.

2. Confusion on 'Realism'
Moreland claims:

> My own eclectic view incorporates a chastened form of rational realism.[118]

---

[116] Moreland (1989) p. 42.
[117] Moreland (1989) p. 101.
[118] Moreland (1989) p. 141.

We are sympathetic, but think it insufficiently chastened because he claims:

> If Kant and his contemporary followers are correct, then science as it is understood in classical realist terms, is not possible because one of the major preconditions for science, the existence of order that can be discovered in the (mind-independent) world (and not created by the knowing subject itself) is an illusion.[119]

Of course Kant is not a 'classical realist' if by this one means a naïve representative realist. But neither Kant nor Putnam is denying that there is a 'real' world that is given to us. We do not 'create' our own world, it is just that we (inevitably) experience reality through the medium of human sensory experience. To Kant this is 'empirically real' but 'transcendentally ideal'. It is a false dichotomy to suggest that *either* order is in the 'mind-independent world' *or* it is 'created by the knowing subject'. Kant surely cannot be taken to mean that our minds could somehow create order where there were none at all in 'things-in-themselves? Though we *have* to perceive in terms of cause-effect, space-time, number etc this does not mean that science is anything but dealing with 'reality'. As Christians we readily accept that, for example, our perception of 'time' may differ from how it is in itself or how God perceives it. This does not imply it is unreal.

Associated with this is Moreland's statement:

> Science presupposes that language is an adequate medium for referring to and stating truths about the world.[120]

What is an 'adequate medium' and who decides what 'science presupposes'? Of course we *have* to use language – we cannot use anything else. But scientists at least since Bacon have recognised the problems with language. Bacon's 'idols of the tribe' and 'idols of the market place' refer to the inherent problems of human perception and language – and in later figures like Whewell the implications were worked out of both.

We too are critical realists, but we have problems with Moreland's apparent criteria as to *what* should be taken in an anti-real manner:

---

[119] Moreland (1989) p. 112.
[120] Moreland (1980) p. 122.

When science and a theological statement or biblical interpretation come into conflict, part of the solution may be in adopting an antirealist view of the scientific statement... An antirealist approach should be taken toward some scientific theory in those cases where the phenomena described by that theory lie outside the appropriate domain of science, or the scientific aspect of some phenomenon is inappropriately taken to be the whole phenomenon itself.[121]

There were those who sought to take early Copernicanism in an anti-real sense (ie that the orbits of planets around the sun were convenient mathematical models and not real). Is this what he means? Did it help? On the second criteria, he cites Paul Churchland's claim that 'a type of mental state, namely human joy, is really identical to a type of physical state, namely, resonances in the lateral hypothalmus.' We would see this not as a part of science to be interpreted in an anti-real manner, but as a dangerous confusion of science and metaphysics. The Churchlands' view is ultimately incoherent and untenable, it confuses basically different categories. The 'critical' part of modern realism is a recognition that because we use human senses and language all description involves perspective. It is not a let-out to avoid difficult scientific concepts.

3. Misrepresentation of Historical Views
There are two aspects of Moreland's misunderstanding of nineteenth century creationism:
1. He thinks that they thought it legitimate to start their science from the Bible.
2. He thinks that they thought it legitimate to introduce supernatural creation *as part of their science.*

Moreland seems to rely crucially on Neal Gillespie[122] for his treatment. As we saw in the last section, Gillespie adopts a quite untenable 'positivists' verses 'creationists' model which reflects his own positivism, his lack of understanding of the real position of many of the scientists in that period, and a total confusion of what the term 'positivism' is supposed to mean. Thus misled, Moreland constructs a model where there are two rival *'epistemes'* (ie approaches to discovering truth). One is 'creationist' (which uses the Bible as a source for deriving truths

[121] Moreland (1989) p. 206.
[122] Gillespie (1977).

of science and has God as part of science) and the other is 'positivist' (which rules out all supernatural agency whether inside science or outside).

Here is his statement of the first point:

> Even up to the 1850's and beyond, many men of science believed it was reasonable to hold a discontinuous, typological view of nature and to believe that the Bible recorded the actual history of the creation of life and could thus serve as a guide for doing science...The creationists believed that science was logically and theoretically obligated to theology and that it was legitimate to consult the early chapters of Genesis as a guide for biology and geology... Thus Darwin's theory signalled the epistemic breakdown of theology as a vehicle for doing science.[123]

Can he name a *single one* such creationist of any note? We are familiar with all the major U.K. and many of the U.S.A. scientist-creationists in this period, and know of no one for whom this was true. This is not a matter of 'perspective', Moreland's statement is simply, demonstrably, false. He admits, of course, that he is 'not a historian of science'[124], but to base a radically new philosophy on so demonstrably a false premise about historical scientist-Christians is breathtaking. The only scientists Moreland names as 'creationists' are Sedgwick, Buckland and Agassiz.[125] All three would have vehemently rejected this supposed '*episteme*'. Sedgwick was the only clear Evangelical of the three, and adamantly and explicitly denied the *episteme* which Moreland apparently ascribes to him. Like all the other 'creationists' amongst scientists of the period Sedgwick took a Baconian approach.

There were at least *four* distinct views amongst mainstream scientists:

1. (eg Adam Sedgwick, Hugh Miller) empirical science revealed emergence of species suddenly and by no known process. 'Creation' was the term used to describe this unknown process.
2. (eg Asa Gray) empirical science revealed evolution by natural selection, which was therefore accepted as God's

---

[123] Moreland (1989) p. 216.
[124] Moreland (19940 p. 62.
[125] Moreland (1989) p. 216, p. 224 quoting Kitcher.

method of creation – and he was believed to guide the process.

3. (eg Saint George Mivart) empirical science revealed a Lamarckian form of evolution, accepted as describing God's method of creation.

4. (eg Robert Grant, T H Huxley) supernatural agencies to be ruled out *a priori*, thus *some* form of evolution was necessary.

None of these did what Moreland said and started from the Bible or assumed it could be used to derive geology and biology. They might, of course, get some *inspiration* from ideas in the Bible – and if this is *all* he means[126] this is fine. But so-called modern 'scientific creationists' usually claim that they can derive known truth about science from Scripture – which is certainly *not* what great past scientists did.

On the second point Moreland says:

> Scientists of other generations recognised that God was a legitimate actual or hypothetical source of explanation in science.[127]

Perhaps Newton's view of God making corrections to the solar system might count in this way (though they were arrived at empirically not from Scripture), but the 19th century scientists most certainly did not believe that 'supernatural creation' or 'God' were a part of their *science*. Science concerned natural processes, God was part of a wider world-view.

Let us make no mistake. What Moreland and some of his disciples are doing is basically throwing out the approach taken by all the major scientist-Christian figures of the scientific revolution and the rise of modern science.

4. God, Quarks and Continental Plates

Continental plates are 'real', physical and (in principle) observable in the same sense as elephants. Quarks are theoretical and unobservable but physical. God is neither physical nor observable (in this sense) but metaphysical. To suggest (as in the Moreland quote above) that 'God' is a theoretical concept on a level with continental plates and quarks is to make total confusion. God is excluded from science not

---

[126] This could be the implication of page 229.
[127] Moreland (1989) p. 224.

because he is unobservable, but because he is the *author of* natural processes rather than a *part of* them.

Moreland's 1994 book *The Creation Hypothesis* extends and repeats the same ideas. More emphasis is put on the supposed difficulties of 'demarcation' between science and non-science – much of this based on the views of the anti-realist Laudan.[128]

One rather odd new assertion is made:

> These brothers and sisters are convinced that a proper interpretation of the biblical text renders most reasonable some form of theistic evolution.[129]

We can think of *no one* who adopts what Moreland calls 'theistic evolution' (ie what we would prefer to call 'evolutionary creationism') on the basis just that it is the 'most reasonable' interpretation of the biblical text. The suggestion seems absurd, for they would then be beginning their science from the Bible rather than observation. Our friends, eg Prof R J Berry, Prof Douglas Spanner, Dr Denis Alexander and the many others who are evolutionary creationists, believe that the language of Genesis is neutral as regards the mechanism, if any, used for creation of species. Their conclusions about the mechanism are based on empirical observation, not exegesis. Moreland then goes on to refer vaguely to:

> Christian intellectuals, including Old Testament scholars' who do not believe that Genesis is consistent with evolution as it is usually presented.

This is a clever phrase. If 'as it is usually presented' means here 'as presented by materialist atheists who mix it with metaphysics and assume that the world is undesigned', then of course *any* Christian theist will find it incompatible with Genesis. This, however, is because it is no longer part of science but part of Denkinsland. But which Old Testament scholar would deny that God could have used a natural process to create species if he so chose? Let us have some names. We should be pointing out that such materialist atheists mix up their science and their metaphysics – not denying that there is any demarcation.

---

[128] Moreland (1994) pp. 72, 78, 99 etc.
[129] Moreland (1994) p.13.

Much of Moreland's contribution repeats his earlier views. We agree with him, of course, that *total* separation of science and theology is absurd. We agree that the physicalism of the Churchlands is incoherent, and that the Christian versions of physicalism are inconsistent with divine action. We agree that scientism (in its strong or weak form) is foolish. But none of this is to deny the basic Baconian views which underlay the great scientist-Christian input to the scientific revolution. We actually agree with the quoted views of the affable atheist Michael Ruse:

> Even if Scientific Creationism were totally successful... it would not yield a *scientific* explanation of origins. Rather, at most, it could prove that science shows there can be no scientific explanation of origins.[130]

This would exactly state the views of Whewell, Sedgwick, and other great 'creationists' of the nineteenth century – though they wouldn't have thought much of Ruse's moral philosophy! 'Science' is an attempt to 'explain' individual phenomena using humanly constructed laws which reflect natural processes. The two key points about this are that:

1. Direct type-ii miracle acts of God are not part of it.
2. There is no *a priori* guarantee that it will succeed (ie because a type-ii miracle may be involved).

These points apply both to the origin of species and to particular healing miracles. This relates to some of our earlier comments in Section 5 on a supposed concept of 'Healing in the Scientific Sense'. The Baconian theist assumes neither that immediate supernatural agency is to be ruled out, nor that it is a part of science.

In Moreland's most recent chapter in Dembski (1998), we find little to dissent from – we too believe that God has a freedom for libertarian action. It seems to us a part of theism.

The Fruitfulness of 'Theistic Science'

The first question we may ask is whether 'creation science' has shown any scientific advance over the decades. Moreland raises the question and claims:

---

[130] Quoted in Moreland (1989) p. 42.

Modern creation scientists' model differs in several respects from that of their counterparts.[131]

We do not believe that Duane Gish and those like him are in any sense the 'modern counterparts' of 'creationist' scientists like Hitchcock, Sedgwick, Owen, Guyon, etc who made real contributions to empirical science and would have emphatically disowned 'scientific creationism'. All that Moreland mentions as an 'advance' is that the modern 'scientific creationists' no longer accept the absolute fixity of species. They have done nothing eg to show how a short duration flood could build the rocks of the Grand Canyon or the Himalayas. In mainstream geology an elaborate picture has emerged of moving plates and the impact of India on Asia, which, using known laws of physics and suitable starting conditions, may explain physical features like the Himalayas and Tibet and various features of similarities and differences in animal distributions. This involves a complex pattern of prediction, detailed measurement, etc. An elaborate picture, involving predictions and correlation of phenomena, has emerged of the meteor impact in the Yucatan basin which apparently ended the Cretaceous period. Where are any comparable developments in 'scientific creationism'? We know of none.

Is Moreland's so-called 'theistic science' potentially fruitful? One is not reassured to read:

> Creationists and evolutionists do not need to attempt to solve a problem, say a gap in the fossil records, in precisely the same way... Creationists may elevate the virtue 'solves the theological or philosophical internal and external conceptual problems' above the virtue 'offers solutions yielding empirically fruitful lines of new research.' There is nothing unscientific about this at all.[132]

One wonders where this would have left, say, Kepler or Galileo if, when astronomy or physics raised new theological or philosophical problems, it was thought better not to pursue them. And what about the gaps? What 'research' can be done if the gaps are filled miraculously and according to God's libertarian will? Nineteenth century creationists recognised that filling the then 'gaps' with preternatural processes was not a

---

[131] Moreland (1989) p. 230.
[132] Moreland (1994) p. 63.

'scientific' explanation but an admission of a lack of one – and it was therefore perfectly proper to continue to seek one. But if 'design' is an alternative *scientific* explanation, then it would explain the phenomena perfectly and there would be no possibility of getting a better scientific explanation.

Intelligent Design

We have looked in some detail at the views of J P Moreland, whom we take as seminal in the 'Intelligent Design' movement. We like his spirit of tolerance in writing, but think his system deeply flawed and based on some demonstrably untrue historical premises.

It should not, however, be thought that we are unsympathetic to all the ideas of the movement. Like them, we reject scientism and physicalism. We also, in our own earlier books invoked the argument from design.[133] Like Dembski, we used a form of Bayes theory – though recognising its shortcomings – to argue the 'high probability' of intelligent design of our universe.[134] In *The Design Inference* Dembski describes his 'design filter' which essentially infers intelligent design if any other assumption would imply that an event with low probability has occurred. He looks at Dawkins and Kauffman in this context, pointing out their acceptance of the form of argument – though they assert that the probability of life forming without conscious design would actually be high. His technical descriptions of probability, Bayes theorem, and significance are correct and well written summaries. We agree with his more technical version of Swinburne's counter to the strong anthropic principle.[135] His final statement of 'the Design inference' is fair enough, except that it begins with the sentence:

> Suppose a subject S has identified all the relevant chance hypotheses H that could be responsible for some event E...[136]

Obviously in practice one could not *be* sure that all had been so identified, and in our view it would be the job of natural science to continue to look for some – even though as theists we accept

---

[133] Forster and Marston (1971), (1989), (1995).
[134] Forster & Marston (1989) p. 427, compare Dembski (1998b).
[135] Dembski (1998b) pp. 185-6.
[136] Dembski (1998b) p. 222.

that they may never be found. Our only real quibble might be over evolution. Dembski states:

> Along with most evolutionists, Dawkins holds that regularity and chance together are adequate to explain life.[137]

Actually, the figures cited by his friend Philip Johnson[138] show that the majority of evolutionists (in America at least) do *not* believe that evolution operated undesigned.

We also find much to agree with in his more popular *Mere Creation*. In this, Dembski defines 'naturalism' in terms of 'the self-sufficiency of nature' and calls it 'pure poison' because God need not exist.[139] We have some sympathy with this view, though we would insist that it is quite a different question as to whether *methodological* naturalism is proper to science. 'Naturalism' properly means a denial of any supernatural or spiritual realities – and should form no part of science. Science, however, does quite properly seek explanations in terms of regularities in natural processes.

We have less sympathy with his comments on what he calls 'theistic evolution'. He claims that whilst, in theory, it is compatible with 'intelligent design', it would imply that 'the natural world provides no evidence that life is designed'.[140] This is not really true. The evolutionary creationists who are friends of ours all assert that the 'fine tuning' in the basic constants of the universe constitute a 'design argument' – it 'looks as though someone were expecting us' or in Hoyle's famous words 'a super-intellect has been monkeying with the laws of physics'. Even if there were conclusive evidence for organic macro-evolution (which is debatable), it would not destroy the design argument. Theism would still make the most sense of our universe and our consciousness – consciousness would still not be 'reducible' to matter. Scripture itself, moreover, does not make 'intelligent design' arguments in the way in which Dembski, Swinburne, and we ourselves do; Paul appeals to the orderliness and structure of nature not to improbabilities of chance. It cannot, therefore, be *essential* to Christian faith to be

---

[137] Dembski (1998b) p. 58.
[138] Johnson (1997) p. 15.
[139] Dembski (1998) p. 14.
[140] Dembski (1998) p. 20.

able to make such arguments. The basic point Dembski seems to miss is that the evolutionary creationist does not adopt her/his position to 'find solace' (his term) from intelligent design or to 'find solace' from the evolutionary establishment – but because (s)he thinks it most likely to be *true*. Truth is a matter of evidence, not solace.

If there is good evidence for 'gaps' in natural processes, then we are happy to accept a preternatural explanation and to use this as evidence. But we should not insist that such gaps are essential to Christian faith. We don't think Dembski is doing this, but at times he seems to come close.

One useful section in Dembski's book is that by philosopher of science Del Ratzsch. Though we are not quite sure *who* decided that 'evolution is, notoriously, supposed to be undirected', Ratzsch's careful analysis of the difference between evolutionary creationism and 'intelligent design' is very useful – we hope Phillip Johnson reads it.

Much of the rest of the book consists of articles pointing out specific problems in current evolutionary theory. We have every sympathy with this, but lack the technical competence to comment further.

'God of the Gaps' Revisited

We have argued that pure determinism is incompatible with meaningful theism or personal responsibility. However, in a quantum world, we argued that there are permanent 'gaps' in determinism within which volition (human and divine) may operate. Suppose, however, that we think about 'gaps' which involve type-ii miracles or preternatural events of creation? We have argued that there is no reason for the theist or theologian to believe *a priori* that these 'must have' happened – and that nineteenth century creationists did not take such a line. We would, however, argue that there *may be* such gaps. Does this constitute 'god-of-the-gaps' theology? To us, the 'god-of-the-gaps' epithet (always used, of course, in derision) properly applies to anyone who *restricts* God to working in gaps in natural processes. But surely it cannot properly be applied to someone who just believes that there *are* gaps in such natural processes? If, as we believe, Jesus really did turn water into wine, we are frankly sceptical that any 'advance in science' will remove the 'gap' in natural sequences – but God did not work through Jesus *only* in gaps. In an article, Howard van Till states:

> The concepts of 'special creation' and 'gaps' in the developmental economy of the created world go hand in hand. In the tradition of 'God-of-the-gaps' theology, holding to such gaps plays a crucial apologetic role – gaps in the world's developmental economy could have been bridged, it is commonly argued, only by the miraculous interventions of an all-powerful creator God...[141]

Now here 'God-of-the-gaps' theology seems not to mean someone who thinks God works *only* in gaps, but anyone who thinks there are such gaps at all. We would find this unacceptable, and do not believe that Christians can apply it consistently. When the apostle Paul appealed to the 'gap' in natural processes associated with the resurrection of Jesus (eg Acts 17:31) some laughed, and presumably the Epicureans found it unacceptable because they did not believe in the possibility of such gaps. So was Paul adopting a 'god-of-the-gaps' theology? We do not believe so. The Resurrection was not, of course, a 'knock down proof' of Christianity. Sceptics could always find *some* explanation, however implausible. But apparent type-ii miracles like those done in Jesus' ministry, his Resurrection, and those seen today, do offer a powerful evidence for a personal God. Most reasonable people would see it as an 'evidence' for something beyond the physical if (say) a person is healed apparently against all scientific explanation. If it turns out that (say) the origins of life are a 'jump' which science proves unable to explain, why is this not similarly to be seen as evidence?

Van Till argues for the 'functional integrity' of creation. Granted this is a better phrase than Kaiser's 'relative autonomy', but does it simply mean that all events are in principle predictable according to regular scientific laws? We are as suspicious of any *a priori* assumption of this as of the opposite *a priori* assumption that there 'must be' creative 'gaps'. We would also question the possible assumptions of Denis Alexander who says Behe:

---

[141] Van Till (1996).

allows us to plug the gaps in our knowledge with the concept of a designer-God, an idea which is clearly a hostage to fortune; since Behe's designer God will inevitably shrink, in this view, as scientific explanations become ever more complete.[142]

This seems to contain several unwarranted assumptions. It assumes that the *only* role for Behe's 'designer God' is in the gaps – which is untrue (although admittedly at times Behe's language is ambiguous). It assumes that 'explanations will become more complete' and that this means the gaps will 'inevitably' shrink. This has not been the case over the last half century – the mechanism of DNA has turned out to be unbelievable complex and the prospects of a workable model for origins of life in terms of natural processes are bleaker than ever. Increased knowledge may fill in some gaps whilst uncovering bigger ones – as we remarked earlier one can scale one peak only to find that even higher ones stretch out above. Alexander also seems to be saying that there are *in fact* only gaps in our present *knowledge*, ie the 'gaps' are not features of nature which will turn out to be even in principle irreducible to analysis and prediction by scientific law. This *may* be true, but on what basis can we assume it *a priori*?

The early fathers did not generally reject spontaneous generation, and a case can be made that they may have found evolution acceptable – but this is not to say they would have found it *essential* to maintain this 'functional integrity'. 'Functional integrity' sounds dangerously like another term for 'physicalism' – and we have already given our reasons for rejecting this. To us, 'gaps' in natural processes are neither impossible nor essential – and that seems to us the most consistent view for theists to take.

---

[142] Alexander (1998). Much in this article is, however, useful, including a critique of Dawkins.

11

Genesis and Science Today

Synthesising Paradigms

The fundamental point of this chapter is to try to see how we may be able to bring together the Genesis teachings on creation and the findings of modern science. Before actually doing this, we need to think a little about the nature of the exercise itself.

In Section 10 we explained our critical realist views of science that are fairly common today. 'Scientific laws' are humanly created systems involving humanly invented concepts and language, which help us to explain and predict our experiences. We build 'paradigms'[1] which involve concepts, models, rules and exemplars, and through which we 'perceive' phenomena. As we know, these paradigms can sometimes change in a major way, as for example the change from Newtonian to the modern physics of relativity and uncertainty. It is, of course, possible that some such 'paradigm changes' may occur in the future. So does this mean that we can never really know anything? A point we ought to note on this is that at a certain level events are unchanged by the way they are perceived. The cavewoman knew very well that if she released a rock it fell - and if it fell on her foot it hurt. This fact remained known and unchanged throughout the successive interpretations of gravity brought forward by Aristotle, Newton and Einstein, and the development of theories of nerve communication.

We would want to apply parallel ideas to the enterprise of setting up a kind of 'super-paradigm' which synthesises physical and theological understanding. 'In the beginning God made the heaven and the earth.' This truth is unaffected whether one conceives the earth as a disc beneath a tent, a static globe, or a rotating globe hurtling through space. The Bible, properly read and understood, contains none of these particular physical concepts, though any particular generation synthesising its knowledge could combine the theological truth with the stage of

---

[1] A term popularised by T S Kuhn (1970).

science it had reached. There was nothing wrong at all in (say) scholastic Christians of the 13thC synthesising a 'super-paradigm' of their Aristotelian science and their theology. Their mistake would have been to imagine that this was the *only* physical theory consistent with their theology. As we have seen, key figures like Grosseteste and Aquinas were both entirely clear that this was not the case.

To take a second example, the Bible indicates that humans have a freedom to choose. Whether this is thought to be through interaction in the pineal gland (as Descartes), or is some property which we see as part of uncertainty physics and chaos theory, the fact of human freedom is unaltered.

Throughout history, thinking Christians have tried to synthesise a 'super-paradigm' which combines the teachings of Genesis 1-11 with their current ideas of science. There was nothing silly or misguided in doing this even if some of their science turned out later to be mistaken. In this respect we are continuing the tradition of (say) Clement, Origen, Augustine, Grosseteste, Aquinas, Bacon, Descartes, Boyle, Wesley, the nineteenth century Evangelicals and the early Fundamentalists. Their particular 'super-paradigms' might have error (eg a scholastic system implied a static and young earth because both were reasonable inferences from what was then known). We are not following their *systems* but their *approach*.

We have in this book given priority to establishing the biblical framework on origins, without consideration to science. In one sense our treatment has been 'distorted' by the need to deal with the modern young-earth creationist 'super-paradigm'. We take no delight in criticising the theological system of fellow Christians, and wish to dwell in fellowship with any who hold that view. To many however both Christians and the uncommitted (though perhaps more in America than in the UK) the young-earthers are seen as representing 'traditional' and 'Bible based' Christianity. In order to defend a traditional and Bible-based 'super paradigm', therefore, we have needed to deal in some detail with this misapprehension. What we have shown is that they and their fellow travellers misunderstand science history (Section 9), and do not represent the general mainstream of Bible-believing faith in their particular literal approach to

Genesis (Section 7) or in their understanding of the faith-science links and 'doing science from the Bible' (Section 9). Even without looking at their specific 'science' we would reject their system as inconsistent and unbiblical. At this point, then, we come finally to look at the actual scientific evidence – and to finish on the positive note of suggesting our own tentative super-paradigm to harmonise this with biblical faith.

We will give only the barest outline of our understanding of the current state of the scientific evidence. To many readers it will be irrelevant – they are not prepared to even think of writing off most of mainstream science. For the others, we may invite those better qualified than us to put material on our web site. This, however, is how we see it.

Scientific Evidence: The Big Bang

We looked in Section 4 of some of the ideas of 'the 'Big Bang' theory. A 1998 young-earth book asks sardonically:

One wonders, for example, if a religious group first put forward Big Bang cosmology, how would evolutionists have reacted?[2]

Well actually, the undoubted originator of the Big Bang theory *was* a Belgian Priest, Georges LeMaître – what one really wonders is how Christian young-earthers so unfamiliar with the subject can write on it.

Though initially some cosmologists like Fred Hoyle tried to reject the Big Bang theory (largely for fear that it supported the idea of creation), it is now universally accepted. The red shift in light from distant galaxies and the discovery of a predicted incidence of 'background radiation' are the major evidences for it. The physics associated with it enables detailed prediction of stellar evolution, and our observations of stars and galaxies are what we would expect - showing stars in different stages of a well worked out cycle.[3] There remain some anomalies, but the general evidence that the universe is some 10-14 billion years old and millions of light years across is overwhelming.

---

[2] Ankerberg & Weldon (1998) p. 249.

[3] Paul Marston, of course, is presently in a Department of Physics, Astronomy and Mathematics in the Science Faculty of a British university. See also van Till (1986) Chs. 6-7.

Astronomy involves logical reconstruction of the past, but it also enables prediction. In February 1987, a particularly spectacular type-II supernova (1987a) caused a flurry of observation as scientists rushed to test theoretical predictions based on their models of the life-cycles of stars. This shows the way in which experimental physics, historical astrophysics, theoretical stellar dynamics, etc, all form part of one continuous scientific whole. The end object is to make sense of the universe in terms of physical cause-effect laws.

Henry Morris once claimed that 'as long as man has been observing the sky, the stars have stayed absolutely the same'.[4] This statement revealed an amazing ignorance of some of the key events in the history of astronomy, eg the nova of 1572 (carefully recorded by Tycho in his *De Stella Nova* (1573)) and the supernova of 1604 (carefully recorded by Kepler in his *De Stella Nova in Pede Serpentapii* (1606)). Presumably, this was pointed out to Morris, who maintained the same approach but toned down the actual claim in later books. Study of stellar evolution is, however, an integral part of astrophysics, and it seems quite extra-ordinary for a hydraulics engineer to continue to write off huge areas of physics in this way.

In general young-earthers who wish the whole universe to be only about 6000 years old can only either relapse into 'Gossism' or come up with the wildest ideas - such as a radical reduction in the speed of light. The 'evidence' for this latter comes in a paper by Barry Setterfield which is a statistical nonsense.[5] Writing in the young-earth *Creation Research Quarterly*, G E Aardsma and D R Humphreys stated that the speed of light hypothesis 'is not warranted by the data upon which the hypothesis rest' and cite various fundamental problems and unintelligibility's within it.[6] The whole idea is plain moonshine, and conflicts at every level with the physics which has been built up over the last four centuries.

---

[4] Morris (1974) p. 234.
[5] Setterfield (1987): the worst piece of pseudo-statistics we have ever read. Bowden (1998) dedicates his book to Setterfield.
[6] Aardsma & Humphreys (1988).

Scientific Evidence: the Age and Nature of Strata

On geology there are two basic issues for Christians. The first is whether the existing strata (which no one denies exist) were laid down over long periods of time (mainstream geology) or all within a period of a few weeks during one short flood a few thousand years ago (flood geology). The second is whether or not it is possible actually to date the time periods concerned in the millions of years commonly claimed.

Flood geology is supported by a very small minority of scientists, all committed to the young-earth creationist viewpoint. In our own view there are both good historical and good contemporary reasons to believe that geological strata were laid down over long periods of time. The historical reasons are as follows:

i.   The mainstream theory developed over a period of many decades of solid empirical study.

ii. Any alternative Flood-geology theory was consistently found to be at variance with observation by scientific specialists, many of whom were committed Bible-believing Christians.

iii. A large volume of consistent and detailed study has been based on the theory.

Sometimes, of course, accepted scientific theories are later rejected, but not in these kinds of circumstances.

As we have noted, geology is, again, a historical science – but there is nothing strange about inferring the past from present observation as we do it all the time. Here are some relevant features:

1. **Radiometric dating:** It must be pointed out that all such methods were developed well after Christian geologists of the eighteenth and nineteenth centuries concluded that the earth was very ancient, and the actual timescale now often placed at the side of the geological column was developed many years after the column itself. The arguments about the accuracy of such methods are highly technical, and it has to be remembered that there are various different methods and though some may be more reliable than others they all point to an ancient earth.

2. **Heat flow from crystallising magma:** Davis Young asserts that there are rocks for which the cooling time may be calculated in tens or hundreds of thousands or even a million years.[7]

3. **Plate tectonics:** Current evidence is greatly in favour of the idea that continents are parts of plates which move across the surface of the globe. The impact of India as it moves north has been shown to be a means by which the Himalayas were created and the Tibetan plateau produced. There is simply no room for this on the Flood-geology model, as plate tectonics necessitates great periods of time after many of the strata have been laid down.

4. **Coral-reefs:** Particularly large coral-reefs (such as one in Wisconsin) would have required a very long time to grow. The fact that the coral remains are all the right way up rules out the possibility that it somehow piled up during one big flood.

5. **Palaegeographic reconstructions:** Sometimes young-earth creationists have thrown out the challenge that fossil-bearing rocks are not being formed today. This is simply untrue: geologists can cite examples today of most situations which are deemed to have given rise to structures in the strata. Arthur Fraser gives one such detailed example relating to the Torridonian sediments. There is clear evidence of raised shore lines, river-basins, etc - all within thousands of feet of rock (and all according to the young-earth model laid down in a one-year flood!).[8] Often predictions can be made and tested based on such reconstructions.

6. **Thickness:** Volumes of fossil-carrying rock are immense. The total amount of water on the globe today simply could not carry this volume of material as sediment - a problem recognised by the eighteenth-century Christian naturalists and confirmed over and again.

7. **Layering:** Different rock types are laid under different conditions. Metamorphic are originally laid down under

---

[7] Young (1977) p. 184.
[8] In Burke (1985) p. 19.

water, then changed by heat. Conglomerates are mixtures of consolidated gravel and pebbles, laid down under conditions of shallow water and vigorous cur-rents possible under flooding. Fine grained sedimentary rock can be laid down as sediment (sand), which settles out of water and is consolidated -or in desert conditions. The point is that such types of rock, laid down under different conditions, are found in layers - often up to a thousand in number - with sharp lines of demarcation between them. This indicates long periods of deposition followed by consolidation.

8. **Fossil volume:** The sheer volume of fossils in some rocks is difficult to explain other than as a result of long periods of deposition.

9. **Fossil layering:** There is a clear zoning of fossils in the rocks irrespective of whether these zonings are time-based or invariant. In general these zones follow a clear deposition order. Where they do not, there are often clear signs of folding, either in the inversion of specimens or in tracing along to actual folds. Mainstream geology explains this as a time-sequence.

What about the young-earth model? On radiometric dating, young-earthers advance various technical reasons to doubt the methods for longer periods. As noted. however. such dating is in no way important to the development of mainstream geology. On the other points in (3)-(9), they have all kinds of problems. On the 'volume' kinds of argument, even simple calculations indicate the impossibility of laying down so much rock and fossil in one year - without a hefty dose of apparently pointless miracles. On the 'structures' types of argument, in four decades of the theory (even discounting Price's earlier versions) young-earthers have produced no detailed explanations of how various structural features of the strata could conceivably have been produced by rushing flood waters. On the layering of rocks, for example, an area containing 30,000 such layers would require about eighty distinct strata to be laid each day during a one-year flood often under contrasting conditions.[9] On the correlation of fossils they have various ideas, of which the only one with any

---

[9] CF Hayward (1985) p. 124.

plausibility is that of ecological zoning. If animals, they say, were overwhelmed in their natural habitat, then similar animals would be found in similar rocks. This sounds plausible, yet in all levels of strata, creatures of varying habitats are found. What distinguishes, say, Eocene from Carboniferous is not the habitat but the particular organisms. In any detail their model simply does not fit. Why, for example, do coal seams not contain modern plants? Why is it that none of the 300 or so ancient caves found in Europe with brilliant pictures of mammoths, deer, bison, etc contain any of dinosaurs?

Young-earth creationists often cite lists of supposed difficulties for mainstream geology, but many of these are actually perfectly explicable on mainstream principles. For example they endlessly repeat the 'problem' that the complete geological column is not found anywhere. But for this to happen would require somewhere to have been continuously underwater in conditions of deposition for all earth history – a highly unlikely phenomenon. Others are supposed problems based on early conjectures long since disproved or absorbed by specialists in the field. All too frequently, too, young-earth creationists copy the citations from one to another - with the certainty of expression increasing with each re-quotation Here are some favourite ones:

1. **Fossil graveyards:** These are frequently cited as a problem, but in fact it has long been recognised that they are caused by local catastrophes and no problem at all for mainstream geology.

2. **Polystrate trees:** These are fossilised trees which stand upright in the strata. The argument goes that they could not do this if strata formed slowly over millions of years. In fact, of course, no geologist says that all strata were laid down slowly, and most such trees present no particular problem. Some young-earthers have so misunderstood their theme as to cite it as a problem that the 'same plant and insect forms which are found at the top of the seam are found at the bottom.'[10] Actually, it would be a far greater problem if they didn't, for then the tree would span

---

[10] Price (1979) p. 49.

geological ages. The need to further explore exact conditions of fossilisation for such trees is a very minor problem compared with the massive problems in Flood geology.

3. **The shrinking sun:** Howard J Van Till has presented details of the way in which some early suggestions (1979) about variations in the sun's size - soon abandoned by the scientific community - were taken up by a young-earth creationist in 1980. He took the results as definite, projected them back indefinitely and concluded that if this sun were really very ancient, then it would have been big enough to fry the earth.[11]

4. **The moon dust:** In a 1960 article in Scientific American, H Petterson conjectured about the amount of cosmic dust which might have settled on the moon, assuming it to be as old as astronomers said. The moon landing-craft was prepared for dust, but in fact no thick layer of dust was found. This was taken by young-earth creationists as proof that the moon (and therefore earth) was young. By the late 1970s, however, actual measurements of amounts of the dust in space had been made, and these showed that the layers which had accumulated on the moon were well in accord with the age usually ascribed to it. Young-earth creationists, however, ignore this later work, and continue citing earlier conjecture as though it were relevant.[12]

5. **Magnetic field:** Few young-earth books on age fail to quote Dr Thomas Barnes' work in 1973 which took the 150 years of data on changes in the earth's magnetic field, extrapolated it back exponentially for 20,000 years, and proclaims that this gave an impossible figure, so the earth must be young! Actually, there is now clear evidence that the earth's field fluctuates; it is not getting less. Yet, later papers by Barnes and others continue to cite early sources (even including Jacobs' key 1962 book, which was totally changed in later editions). The claim is still made in the

---

[11] Van Till (1986).
[12] See eg Hayward (1979) p. 142.

1996 reprint of Morris' Scientific Creationism as one of the main proofs of a young earth.[13]

6. **Footprints:** Young-earth creationists have repeatedly claimed that human footprints found in Paluxy rock beds alongside dinosaur tracks are a problem for conventional geology. Yet, in 1986, one of their main experts on this, John D Morris, showed great integrity by admitting that they had been mistaken. There was, in fact, no scientific evidence for such tracks Their film *Footprints in Stone,* was to be withdrawn – though arguments for the idea still pop up even so.[14]

7. **Human remains:** A number of human skeletons have been claimed to have been found in early strata. Alan Hayward looked at these, showing the clear evidence that each one is no such thing.[15]

8. **Surtsey:** Professor Andrews and others make much of the development of landscape on the volcanic island of Surtsey, formed in the late 1960s. Actually, all Andrews cites is geologists' 'first impressions as they wandered about'. As Christian geologist Arthur Fraser points out conventional geology has no difficulty in explaining Surtsey, and the conditions which resulted in some superficial features of age could not explain more structural features found in genuinely old rocks.[16]

Alan Hayward follows various other problems which young-earth creationists raise about mainstream geology, finding similar features in each one. What is, perhaps, most sad is that often such supposed problems continue to be quoted and re-quoted long after they have been conclusively refuted in mainstream Christian literature.

It is not worth following all this further. We see no reason at all to doubt that the basic theories of modern geology are correct though doubtless they will continue to be amended. We may remain sceptical about the precision of some of the radioactive

---

[13] Morris (1996 repr of 1985) p. 157.

[14] Eg Ian Taylor (1991) p. 109.

[15] Hayward (1979) p. 146.

[16] Cf Burke (1985) where this is discussed.

dating methods, but the bulk of church leaders have been right in believing for the last couple of centuries that the age of the earth is greatly in excess of 10,000 years.

Scientific Evidence: Evolution

Few if any would believe that no evolution at all has taken place. The Galapagos are comparatively recent volcanic islands - and no one believes that God created separately each species of finch and placed them there at that time. All the species evolved from one original type (or 'kind' as some prefer to call it). Micro-evolution, involving a mutated change in genetic coding, is a fact - and is seen in domestic species no less than in Darwin's Galapagos finches.

But what of more major changes? A range of possibilities exists:

1.Neo-Darwinism

All modern species evolved from one or a few original life forms by the main mechanism of natural selection operating on small genetic mutations. Classically, this view is represented by R A Fisher, Julian Huxley and John Maynard-Smith, and has been developed on a gene level by Richard Dawkins. Within its broad field there are figures like Stephen Jay Gould and Niles Eldredge, who suggest that evolution has proceeded in a series of 'lurches' rather than smoothly. There are also those who have suggested that genetic drift, or an in-built chemical programming, may be as important as natural selection. Whilst sometimes these may describe themselves as 'giving an alternative paradigm', we must realise that they are all variations within a theme.

A very different form of evolutionism (as we have seen) is that presented by Henry Morris. He supposes major structures in animals (specialisation for predatory habits) to have evolved by natural selection over a couple of thousand years between Eden and the flood. On the one hand, Henry Morris argues that complex organs could not possibly evolve through evolution, that mutations are practically all harmful, that random genetic change has 'only an infinitesimal chance of improving the functioning of the system', etc. On the other hand, he believes a non-divinely directed process of evolution by random mutation and natural selection. over just a few thousand years, has produced all the elaborate mechanisms of attack and defence in living creatures which would have been unnecessary before the Fall. Morris may call this process 'degeneration' rather than evolution, but this is a moral judgement not a comment on the newness and complexity of the structures involved. Few of us who watch any television nature programmes can fail to be aware of the great number of very elaborate specialist structures for defence, attack and predatory habit. In some cases it is hard to imagine how some vegetarian version of the creature could meaningfully be called the same 'kind' - and even harder to believe one could have evolved into the other in just a few thousand years.

We appreciate the motives which have led Morris and his associates into such a self-contradictory situation, and share his earnest desire that God should be glorified. But he is in the strange position of being, at one and the same time, one of the most extreme evolutionists and one of the most anti-evolutionists we know. We simply cannot make coherent sense of it. We find this version frankly incredible, and will consider only versions of the more 'orthodox' neo-Darwinism.

We have no strong view on whether or not macro-evolution (by natural selection) was the mechanism used by God to create major orders of animals. Here are some of the scientific arguments for it:

i.   **Arguments from micro-evolution** Arguments by analogy to domestic breeding (eg of dog variety) or laboratory breeding of invertebrates.

ii. **Arguments from resemblance** Arguments centred around the similarities of bone structure, embryo, behaviour and biochemistry of divergent species and genera.

iii. **Arguments from genetic resemblance.** It is frequently pointed out that the DNA of (say) a chimpanzee is 99% the same as that of a human.

iv. **Arguments from palaeontology** Arguments from the development found in fossil forms towards present-day species.

v. **Arguments from genetic mechanism** Arguments that look
   in detail at genetic processes and deduce from this the
   effects of genetic mutation within a wider model of natural
   selection.

The arguments from micro-evolution are unconvincing.
Generally the results remain interfertile, and do not change basic
structures. Micro-evolution results are compatible with a view
based on gene pools which sees selective breeding as able to
push a species only to a limit on a particular characteristic, at
which point further change becomes infinitely slow. The
argument gives, as Darwin himself used it, a powerful analogy
but nothing more.

   The arguments from resemblance do not provide any proof. It
would be quite possible to believe that God used variations on a
theme - much as Bach in his music - in a creative process not
involving direct descent. What, perhaps, constitutes a rather
stronger line of argument is that, looking, for example, at the
forelimbs of various mammals, in the words of Stephen Jay
Gould: 'An engineer, starting from scratch, could design better
limbs in each case.'[17] Adaptation of a common pattern is less
efficient in engineering terms than a purpose-built model.
Conceivably, of course, the Creator may have valued symbolic
unity of all the divergent living creatures more than he valued
engineering efficiency, but it does seem to offer some argument
for genetic descent. Genetic resemblances may be a stronger
argument than the general ones, but we know, of course, that
very small changes in coding can make a macro difference in
structure. It is not a proof of a totally natural descent of the
human from the ape-like creature. In principle, genetic
similarities are not really much different in form of argument
than the nineteenth century ones from body structure. They do,
however, enable us to better see how a small genetic mutation
could have produced new species – except that few details of
this have yet been worked out. There are also argument from
'junk' DNA – the fact that many of the DNA sequences seem
never to be 'switched on'. Though the past history of arguments
from 'vestigial organs' (many of which turn out to have some

---

[17] In Montagu (1984) p. 122.

function) may make us wary, such arguments from DNA do seem to carry some weight.

The arguments from fossils have always been controversial. In general terms the fossil record does show development: invertebrates began in the Cambrian period, fish in the Silurian, amphibians in the Devonian, reptiles in the Permian, and mammals not until the Cretaceous. What, however, we do not find is a slow gradation of fossil forms. In Darwin's day the incompleteness of the fossil record was invoked to explain the 'gaps'. Nearly one and a half centuries later this wears a bit thin – though Gould and Eldredge's theory of 'punctuated equilibria' has provided an escape clause for it. New species evolve rapidly in thousands or tens of thousands of years, and may then last for ten million almost without change. This would then explain the 'sudden' origin of new species in the fossil record, and failure to change thereafter. It must, of course, be noted that Gould is not saying that there are no transitional forms, nor that change was instantaneous (though, to his justifiable annoyance, he is sometimes quoted as though he were). But the implication of the theory, if true, is that the fossil record never is likely to tell us whether new species appeared literally instantaneously or, as Gould supposes, in a rapid evolutionary 'lurch'. Missing links may be found, but missing chains are likely to stay missing.

Finally, what of arguments from genetical processes'? Christian Professor of Genetics R J Berry points out that, whilst Darwin knew nothing of such processes, it is incorrect to assume that nothing is known today.[18] He claims that it is now possible to reconstruct the speciation process in the laboratory. This obviously increases the circumstantial evidence for macro-evolution as a past event.

Our own view is that there is good circumstantial, though not conclusive, evidence that macro-evolution occurred. We remain open to the degree to which type-i or type-ii miracles were involved.

---

[18] Eg in Berry (1988) p. 114.

Scientific Evidence: Human Origins

There is now a fairly clear consensus on some aspects of the origins of modern humans. The evidence comes from several sources:

1. Evidence of skeleton finds and associated artefacts.
2. Evidence of from mitochondrial DNA (mDNA) which enables a trace of female descent.
3. Evidence from Y chromosomal studies which enables a trace of male descent.
4. Evidence of similarity and diversity in present human DNA.

Modern microbiologists have identified 'mitochondria', minute organelles in the human cell which are the site of much of its energy metabolism. Mitochondria have their own DNA (with about 16,000 bases), distinct from that of the cell nucleus. The mitochondria, therefore, have their own evolutionary development – not obviously connected with the major physiological developments shown in the organism carrying them. These can be used to trace family trees for the mitochondria, which are also, of course, the family trees for the organisms. This technique has been applied to human fossils. The human *male* sperm does not have room to package mitochondria, and they are contributed to the organism only through the *female* ovum. Tracing back to try to find the time of a single ancestral female, Allan Wilson came to a surprising result:

> The transformation of archaic to anatomically modern forms of Homo Sapiens occurred first in Africa, about 100,000 to 140,000 years ago, and that all present-day humans are descendants of that African population.[19]

What was surprising to palaeontologists used to thinking in terms of millions of years, was how recent this was. Whilst there are still some uncertainties about mitochondrial DNA, its general results seem now fairly well accepted. Richard Leakey, a traditional 'bone based' anthropologist, has described how those from his background have had to come to terms with

---

[19] Wilson in *Science* (1987) vol 237 (2nd October) p. 1292 (see also Wilson et al (1987)).

this.[20] He points out that Wilson's initial 1987 results were based on only 145 individuals, and was heavily criticised.[21] By April 1992 they had checked some 4,000 individuals with the same results.[22] Leakey summarises:

> The mitochondrial DNA in each human being can be traced back to a single female who lived in Africa over 100,000 years ago.[23]

The Y is the second smallest human chromosome having an estimated size of 60 million base pairs of DNA. In the 1990s there began an explosion of publications based on comparisons of Y chromosomes, Various authors have attempted to estimate the time since the last common human Y chromosome consistent with the absence of observed variation. Studies agree that this was less than 250000 years, most give less, and one study summarises:

> A coherent picture is now beginning to emerge that places both our common ancestral Y chromosome and mitochondrial DNA molecule in the late middle Pleistocene, only slightly before the hypothesised origin, based on fossil data, of anatomically modern humans.[24]

So 'Mitochondrial Eve' and 'Y-Chromosomal Adam' (as some have dubbed them), both come from about the same period and lived somewhere in Africa!

Before Christians run away with the idea that scientists now picture these two individuals as alone in the world, we have to note that the following two statements are NOT equivalent:

1. All humans ever born descend from two individuals Adam and Eve.
2. All present humans have a common female ancestor M-eve and a common male ancestor y-adam.

To illustrate this consider the diagrams of Model 1 and Model 2 below.

In the first diagram (Model 1) every human living in all generations descend from 'Adam' and 'Eve'. In the second

---

[20] Leakey (1992) Ch. 13.

[21] Eg Gee (1992), Hedges (1992).

[22] Wilson & Cann (1992).

[23] Leakey (1992) p. 220.

[24] Hammer and Zedura (1996) p. 125.

diagram every 3rd generation female descends in the female line from M-Eve (Mitochondrial Eve), and every 3rd generation married male in the male line from y-adam (Y-chromosome Adam). The dotted boxes show this descent. By the fourth generation everyone will have M-Eve *and* y-adam as ancestors – but many will actually have *all three* of the original couples as ancestors.

Model 1: Only One Ancestral Pair

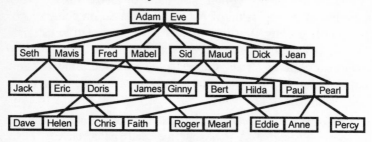

Model 2: Multiple Ancestors

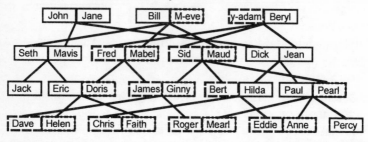

The evidence that we all have a common female and male ancestor in the very recent past tends to suggest that there was a narrow 'bottleneck' around this time. The scientists, however, are not seeing this as a type-A model but a type-B. Geneticist Francisco Ayala argues that diversity in other parts of the human genome and theories of gene coalescence point to a minimum breeding population of around 4,000 (implying a total population of some 15,000).[25] Some of the statistics used may need refinement, but we do have to be clear that the second model is what scientists are suggesting. Ayala also states:

---

[25] Ayala (1995) p. 1395; see also Ayala's chapter in Warren Brown (1998).

The deepest split in the genealogy is dates at ~156,000 years ago, which thus estimates the time when modern humans spread from Africa throughout the world.

Neanderthal man, who appeared some 200,000 years ago, was once widely pushed as a human ancestor. A recent study now says:

> Neanderthals are strikingly different from modern humans in almost every area of the skeleton... Neanderthal belonged to a species entirely different from our own with a relatively remote common ancestry.[26]

Neanderthals overlapped in time with modern man though died out in Europe around 34,000 years ago soon after modern man appeared there. DNA evidence now seems to show that there was no interbreeding between the two groups, and also (incidentally) that the suggestion of some Christians that Neanderthals are sick or degenerate moderns is untenable.

Most palaeontologists assume that modern man evolved from *Homo Erectus,* though there seems no way to test this. However they appeared, *Homo Sapiens Sapiens* spread out from Africa as hunter-gatherers. Modern races could have developed from local 'bottlenecks' around 70,000 or less years ago.[27] They reached Australia around 35-50,000 years BP, Europe some 30-40,000 years BP, and crossed the Bering land bridge to America just before it disappeared as the ice age water melted some 12,000 years ago.[28] Recent suggestions that modern Europeans reached America in 25,000 BC[29] are not at present generally accepted.

This Palaeolithic ice age saw the explosion of the brilliant art found in caves. People sometimes have the impression of 'cavemen' as living in shallow tiny and bleak caves. One of the present authors visited a Palaeolithic cave in Northern Spain and was astounded at the almost cathedral like spaciousness and the pleasant even temperature. Just as stunning was the art - antelopes, bison, mammoths, horses and human hands (no

---

[26] Tattersall (1998) p. 158.
[27] Cf Stanley Ambrose (1998).
[28] See eg Jones (1993) p. 162, Hammer and Zegura (1996).
[29] Cf Roger Lewin (1998).

dinosaurs though!). Some 300 such caves - large and small - have been found in Europe with Palaeolithic art.[30]

The change from hunter-gathering to agriculture seems to have begun in the Levant (roughly modern Israel) and arose out of Natufan culture. One recent study asserts:

> no field project outside of the Levant has yet exposed any indication of a prehistoric entity that resembles the Natufan.[31]

During the Late Glacial maximum (up to c 12,500 BC) the area was cold and dry, although there were coastal forests. Climatic chances around 11,000 BC provided a wealth of food resources, and the Natufan culture emerged around 11,000-10,800 BC. The Levant then contained an oak-dominated parkland and woodland that provided the highest biomass of foods exploitable by humans. The people ate a wide variety of fruits, seeds and vegetal foods, and hunted gazelle, wild goats and cattle, and pigs. The Natufans lived in semi subterranean houses, in settled villages. In the younger Dryas period (9,000 to 8,300 BC) saw colder, dryer conditions, and this may have stimulated a move to cultivation rather than harvesting natural produce. This was the 'Neolithic' or new stone age, a development of Natufan culture. One interesting find is that Jericho seems to contain evidence of communal building and a tower (possibly with a mud brick shrine on its top) with an unknown function.[32]

Neolithic culture spread throughout the world - although there were, of course, still areas where hunter-gatherers predominated.

Geneticist Steve Jones, who is not a Christian, notes that the new farmers had a far more restricted diet than hunter gatherers, and also makes the interesting comment:

> Hunter gatherers had an easier life than the first farmers. The modern King Bushmen who still live in this way only need to work for fifteen hours a week to feed their families, far fewer than those who have moved to the farming economy and less than the time which most western industrial workers have to spend at work to buy food... Perhaps the extra work involved explains the Bible's disparaging tone about the new economic system: Adam, on the expulsion from his hunter-gatherer Eden was admonished, 'Cursed

---

[30] See Bahn (1996) pp. 204-5.
[31] Ofer Bar-Yosef (1998) p. 160.
[32] Ofer Bar-Yosef (1998) p. 170.

is the ground because of you... therefore the Lord God sent him forth from the Garden of Eden to till the ground from which he was taken.'[33]

Jones also points out that the Biblical Cain 'set bounds to fields' and 'with agriculture the idea of ownership of land was born.' When one group of 20th century Kenyan hunter-gatherers settled into farming:

> Great inequalities of wealth soon appeared depending on who obtained the best land. When harvests were bad the poor starved while the rich grew fat. Competition among males to gain a mate increased, so that the beginning of farming marked a new campaign in the battle of the sexes...'[34]

He sees the process as extending to form competing nation states - a comparatively recent phenomenon. Another non-Christian, Richard Leakey, also argues that hunter-gatherers were fundamentally peaceful, that increased bloodshed and strife came with farming, and that military strife is rare in paintings of 5,000-10000 years ago and absent in pre-Neolithic times.[35]

As far as concerns evidence for any kind of cataclysmic flood, it is well known that cultures throughout the world tend to have versions of a great flood story. As to the location of the Genesis flood, we have little clue other than that the ark came to rest on the 'mountains' (plural) of Arrarat (Gen 8:4), ie somewhere in the range of what is now Turkey. A 1999 joint Time-Life and BBC TV programme, presented by Cambridge Archaeologist Dr Kate Spence, gave the increasingly plausible hypothesis of two academics from Columbia university: Drs Bill Ryan and Walter Pitman.[36] This is that, around 5600 BC there was a catastrophic inundation in the Black Sea area. As waters rose at the end of the last ice age, a sudden breach in a previous Bosphorous land portal, caused a cataclysmic marine flood in the previous fertile area around a much smaller lake in the present Black Sea area. Descendants of the survivors are likely to have reached Nineveh, where the Gilgameresh version of the flood story was

---

[33] Jones (1993) p. 166.
[34] Jones (1993) p. 173.
[35] Leakey (1992) p. 233.
[36] There is also a booklet.

found in a 7th century BC library. It is possible that it relates in some way to the Genesis account. David Rohl's suggestions[37] for a flood at a somewhat later date are also interesting, but, unless there is a more widespread acceptance amongst experts of his radical redating of the period, any conclusion would be premature. A third suggestion was recently made by research hydrologist Ward Sanford to the Affiliation of Christian Geologists.[38] Sanford suggests that the flood might have been a massive marine inpouring to the present Persian Gulf over some months. All these suggestions would need more work.

As for the various claims that the ark has been 'found' on some or the other mountain in the area, we remain very sceptical. Some are manifestly natural outcrops, others are not the shape described in Genesis, and none is convincing.

Adam and Anthropology

How can Genesis 1-3 (or perhaps one might say Genesis 1-11) be related to current scientific ideas? Any synthesis must, of course, be tentative, for as Bacon said, our interpretations of God's word (in theology) and of God's works (in science) can both be mistaken. Nevertheless it is right, as we have argued, to look for harmony. On the basic question of the origins of the first humans there are three possible alternatives:

1. The first humans formed instantaneously from basic elements in a spectacular type-ii miracle.
2. The first humans resulted from a crucial genetic mutation from previous primates.
3. There were no particular 'first' humans, human qualities emerged slowly in a particular breeding population.

It should be noted that some 'Fundamentalists' who are often cited as ardent 'creationists' (eg G F Wright[39]) have actually been open to the second of these. We are, of course, often told how similar is the DNA of humans to that of other primates, so who knows what kind of change could be crucial to a 'threshold' change? Supposing that *homo sapiens sapiens* did descend from

---

[37] Rohhl (1998) Chs. 4-5.
[38] Not yet published – see our website for any news.
[39] CF Numbers (1992) p. 34. This view was not uncommon.

homo erectus, there is presently very little evidence to show what this process might have looked like or how 'sudden' it was. There may be questions about the point at which consciousness of sin entered the human race, as there are about the human individual. We don't feel that presently enough is known empirically to enable a sensible synthesis to be made.

Aside from issues of the process, the following (as we explored in Section 8) are possible views of whether 'Adam and Eve' were individuals:

1. **Adam and Eve as Literal Progenitors:**
   - Model-A: All of the species *homo sapiens sapiens* descend from one original pair (traditional Adam and Eve).
   - Model-B: All modern humans share a common ancestral pair.
2. **No individual Adam and Eve:** This is the view that 'The Man' and 'the Woman' in Genesis 2-3 are not meant to refer to individuals at all, but are a graphic portrayal of Everyman's condition of sin and separation from God.
3. **Individuals as Federal Heads:** This is the view that 'the man' in Gen 2-3 was a literal individual but not a physical ancestor of all modern humans. Rather he was a federal head, whose particular sin was a benchmark transgression of an explicitly recognised moral law, epitomising the condition of the old humanity.

In what ways can the 'traditional' (1) model-A be held? One is in a radical rejection of current anthropology, in the style of Lubenow.[40] Lubenow writes courteously, but follows standard young-earth rejection of what he calls 'the double revelation theory'[41] - ie the approach to science and faith taken by all scientist-Christians of note since the scientific revolution. He credits Neal Gillespie's muddled analysis of Darwin as though it makes sense[42], and makes the common young-earth assumption that somehow 'evolutionists' have inveigled their ideas into assessments of earth age, solar age, and other 'ancient universe'

---

[40] Lubenow (1992) – reprinted 1998.
[41] Lubenow (1992) p. 244.
[42] Lubenow (1992) p. 191.

ideas first developed by scientists who all rejected evolution. He rightly notes that his assertions that Exod 20:11 settles the earth age issue are made 'at risk of being called simplistic'.[43] However, he does present well the current confusion and disarray amongst paleoanthropologists on a supposed line of descent for humankind. One does not need to accept the whole untenable young-earth package in order to recognise flaws both in the dating techniques and in the prevailing ideas on human development. We would therefore recognise the possibility of the final emergence of some radically different view of origins – though are unconvinced by that given by Lubenow himself.

But can Gen 2-3 be reconciled with current scientific 'orthodoxy'? If one wants to keep an (1) Model-A 'traditional' Adam and Eve model, then it would seem that Gen 2-3 has to be pushed back to sometime at least around 150,000 years ago – and if Ayala is right then much earlier. Christian anthropologist James Buswell takes this view.[44] It would, however, imply a fairly radical break between Genesis 3:24 and Genesis 4:1 since people in 150,000 BC did not grow crops, even less 'found cities'. Genesis 4 onwards seems to clearly describe a settlement and farming culture that is Neolithic or later.

So can we put a Model-A 'Adam and Eve' in Neolithic times? The Christian anthropologist E K Victor Pearce gives a fair amount of detail correlating the subsequent chapters of Genesis with the results of the scientific finding of the Iron Age etc, and presents evidence to show that the biblical genealogies fall well within the ranges of years needed to fit within present margins of scientific accuracy on dating.[45] The person named 'Adam' in the start of the genealogies of 5:1 must indeed be late Natufan or early Neolithic. Pearce himself suggested that 'man' in Genesis 1 was a hunter-gatherer whilst the 'man' and 'woman' in Genesis 2-3 were Neolithic. He also suggested that we might all descend from that Neolithic pair, the world being repopulated with a second wave of migration. This is possible, but all the recent evidence seems to indicate that we do *not* all descend

---

[43] Lubenow (1992) p. 225.
[44] Buswell (1975) – but similar views were confirmed by him to us in personal conversations in the summer of 1998.
[45] Pearce (1993) ch. 8.

from a second wave of (Neolithic) migration. There was migration, but the evidence seems to point to genetic continuity in other parts of the earth. On current evidence even a (1) Model-B type Adam and Eve are unlikely – though it may be possible.

The second approach (2) has been argued - seeing the account as meant to teach theology rather than proto-history. This would imply a transition from issues of timeless spiritual truth in Genesis 2-4 to a truly proto-historical treatment of genealogies. We do not, however, presently know of any attempt to follow this line convincingly, and it is not our own understanding.

The third approach (3) is to adopt a 'Federal Head' approach, and think of 'the man' and 'the woman' of Genesis 2-3 as real individuals located around the late Natufan period. 'Eden' would be the plentiful and pleasant forests of Levant (which includes Israel),[46] and 'the man' was to 'cultivate' (or 'serve') and 'guard' the garden. The verb to 'serve' seems to indicate an intended ecological role, whilst the word 'guard' means to 'exercise great care over to the point if necessary of guarding.'[47] The fall into sin is also a failure to rise to the task of serving and guarding the environment. The breaking of God's moral law is associated, of course, with a breakdown in human relationships - typified by that deepest of relationships the marriage bond. This progresses to the nuclear family - and the violence is exacerbated by the move to farming and settlement typified by Cain. The Adam-Eve-Cain-Abel story may relate to particular benchmark individuals - but they are also the story of mankind.

On this view, what Paul is saying in Romans is that the individual 'Adam' sinned in breaking an expressly revealed command. Paul states:

> death spread to all men because all men sinned - sin indeed was in the world before the law was given, but sin is not counted where there is no law. Yet death reigned from Adam to Moses even over those whose sins were not like the transgression of Adam who is a type of the one who was to come...' (Rom 5:12-14)

---

[46] There is no consensus identifying the river in Eden which splits into four - so we cannot say where this was though it is around this area.

[47] Hamilton (1990) p. 171.

Accepting, for the present, that Paul is indeed taking Adam as an individual and not an 'Everyman' type for the Messiah, 'Adam' was given an express command. In a sense this *was* a 'law', but after the expulsion from Eden it obviously could no longer apply as the situation had changed (ie there was no forbidden fruit). Since the 'law' came only with Moses, and since sin 'does not count if there is no law', would this mean that between Adam and Moses no one sinned? Obviously not, according to Paul. Even without a specific revealed command to break, individuals still 'opted in' to the sin epitomised in a more explicit sense by Adam, sin revived and they (spiritually) died.

Now all Christians believe that those with faith in God - before and after the time of Christ - are saved through his one righteous act of going to the cross. It is by faith that we 'opt in' to God's free gift of grace. It is by sinning that we 'opt in' to the 'old Adam'. Paul specifically illustrates this in terms of the ones who were 'between Adam and Moses', of whom else should he speak in those days and to that audience? Is it essential to his theme, though, to reject the idea that contemporaries or those before Adam could 'opt in' to this sin principle he represents? It would, after all, only be analogous to the time-independent effect of the 'one righteous act' of Christ?

We are not, of course, saying that the apostle had this explicitly in mind when he wrote the Epistle to the Romans. Today, questions are being asked which would not have occurred to Paul, based on information that he did not have. What we are saying is that the doctrine he puts forward may be perfectly compatible with such a suggestion.

What is central to Pauline doctrine is that all men and women have sinned, and as part of the 'old Adam' or 'old humanity' stand under the judgement of God. This is true whether (like Adam and the Jews after Moses) they broke specific commands, or simply went against their own consciences (cf Rom 2:24-25). All need the salvation which is there through the righteous act of Jesus the Messiah - of whom Adam (with his archetypal act of specific sin) is a 'type'. Adam is not merely representative 'old man' but also a representative (in Paul's thinking) of the Jews - as they too had explicit 'revealed' commands. Similarly Jesus is not only representative second Man (New Man) but also, as Jesus *the Messiah*, representative Jew.

If we adopt this basic approach, a very interesting recent book by David M Rohl[48] suggests an actual location for 'Eden'. Rohl advocates a radical redating of ancient chronologies which at present is not generally accepted, but irrespective of this his book presents some evidence on 'Eden' based on the work of the late Reginald Arthur Walker. He assumes (as the biblical writers seem to) that the Noachic flood brought no radical change in the earth's surface and that the present Tigris and Euphrates are the ones meant in Gen 2:14. The Genesis text describes a location where 'water sprang up in certain places and flowed across the land' (Gen 2:6). Rohl suggests that a location at the side of the present Lake Urmia is just such a location. Gen 2:10 states that four rivers divided up from the same fundamental source. The region Rohl identifies is marked by some major water springs, and the Tigris and Euphrates do indeed source from the NW and SW respectively. Rohl identifies the Genesis *Gihon* with the *Aras/Araxes* (sourcing on the NE of the area) and the Pishon with the Uizhun:

> Which rises from several springs located near Mount Sahand (an extinct volcano east of Lake Urmia).[49]

Local soil is 'red' which reflects the word for earth (similar to 'Adam') which implies a red colouring. This location is in Armenia, not in the immediate vicinity but but within the general Middle East region in which the Natufan culture emerged. Rohl also makes various suggestions about a localised flood in the area, though we would need more archaeological information to consider this in an informed way. The Eden location, however, may well have some validity. Certainly it sounds as though in that period the area could have seemed like a 'paradise' with lush vegetation.

We have, of course, to add that – in the tradition of Augustine and those who followed him in the first one and a half millennia of the church – we would want to take 'some parts literally and some parts allegorically' about Eden. As Origen said, God did

---

[48] David M Rohl (1998).

[49] Rohl (1998) p. 53.

not plant a garden 'in the manner of a gardener'. He did not walk literally 'in the cool of the evening' in the garden – leaving footprints in the soil. This last is an image of a rich landowner who would come out in the cool of the evening to stroll in his property and see how the tenants or servants had been doing. It is a metaphorical or symbolic way of speaking – but it relates an intended truth about God. The origins of present human culture may indeed have originated here – together with a new awareness of sin. But the form of the account in Genesis 2-3 is intentionally a narrative saga. It is not a historical description in the manner (say) of Luke's gospel. The depiction of a 'tree' of knowledge of good and evil is no more intended 'literally' than God digging holes to plant trees or later tramping through the garden in the evening. But what more obvious a symbol than two 'trees' in a vegetation paradise such as it would have been?

We would not wish to be at all dogmatic in our synthesis. Both science and theology are too uncertain to do this. But what we do believe is that the traditional approach to Genesis is looking beneath the surface to find its real meaning. It is interesting to find that non-Christians like Richard Dawkins, Steve Jones and Richard Leakey (amongst many others) not only share the Bible's view of what is different to humankind (language, community and morality) but repeatedly return to its imagery. It is saying profound things both to individuals and to society. Some earlier generations' false optimism with the supposed future of an earthbound humanity in utopia is now largely dead. We recognise, what the Bible always knew, that the condition of the old humanity is hopeless without a radical breakthrough represented in the cross and resurrection. Humanity has the unique capacity to rise. The way to it is through Jesus - though it cannot arrive at perfection in the present human environment.

So What?

Though we hope readers have found it interesting, this book has not been written merely to interest. We have sought to show that a true, biblical Christianity, which takes the approach (though not always the specific conclusions) of mainstream Christian leaders throughout history, is compatible with the broad sweep of modern science. There may, of course, be aspects both of theology and science which are presently mistaken. But our contention is that in general a synthesis of the two may be constructed which 'makes the best sense' of our human experiences. This, however, has implications. If God really is there, and Jesus really did die on the cross for the sins of the world, then this places a demand for a response on every human being. The New Testament is not interested in 'belief' in merely intellectual terms. A 'faith' in Christ means a repentance, a renouncing of sin, and an acceptance of the work of Christ on the cross for oneself. We will repeat here what we wrote at the end of our last book *Christianity, Evidence and Truth*. Its relevance is no less whether at the end of a more popular book, or one which goes into greater depth. Jesus once said: 'Unless you turn and become like little children you will never enter the kingdom of heaven.' (Mat 18:3).

To become a Christian a person must begin talking personally to God who is himself a person.
1. Confessing his or her failings and confirming a willingness to do God's will.
2. Thanking God for the forgiveness offered through Christ's work in dying for him or her.
3. Asking Christ to enter his or her life and share it.
It is good to put one's prayer to God in one's own words. Some people, however, may find this difficult at first, so here is a prayer of commitment which could be used:

Heavenly Father

I am sorry that I have not come to you before, and I repent of not living in your world in your way. Now I want to do your will.

Please forgive me for the things I have done wrong.

I thank you for sending your son, Jesus, and accept his death for my wrongdoing. I accept your forgiveness and receive your son Jesus into my life as my Saviour and my Lord. I intend henceforward to live for you as his disciple.

Thank you for the help of your Holy Spirit in leading me to this point of decision. I ask you now for him to fill me with power to live and love for you day by day.

Amen

BIBLIOGRAPHY

Aardsma, G E & Humphreys DR (1988)
'Has the speed of Light Decayed recently?' *Creation Research Quarterly,* vol
  25 (1988) pp 36-45
Alexander, Denis (1998) *Does evolution have any religious significance?*
  (Public Lecture 2nd March 1998) CiS (also on www.csis.org.uk)
Allegro, John (1973) *The Sacred Mushroom and the Cross* Hodder
Ambrose *Hexameron* in *The Fathers of the Church* (Tr J J Savage, 1961)
  Cath U of Am Pr
Ambrose, Stanley (1998) 'Later Pleistocene population bottlenecks...' *Journal
  of Human Evolution* vol 34 no 6 (June 1998) pp. 623-651
Anderson, Leith (1992) *A Church for the Twenty-first Century* Bethany House
Anderson, Norman (1990) *Islam in the Modern World, A Christian
  Perspective* Apollos
Andrews, E H (1977) *Is Evolution Scientific?* Evangelical Pr
Andrews, E H (1978) *From Nothing to Nature* Evangelical Pr
Andrews, E H (1980) *God, Science and Evolution* Evangelical Pr
Andrews, E H (1986) *Christ and the Cosmos* Evangelical Pr
Andrews, E H et al (Eds) (1986) *Concepts in Creationism* Evangelical Pr
Andrews, E H, Gitt, W, & Ouweneel, W J (Eds) (1986) *Concepts in
  Creationism* Evangelical Pr
Ankerberg, John & Weldon, John (1998) *Darwin's Leap of Faith* Harvest
  House
Aquinas, Thomas *Summa Theologicae* (Tr Dominican Fathers, 1912)
    Paternoster
Armstrong, D M (1968, 1993) *A Materialist Theory of the Mind* Routledge
Ashwell, A (1880-2) *A Life of Samuel Wilberforce* Murray
Atkins, P (1981) *The Creation* W H Freeman
Atkinson, David (1980) *The Message of Genesis 1-11* IVP
Augustine *The Literal Meaning of Genesis* (Tr J H Taylor, 1982) Newman
Ayer, A J (1936, 1946) *Language Truth and Logic* Gollancz
Ayer, A J (1956) *The Problem of Knowledge* Penguin
Ayer, A J (1978) *Interview in 'The Listener'* 2nd March 1978
Bacon, Francis (1605) *Of the Advancement of Learning*
Bacon, Francis (1620) *Novum Organum*
Bacon, Francis (1734) *Valerius Terminus*
Bahn, Paul G (1996) 'New Developments in Pleistocene Art' *Evolutionary
  Anthropology* Vol 4 No 4 (1995-6)
Baker, John A (1964) *The Theology of Jewish Christianity* (Tr from Jean
  Dalielou) Darton
Balleine, G R (1908) *A History of the Evangelical Party in the Church of
  England* Longmans
Barbour, Ian (1966) *Issues in Science and Religion* SCM
Barbour, Ian G (1974) *Myths, Models and Paradigms* SCM
Barbour, Ian G (1998) *Religion and Science* SCM
Barclay, Oliver (1997) *Evangelicals in Britain 1935-1995* IVP

Barnes, Eric Christian (1998) 'Probabilities and Epistemic Pluralism' *Brit J Phil Sci,* 49 (1998) 31-47

Barnes, Thomas (1973) *Origins and Destiny of the Earth's Magnetic Field* Creation Life

Barnett, Paul (1986) *Is the New Testament History?* Hodder

Bartholomew, J (1984) *God of Chance* SCM

Bartholomew, M (1973) "Lyell and Evolution" *British Journal for the History of Science* Vol 6:23 (1973) p. 266

Bartholomew, Michael (1980) 'The Singularity of Lyell' *History of Science* (1980) pp. 276-293

Bar-Yosef, Ofer (1998) 'The Naftufian Culture in the Levant, Threshold to the Origins of Agriculture' *Evolutionary Anthropology* Vol 6 No 5 (1998) pp. 159-170

Basil *Hexameron* (Tr A Clare, 1963) Cath Un of Am Pr

Bayes, Thomas (1763) *Essay Towards Solving a Problem in the Doctrine of Chances*

Baynes, K & Bohman, J (1987) *After Philosophy: End or Transformation* MIT

Bebbington, David (1990) *Patterns in History* Apollus

Behe, Michael (1996) *Darwin's Black Box* Free Pr

Berry, R J (1982) *Neo-Darwinism* Edward Arnold

Berry, R J (1988) *God and Evolution* Hodder

Berry, R J (1996) *God and the Biologist* Apollos

Berry, R J & Jeeves, M (1998) *Science, Life and Christian Belief* Apollos

Beveridge, W I (1968) *The Art of Scientific Investigation* Heinemann

Beveridge, W I (1968) *The Art of Scientific Investigation* Heinemann

Black, Max (1971) *A Companion to Wittgenstein's Tractatus* CUP

Blackburn, Simon (1996) *Oxford Dictionary of Philosophy* OUP

Blackmore, Vernon & Page, Andrew (1989) *Evolution, the Great Debate* Lion

Blaiklock, E M (1983) *Man or Myth?* Anzea

Blake, R M et al (1960) *Theories of Scientific Method* U of Wa Pr

Blocher, Henri (1984) *In the Beginning* IVP

Blomberg, Craig (1987) *The Historical Reliability of the Gospels* IVP

Bloor, D (1976) *Knowledge and Social Imagery* Routledge

Born, M (1949) The Natural Philosophy of Cause and Chance OUP

Boslough, John (1985) Stephen Hawking's Universe Collins

Bowden, M (1982) *The Rise of the Great Evolution Fraud* Sovereign Pr

Bowden, Malcolm (1998) *True Science Agrees With The Bible* Sovereign Pr

Bowler, Peter (1976) *Fossils and Progress* Science History Pub

Bowler, Peter (Pb Edn. 1992) *The Eclipse of Darwinism* John Hopkins

Bowler, Peter (1984) *Evolution: The History of an Idea* U of Ca Pr

Boyd, R et al (1991) *The Philosophy of Science* MIT

Boyle, R (1688) *A Disquisition...*

Boyle, Robert *Of the High Veneration Man's Intellect Owes to God*

Boyle, Robert (1690) , *The Christian Virtuoso*

Boyle, Robert (1744) *Works* Miller

Braithwaite, R B (1953) *Scientific Explanatio* Harper

Broadbent, E H (1931) *The Pilgrim Church* P&I

Brooke, John Hedley (1991) *Science and Religion* CUP

Brooker, Peter (1992) *Modernism/Postmodernism* Longman

Brooks, Jim (1985) *Origins of Life* Lion

Brown, Colin (1984) *Miracles and the Critical Mind* Paternoster

Brown, Colin (1985) *That You May Believe* Paternoster

Brown, Colin (1987) *History & Faith* IVP

Brown, Colin (Ed) (1978) *The New International Dictionary of New Testament Theology* 3 Vols Paternoster

Brown, F K (1961) *Fathers of the Victorians* CUP

Brown, H I (1987) *Observation and Objectivity* OUP

Brown, R K (1961) *Fathers of the Victorians* CUP

Brown, Warren (Ed) (1998) *Whatever Happened to the Soul?* Fortress Pr

Browne, Janet (1995) *Charles Darwin, Voyaging* Pimlico

Bruce (1943, 1961) *The New Testament Documents, Are They Reliable?* IVP

Bruce, F F (1984) *Jesus and Christian Origins Outside the New Testament* Hodder

Bruce, F F (1988) *The Canon of Scripture* Chapter House

Brueggemann, Walter (1982) *Genesis* John Knox Pr

Bryan, William Jennings & Mary Baird *The Memoirs of William Jennings Bryan* Winston

Buchwald, Jed Z & Smith, George E (1997) 'Thomas S Kuhn 1922-1996' *Philosophy of Science*, 64 (June 1997) 361-376

Buckland, William (1820) *Vindiciae Geologicae* OUP

Buckland, William (1823) *Relinquiae Diluvianae* John Murray

Buckland, William (1836) *Geology and Mineralogy Compared with Reference to Natural Theology* Pickering

Buffon, G I (1778) *Epoques de la Nature*

Burchfield, Joe (1975) *Lord Kelvin and the Age of the Earth* McMillan

Buridan, Jean *Quaestiones Super Octo Physicorum*

Burke, Derek (Ed) (1985) *Creation and Evolution* IVP

Burnett, Thomas (1684) *The Theory of the Earth* MARC

Buswell, James (1975) "Creationist Views on Human origins' *Christianity Today* 8 August 1975

Caird, G B (1980) *The Language and Imagery of the Bible* Westminster

Calvin, John *Commentary on Genesis,* (Tr J King , 1965) Banner of Truth

Campbell, Neil A *Biology* (3rd edition, 1993) Cummings

Cannon, S F (1978) *Science in Culture* Dawson

Carr, E H (1987) *What is History?* Penguin

Cassuto, U (1961) *A Commentary on the Book of Genesis Part 1* (Tr I Abrahams)

Chalmers, A F (1982) *What is This Thing Called Science?* OUP

Chalmers, David (1996) *The Conscious Mind: In Search of a Fundamental Theory* OUP

Chalmers, Thomas (1814) *The Evidence and Authority of the Christian Revelation* Blackwood

Cicero *The Nature of the Gods*

Clark, Harold W (1966) *Crusader for Creation* Pacific

Clark, J W & Hughes T M (1890) *The Life and Letters of Adam Sedgwick* 2 Vols CUP

Clark, R E D (1961) *Christian Belief and Science* English U Pr

Clayton, Philip (1997) *God and Contemporary Science* Eerdmans

Cohn, Norman (1996) *Noah's Flood* Yale U Pr

Colish, Marcia (1994) *Peter Lombard* (Vol 1) Brill

Colson F H & G H Whitaker (1991) *Philo* Vol 1

Copernicus, Nicolas (1543) *Revolutions of the Heavenly Spheres*

Coppleston, F C (1964) *A History of Philosophy* Image

Coppleston, F S (1989) *Christ or Mohammed?* Islam's Challenge

Cottingham, John (Ed) (1992) *The Cambridge Companion to Descartes* CUP

Couvalis, George (1997) *The Philosophy of Science* Sage

Cranfield, C E B (1980) *Romans* 2 Vols T & T Clark

Cray, G et al (1997) *The Post-Evangelical Debate* Triangle

Crick, Francis (1994) *The Astonishing Hypothesis: The Scientific Search for the Soul* Touchstone

Croft, L R (1988) *How Life Began* Evangelical Pr

Crouzel, Henri (1989) *Origen* T & T Clark

Cupitt, Don (1984) *The Sea of Faith* BBC

Darrow, Clarence (1934) *The Story of My Life* Scribner

Darwin, Charles (1859) *The Origin of Species* Murray

Darwin, Francis (1887) *The Life and Letters of Charles Darwin* London

Davies, Paul (1980) *Other Worlds* Dent

Davies, Paul (1992) *The Mind of God* Penguin

Davies, Paul (1983) *God and the New Physics* Penguin

Dawkins, R (1989) *The Selfish Gene* (2nd Edn.) OUP

Dawkins, R (1995) *River Out of Eden* Penguin

Dawkins, R (1986) *The Blind Watchmaker* Penguin

Dawkins, R (1996) *Climbing Mount Improbable* Penguin

Dawkins, R (1998) *Unweaving the Rainbow* Penguin

Dawson, J W (1880) *The Origin of the World According to Revelation and Science* (2nd Edn.) Hodder and Stoughton

Day, Allan (1998) 'Interpreting the Biblical Creation Accounts' *Science and Christian Belief* October 1998 pp. 115-144.

Deedat, Ahmed (1987) *Crucifixion or Cruci-fiction?* IPC

Delizsch, F (1888-9) *A New Commentary on Genesis* Clark

Deluc, Andre (1809) *An Elementary Treatise on Geology*

Dembski, William A (1998) *Mere Creation* IVP

Dembski, William A (1998b) *The Design Inference* CUP

Dennett, Daniel (1991) *Consciousness Explained* Penguin

Dennett, Daniel (1995) *Darwin's Dangerous Idea* Penguin

Dennet, Daniel (1996) *Kinds of Minds* Weidenfeld

Denton, Michael (1985) *Evolution: A Theory in Crisis* Burnett

Descartes, Rene (1637) *Discourse on Method*

Descartes, Rene (1641) *Meditations*

Desmond, A (1982) *Archetypes and Ancestors* Blond & Briggs

Desmond, A (1969) *The Politics of Evolution* U of Chicago Pr

Desmond, A & Moore, James R (1992) *Darwin* Michael Joseph

Dewar, Douglas (1938) *More Difficulties of the Evolution Theory* Thynne

Douglas, J D (Ed) (1980) *The Illustrated Bible Dictionary* IVP

Drake, Ellen T (1981) 'The Hooke Imprint on the Huttonian Theory', *American Journal of Science* (1981), 281, 963-973

Drake, Stillman (1957) *Discoveries and Opinions of Galileo* Anchor

Drake, Stillman (1980) *Galileo* OUP

Drake, Stillman (1981) *Galileo at Work* U of Chicago Pr

Draper, J W (1875) A *History of the Conflict Between Religion and Science* Henry S King

Duhem, P (1906) *The Aim and Structure of Physical Science* Princeton

Duhem, P (1906) *The Aim and Structure of Physical Theory* (1954 Edn.) Princeton

Dunn, Jame D G (1988) *Word Bible Commentary: Romans 1-8* Word

Durant, John (Ed) (1985) *Darwinism and Divinity* Blackwell

Dyson, Freeman (1979) *Disturbing the Universe* Harper

Eccles, John (1980) *The Human Psyche* Springer-Verlag

Eccles, John and Popper, Karl (1977) *The Self and Its Brain* Springer-Verlag

Edersheim, Alfred (1900) *The Life and Times of Jesus the Messiah* Longmans

Eddington, Arthur (1928) *The Nature of the Physical World* CUP

Einstein, Albert (1954) *Ideas and Opinions* (1973 edition used) Dell

Elton, G R (1969) *The Practice of History* Fontana

Faber, G S (1823) *Genius and Object*

Fantoli, Annibale (1994) *Galileo* Vatican Observatory Foundation

Feathers, James A (1996) 'Luminescence Dating and Modern Human Origins' *Evolutionary Anthropology* Vol 5 No 1 (1996) pp 25-35

Fergusson, David (1998) *The Cosmos and the Creator* SPCK

Feyerabend, P (1975) *Against Method* Verso

Feyerabend, Paul (1975) Against Method (3rd Edn. 1993) Verso

Feyerabend, Paul (1995) *Killing Time* U of Chicago Pr

Filby, F A (1964) *Creation Revealed* P & I

Finan Thomas & Twomey, Vincent (1995) *Scriptural Interpretation in the Fathers*

Finetti, B de (1939) 'Foresight, its logical laws its subjective sources' in Kybug, H E & Smolker, H E *Studies in Subjective Probability* Wiley

Finocchiaro, Maurice (1989) *The Galileo Affair* U of Ca Pr

Finn, S (Tr) (1996) *Gregor Mendel: The First Geneticist*

Fleming, Ambrose (1933) *Evolution or Creation?* Marshall

Forster, Roger and Marston, Paul (1973,1989) *God's Strategy in Human History* STL/Tyndale House/Bethany/Highland

Forster, Roger and Marston, Paul (1989) *Reason and Faith* Monarch

Foster, John (1991) *The Immaterial Self: A Defence of the Cartesian Dualism* Routledge

France, R T (1985) *Matthew* IVP

Fuller, Michael (1995) *Atoms and Icons* Mowbray

Gaebelein, A C (1913) *The Annotated Bible: The Pentateuch*

Gale, Barry (1982) *Evolution Without Evidence* Univ of New Mexico Pr

Galileo, Gallilei (1615) *Letter to the Grand Duchess Christina* Tr Drake (1957)

Galileo, Gallilei (1632) *Dialogue on the Two World Systems*

Galton, Francis (1874) *English Men of Science* Macmillan

Geach, Peter T (1977) *Providence and Evil* CUP

Gee, Henry (1992) 'Statistical Clouds Over African Eden' Nature 355 (1992) 583

Geisler, N L (1976) *Christian Apologetics* Baker

Geisler, N L (1979) *Miracles and Modern Thought* Zondoveran
Gillespie, Neil C (1977) *Charles Darwin and the Problem of Creation* U of Chicago Pr
Gillies, Donald (1993) *Philosophy of Science in the Twentieth Century* Blackwell
Gillispie, Charles C (1951) *Genesis and Geology* Harper & Row
Glymour, Clark (1981) *Theory and Evidence* U of Chicago Pr
Goodwin, Brian (1994) *How the Leopard Changed Its Spots* Weidenfeld
Goldernstein, J (1995) *Albert Einstein: Physicist and Genius* Aesop
Gordon, E O (1894) (Ed), *The Life and Correspondence of William Buckland*
Gorman, Michael (1997) "The Commentary on Genesis of Claudius of Turin and Biblical Studies under Louis the Pious" *Speculum*, 1997, (72) 279-329
Gosse, P H (1857) *Omphalos*
Gott, Ken and Lois (1995) *The Sunderland Refreshing* Hodder
Gower, Barry (1997) *Scientific Method* Routledge
Graves, Don (1996) *Scientists of Faith* Kregel
Gray, Asa (1861) *Natural Selection...* Trubner
Gray, Asa (1880) *Natural Science and Religion* Scribner
Gray, James M (1920) *Synthetic Bible Studies* Oliphant
Gribbin, John and Rees, Martin (1990) *Cosmic Coincidences* Black Swan
Griffin, David (1975) *God, Power and Evil* Westminster
Gunton, Colin (1993) *The One, The Three and the Many* CUP
Guth, Alan (1997) *The Inflationary Universe* Vintage
Guthrie, Donald (1974) *New Testament Introduction* Tyndale
Hacking, Ian (1981) *Scientific Revolutions* OUP
Hacking, Ian (1983) *Representing and Intervening* CUP
Hailperin, Herman (1960) *Rashi and the Christian Scholars* U of Pitsbg Pr
Hall, D H (1976) *History of Earth Sciences During the Scientific and Industrial Revolutions* Elsevier
Hallam, A (1983) *Great Geological Controversies* OUP
Hamilton, Victor P (1990) *The Book of Genesis Chapters 1-17* Eerdmans
Hammer, M F and Zegura, S L (1996) 'The Role of the Y Chromosome in Human Evolutionary Studies' *Evolutionary Anthropology* Vol 5 No 5 (1996) pp. 116-131
Hanson, N R (1958) *Patterns of Discovery* CUP
Hart, David (1995) *One Faith?* Mowbray
Hartshorne, Charles (1948) *The Divine Relativity* Yale U Pr
Haught, John (1995) *Science and Religion* Paulist
Hawking Stephen (1988) *A Brief History of Time* Bantam
Hawking, Stephen (1993) *Black Holes and Baby Universes* Bantam
Hawthorne, Tim (1987) *Windows on Science and Faith* IVP
Hays, Arthur Garfield (1967) *Let Freedom Ring* Liverlight
Hayward, Alan (1985) *Creation and Evolution* SPCK
Hedges, S et al (19920 'Human origins and the analysis of Mitochondrial DNA Sequences' *Science* 255 (February 1992) pp. 737-739
Heeren, Fred (1998) *Show Me God* Day Star
Heidel, Alexander (1951) *The Babylonian Genesis* U of Chicago Pr
Heisenberg, W (1971) *Physics and Philosophy* Allen & Unwin
Hellman, Geoffrey (1997) *Philosophy of Science,* 64 (June 1997) 191-221

Helm, Paul (1993) *The Providence of God* IVP

Helm, Paul (1987) *Objective Knowledge* IVP

Helm, Paul (1988) *Eternal God* OUP

Henbest, N (1987) 'Brightest Supernova for Four Centuries' *J Brit Aston Assoc* Vol 97: 3 (1987) pp. 130-2

Herbert, Lord Edward (1624) *On Truth*

Herschel, John (1831) *A Preliminary Discourse on Natural Philosophy*

Hesse, Mary (1966) *Models and Analogies in Science* Sheed

Hesse, Mary (1974) *The Structure of Scientific Inference* U of Ca Pr

Hewitt, J W (1932) 'The Use of Nails in the Crucifixion" *Harvard Theological Review*, Vol 25, 1932 pp 29-45

Highfield, R & Carter, P (1993) *Private Lives of Albert Einstein* Faber

Himmelfarb, Gertrude (1959) *Darwin and the Darwinian Revolution* Norton

Hodge, A A (1890) *Evangelical Theology* (Repr 1976 Banner of Truth)

Hodge, Charles (1974) *What is Darwinism?* Scribner

Holder, Rodney J (1993) *Nothing But Atoms and Molecules* Monarch

Holder, Rodney D (1998) "Hume on Miracles: Bayesian Interpretation, Multiple Testimony and the Existence of God", *Brit J Phil Sci*, 49 (1998) 49-65)

Holland, R F (1965) 'The Miraculous', *American Philosophical Quarterly*, ii 1965 p. 43-51

Hooykaas, R (1959) *The Principle of Uniformity in Geology, Biology and Theology* Brill

Hooykaas, R (1963) *Natural Law and Divine Miracle* Leiden

Hooykaas, R (1972) *Religion and the Rise of Modern Science* Scottish Academic Pr

Houghton, John (1988) *Does God Play Dice?* IVP

Hovencamp, Herbert (1978) *Science and Religion in America 1800-1860* U of Pa Pr

Howson, Colin & Urbach, P (1993) *Scientific Reasoning: The Bayesian Approach* (2nd Edn.) Open Court

Howson, Colin (1995) 'Theories of Probability' *Br J Phil Sci*, 46 (1995) 1-32

Hull, D (1973) *Darwin and His Critics* Harvard U Pr

Hume, D (1748) *An Enquiry Concerning Human Understanding*

Hume, D (1739) *A Treatise of Human Nature*

Hutchinson, James E (1993) *Religion and the Natural Sciences* Harcourt

Huxley, Julian & Ketterwell, H (1965) *Charles Darwin and His World* Thames & Hudson

Huxley, T H *(1894, 1898) Collected Essays* 2 Vols MacMillan

Irvine, W (1956) *Apes, Angels and Victorians* Weidenfeld

Irzik, Gurol and Grunberg, Teo (1995) 'Carnap and Kuhn: Arch Enemies of Close Allies?' *Brit J Phil Sc*, 46 (1995) 285-307

Ito,Yushi (1988) 'Hooke's Cyclic Theory of the Earth in the Context of Seventeenth Century England', *British Journal for the History of Science* (1988) 21, 295-314

Jackson, F (1982) "Epiphnemenal qualia" *Philosophical Quarterly* 32 pp. 127-36

Jaki, Stanley L (1970) *Brain, Mind and Computers* Herder & Herder

Jaki, Stanley L (1978) *The Roads of Science and the Ways to God* Scottish Academic

Jaki, Staley L (1986) *Science & Creation* (Rev Edn.) Scottish Academic

Jaki, Stanley L (1996) *Bible and Science* Christendom

Jaki, Stanley L (1998) *Genesis 1 Through the Ages* (2nd Edn.) Scottish Academic

Jeeves, Malcolm (1994) *Mind Fields* Apollos

Jeeves, Malcolm (1997) *Human Nature at the Millennium* Apollos

Jeeves, Malcolm & Berry, R J (1998) *Science, Life and Christian Belief* Apollos

Jenkins, D E (1987) *God, Miracle and the Church of England* SCM

Jenson, J V (1970) 'The X-Club', *British Journal for the History of Science* (1970), 59, 179, 63-72

Johnson, P E (1991) *Darwin on Trial* Monarch

Johnson, P E (1997) *Testing Darwinism* IVP

Jones, D Gareth (1981) *Our Fragile Brains* IVP

Jones, Steve (1993) *Language of the Genes* Flamingo

Kaiser, Christopher (1991) *Creation & History of Science* Vol 3 Marshall

Kaufmman, Stuart (1995) *At Home in the Universe* Penguin

Kepler (1609) *Astronomia Nova*

Kidner, Derek (1964) *Proverbs* Tyndale Pr

Kidner, Derek (1967) *Genesis* Tyndale Pr

Kiljn, A (1983) *The Old Testament Pseudepigrapha,* Vol 1

King, John (1969) *A Commentary on Genesis: John Calvin* Banner of Truth

Kitcher, P (1982) *Abusing Science: The Case Against Creationism* MIT Pr

Kittel, G (1964-74) *Theological Dictionary of the new Testament* Paternoster

Kline, M (1958) 'Because It Had Not Rained' *Westminster Theological Journal* Vol 20 (1958) p. 15

Koestlerm, A (1959, 1972) *The Sleepwalkers* Hutchinson/Penguin

Kuhn (1990) 'The Road Since Structure' *PSA* 1990 Vol 2 pp. 3-13 reprinted in Tauber (1997)

Kuhn, T S (1970) *The Structure of Scientific Revolutions* (2nd Edn.) U of Chicago Pr

Kukla, Anndre (1994) 'Scientific Realism, Scientific Practice and the Natural Ontological Attitude' *Brit J Phil Sci,* 45 (1994) 955-975

Kutrtz, J H (1857) *Bible and Astronomy* (3rd Edn.)

Kyle, Melvin Grove (1912) *The Deciding Voice of the Monuments in Biblical Criticism*

Lacey, A R (1996) *A Dictionary of Philosophy* Routledge

Lakatos, I & Musgrave A (1970) *Criticism and the Growth of Knowledge* CUP

Laplace, Pierre-Simon Marquis de (1812) *Analytic Theory of Probability*

Laslett, P (1950) *The Physical Basis of Mind* Blackwell

Laudan, Larry (1981) 'A Confutation of Convergent Realism' *Philosophy of Science*, 48 (1981) 19-48 (also in Boyd (1990) Ch 12 and elsewhere)

Laudan, R (1987) *From Mineralogy to Geology: The Foundations of a Science 1650-1830* U of Chicago Pr

Lawrence, D H (1915)*The Rainbow* Phoenix edition Heinemann

Leakey, R (1992) *Human Origins Revisited* Little Brown

Lewin, R (1987) 'The Unmasking of Mitochondrial Eve' *Science* Vol 238 (and October 1987) pp. 2-8

Lewin, R (1998) 'Young Americans' *New Scientist* No 2156 (17 October 1998)

Lewis, C S (1960) *Miracles* (1st Edn. 1947) Fontana

Lewis, Jack P (1968) *A Study of the Interpretation of Noah and the Flood in Jewish and Christian Literature* Leiden

Lhwyd, E (1699) *Lithophylactii Britannici Ichnographia*

Lindberg D C & Numbers R L (1986) *God and Nature* U Cal Pr

Livingstone, David (1987) *Darwin's Forgotten Defenders* Eerdmans/Scottish Academic

Losee, J (1993) *A Historical Introduction the Philosophy of Science* Opus

Lubenow, Marvin L (1992) *Bones of Contention* Baker

Lucas, Ernest (1989) *Genesis Today* Scripture Union

Luntley, Michael (1995) *Reason, Truth and Self* Routledge

Luther, Martin *Lectures on Genesis* in *Luther's Works* (Tr J Pelikan, 1959-86) Concordia

MacKay, D M (1980) *Brains, Machines and Persons* Collins

MacKay, D M (1963) *Science and Christian Faith Today* Falcon

MacKay, D M (1965) *Christianity in a Mechanistic Universe* IVP

MacKay, D M (1974) *The Clockwork Image* IVP

Mackay, D M (1978) *Chance and Providence* OUP

MacKay, D M (1980) *Brains, Machines and Persons* Collins

Majerus, Michael, Amos, William & West, Gregory (1996) *Evolution: The Four Billion Year War* Longman

Malcolm, Norman (1968) "The Conceivability of Mechanism" *The Philosophical Review* lxxvii pp 45-72

Marcus, Ralph (1929, 1953) *Philo*

Marshall, I Howard (3rd Ed 1988) *Luke - Historian and Theologian* Paternoster

Marshall, I Howard (Ed) (1979) *New Testament Interpretation* Paternoster

Marston, Justin (1997) *Report on a National Survey of Student's Opinions on Science and Faith* [www.csis.org.uk]

Marston, Justin (1998) *Early Hebrew Understandings of Genesis 1-3* (Paper at summer CIS/ASA Conference in Oxford)

Marston, Paul (1980) *The Biblical Family* Cornerstone

Marston, Paul (1984) *Science, Methodology and Religion in the Work of Adam Sedgwick* PhD Thesis Open University

Marston, Paul (1984) *God and the Family* Kingsway

Marston, Paul 'Review: H I Brown's Observation and Objectivity' *Nature*, 333, (April 1988)

Mauro, Philip (1922) *Evolution at the Bar*

Mayo, Deborah (1997) 'Duhem's Problem, the Bayesian Way and Error Statistics' *Philosophy of Science*, 64, (June 1997) 222-244

Mayo, Deborah G (1996) 'Ducks, Rabbits and Normal Science' *Brit J Phil Sci*, 47 (1996) 271-290

McCluskey, Stephen C (1998) *Astronomies and Cultures in Early Medieval Europe* CUP

McCosh, James (1872) *Christianity and Positivism*

McGrath, Alister E (1996) *A Passion for Truth* Apollos

Medawar, P B (1969) *Induction and Intuition in Scientific Thought* Methuen

Meeham, Brenda M (1967) "A C Dixon: An Early Fundamentalist" *Foundations*, x, 1967, No 1

Metzger, Bruce (1981) *The Manuscripts of the Bible* OUP

Metzger, Bruce (1987) The Canon of the New Testament OUP

Midgley, Mary (1981) *Heart and Mind* Methuen

Midgley, Mary (1994) *The Ethical Primate* Routledge

Mill, J S (1843) *A System of Logic*

Millard, Alan (1990) *Discoveries from the Time of Jesus* Lion

Miller, Hugh (1849) *Footprints of the Creator*

Miller, Hugh (1857) *The Testimony of the Rocks* (1st Edn. 1849)

Monod, Jacques (1970) *Chance and Necessity* Collins

Montagu, Ashley (1984) *Science and Creationism* OUP

Moore, James R (1979) *The Post Darwinian Controversies* CUP

Moreland, J P (1989) *Christianity and the Nature of Science* Baker

Moreland, J P (1994) *The Creation Hypothesis* IVP

Morgan, G Campbell (1947) (3rd Edn.) *Great Chapters of the Bible*

Mormann, Thomas (1997) 'Review' *Br J Phil Sci*, 48 (1997) 306-309

Morris H M (1977b) (2nd Edn.) *The Beginning of the World* Accent

Morris H M (1984) *A History of Modern Creationism* Master

Morris H M (1984b) *A Biblical Basis for Modern Science* Baker

Morris, H M (1974) *Many Infallible Proofs* Creation Life

Morris, H M (1976) *The Genesis Record* Baker

Morris, H M (1977) (2nd Edn.) *Evolution and the Modern Christian* Baker

Morris, H M (1982) *Men of Science, Men of God* Master

Morris, H M (1985) (2nd Edn.) *Scientific Creationism* (reprinted 1996) Master

Morris, H M (1988) *Science and the Bible* (Revised Edn.) Scripture Pr

Morris, H M and Whitcomb, John C (1961) *The Genesis Flood* Baker

Morris, Leon (1987) *Revelation* Tyndale

Mortensen, T J (1996) *British Scriptural Geologists in the First Half of the Nineteenth Century* PhD Thesis Coventry University/Wycliffe Hall

Muggeridge, Malcolm (1968) *Another King* St Andrews Pr

Mullins, E Y (1905) *Why Is Christianity True?*

Murray, John (1965) *The Epistle to the Romans* Eerdmans

Musgrave, Alan (1993) *Common Sense, Science and Scepticism* CUP

Nagel, T (1974) "What is it like to be a bat?" *Philosophical Review* 83 pp. 435-50

Newton-Smith, W (1981) *The Rationality of Science* Routledge

Neve, M and Porter, R (1977) 'Alexander Catcott', *British Journal for the History of Science* (1977), x, 1, 37-60

Nickles, T (Ed) (1980) *Scientific Discovery, Logic and Rationality* Reidel

Nietzsche, F (1884) *Thus Spoke Zarathustra* (Tr R J Hollingdale 1961) Penguin

Numbers, Ronald L (1992) *The Creationists* U of Ca Pr

O'Connor, J (Ed) (1969) *Modern Materialism: Readings on the mind-Body Identity* Harcourt

O'Hear, Anthony (1989) *An Introduction to the Philosophy of Science* OUP

O'Hear, Anthony (1997) *Beyond Evolution* OUP

Oberdan, Thomas (1998) "The Vienna Circle's 'Anti-Foundationalism'" *Brit J Phil Sci 49 (1998) 297-308*

Origen *Homilies on Genesis and Exodus* (Tr R E Heine, 1982) Cath Un of Am Pr

Origen *First Principles* (Tr G W Butterworth, 1936) SPCK

Orr, James (1910-15) *Science and Christian Faith* and *The Early Narratives of Genesis* (Vols 4 & 6 in *The Fundamentals*) Testimony publishing Company (Chicago)

Oswalt, John N (1986) *The Book of Isaiah* Eerdmans

Paley, Wiliam (1802) *Natural Theology*

Panneberg, Wolfhart (1993) *Towards a Theology of Nature* Westminster/John Knox

Papineau, David (1996) *The Philosophy of Science* OUP

Paul, I (1986) *Science and Theology in Einstein's Perspective* Scottish Academic Pr

Peacocke, A (1993) *Theology for a Scientific Age* Blackwell

Peacocke, A (1979) *Creation and the World of Science* Nelson

Peacocke, A (1985) *Reductionism in Academic Disciplines* Nelson

Peacocke, A (1986) *God and the New Biology* Dent

Pearce, E K Victor (1969) *Who Was Adam?* (Second Edn.) Paternoster

Pearce, E K Victor (1993) *Evidence for Truth: Science* Evidence Programmes

Pearcey, Nancy & Thaxton, Charles (19940 *The Soul of Science* Crossway

Pearl, Chaim (1971) *The Medieval Jewish Mind* Vallentime

Pember, G H (1876) *Earth's Earliest Ages*

Penfield, Wilder (1975) *The Mystery of the Mind* Princeton University Pr

Philo *Volume 1* (Tr F H Colson and G H Whitaker 1991) Harvard U Pr

Pinker, Steven (1994) *The Language Instinct* Penguin

Pinnock, Clark et al (1994) *The Openness of God* IVP/Paternoster

Planck, Max (1937) *The Universe in the Light of Modern Physics* (2nd Ed) Unwin

Plantinga, Alvin & Wolterstorff, Nicholas (1983) *Faith and Rationality* Notre Dame

Plantinga, Alvin (1993) *Warrant and Proper Function* OUP

Polanyi, Michael (1958) *Personal Knowledge: Towards A Post-Critical Philosophy* Routlege

Polkinghorne, John (1988) *Science and Creation* SPCK

Polkinghorne, John (1989) *Science and Providence* SPCK

Polkinghorne, John (1998) *Science and Theology: An Introduction*

Pollard, G (1958) *Chance and Providence* Faber and Faber

Poole, M (1992) *Miracles* Scripture Union

Poole, M (1994) *A Guide to Science and Belief* Lion

Poole M (1670) *Synopsis*

Popper, Karl (1956) *The Logic of Scientific Discovery* Hutchinson

Popper, Karl (1965) *Conjectures and Refutations* (1st Edn. 1963) Routledge

Popper, Karl and Eccles, John (1978) *The Self and Its Brain*

Porter, R (1977) *The Making of Geology* CUP

Porter, R (1976) 'Charles Lyell and the Principles of the History of Geology', *British Journal for the History of Science* (1976), ix, 2, 32 9 91- 10 3

Preston, John (1996) 'Feyerabend's Retreat from Realism' *Philosophy of Science,* 64 (1997) S421-431

Price, George McCready (1906) *Illogical Geology: The Weakest Point in the Evolution Theory*

Price, George McCready (1911) *God's Two Books: Plain Facts About Evolution, Geology and the Bible*

Price, George McCready (1913) *The Fundamentals of Geology*

Price, George McCready (1917) *Q.E.D. Or New Light on the Doctrine of Creation*

Price, George McCready (1923) *The New Geology*

Price, George McCready (1925) *The Predicament of Evolution*

Price, George McCready (1926) *Evolutionary Geology and the New Catastrophism* (4th Edition of "Illogical Geology")

Price, Roger (1979) *The Age of the Earth*

Putnam, Hilary (1975) *Mind, Language and Reality* CUP

Putnam, Hilary (1976) *Meaning in the Moral Sciences* Routledge

Putnam, Hilary (1981) *Reason, Truth and History* CUP

Putnam, Hilary (1982) *Reason, Truth and History* CUP

Putnam, Hilary (1983) *Realism and Reason* CUP

Putnam, Hilary (1989) *Representation and Reality* MIT

Putnam, Hilary (1990) *Realism with a Human Face* Harvard U Pr

Quine, W V (1951) "Two Dogmas of Empiricism' in *From a Logical Point of View* (1961) Harper

Quine, W V (1960) *Word and Object* Wiley

Raedts, Peter (1987) *Richard Rufus of Cornwall and the Tradition of Oxford Theology* OUP

Ramm, Bernard (1955) *The Christian View of Science and Scripture* (Second impression) Paternoster

Ramsay, William (1895) *St Paul the Traveller and Roman Citizen* Hodder

Ramsay, William (1915) *The Bearing of Recent Discovery.*

Ramsey, F P (1978) *Foundations: Essays Philosophy, Logic, Mathematics and Economics* Routledge

Rattray-Taylor, G (1983) *The Great Evolution Mystery* Secker & Warburg

Rautsch, Del (1986) *Philosophy of Science* IVP

Ray, John (1691) *The Wisdom of God Manifested in the Works of Creation*

Ray, John (Tr 1876) *Reflections on the Study of Nature*

Reichenbach, Hans (1949) *The Theory of Probability* U of Ca Pr

Renan, J E (1863) *Life of Jesus*

Rhappaport, R (1978) 'Geology and Orthodoxy', *British Journal for the History of Science* (1978) xi, 19 8

Rheticus, Joachim (1540) *Narratio Prima*

Richardson, W M & Wildman, W J (1996) *Religion and Science* Routledge

Ridley, M (1985) *The Problems of Evolution* OUP

Roberts, M (1986) 'The Roots of Creationism' *Faith and Thought* Vol 112 I (1986) pp. 21-36

Roberts, M (1997) Review of Behe's Dawsin's Black Box, in *Science and Christian Belief,* October 1997 pp. 191-2

Robert, M (1998) Darwin's Black Box Reconsidered in *Science and Christian Belief* October 1998 pp. 189-195.

Robertson, J (ed) (1905) *The Philosophical Works of Francis Bacon*
    Routledge
Robinson, George L (1906) *Leaders of Israel*
Robinson, John A T (1961) *Honest to God* SCM
Robinson, John A T (1976) *Redating the New Testament* SCM
Robinson, John A T (1977) *Can We Trust the New Testament?* Mowbrays
Robinson, John A T (1985) *The Priority of John* Macdonald
Rohl, David (1998) *Legend: The Genesis of Civilisation* Random House
Rosenkrantz, R D (1977) *Inference, Method and Decision: Towards a
    Bayesian Philosophy of Science* Reidel
Rudwick, M (1972) *The Meaning of Fossils* Elsevier
Rudwick, M (1977) 'Lyell's Chronological Model', *ISIS* (1977) 9 2439 440-3,
Rudwick, M (1974) 'Charles Lyell and His London Lectures on Geology',
    Royal Society Notes and Records (1974), 29, 231-263
Rudwick, M (1982) 'Charles Darwin in London: The Integration of Public and
    Private Science', *ISIS* (1982), 73
Ruse Michael and Wilson E O (1993) "The Evolution of Ethics" in Hutchinson
    (1993)
Russell, Colin A (1983) *Science and Social Change 1700-1900* Macmillan
Russell, Colin A (1985) *Crosscurrents* IVP
Ryle, Gilbert (1949) *The Concept of Mind* Hutchinson
Sailhamer, John (1996) *Genesis Unbound* Multnomah
Sampson, Philip et al, (1994) *Faith and Modernity* Regnum
Sanday W and Headlam AC (1902) *A Critical and Exegetical Commentary on
    the Epistle of the Romans* (5th Edn.)
Sanders, E P (1995) *The Historical Figure of Jesus* Penguin
Sarna, Nahum M (1966) *Understanding Genesis* Schocken
Sartre, Jean-Paul (1946; English Tr Philip Mairet, 1948) *Existentialism and
    Humanism*
Sartre, Jean-Paul (1964) *Words* (Edition used: Penguin 1967) Hamilton
Sarup, Madan (2nd Ed 1993) *An Introductory Guide to Poststructuralism and
    Postmodernism* Harvester
Savage, John J (1961) *Saint Ambrose: Hexameron, Paradise and Cain and
    Abel* Catholic U of Am Pr
Schaeffer, Francis (1972) *Genesis in Space and Time* IVP
Schonfield, Hugh (1965) *The Passover Plot* Hutchinson
Scopes, John T & Presley, James (1967) *Centre of the Storm* Holt
Searle, J (1984) *Minds, Brains and Science* BBC
Searle, J (1990) "Is the brain's mind a computer program? *Scientific American*
    262 p.26-31
Searle, John (1997) *The Mystery of Consciousness* Grantna
Secord, James A (1991) 'The discovery of a vocation: Darwin's early geology'
    BJHS, 1991, 24, 133-157
Sellars, Wilfrid (1963) *Science, Perception and Reality* Routledge
Selvidge, M J (1984) *Fundamentalism Today* Brethren Pr
Setterfield, Barry (1987) *The Atomic Constants, Light and Time* Stanford
    Research International
Shapere, Dudley (1984) *Reason and the Search for Knowledge* Reidel
Sharratt, Michael (1994) *Galileo: Decisive Innovator* CUP

Sherrington, C S (1933) *The Brain and Its Mechanism* CUP

Sherrington, C S (1940) *Man on His Nature* CUP

Simeon (1819-28) *Horae Homileticae* London

Smart, J J C (1994) "Mind and Brain" pp 19-23 in Warner & Tadseuz (1994)

Smart, Ninian (1986) *Concept and Empathy* Macmillan

Smith, John Pye (1839) *On The Relation Between the Holy Scriptures and Some Parts of Geological Science*

Smyth, Marina (1996) *Understanding the Universe in Seventh- Century Ireland* Boydell

Sorrel, Tom (1991) *Scientism* Routledge

Spanner, Douglas (1987) *Biblical Creation and the Theory of Evolution* Paternoster

Spong, John Shelby (1994) *Resurrection, Myth or Reality?*

Stanesby, Derek (1985) *Science, Reason & Religion* Croom Helm

Stannard, Russell (1982) *Science and the Renewal of Belief* SCM

Stanton, Graham (1997) *Gospel Truth?* Fount

Staub, Jacob J (1982) *The Creation of the World According to Gersonides* Scholars Pr

Stern, C and Sherwood, E R (1967) *The Origin of Genetics: A Mendel Source Book* Freeman

Stillingfleet, E (1662) *Origines Sacrae*

Stirton, William R (1997) 'Anti-Realism, Truth-Conditions and Verificationism' *Mind,* 106, Pct 1997, 697-776

Strinati, Dominic (1995) *An Introduction to Theories of Popular Culture* Routledge

Stock, E (1899-1916) *The History of the Church Missionary Society* 4 Vols London

Strauss, D F (Tr 1846) *Life of Jesus* (original in 1835-6, Tr 1846, 2nd Edn. 1892)

Suppe, Frederick (ed.) (1977) *The Structure of Scientific Theories* 2nd Edn. U of Ill Pr

Swinburne, Richard (1994) *Body and Soul* in Warner & Tadeusz (1994)

Swinburne, R (1979) *The Existence of God* OUP

Swinburne, R (1981) *Faith and Reason* Clarendon

Swinburne, R (1993) *The Coherence of Theism* Clarendon

Swinburne, R (1994) *The Christian God* Clarendon

Swinburne, R (1996) *Is There a God?* OUP

Swinburne, Richard (1986) *The Evolution of the Soul* Clarendon

Tattersall, Ian (1998) 'Neandethal Genes: What Do They Mean?' *Evolutionary Anthropology* Vol 6 No 5 (1998) pp. 157-158

Tauber (1997) *Science and the Quest for Reality* McMillan

Taylor C (1987) "Overcoming Epistemology" in Baynes & Bowman (1987) pp. 464-88

Taylor, Ian (1991) *In the Minds of Men* TFE (3rd Edition)

Taylor, John (1998) "Science, Chrisitanity and the Postmodern Agenda" *Science and Christian Belief* October 1998 pp. 163-178

Templeton, John Marks (1994) *Evidence of Purpose* Continuum

Thackeray, A & Morrell, F J (1981) *Gentlemen of Science* Clarendon

Thiede, Carsten & D'Ancona, Matthew (1996) *The Jesus Papyrus* Weidenfeld

Thiede, Carsten (1992) *The Earliest Gospel Manuscript?* Paternoster

Thiering, Barbara (1992) *Jesus the Man* Doubleday

Thomas, W H Griffith (1946) *Genesis*

Tindale, Matthew (1730) *Christianity as Old As Creation*

Toland, John (1696) *Christianity Not Mysterious*

Tomlinson, David (1995) *The Post-Evangelical* Triangle

Toon, P (1979) *Evangelical Theology 1833-1856* Marshall,

Torrens:, Hugh (1988) 'Hawking History - A Vital Future for Geology's Past'
    Modern Geology (1988) 139 pp 83-93

Torrey, R A (1907) *Difficulties in the Bible* Moody

Tosh, John (1991) *The Pursuit of History* Longman

Trigg, Roger (1993) *Rationality and Science* Routledge

Trigg, Roger (1998) *Rationality and Religion* Blackwell

Tully, Mark (1996) *An Investigation into the Lives of Jesus* Penguin

Van de Fliert, R (1978) 'Fundamentalism and the Fundamentals of Geology',
    ASA Journal, 'Origins and Change' (1978)

Van Fraasen (1980) *The Scientific Image* Clarendon

Van Inwagen, Peter (1983) *An Essay on Free Will* Clarendon

Van Leeuwen, Mary Stewart (1985) *The Person in Psychology* IVP

Van Till, Howard (1986) 'The Legend of the shrinking Sun' *ASA Journal , vol
    38 (30 (1986) pp 123-32*

Van Till, Howard J (1986) *The Fourth Day* Eerdmans

Van Till, Howard (1988) *Science Held Hostage* IVP

Van Till, Howard (1996) 'Basil, Augustine and the doctrine of creation's
    functional integrity' *Science and Christian Belief 8 (1), 21-38, April 1996*

Veith, G E (1994) *Guide to Contemporary Culture* Crossway

Von Daniken, Erich (1968) *Chariots of the Gods* Souvenir

Von Mises, Richard (1957) *Probability, Statistics and Truth* (1st Edn. 1939)
    Allen & Unwin

Von Rad, Gerhard (1972) *Genesis* (Tr J H Marks) SCM

Walker, B (1983) *Gnosticism* Aquarian Pr

Ward, Keith (1996) *God, Chance and Necessity* One World

Ward, Keith (1996) *Religion and Creation* Clarendon

Ward, Keith (1998) *God, Faith and the New Millennium* One World

Warner, Richard and Szubka, Tadeusz (1994) *The Mind-Body Problem*
    Blackwell

Watson, Gary (Ed) 1982) *Freewill* OUP

Watson, J B (1919) *Psychology from the Standpoint of a Behaviourist*

Watts, Fraser (1998) *Science Meets Faith* SPCK

Weaver, John David (1994) *In the Beginning God* Regents College

Wenham, John (1993) *Christ and the Bible* Eagle

Wenham, Gordon J (1987) *Genesis 1-15* Word Bible Commentary

Wenham, John (1991) *Redating Matthew, Mark and Luke* Hodder

Wenham, John (1993) (2nd Ed) *The Easter Enigma* Paternoster

Wesley, John (1756) *The Doctrine of Original Sin* (Repr. In *Works* (1986) ix
    pp. 1921-464)

Wesley, John (1872 Ed) *Works* (Repr. (1986) Hendrickson)

Westfall, Richard (1958) *Science and Religion in Seventeenth century England*
    U. Mich Pr

Westermann, C (1971) *Creation* (Tr J J Scullion) SPCK

Westermann, C (1974) *Genesis Band 1*

Westfall, R S (1973) *Science and Religion in Seventeenth Century England* U Mich Pr

Whewell, William (1840) *The Philosophy of the Inductive Sciences*

Whiston, William (1696) *A New Theory of the Earth*

Whitcomb, J C & DeYoung, Donald (1978) *The Moon: Its Creation, Form and Significance* BMH Books

White, A D (1896) *A History of the Warfare of Science With Theology*

White, E G (1864) *Spiritual Gifts: Important facts of faith in connection With Holy men of Old* (7thDayPub)

White, E G (1888) *The Great Controversy Between Christ and Satan*

White, E G (1890) *Patriarchs and Prophets*

White, E G (1903) *Education*

White, E G (1929) *Principles of True Science*

White, Michael and Gribbin, John (1995) *Darwin: A Life in Science* Simon & Schuster

Whitehead, A N (1929) *Process and Reality*

Wilkinson, David (1993) *God, The Big Bang and Stephen Hawking* Monarch

Wilson, A et al (1987) 'Mitochondrial DNA and Human Evolution' Nature Vol 325 (1st January 1987) pp. 31-33

Wilson, Allan C & Cann, Rebecca L (1992) 'The Recent African Genesis of Humans' *Scientific American,* (April 1992) pp. 68-73

Wilson, A N (1992) *Jesus* Sinclaire-Stevenson

Wilson, Ian (1984) *Jesus the Evidence* Weidenfeld

Wiseman, P J (1985) *Ancient Records and the Structure of Genesis* (Reprinted from 1936) Nelson

Wittgenstein, Ludvig (1921) *Tractatus Logico-Phosophicus* (Tr Pears and McGuiness 1922) Routledge

Wittgenstein Ludvig   *Lectures on Religious Belief*

Wolfe, David L (1983) *Epistemology: the Justification of Belief* IVP

Wolfe, Stephen L (1993) *Molecular and Cellular* Wadsworth

Wolpert, Lewis (1992) *The Unnatural nature of Science* Faber

Woodward, John (1695) *An Essay toward a Natural History of the Earth*

Woolston, Thomas (1720) A Discourse on the Miracles of our Saviour

Wright, G F (1896) *Scientific Confirmations of Old Testament History*

Wright, John (1994) *Designer Universe* Monarch

Wright, N T (1991) *The Climax of the Covenant* T & T Clark

Wright, N T (1992) *The New Testament and the People of God* SPCK

Wright, N T (1996a) *The Original Jesus* Lion

Wright, N T (1996b) *Jesus and the Victory of God* SPCK

Wright, Tom (N T) (1997) *What St Paul Really Said* Lion

Wright, Nigel (1996) *The Radical-Evangelical* SPCK

Young, Davis A (1992) *Christianity and the Age of the Earth* Zondervan

Young, Davis A (1995) *The Biblical Flood* Eerdmans

Young Davis A (1987) 'Scripture in the Hands of the Geologists', *Westminster Theological Journal* (1987), 49, 1-34, 257-304

Young, E J (1966) *Genesis 3* Banner of Truth

Young, E J (1964) *Studies in Genesis One* Presbyterian & Reformed

Young, E J (1976) *In the Beginning* Banner of Truth
Youngblood, Ronald (1980) *How it all Began* Regal
Yule, J D (1976) *The Impact of British Religious Thought in the Second Quarter of the Nineteenth Century* (PhD Thesis, Cambridge 1976)
Zacharias, Ravi (1996) *Deliver us From Evil* Word

Don't forget we may be contacted through our website:
www.reason-science-and-faith.com

You may also find interesting:
www.cis.org.uk (Christians in Science).
www.csis.org.uk (Christian Students in Science).

GLOSSARY

This Section contains some very brief definitions of key terms. Where relevant, page numbers are given where there are more detailed definitions or discussions in the book.

Actualism: Reconstructing past based on present processes (337).

Allegory: A 'story in which the meaning is represented symbolically.' Early Jews/Christians distinguish the allegorical and literal levels of interpretation – but in the literal level take some major parts of Gen 1-3 passages as meant figuratively (192)

A priori: Knowledge available in advance of experience.

Age-Day: Identifies Genesis 'days' with geological epochs (219).

Anthropology: Study of human societies, especially early ones.

Anthropomorphic: Metaphorical/symbolic ascription of human characteristics to God.

Baconian: Emphasis on empirically based induction of scientific laws, done in slow methodical way (cf 'Two-books') (360).

Bayesian: View of probability in which probabilities of statements being 'true' are adjusted in light of experience (381).

Behaviourism: Only behaviour (not mental processes) is real enough to study systematically (68)

Cartesian Dualism: Some kind of dualist interactionism (qv).

Chance: We distinguish: **Chance₁:** in sense used in the theory of probability. **Chance₂:** in sense of openness in the Uncertainty Principle in physics. **Chance₃:** in sense of lack of design (108).

Charismatic: An emphasis on the 'charismata' or spiritual gifts like healing and speaking in tongues 31).

Compatibilism: Holds that freewill consists merely in a lack of *external* constraint on the agent who may be deterministic (80).

Creationism: Belief that God created the world. Used in restricted (inconsistent) sense by some to imply type-ii miracles in creation, but should also include evolutionary creationists (241).

Critical Realism: See 'Realism'.

Deism: God created the world but it now runs autonomously (129).

Denkinsland: Our term for views of Richard Dawkins, Daniel Dennett and Peter Atkins (43).

Design Theory: Belief that 'design' is a scientific term, present when no obvious physical causal chain exists (151)

Determinism: Belief that state of a system at time t determines with certainy its state at time t+n (79).

Dualism: Belief that there are two basic kinds of reality (67).

Dualistic Interactionism: Mind and matter are two distinct kinds of reality which interact causally (67).

Eclectic: Gathering ideas from diverse sources.

Empiricism: Knowledge by observation and experience.

Enlightenment: 18thC movement exalting human reason (19).

Epiphenominalism: Mental properties are accidental by-products of the physical brain (68).

Evangelicalism: Acceptance of the inspiration of the Bible and need for personal acceptance of the atoning work of Christ.

Evolutionary Creationism: Belief that God chose to use a process of evolution in order to create different species.

Exemplars: Scientific experiments seen as exemplifying particular scientific ideas.

Exegesis: Critical explanation of a text of the Bible

Existentialism: Emphasis on humans as free agents able to choose their own essence.

Federal Head: Someone seen as unifying and representing a humanity which is corporate (443).

Figurative: Metaphorical not literal language - dealing with real events and issues in symbolic terms.

Flood-Geology: Assumption that all the strata were laid down in one large recent flood (ie of Noah) (219).

Foundationalism: That some basic beliefs are self-justifying (387).

Framework Theory: The Genesis days are neither literal nor chronological but a dramatic device used by the writer (219).

Functionalism: Focuses on *function* of mental states in terms of input and output rather than inner experience (68).

Fundamentalism: Nickname arising from the *Fundamentals* series (1909-12) which were evangelical but not literalistic (227).

Gap-Theory: posits a 'gap' between Gen 1:1 and1:2, with the days as days of reconstitution of a devastated earth (219)

God-of-the-gaps: God operates only in gaps in the regular natural sequences (130/418).

Gossism: God created the world with apparent age - may include apparent geological history which didn't actually happen (223).

Humanism: Highly valuing human culture – originally in Christian context but later instead of it (54).

Idealism: Only 'ideas' or experiences are real (qv phenomenalism).

Identity Theory: Conscious phenomena are identical with brain states (see also type and token identity theory) (68).

Immanent: Divine property of being present throughout creation.

Instrumentalism: Scientific laws are really no more than useful instruments for prediction, they are not 'true' or 'untrue'. (380)

Liberal: (theological) Accepts parts of the Bible are not inspired by God or accurate (26).

Logical Empiricism: Softer and later term for Logical Positivism.

Logical Positivism: Belief that any statement not verifiable by direct observation is meaningless (366).

Materialism: Generally the same as physicalism (qv).

Memes: Ideas which compete for survival like genes do (45).

Metaphysics: Questions arising out of but going beyond those about the physical world and the remit of science (58).

Miracles: Events especially significant as intended by God: **Type-i:** Those which involve no alteration in the regular physical cause-effect sequences **Type-ii** Those involving alteration in the usual physical cause-effect sequences (132).

Mitochondrial-Eve: Single female ancestor posited on basis of evidence from mitochondria in human DNA (434).

Modernism: Strong belief in truth of and progress through science and technology (21).

Naturalism: View of reality which excludes the supernatural or spiritual, there is only the physical (129).

Neptunism: Early geological theory that most strata laid down under water, and that process overall had direciton (327).

Nominalism: Belief that universal concepts are just mental constructs and do not relate to anything 'real' except in thought.

Omnipotent: Capacity of God to do anything not a contradiction in terms of contrary to his nature (159).

Omniscience: Divine characteristic of knowing everything which there is to know (which may not include all the future) (159).

Organic: Relating to the molecules in a living being.

Pantheism: God is immanent in but not outside the world (129)

Paradigm: Set of conscious ideas and also unconscious approaches which interpret a set of phenomena (370)

Pentateuch: The first five books of the Bible (includes Genesis).

Perspectivalism: Mental and physical phenomena are equally real but different perspectives or dimensions of the same event (68).

Phenomenalism: The only reality is experiences and there is no necessity to assume anything 'behind' experiences which 'causes' them (379).

Physicalism: (i) Belief that the only reality is the physical (ii) Belief that the physical sequence is totally regular (25).

Postmodernism: We take this as a form of 'relativism' (qv) (22).

Preternatural: From beyond nature.

Process Theology: God changes and reacts to the universe, though it is unclear if or how he acts in it (151).

Property Dualism: There is one reality but it has 'mind' and 'matter' properties which are irreducible to each other

Qualia: Individual sensation in human experience of eg red (74).

Quarks: Smallest parts of matter, going to make up particles.

Quantum Physics: Deals with the peculiar wave-particle properties of 'quanta' or packets of energy. Uncertain and probabilisitc outcomes are involved (cf uncertainty).

Rabbi: A recognised Jewish teacher and expounder of Scripture.

Rationalism: Belief that pure reason can provide knowledge.

Realism: Belief that concepts used in science and common experience relate to 'real' entities. 'Critical Realism' emphasises that all human descriptions of such involve perspective (374).

Reductionism: The 'reduction' of one system of ideas to another eg biology to physics. For types of reductionism see (62).

Reformed: Taking views of Reformers eg Calvin & Luther (35).

Relativism: There is no absolute 'truth' or 'reality', both are relative to different traditions, cultures or epochs (22).

Sabbath: Seventh day to be 'kept holy' by Jews. The early church rested instead on Sunday to commemorate the resurrection.

Scholastic: Late medieval theology with Aristotle's physics (213)

Scriptural Geologist: Does geology from Genesis rather than observation (219).

Scripture: =The Bible – a description often used by those who (like us) accept the Bible as authoritative.

Semi-Deism: God made the world to run autonomously and only occasionally 'interferes' for outside in its processes (129).

Spontaneous Generation: Formation of new life directly from chemicals without reproduction.

Subjective Belief: Arises from individual assessment without obvious rationale. May involved degrees of certainty (382 etc).

Subjectivism: Similar to 'relativism' – everything is subjective.

Supernatural: A force above nature – whether theistic or magical.

Targums: Early Jewish free renderings of Old Testament in the common (Aramaic) language (103).

Tautology: Something which is true by definition.

Theism: God is both external to and immanent in the created world, which owes its continued existence to God ( )

Theistic evolutionist: Belief that a God is behind evolution. We prefer the term evolutionary creationist.

Thermodynamics 2nd Law: Entropy (ie disorder) in any closed physical system increases over time.

Token Identity Theory: *Every* mental event is identical with *some* physical event (also called token physicalism) (68).

Transcendent: Divine property of being outside and above the created order.

"Two Books" Baconian view that theology interprets Scripture and science interprets nature, both are fallible, both ultimately point to God, but the two should not be mixed.

Type: A 'type' in theology is where an incident or individual is seen as a picture of something else (eg Gal 4:24) (300, 443)

Type Identity Theory: Every psychological *type* of mental event is identical with a particular *type* of physical event (68).

Vulcanism: Early geological theory holding water deposition and molten origins of rocks, in cyclical non directional system (327).

Uncertainty Principle: In physics do not have precise position and velocity and paths after impact are in principle predictable only statistically. Particles are more like a probability waves (81).

Uniformitarian: Gratuitous assumption that rates of past geological processes have been constant (467).

Verificationism: View that general statements can be 'verified'.

Warrant: Satisfactory justification for a belief (386).

Y-Chromosomal Adam: Single male ancestor posited on basis of variations in human Y-chromosomes (434).

Young-earth Creationism: Belief that the earth is only about 6000 or so years old, and creation in 7 literal days (230 etc).

SUBJECT INDEX

PEOPLE & PLACES INDEX

Don't forget we may be contacted through our website:
www.reason-science-and-faith.com

You may also find interesting:
www.cis.org.uk (Christians in Science)
www.csis.org.uk (Christian Students in Science)